T0377998

GOSPEL MEDIA

GOSPEL MEDIA

Reading, Writing, and Circulating Jesus Traditions

◆ ◆ ◆

Nicholas A. Elder

WILLIAM B. EERDMANS PUBLISHING COMPANY
GRAND RAPIDS, MICHIGAN

Wm. B. Eerdmans Publishing Co.
4035 Park East Court SE, Grand Rapids, Michigan 49546
www.eerdmans.com

© 2024 Nicholas A. Elder
All rights reserved
Published 2024

Book design by Jamie McKee

Printed in the United States of America

30 29 28 27 26 25 24   1 2 3 4 5 6 7

ISBN 978-0-8028-7921-9

Library of Congress Cataloging-in-Publication Data
A catalog record for this book is available from the Library of Congress.

For my late father, Kenneth Merlin Elder, who taught me the values of perseverance and dedication above all else

Contents

Acknowledgments ix
List of Abbreviations xii

Introduction 1

PART ONE: Reading 5

1. **Silent and Vocalized Reading** 7
   Scriptio Continua 10
   Neuropsychology of Reading 13
   Silent Reading 15
   Vocalized Reading 25
   Ambiguous Cases of Reading Aloud 26
   Unambiguous Cases of Reading Aloud 33
   Conclusion 36
2. **Solitary and Communal Reading** 38
   Solitary Roman Reading 41
   Solitary Jewish and Christian Reading 43
   Conclusion to Solitary Reading 53
   Communal Reading 54
   Conclusion 76
3. **Reading the Gospels** 79
   The Extended Situation, Textual Self-Consciousness, and Paratexts 80
   Mark 83
   Matthew 91
   Luke 102
   John 113
   Conclusion 119

PART TWO: Writing 123

4. **Writing by Hand** 125
   Writing Literary Letters by Hand 126
   Writing Letters by Hand in the Novels 129

Writing Letters by Hand in the Papyri 132
Writing Literary Compositions by Hand 136
Conclusion 143

5. **Writing by Mouth** 144
   Dictating Literary Letters 147
   Dictating Papyri Letters 152
   Dictating Literary Compositions 160
   Texts Derived from Oral Events 165
   Conclusion 170

6. **Writing the Gospels** 172
   Mark 172
   Matthew and Luke 185
   John 201
   Conclusion 206

PART THREE: Circulating 209

7. **Publication and Circulation** 211
   The Complexity of Publication 214
   Unpublished Material, Partial Release, Limited Circulation 222
   "Not for Publication" and "For Publication" 228
   Conclusion 234

8. **Circulating the Gospels** 236
   Circulating the Synoptics 237
   Circulation in Codex and Roll 250
   Circulating John 257
   Conclusion 271

Conclusion 273

Appendix: Papyri Letters 277
Appendix: Tables to Chapter 6 283
Glossary of Terms 289
Bibliography 293
Index of Authors 311
Index of Subjects 314
Index of Scripture 316
Index of Other Ancient Sources 320

Acknowledgments

The book that you hold in your hands or read on your screen is, like most texts, a communal product. As such, I wish to thank the communities and individuals who have had an impact on its conception, production, revision, and publication.

First and foremost, I am ever grateful for my family, my closest community. This book was written through many milestones and hardships: three new jobs, two moves and the restoration of two historic homes, a global pandemic, unanticipated homeschooling, and a victory over cancer. These familial trials and triumphs influence the book in subtle, significant ways. Beth, Brooks, Kit James, Nettie, and Lucy, thank you for who you are: the most important people in my life.

Second, many academic networks, institutional and otherwise, have impacted the content and form of this book. The preliminary research and writing began while I was a visiting assistant professor at Marquette University, where I also completed my doctorate. The faculty welcomed me warmly as I moved from one side of the table, as a graduate student and advisee, to the other, as a faculty member. Julian Hills, Joshua Burns, Deirdre Dempsey, Michael Cover, Jeanne-Nicole Mellon Saint-Laurent, Andrei Orlov, Karen Ross, Jen Henerey, Paul Cizek, Tyler Stewart, David Burnett, Chris Lilley, Shaun Blanchard, Tim Gabrielson, and Chris Ganski, thank you for the positive influence that you have had on my life, thinking, scholarship, and teaching.

Many of the ideas presented in this book were first presented orally in various venues. The Book History and Biblical Literature, Synoptic Gospels, The Bible in Ancient (and Modern) Media, and the Gospel of Mark sections of the annual Society of Biblical Literature meeting were all productive spaces to share and have sharpened the book's content. Thank you to Matthew D. C. Larsen, Daniel Picus, Patricia A. Rosenmeyer, Stephen Carlson, and Raymond F. Person for the opportunity to present in these spaces and for the feedback that you offered in them. Every year I eagerly anticipate the Midwest Regional Meeting of the Society of Biblical Literature. I am grateful for several people who offered insight in that venue: Dale Walker, Clare Rothschild, Matt Calhoun, Jeremiah Coogan, and Brandon Massey. The "Word

Became Flesh: The Question of Performance Criticism as Method" conference at Loyola University Chicago was especially instrumental for articulating the arguments in part 1 of this book. Thank you to Megan Wines and Zechariah Eberhart for organizing this formative event, and to Christopher Skinner, Kelly Iverson, Daniel Smith, Bill Shiell, Kathy Maxwell, Scott Brevard, Edmondo Lupieri, Olivia Stewart Lester, and Jon Hatter for your contributions to it. The University of Dubuque Theological Seminary has supported me in writing the majority of this book. I am especially grateful to my colleagues Annette Huizenga, Matt Schlimm, Chris James, Susan Forshey, and Mary Emily Duba for their encouragement.

Third, a debt of gratitude is owed to those who were involved in the publication of the book. I am grateful for the patience of the book's editors, Trevor Thompson and Laurel Draper. I am thankful for the copyeditor, Kathy Noftsinger, who improved the rhetoric, flow, and style of the written words. Anonymous and unacknowledged persons often stand behind written works. Though I will likely never know their names, I wish to thank those who were involved in the physical and electronic production and distribution of this book.

Finally, there are two artists to thank for two albums that serve as this book's soundtrack. The first is Tacocat for *This Mess Is a Place*, which was on loop during much of the initial research and the ominous task of getting the first words on the blank screen. Written in the wake of the 2016 presidential election, *This Mess Is a Place* manifests deep existential anxiety in cloying pop-punk guise. At times the angst is unresolved, as in "Crystal Ball," which cheerfully laments "What a time / To be barely alive." At other times the listener is admonished by subversive lyrics set atop saccharine instrumentals, as in the chorus of the album's opening track: "Just remember if you can / Power is a hologram / And every reality / Every little reality / Is rippin' at the seams." Tacocat's ruminations on genuine agony offer pinpricks of defiant hope, and these provided motivation in the trying circumstances through which this book was written.

The second album is Margot & The Nuclear So and So's 2018 *Vulgar in the Chapel*, an acoustic LP of demos that commemorates the ten-year anniversary of the band's cult-classic sophomore album(s) *Animal!* / *Not Animal*. As stripped-down, acoustic versions of the orotund takes in their "original" release, I returned frequently to these tracks as background noise. The circumstances surrounding the release of *Animal* and *Not Animal!* raise questions about publication, authorship, pluriform traditions, and intellectual property in the twenty-first century that are akin to those this book addresses with respect to the first century. Fans of Margot know well the peculiarities surrounding the 2008 release of *Animal!* and *Not Animal*. The double release resulted from a rift between the band and their label, Epic Records. *Animal!* was the band's preferred version of the album, while *Not Animal*, as its title suggests, was the takes, collection, and arrangement of songs that Epic Records selected. Both albums were released simultaneously in multiple media forms, the former on vinyl and the latter, the label's "official" album, digitally and on compact disc. The band's now-defunct Myspace page once offered their listeners the following caveat: "Remember, *Animal!* is our second album, while Not *Animal* is a label compiled collection of songs. We HIGHLY recommend listening to *Animal!* first." Like the canonical gospels, *Animal!* and *Not Animal* are overlapping discourses that compete with one another. They are pluriform traditions with multiple "publications" and "re-publications." The most recent of these, *Vulgar in the Chapel*, made a significant impact on this book.

Abbreviations

PRIMARY SOURCES

Ad Amicos	Marcus Aurelius, *Epistolae ad amicos*
Ad Antoninum Imp.	Fronto, *Epistolarum ad Antoninum Imperatorem*
Ad Autolycum	Theophilus of Antioch, *To Autolycus*
Ad M. Caes.	Fronto, *Epistolarum ad Marcum Caesarem*; Marcus Aurelius, *Epistolarum ad Marcum Caesarem*
Adv. Col.	Plutarch, *Adversus Colotem*
Ad Verum Imp.	Fronto, *Epistolarum ad Verum Imperatorem*
Adv. Haer.	Irenaeus, *Against Heresies*
Adv. Marc.	Tertullian, *Against Marcion*
Ag. Ap.	Josephus, *Against Apion*
Alex.	Plutarch, *Alexander*
Alex. fort.	Plutarch, *De Alexandri magni fortuna aut virtute*
Amic.	Cicero, *De amicitia*
Ann.	Tacitus, *Annales*
Ant.	Josephus, *Jewish Antiquities*
Apol.	Tertullian, *Apology*
1 Apol.	Justin Martyr, *First Apology*
2 Apol.	Justin Martyr, *Second Apology*
3 Apol.	Justin Martyr, *Third Apology*
Att.	Cicero, *Epistulae ad Atticum*
Att. Noc.	Gellius, *Attic Nights*
Bell. Civ.	Appian, *Civil Wars*
Brut.	Plutarch, *Brutus*
Catech.	Cyril, *Catechetical Lectures*
Cat. Maj.	Plutarch, *Cato the Elder*
Cat. Min.	Plutarch, *Cato the Younger*
Chaer.	Chariton, *Chaereas and Callirhoe*
Cherubim	Philo, *On the Cherubim*
Cic.	Plutarch, *Cicero*
Comm. on Matt.	Jerome, *Commentary on Matthew*
Conf.	Augustine, *Confessions*

Contempl. Life	Philo, *On the Contemplative Life*
Contr.	Seneca the Elder, *Controversiae*
Creation	Philo, *On the Creation of the World*
De Fer. Als.	Fronto, *De feriis alsiensibus*
Deipn.	Athenaeus, *Deipnosophistae*
Demetr.	Plutarch, *Demetrius*
De vir.	Jerome, *De Viris Illustribus*
Dial.	Justin Martyr, *Dialogue with Trypho*; Tacitus, *Dialogus de oratoribus*
Dreams	Philo, *On Dreams*
Embassy	Philo, *On the Embassy to Gaius*
Ep.	Jerome, *Epistle*; Pliny the Younger, *Epistle*; Seneca, *Epistulae morales*
Eph.	Ignatius, *To the Ephesians*
Epict. diss.	Arrian, *Epicteti dissertationes*
Epigr.	Martial, *Epigrams*
Eq.	Aristophanes, *Knights*
Eternity	Philo, *On the Eternity of the World*
Fin.	Cicero, *De finibus*
Flaccus	Philo, *Against Flaccus*
Good Person	Philo, *That Every Good Person Is Free*
Her.	Ovid, *Heroides*
Herm. Vis.	Visions of Hermas
Hipp.	Euripides, *Hippolytus*
His. rom.	Dio Cassius, *Roman History*
Hist. eccl.	Eusebius, *Ecclesiastical History*
Hom. in Ex.	Origen, *Homily in Exodus*
Hom. in Gen.	Origen, *Homily in Genesis*
Hom. in Lev.	Origen, *Homily in Leviticus*
Hom. in Num.	Origen, *Homily in Numbers*
Hom. Jo.	John Chrysostom, *Homiliae in Joannem*
Ind.	Lucian, *The Ignorant Book-Collector*
Inim. util.	Plutarch, *De capienda ex inimicis utilitate*
Inst.	Quintilian, *Institutio oratoria* (*The Orator's Education*)
Judic.	Claudius Ptolemy, *Judiciaris*
J.W.	Josephus, *Jewish War*
Leg.	Philo, *Legum allegoriae*
Leuc. Clit.	Achilles Tatius, *The Adventures of Leucippe and Cleitophon*
Life	Josephus, *The Life*

Luc.	Plutarch, *Lucullus*
Lys.	Plutarch, *Lysander*
Magn.	Ignatius, *To the Magnesians*
Metam.	Apuleius, *Metamorphoses*
Moses	Philo, *On the Life of Moses*
Or. Graec.	Tatian, *Oratio ad Graecos*
Phil.	Ignatius, *To the Philadelphians*
Planting	Philo, *On Planting*
Posterity	Philo, *On the Posterity of Cain*
Prelim. Studies	Philo, *On the Preliminary Studies*
Probl.	Aristotle, *Problems*
1QSa	Community Rule (Rule of the Congregation)
Quint. fratr.	Cicero, *Epistulae ad Quintum fratrem*
Sacrifices	Philo, *On the Sacrifices of Cain and Abel*
Sat.	Horace, *Satires*; Juvenal, *Satires*
Spec. Laws	Philo, *On the Special Laws*
Strom.	Clement, *Miscellanies*
Suas.	Seneca, *Suasoriae*
Suav. viv.	Plutarch, *Non posse suaviter vivi secundum Epicurum*
Trin.	Augustine, *The Trinity*
Tusc.	Cicero, *Tusculanae disputationes*
Virtues	Philo, *On the Virtues*
Vit. Apoll.	Philostratus, *Vita Apollonii*
Vit. Plot.	Porphyry, *Vita Plotini*

PAPYRI (DUKE DATABASE OF DOCUMENTARY PAPYRI)

P.Abinn.	*The Abinnaeus Archive: Papers of a Roman Officer in the Reign of Constantius II*
P.Brem.	*Bremer Papyri*
P.Giss.	*Giessen Papyri*
P.Lond.Lit.	*Catalogue of the Literary Papyri in the British Museum*
P.Mert.	*A Descriptive Catalogue of the Greek Papyri in the Collection of Wilfred Merton*
P.Mich.	*Michigan Papyri*
P.Oxy.	*Oxyrhynchus Papyri*
P.Yale	*Yale Papyri in the Beinecke Rare Book and Manuscript Library*
SB	*Sammelbuch griechischer Urkunden aus Aegypten*

OTHER ABBREVIATIONS

AB	Anchor Bible
ABRL	Anchor Bible Reference Library
AJP	*American Journal of Philology*
AYBC	Anchor Yale Bible Commentary
BDAG	Danker, Frederick W., Walter Bauer, William F. Arndt, and F. Wilbur Gingrich. *Greek-English Lexicon of the New Testament and Other Early Christian Literature.* 3rd ed. Chicago: University of Chicago Press, 2000
BECNT	Baker Exegetical Commentary on the New Testament
BETL	Bibliotheca Ephemeridum Theologicarum Lovaniensium
BGU	*Aegyptische Urkunden aus den Königlichen Staatlichen Museen zu Berlin, Griechische Urkunden.* 15 vols. Berlin: Weidmann, 1895–1937
BHT	Beiträge zur historischen Theologie
BJP	Boudon-Millot, Véronique, Jacques Jouanna, and Antoine Pietrobelli. *Galien, Œuvres, Tome IV: Ne pas se Chagriner.* Paris: Les Belles Lettres, 2010
BL	Berichtigungsliste der griechischen Papyrusurkunden aus Ägypten
BNTC	Black's New Testament Commentaries
BT	*The Bible Translator*
BTB	*Biblical Theology Bulletin*
BZ	*Biblische Zeitschrift*
CBET	Contributions to Biblical Exegesis and Theology
CBQ	*Catholic Biblical Quarterly*
CJ	*Classical Journal*
ClAnt	*Classical Antiquity*
ClQ	*Classical Quarterly*
ConBNT	Coniectanea Neotestamentica or Coniectanea Biblica: New Testament Series
CP	*Classical Philology*
DCLS	Deuterocanonical and Cognate Literature Studies
GKC	*Gesenius' Hebrew Grammar.* Edited by Emil Kautzsch. Translated by Arther E. Cowley. 2nd ed. Oxford: Clarendon, 1910
GRBS	*Greek, Roman, and Byzantine Studies*

HNT	Handbuch zum Neuen Testament
HThKNT	Herders theologischer Kommentar zum Neuen Testament
HTR	*Harvard Theological Review*
ICC	International Critical Commentary
Int	*Interpretation*
JBL	*Journal of Biblical Literature*
JECS	*Journal of Early Christian Studies*
JEH	*Journal of Ecclesiastical History*
JETS	*Journal of the Evangelical Theological Society*
JSNT	*Journal for the Study of the New Testament*
JSNTSup	Journal for the Study of the New Testament Supplement Series
JSOTSup	Journal for the Study of the Old Testament Supplement Series
JTS	*Journal of Theological Studies*
LCL	Loeb Classical Library
LEC	Library of Early Christianity
LNTS	The Library of New Testament Studies
LSJ	Liddell, Henry George, Robert Scott, Henry Stuart Jones. *A Greek-English Lexicon*. 9th ed. with revised supplement. Oxford: Clarendon, 1996
m.	mishnah
Neot	*Neotestamentica*
NICNT	New International Commentary on the New Testament
NIGTC	New International Greek Testament Commentary
NovT	*Novum Testamentum*
NovTSup	Supplements to Novum Testamentum
NTL	New Testament Library
NTS	*New Testament Studies*
OtSt	*Oudtestamentische Studiën*
PG	Patrologia Graeca. Edited by J.-P. Migne. 162 vols. Paris, 1857–1886
PVTG	Pseudepigrapha Veteris Testamenti Graece
RevScRel	*Revue des sciences religieuses*
SBLDS	Society of Biblical Literature Dissertation Series
SBLSBS	Society of Biblical Literature Sources for Biblical Study
SC	Sources Chrétiennes

Smyth	Smyth, Herbert Weir. *Greek Grammar*. Revised by Gordon M. Messing. Cambridge: Harvard University Press, 1956
SNTSMS	Society for New Testament Studies Monograph Series
SP	Sacra Pagina
STDJ	Studies on the Texts of the Desert of Judah
THKNT	Theologischer Handkommentar zum Neuen Testament
UNT	Untersuchungen zum Neuen Testament
VC	*Vigiliae Christianae*
VCSup	Vigiliae Christianae Supplements
VT	*Vetus Testamentum*
WBC	Word Biblical Commentary
WUNT	Wissenschaftliche Untersuchungen zum Neuen Testament
ZNW	*Zeitschrift für die neutestamentliche Wissenschaft und die Kunde der älteren Kirche*

Introduction

Reading, writing, and circulating texts are all social acts. They are complex and culturally constructed. Individuals and groups read, write, and circulate discourses differently in different times and contexts. This book engages the mechanics and sociality of reading, writing, and circulation in the canonical gospels' context. It argues that the complexity of ancient media practices is reflected in the reading, writing, and circulation of these written Jesus traditions. The gospels were not all read, written, or circulated the same way. They are characterized by media diversity.

New Testament scholarship has often flattened this diversity. It simplifies ancient reading, writing, and circulation by presenting them in binary oppositions. Texts were either influenced by orality or they were influenced by textuality. Persons either read aloud or they read silently. Composition was either by dictation or by hand. Traditions were either read publicly to groups or read privately by individuals. Texts were either distributed in codices or in bookrolls. But the evidence simply does not fit these oppositions. The sources paint a colorful and complex portrait. This book colorizes the media in which Jesus was re-presented. The black-and-white categories constructed around gospel media are filled with vivid tones. I hope to brighten the drab media myths that mar gospels scholarship. We are left with a lively, compelling, and captivating portrait of how Jesus traditions were written, read, performed, and circulated.

Each chapter of the book addresses a media myth and attempts to rectify it. "Myth" does not mean "false." It connotes an idea that exercises powerful influence though is left unscrutinized. Many of these myths concern the mechanics of reading, writing, and circulation. Recent scholarship in both classics and biblical studies has focused on the sociality of reading in ancient communities and contexts.[1] The mechanics of reading, writing, and publication have been overshadowed. Questions about whether texts were written by hand or by mouth and whether they were read aloud in communal events or silently

---

1. Largely under the influence of William A. Johnson's *Readers and Reading Culture in the High Roman Empire: A Study of Elite Communities* (Oxford: Oxford University Press, 2010).

by individuals in private settings have been cast to the periphery to focus on the social contexts of reading. This book addresses both this sociality and the mechanics of ancient media. The two are inseparable. The latter impacts the former and vice-versa. How texts are read, written, and circulated varies on the basis of social factors, and different modes of reading, writing, and circulation have different social effects.

In all the media myths addressed, there are elements of reality to be expanded and complexified. The eight chapters are divided into three parts, one part each on reading, writing, and circulation. The initial chapters in each part examine the mechanics and sociality of media in the gospels' context. The final chapters in each part then address the canonical gospels themselves.

Part 1 engages reading practices, countering common assumptions that reading was always aloud and communal. It demonstrates that literate persons also read silently and in solitary settings. There was not a normalized manner or context for reading. When it comes to the gospels, they were likewise read in both communal and individualized events. Each canonical gospel indicates that it is a unique kind of text that made for a unique kind of reading event.

Part 2 surveys how persons wrote in antiquity. It argues that both dictation and handwriting were common compositional modes. Moreover, writing by mouth and writing by hand were not mutually exclusive. Some ancient texts demonstrate both oral and written characteristics simultaneously. With respect to the gospels, we should not expect that each one was composed the same way. Matthew, Mark, Luke, and John betray a variety of compositional modes.

Part 3 addresses how texts were circulated in antiquity, contesting the notion that they were distributed following a concentric-circles model. In such a model, texts gained more influence as they moved outward and acquired more readers. While this is the case for some discourses, many were circulated haphazardly. The gospels did not follow a standard model of circulation but were distributed in various physical forms and socially constructed ways.

The gospels contain no direct statements about how they were read, written, or circulated. Writers, both ancient and modern, do not often declare such things in their texts because reading, writing, and publication are culturally constructed. Their mechanics and processes are assumed by those who participate in the culture. To understand the gospels' media context, we are dependent on occasions in other texts when these processes and mechanics are mentioned, imagined, or expressed by their physical forms. This happens in various kinds of texts contemporaneous with the gospels: Second Temple Jewish literature, other New Testament and early Christian texts, Greco-Roman literature, collected letters from Roman "elites," personal papyri letters, the writings of Galen the physician, and ancient novels. This book engages all of these to describe and reimagine the gospels' media culture. The final four corpora merit brief commentary.

The primary "elite" letter writers engaged are Pliny the Younger, Cicero, Marcus Aurelius, and Marcus's tutor, Fronto. In most cases, these letters are personal and come from collected correspondence. There is much social and literary posturing in all the correspondences, which makes it difficult to determine whether the events and practices mentioned in them actually occurred. For example, daily routines are described that include a regimen of reading, composing, and editing. Did these authors really follow the prescriptions described in these routines? Whether they did or not, the description of such programs tells us how these authors *imagined* composition, reading, and publication. For example, even if Pliny the Younger's account of reading speeches aloud to aid digestion is literary posturing, it demonstrates that he can envisage such an act taking place to accomplish such an end (Pliny the Younger, *Ep.* 9.36).

The same is true of the novels, which sometimes present reading and writing in narrativized form. The actions are entirely imagined but they reflect the media realities of how persons read and wrote. In *Callirhoe*, for instance, Chaereas writes a letter to his wife in his own hand in solitude. This suggests that the novel's author knows this to be a way that persons composed letters. Imagined practices are as revelatory about the gospel's media culture as actualized practices.

Evidence of "on the ground" practices come from personal papyri letters authored by otherwise unknown individuals from antiquity. These are physical artifacts that offer confirmation of what is imagined in the novels and other texts. Letters are imagined to be handwritten by their senders in the novels. Letters are in actuality handwritten by their sender in the nonliterary papyri.

As with the "elite" letters, there is much literary posturing in Galen the physician's massive body of work.[2] We cannot trust everything he says about

---

2. It is a mess to access and cite Galenic texts. Many of Galen's works are collected and available in Karl Gottlob Kühn, *Claudii Galeni opera omnia*, 22 vols. (Leipzig: Car. Cnoblochii, 1821–1833), but the texts therein are wanting. Commonly scholars will reference a text on the basis of its page number in Kühn's collection in addition to its versification reference. For example, *Thrasybulus* 1 in Johnston's LCL text and translation includes 806K in the margin, indicating that the Greek text begins on page 806 of the Kühn volume in which it is found. Confusion reigns in referring to Galen's works, because many of the Latin titles are similar to

his own reading, writing, and circulation practices. But again, how he imagines these practices is informative, even if they are not actualized. When he states that a specific oral lecture was reduced to writing by someone in attendance and then dubiously reused, this may or may not actually be the text's origin. Nonetheless, it demonstrates that he and others know this kind of production and circulation to have occurred.

Some of the texts from these different corpora are not readily accessible in a medium like a critical edition. When this is the case, I have provided the primary text, often in block format. Some readers will find this rhetorically distracting, and to you all I apologize. Others will find it convenient. I have not generally followed this same practice for texts that are readily accessible, such as New Testament documents or works available in the Loeb Classical Library. However, there are many occasions when the primary texts themselves do just as much work toward dispelling the media myths addressed in this book as my argumentation from them. In these cases, I have also made the decision to re-present the primary source under discussion.

Finally, there are terms that appear frequently in this book that I wish to define, and I have done so in the glossary. Many of the terms are closely related but are not synonyms.

I define these terms to be precise with respect to the gospels' media culture. This culture is one that is different from our own. It is easy to import unknowingly our own reading, writing, and publication practices into it. By being more exact in terminology, we will be better equipped to describe the mechanics of ancient media that are different from our own, as well as those that are similar. I advise familiarizing yourself with these terms in the glossary before turning to the mechanics of ancient media. We will begin with silent and vocalized reading.

---

one another. I default to citing the most accessible translations and texts of Galen and also reference the edition and page number from Kühn. I use English titles of Galen's texts in italics for clarity's sake, and often reproduce the text for accessibility's sake, because many of them are not readily available. The various conventions for citing Galen are also addressed by P. N. Singer and William A. Johnson (Singer, trans., *Galen: Selected Works*, The World's Classics [Oxford: Oxford University Press, 1997], xliii; Johnson, *Readers and Reading Culture*, 96–97).

PART ONE

Reading

Reading is a social act. It is not an individual affair between person and text. Even when in private and silent, the reader is engaging another person's or persons' thoughts. As William A. Johnson puts it, reading is "a sociocultural *system* in which the individual participates."[1] Individuals and groups participate in the system of reading in a variety of ways.

This was no less true in antiquity than it is today. Ancient reading modes, practices, events, and cultures were as diverse as those in modernity. Persons read privately and silently. They read privately and aloud. Those who were illiterate participated in reading events by having texts read to them in small and large groups. Literate individuals had texts read to them, sometimes by slaves, sometimes by colleagues. Persons were read to out of medical necessity, for the purpose of entertainment, or because they did not want to read themselves. As physical objects with permanence, texts were used in differing ways.

I intentionally employ the verb "used" rather than "read." The most common way for a text to be used is by being read, whether individually or communally, vocally or silently. But texts are more than objects inscribed for the purpose of reading. They can also function as memory aids or apotropaic devices. Not all texts were written for the same reason and not all texts were considered "books." Different kinds of texts were created for different purposes. Singular texts can serve multiple different ends. At one time a text can be used in one manner, such as being read silently by an individual, and at another time a text can be used in an entirely different manner, such as being read aloud by an individual to a gathered group. Still at other times a text could be used without being read at all, such as when it serves a symbolic function.[2]

---

1. William A. Johnson, *Readers and Reading Culture in the High Roman Empire: A Study of Elite Communities* (Oxford: Oxford University Press, 2010), 11.

2. Texts are used for purposes never intended by their producers. The third-century *P.Oxy.* 67.4633, which contains Homeric scholia, was last used in antiquity as a piece of toilet paper, or as Anne-Marie Luijendijk better puts it, as "toilet papyrus" ("Sacred Scriptures as Trash: Biblical Papyri from Oxyrhynchus," *VC* 64 [2010]: 246).

Part 1 of this book surveys the diversity of reading modes and events in antiquity. Its aim is to deromanticize and to complicate understandings of how the gospels were experienced. In New Testament scholarship, exotic notions of communal and vocalized reading continue to exert influence. Many presume that texts were always read aloud in a communal setting in antiquity. This claim is absurd. It does not hold up to textual evidence. Greco-Roman, Second Temple Jewish, and early Christian texts all attest to a variety of reading events. There was not one normative way to read.

Chapter 1 addresses reading modes, namely silent and vocalized reading. I counter the media myth that reading in antiquity was always or usually aloud. Both silent and vocalized reading were well known in private and in public settings. Chapters 2 and 3 examine the sociality of reading, arguing that texts were read in solitary and communal events. Individuals read the gospels to themselves, and groups read the gospels together. There were different kinds of group reading events in antiquity that were private or public to varying degrees.

CHAPTER 1

Silent and Vocalized Reading

Media Myth: Reading was always or usually aloud.
Media Reality: Literate persons read both silently and aloud.

◆ ◆ ◆

In a passage from the *Confessions* that is foundational for the myth that all reading in antiquity was vocalized, Augustine narrates that his teacher, Ambrose, read silently (Augustine, *Conf.* 6.3.3 [Hammond, LCL]). Though Augustine specifically states that the bishop of Milan read silently to himself, the account has been twisted to support the opposite claim: that silent reading was anomalous in Greco-Roman antiquity. This is because Augustine explains *why* Ambrose read silently. The logic runs as follows: Ambrose did not vocalize the text during the reading events that Augustine observed, and Augustine attempts to explain why Ambrose read silently. Therefore, Augustine is puzzled by the bishop's action during these reading events. Therefore, the content of Augustine's surprise is Ambrose's capacity to read silently. Therefore, the ability to read silently was rare in Greco-Roman antiquity.

But Augustine never expresses his surprise at Ambrose's *ability* to read this way. He is surprised that Ambrose did so in a certain social setting. Augustine ponders why Ambrose read silently when his pupils were present.[1] He offers two possibilities: either Ambrose did not have time to explain the passage he was reading to those present or he wanted to save his voice for his other responsibilities. Both have social implications and neither has anything to do with Ambrose's "unique" abilities.

In book 8 of the *Confessions* Augustine reveals that he himself reads silently.[2] Narrating the famous *tolle lege* ("take up and read") incident in which he randomly opens to Romans 13, Augustine writes, "I snatched it up, opened it, and

---

1. Both A. K. Gavrilov ("Techniques of Reading in Classical Antiquity," *ClQ* 47 [1997]: 63) and Carsten Burfeind ("Wen hörte Philippus? Leises Lesen und lautes Vorlesen in der Antike," *ZNW* 93 [2002]: 139) take this as the source of Augustine's surprise.
2. Gavrilov, "Techniques of Reading," 63.

read silently [*in silentio*] the first chapter that my eyes lit upon" (Augustine, *Conf.* 8.12.29 [Hammond, LCL]). If Augustine can read silently, he must not have been surprised that Ambrose could. Augustine might be surprised that Ambrose *was* reading silently, but he is not surprised that Ambrose *was able* to read silently.

Despite Augustine's own capacity to read silently, the Ambrose account has long been the *locus classicus* for the ubiquity of vocalized reading in antiquity.[3] In biblical studies the claim that silent, solitary reading was nonexistent in the New Testament's cultural context came to a head in Paul J. Achtemeier's *Journal of Biblical Literature* article, "*Omne Verbum Sonat:* The New Testament and the Oral Environment of Late Western Antiquity."[4] Marshaling a variety of evidence for vocalized reading in Greco-Roman antiquity, Achtemeier brings his litany to completion with Augustine's anecdote. The account suggests to Achtemeier that still in the fourth century CE silent reading was completely anomalous. He concludes, "Reading was therefore oral performance *whenever* it occurred and in whatever circumstances. Late antiquity knew nothing of the 'silent, solitary' reader."[5]

---

3. The passage was instrumental for the consensus throughout most of the twentieth century in classical and biblical studies that silent reading in antiquity was rare. For a broad sketch of the development and eventual breakdown of this consensus especially in classical studies see W. Johnson, *Readers and Reading Culture*, 9; William A. Johnson, "Toward a Sociology of Reading in Classical Antiquity," *AJP* 121 (2000): 594–600. With respect to *Conf.* 6.3.3, Eduard Norden took the passage to suggest that vocalized reading was the norm in antiquity (*Die Antike Kunstprosa* [Leipzig: Teubner, 1898], 6). Josef Balogh advanced Norden's claim ("*Voces Paginarum*: Beiträge zur Geschichte des lauten Lesens und Schreibens," *Philologus* 82 [1927]: 84–109, 202–40). According to Balogh, not only were literary texts always read aloud, but so also were nonliterary texts, wills, receipts, and the like. For some time Balogh's perspective remained the unchallenged consensus. Now, however, it only faintly lingers in classical studies, having been disputed by two tide-turning articles: Bernard M. W. Knox, "Silent Reading in Antiquity," *GRBS* 9 [1968]: 421–35; Gavrilov, "Techniques of Reading."

4. Paul J. Achtemeier, "*Omne Verbum Sonat:* The New Testament and the Oral Environment of Late Western Antiquity," *JBL* 109 (1990): 3–27.

5. Achtemeier, "*Omne Verbum Sonat*," 17. Again, Achtemeier writes, "It is apparent that the general—indeed, from all evidence, the exclusive—practice was to read aloud" ("*Omne Verbum Sonat*," 15). Harry Y. Gamble similarly writes, "The most important thing to be said is that in the Greco-Roman world virtually all reading was reading aloud; even when reading privately the reader gave audible voice to the texts" (*Books and Readers in the Early Church: A History of Early Christian Texts* [New Haven: Yale University Press, 1995], 203).

Achtemeier's article is frequently cited, and this specific claim is often quoted approvingly in biblical scholarship.[6] Rather than investigate and cite the primary sources themselves, writers cite Achtemeier to contend that all reading in antiquity was vocalized. The assertion exercises powerful influence, though is rarely scrutinized.[7] R. W. McCutcheon's observation rings true of much biblical scholarship: "The belief that ancient readers did not read silently has ossified in the research community outside of Classics, with the result that many scholars are confident about this conclusion although less sure about the arguments that will allow them to arrive at it."[8]

In New Testament studies, the myth of vocalized reading comes in various forms. In its strongest instantiation, it is claimed that literate persons in antiquity did not have the mental capacity to read silently. The reason typically offered is technological: *scriptio continua* necessitated vocalized reading. Weaker forms of the myth claim that there was a "strong preference" for the oral experience of a discourse, even when one was reading alone.

Not all assume that ancient reading was always vocalized. Some rightly emphasize that Achtemeier's claim about the absence of the silent, solitary reader in late antiquity is demonstrably false.[9] We have already seen that

---

6. For example, David Neville, *Mark's Gospel—Prior or Posterior? A Reappraisal of the Phenomenon of Order*, LNTS 222 (New York: T&T Clark, 2002), 116; Ben Witherington III, *Jesus the Sage: The Pilgrimage of Wisdom* (Minneapolis: Fortress, 2000), 153.

7. M. F. Burnyeat has used the concept "myth" regarding Augustine's amazement at Ambrose's silent reading and its sway in classical scholarship ("Postscript on Silent Reading," *ClQ* 47 [1997]: 76). Burnyeat also mentions biblical studies as a corollary discipline that has been affected by the Augustinian myth of silent reading.

8. R. W. McCutcheon, "Silent Reading in Antiquity and the Future History of the Book," *Book History* 18 (2015): 17. While the consensus in classics is now that both silent and vocalized reading were well known in Greco-Roman antiquity, there are some who still argue that reading aloud was the normal or even exclusive practice, such as Stephan Busch ("Lautes und Leises Lesen in der Antike," *Rheinisches Museum für Philologie* 145 [2002]: 1–45).

9. Rafael Rodríguez, for example, encourages biblical scholars to recognize that Achtemeier was "simply wrong" on this point (*Oral Tradition and the New Testament: A Guide for the Perplexed* [London: Bloomsbury, 2014], 43). Shortly after its publication, Frank D. Gilliard responded to Achtemeier's article and cheekily concluded, "The NT era should not be viewed as one in which the exclusive practice was to read aloud. *Non omne verbum sonabat*" ("More Silent Reading in Antiquity: *Non Omne Verbum Sonabat*," *JBL* 112 [1993]: 693). More recently, Larry W. Hurtado has suggested that biblical performance critics oversimplify the historical situation when they claim that vocalized reading was the norm in early Christian contexts ("Oral Fixation and New Testament Studies? 'Orality,' 'Performance' and Reading Texts in Early Christianity," *NTS* 60 [2014]: 326–27).

Augustine must not have been amazed at Ambrose's ability to read silently. The evidence from Augustine runs in the opposite direction. It suggests that silent reading was known in late antiquity.

But it is not only in late antiquity and certainly not only in Christian circles that the ability to read silently is attested. There is no shortage of evidence for non-vocalized reading throughout the Greek and Roman periods, which we shall come to in due course. First, we shall address the typography of *scriptio continua*, which has often been considered a hindrance to silent reading in antiquity, as well as the neuropsychology of silent reading.

The aim is to demonstrate that there is nothing technological or physiological that prevented persons in antiquity from reading silently. We will then turn to primary source evidence that attests to silent reading from the fourth century BCE through the second century CE. The purpose of this survey is twofold. First, to rectify the assumption that all reading in antiquity was vocalized. Second, to demonstrate that there was a diversity of reading practices and habits in Greco-Roman antiquity.

Scriptio Continua

Scriptio continua, the practice of writing without spaces between words and sentences, has served as a technological explanation for the necessity of vocalized reading. The argument from typography traces back to an article published by Josef Balogh in 1927, was taken up and popularized by medievalists, and persists in biblical studies.[10] For example, after claiming that all reading, including private reading, was aloud, Harry Y. Gamble suggests that the "principal reason" for this was *scriptio continua*.[11] According to him, "*Scriptio continua*

---

10. Balogh, "*Voces Paginarum*," 220. McCutcheon demonstrates how Balogh's claim about *scriptio continua* was popularized by medievalists ("Silent Reading in Antiquity"). With respect to biblical studies, while addressing the Ethiopian eunuch's reading Isaiah aloud in Acts 8, Craig S. Keener notes that most reading was aloud in antiquity and that this was "because ancients used a continuous script" (*Acts: An Exegetical Commentary 3:1–14:28* [Grand Rapids: Baker Academic, 2013], 1583).

11. Harry Y. Gamble, "Literacy, Liturgy and the Shaping of the New Testament Canon," in *The Earliest Gospels: The Origins and Transmission of the Earliest Christian Gospels—The Contribution of the Chester Beatty Gospel Codex P45*, ed. Charles Horton, JSNTSup 258 (New York: T&T Clark, 2004), 31.

is most easily read phonetically, with the aid of the ear: the sense of the text arises only as the syllables are pronounced and heard."[12]

While *scriptio continua* might seem difficult for English-speaking moderns to read, this is because we are unpracticed at it and largely unfamiliar with the format. In antiquity, students learned to read the continuous script through a scaffolded process. Not only did they memorize syllable groupings, but extant models of literary works created for students by their teachers possess various "reading aids," including dots above these groupings, accent marks, supralinear strokes indicating where a new word begins, and even spacing between words.[13] Learning to read *scriptio continua* was a practiced process. Vocalizing a continuous script was not any easier than reading it silently.

Recourse to modern textuality and education can confirm that it was not any easier to read *scriptio continua* aloud than silently on two counts. First, moderns who have the capacity to read a punctuated, spaced text silently, can read a text in *scriptio continua* in the same manner, even if they are untrained in doing so.

---

12. Gamble, "Literacy, Liturgy and the Shaping," 31. Achtemeier similarly states, "The sheer physical nature of the written page in classical antiquity militated against its ease of reading" ("*Omne Verbum Sonat*," 10). Whitney Shiner proposes that the typography of *scriptio continua* contributed to low literacy in antiquity and it necessitated that texts be written for memorization and subsequent performance. Shiner does not explicitly state that *scriptio continua* made for difficult silent reading, but he does suggest that texts "were memorized for delivery rather than performed from a text" (*Proclaiming the Gospel: First-Century Performance of Mark* [Harrisburg, PA: Trinity Press International, 2003], 12). On the basis of *scriptio continua*, Kristina Dronsch writes, "A text in antiquity is not revealed through sight but through sound for its effectiveness" ("Transmissions from Scripturality to Orality: Hearing the Voice of Jesus in Mark 4:1–34," in *The Interface of Orality and Writing: Speaking, Seeing, Writing in the Shaping of New Genres*, ed. Annette Weissenrieder and Robert B. Coote, WUNT 260 [Tübingen: Mohr Siebeck, 2010], 122).

13. Raffaella Cribiore, *Gymnastics of the Mind: Greek Education in Hellenistic and Roman Egypt* (Princeton: Princeton University Press, 2001), 134–35; McCutcheon, "Silent Reading," 6–7; Hurtado, "Oral Fixation," 328. Quintilian testifies to the importance placed on learning one's syllable groupings well in the elementary stage of education in *Inst.* 1.1.30–34. Jan Heilmann demonstrates that various diacritics and punctuation marks do not exclusively function as "performative" reading aids, but are primarily to "clarify semantic ambiguities," whatever the mode of reading might be ("Reading Early New Testament Manuscripts: *Scriptio Continua*, 'Reading Aids,' and Other Characteristic Features," in *Material Aspects of Reading in Ancient and Medieval Cultures: Materiality, Presence and Performance*, ed. Anna Krauß, Jonas Leipziger, and Friederike Schücking-Jungblut [Berlin: de Gruyter, 2020], 183–90).

ITISCOMMONTOPRESENTAPORTIONOFTEXTINAMANNER
THATMIMICSGRECOROMANTYPOGRAPHYINORDERTOIN
TRODUCESCRIPTIOCONTINUAASYOUREADTHISPORTION
OFTEXTAREYOUNATURALLYDOINGSOALOUDORAREYOU
DETERMININGTHEWORDANDSYLLABLEBREAKSSILENT
LYINYOURMINDITISPROBABLYTHELATTERANDNOTTHE
FORMER.[14]

If our unpracticed eyes can make out syllable groupings and words silently in this manner of script, then trained ancient eyes will have been able to do so with even greater fluency.[15]

The second way that modern textuality can help dispel the myth that *scriptio continua* must have been read aloud is by recourse to languages that employ a continuous script. Greco-Roman antiquity is not the only literate context in which *scriptio continua* has been used.[16] Modern Thai, for example, uses a continuous script and there is no doubt that it is read silently.[17] It is a modern and Western conceit to suppose that the bibliographic practices that are normative in our own context make for reading practices that will have been impossible in others.

Primary source testimony about reading *scriptio continua* further suggests that literate ancients must have been able to read the script silently. Lucian and Quintilian specifically address vocalized reading. They both presume, however, that reading *scriptio continua* aloud is dependent on one's ability to scan ahead in the text without vocalizing the words one is registering.

In *The Ignorant Book Collector* 2, Lucian states that reading with "great fluency" (πάνυ ἐπιτρέχων) involves keeping one's eye in front of one's mouth (φθάνοντος τοῦ ὀφθαλμοῦ τὸ στόμα) (Lucian, *Ignorant Book Collector* [Harmon, LCL]). This passage is sometimes taken as confirmation that ancient reading was always or usually vocalized.[18] Lucian does in fact suggest that texts are

14. McCutcheon offers a similar experiment in reading *scriptio continua* ("Silent Reading," 8).
15. Because reading unspaced texts was a deeply rooted ancient habit, Alessandro Vatri suggests that reading them was far less difficult for ancient readers than modern Western readers ("The Physiology of Ancient Greek Reading," *ClQ* 62 [2012]: 633–47), as does Heilmann ("Reading Early New Testament Manuscripts," 183).
16. McCutcheon, "Silent Reading," 7–8.
17. McCutcheon, "Silent Reading," 7–8.
18. Balogh, *"Voces Paginarum,"* 84–85, 228; G. L. Hendrickson, "Ancient Reading," *CJ* 25 (1929): 192–93.

read aloud. That is not a matter of debate. The question is if Lucian has in mind an individual reading to himself. Later in this chapter we shall address this passage as to its bearing on vocalized reading in private. More relevant for the immediate purpose is that being able to look ahead in the text without vocalizing the words that one's eyes are upon is necessary for reading aloud. That is, Lucian assumes readers can silently scan ahead in a text.

Quintilian similarly states that reading involves looking forward while declaiming what preceded: "For to look forward to the right (as is universally taught), and so foresee what is coming, is a matter not only of theory but of practice, since we have to keep our eyes on what follows while reading out what precedes, and (most difficult of all) divide the attention of the mind, the voice doing one thing and the eyes another" (Quintilian, *Inst.* 1.1.35 [Russell, LCL]). For both Lucian and Quintilian reading requires registering what is to come while speaking what preceded, and they state that this is a practiced process. Reading a text aloud presumes the ability to read it silently. This dovetails with the neuropsychology of reading, which suggests that ancients who were literate must also have had the mental capacity to read silently.

Neuropsychology of Reading

Reading studies outline three levels of development: (1) reading aloud; (2) subvocalization; (3) silent reading.[19] The three modes of reading are neurologically intertwined. It is wrong to think of differing modes of reading as mutually exclusive.[20] In fact, public performance or reading of written texts presupposes the ability to read silently.[21] This is because of the eye-voice span.[22] An individual reading aloud must look ahead to the text that follows and read it inwardly to declaim it outwardly with proper prosody. The more a reader is practiced, the better they are at doing this. Lucian and Quintilian in the passages quoted above are referring to the eye-voice span, though not by that name.

According to modern studies, silent reading is not only a prerequisite to vocalized reading, but it also offers several practical advantages. One of these is

---

19. Gavrilov, "Techniques of Reading," 58; Eleanor J. Gibson and Harry Levin, *The Psychology of Reading* (Cambridge: MIT Press, 1975), 334–91.
20. Gavrilov, "Techniques of Reading," 59.
21. Gavrilov, "Techniques of Reading," 59.
22. Gavrilov, "Techniques of Reading," 59; Harry Levin and Ann Buckler-Addis, *The Eye-Voice Span* (Cambridge: MIT Press, 1979).

the ability to skim a text, because "good readers everywhere read silently more rapidly than orally."[23] This is relevant to ancient texts that report occasions of an individual reading for several hours on end. For example, in one of his letters to his pedagogue, Marcus Aurelius describes his morning. He reports that he read for four hours that day (Marcus Aurelius, *Ad M. Caes.* 4.6). Are we to imagine that Marcus was reading aloud the entire four hours? It's possible, but would no doubt be physically and mentally exhausting. If ancients could not and did not read silently, they would be both psychologically odd and at a great social disadvantage.[24]

While bookroll technology has sometimes been taken as a hindrance to fluid reading, it might be the case that bibliographic features of the bookroll and *scriptio continua* facilitated reading, both silent and vocalized. When reading, the eye jumps unevenly across the page or screen in what are called "saccades."[25] A reader does not steadily scan from one side of a line of text to the other. In a spaced text, the reader's eye fixates on the beginning of words and naturally takes in their "Bouma shape," or the easily recognized form of a particularly well-known word such as "the" or "and."[26] With each saccade the reader processes approximately fifteen to twenty letters on either side of the word that is fixated upon.[27] The average width of columns in a roll, at about six to nine centimeters, resulted in fifteen to twenty-five characters per line.[28] Johnson proposes that the start of each line was the natural place for ocular fixation.[29] This is not to suggest that column width and *scriptio continua* supported silent reading over and against vocalized reading. The format assisted the saccadic scanning of lines that neurophysiologically characterizes *both* types of reading.

Nothing technological nor neurophysiological prevented persons in Greco-Roman antiquity from reading silently. *Scriptio continua* did not necessitate vocalized reading. In biblical studies we must abandon that myth. Psychological studies show that vocalized reading presupposes the capacity to

---

23. W. S. Gray, *The Teaching of Reading: An International View* (Cambridge: Harvard University Press, 1957), 13.
24. Gavrilov, "Techniques of Reading," 61.
25. W. Johnson, "Toward a Sociology of Reading," 610.
26. W. Johnson, "Toward a Sociology of Reading," 610.
27. W. Johnson, "Toward a Sociology of Reading," 610.
28. Hurtado, "Oral Fixation," 328–29; McCutcheon, "Silent Reading," 7; W. Johnson, "Toward a Sociology of Reading," 611.
29. W. Johnson, "Toward a Sociology of Reading," 611.

read silently. From the neurophysiological perspective, those who could read vocally must also have had the capacity to read silently.

Not only *could* ancients read silently; they *did* read silently. Primary source evidence indicates as much. With respect to late antiquity, we have already seen that both Augustine and Ambrose had the capacity to read in this manner. The following survey will set our chronology back several centuries. Evidence from a variety of genres extending from the fourth century BCE to the second century CE attests to the practice of non-vocalized reading. In some of these texts, an author specifically states that a historical individual read silently, as is the case with Augustine and Ambrose. In other cases, and particularly in fictional texts, the logic of a particular scene is dependent on a character's ability to read silently. If individuals could not and did not read silently or if silent reading was a rare practice, these episodes will not have made narrative sense to their audiences.

Silent Reading

Nearly since the moment it was made in 1927, classicists have been marshaling primary source evidence against Josef Balogh's claim that all reading in Greco-Roman antiquity was vocalized.[30] Many of these passages, some of which unambiguously depict silent reading, are not often marshaled in biblical studies. In the following I offer, and in many cases reproduce, texts that serve as a veritable canon of evidence to silent reading.[31] I do so with the hope that

---

30. Balogh, "*Voces Paginarum.*" For a history of scholarship on silent and vocalized reading in classics see W. Johnson, "Toward a Sociology of Reading," 594–600; W. Johnson, *Readers and Reading Culture*, 4–9; McCutcheon, "Silent Reading," 3–17. There are still some who hold to the minority opinion that ancient reading was always or usually aloud. See the list of notable scholars in McCutcheon, "Silent Reading," 26n31.

31. The texts in this "canon" consist of Euripides, *Hipp.* 874–75; Aristophanes, *Equites* 115–28; Cicero, *Tusc.* 5.116; Pliny the Younger, *Ep.* 4.16; Quintilian, *Inst.* 10.1.8–10; 11.3.2–4; Claudius Ptolemy, *Judic.* 5.2. These are the texts most frequently cited as testimony to silent reading, but they are not the only ones. For others, see especially Gavrilov's catalogue of texts "where silent reading is more or less certainly implied" ("Techniques of Reading," 70–71). I am largely dependent on Gavrilov ("Techniques of Reading"), McCutcheon ("Silent Reading"), and W. Johnson ("Toward a Sociology of Reading"; *Readers and Reading Culture*, 5–9) for these references, and make no claim to having discovered them. To my knowledge, the scene from Chariton's novel *Callirhoe* has not been discussed by classicists, and so might be added to the growing list of texts that testify to silent reading in Greco-Roman antiquity. The same is true of many of the Jewish and Christian texts addressed below.

this evidence continues to become better known in biblical studies.[32] I shall also offer texts from Second Temple Judaism and early Christianity that suggest silent reading was not anomalous in these contexts. Just as the classical evidence is generally unknown to biblical scholars, those working in classics have not often considered the early Jewish and Christian evidence to silent reading.[33]

In most of these texts a literate individual reads to themselves in the presence of other persons. It is the other people's presence that reveals the reading to be silent.

Our survey begins with three passages from the fifth and fourth centuries BCE in Athens.[34] The first is a riddle that assumes silent reading was well known in this context. In book 10 of *The Learned Banqueters* Athenaeus reproduces the riddle:

> It is a female creature that keeps its children safe beneath the folds of its garment. And though they are mute, they raise a resounding cry through sea-surge and the whole mainland to whichever mortals they wish, and even those who are not there can hear them, deaf though their perception is. (Athenaeus, *Deipn.* 10.450–51 [Olson, LCL])

The correct answer is not a city with its politicians, as the riddle-answerer supposes. It is a letter (ἐπιστολή), and the written characters (γράμματα) are her children.

> The female creature is an [epistle], and the children she carries around inside herself are the letters. Even though they're mute, they speak to anyone they want who's far away. And if someone else happens to be standing nearby, he

---

32. It is unfortunate that Gilliard's critical note is not as well known as Achtemeier's article to which it responds (Gilliard, "More Silent Reading in Antiquity"; Achtemeier, "*Omne Vernum Sonat*"). Already in 1993 Gilliard had made a compelling case that Achtemeier's thesis was overstated.

33. The major exception is Augustine's account in the *Confessions* previously mentioned. Much of the debate about silent and vocalized reading has centered on this text, which was first noted by Norden and Balogh considered exhibit A for the abnormality of silent reading (Norden, *Die Antike Kunstprosa*, 5–6; Balogh, "*Pages Vocinarum*," 85–85).

34. The first passage is noted and discussed by both E. G. Turner and Bernard Knox (Turner, *Athenian Books in the Fifth and Fourth Centuries BC* [London: H. K. Lewis., 1952], 14; Knox, "Silent Reading in Antiquity," 432–33).

won't hear [οὐκ ἀκούσεται] the man who's reading. (Athenaeus, *Deipn.* 10.451 [Olson, LCL])[35]

The riddle makes little sense if it is presumed that letters were always read aloud in antiquity. Words and characters (γράμματα) are, according to the riddle, by their very being (ὄντα) unvoiced (ἄφωνα). A letter is read silently since the person who happens to be standing near does not hear the reader (τις πλησίον ἑστὼς ἀναγιγνώσκοντος οὐκ ἀκούσεται). The negated verb "hear" (ἀκούσεται) explicitly connotes silent reading.[36]

There are at least two occasions of silent reading on the stage in fifth-century BCE Athens, one from tragedy and one from comedy.[37] The first is from Euripides's *Hippolytus* 856–70. Theseus finds a tablet attached to his dead wife's hand. The chorus sings about what is sure to be bad news written in the tablet as Theseus is reading it silently to himself in lines 866–73. Theseus proclaims his woe, to which the chorus asks, "What is it?" (Euripides, *Hippolytus* [Kovacs, LCL]). The chorus, and the audience along with it, does not know what is written in the tablet because Theseus has been reading the words silently to himself.

The second Attic passage is Aristophanes's *Knights* 115–50. Two slaves of a man named Demos are hatching a plot to take revenge upon their master's newly acquired servant named Paphlagon who has been making life difficult on them. While it is not entirely clear how this will help the two enact their revenge, they steal Paphlagon's "holy oracle, the one he most closely guarded" (Aristophanes, *Knights* [Henderson, LCL]). The first slave then reads this stolen oracle, and the remainder of the scene is dependent on the oracle being read silently. The dialogue between the two slaves progresses as the first slowly reveals the contents of the oracle to the second while he is preparing a drink. A brief excerpt from their dialogue clearly displays that the first slave is reading silently as the second inquires about the written content of the oracle:

---

35. I have slightly emended Olson's translation, which renders ἐπιστολή as "writing tablet."
36. Knox, "Silent Reading in Antiquity," 433n19.
37. These were first noted by Knox, "Silent Reading in Antiquity," 433–34. Both passages are also taken up by Gavrilov who not only acknowledges his dependence on Knox for them but reinforces Knox's argument and offers an even more radical conclusion, namely that silently reading to oneself was ordinary in the classical Greek and late Roman periods (Gavrilov, "Techniques of Reading," 69).

> **First Slave:** "You're a genius! Give it here so I can read it. And you hurry up and pour a drink. Let's see, what's in here? What prophecies! Give me the cup, give it here quickly!
> **Second Slave:** "Here. What's the oracle say?"
> [...]
> **First Slave:** "Paphlagon, you scum! So that's why you were so watchful all that time: you were shitting in your pants about the oracle concerning yourself!"
> **Second Slave:** "Why?"
> **First Slave:** "Herein lies the secret of his own destruction!"
> **Second Slave:** "Well? How?"
> **First Slave:** "How? The oracle explicitly says that first there arises a hemp seller, who will be the first to manage the city's affairs."
> **Second Slave:** "That's one seller. What's next? Tell me!" (Aristophanes, *Eq.* 117–31 [Henderson, LCL])

The dialogue continues in this manner until the first slave has revealed the entire contents of the oracle. From these two Attic examples, Bernard Knox concludes that in the fourth and fifth century BCE, "silent reading of letters and oracles (and consequently any short document) was taken completely for granted."[38] Moving chronologically closer to the period that the gospels were written and received, we find that the situation does not change.

Ancient novels provide a window into the everyday practices of antiquity. At times these texts are highly dramatic and even fantastical. They also depict banal realities of ancient life in a way that more technical, non-prose literature does not. When it comes to media, they offer insight into how ancients imagined reading and writing practices to work. There are several occasions in the novels where an episode's narrative logic depends on a character reading silently. I call attention to two of these: Achilles Tatius's *The Adventures of Leucippe and Cleitophon* and Chariton's *Chaereas and Callirhoe*.[39]

The Adventures of Leucippe and Cleitophon was written in the mid- to late second century CE, and appears to have been one of the more popular novels.[40] The female protagonist, Leucippe, and her mother have been sent

---

38. Knox, "Silent Reading in Antiquity," 434.

39. The former is noted in Gavrilov's appendix of texts that "certainly imply" silent reading ("Techniques of Reading," 71).

40. The popularity of the novel is attested by the seven papyri fragments of it that are extant, by which the novel is also dated (see John J. Winkler's introduction to *Leucippe and*

from Byzantium to live with the male protagonist, Cleitophon, and his father because of war with Thrace. As the trope goes, early in the story Cleitophon sees Leucippe and instantly falls in love with her.[41] In an effort to steal glimpses of his new crush, Cleitophon, who narrates in the first person, feigns reading a book as he walks around the house: "I took a book, and bent over it, and pretended to read; but every time that I was at the door, my eyes, off the book, ogled her slyly" (Achilles Tatius, *Leuc. Clit.* 1.6 [Gaselee, LCL]).

If all reading was vocalized, Cleitophon could not "pretend to read" (ἐγκεκυφὼς ἀνεγίνωσκον) as he steals glances of Leucippe. Surely if he were reading aloud and then took his eyes off the text every time he passed Leucippe, Cleitophon's cover would be blown. The logic of the scene depends on Cleitophon silently reading to himself rather than vocalizing the text.

The case is similar in a scene in Chariton's novel *Chaereas and Callirhoe*, dated to the first century CE (Chariton, *Chaer.* 2.481).[42] In *Chaer.* 4.5.7–10, the male protagonist, Chaereas, has written a letter to his wife Callirhoe. As so often happens in the novels, the two lovers are separated by a series of unfortunate events. At this point in the story, Callirhoe has been taken by grave robbers and sold to Dionysius, who in turn has made her his wife. During a banquet that he is hosting and while he is surrounded by other persons, Dionysius receives several letters, one of which is written to Callirhoe from Chaereas, whom Dionysius previously thought was dead. With the unsealed letters opened before him, Dionysius happens to see (εἶδεν) the words "To Callirhoe from Chaereas: I am alive" (Chariton *Chaer.* [Goold, LCL]). The shocking news causes Dionysius to pass out. Even as he faints, he keeps his wits about him and grasps the letters out of fear that someone else might see.

Clitophon in B. P. Reardon, ed., *Collected Ancient Greek Novels* [Berkeley: University of California Press, 1989], 170). In contrast, there is only one fragment of Heliodorus's *Aethiopica* and none of Xenophon's *Anthia and Habrocomes* or Longus's *Daphnis and Chloe* (Reardon, *Collected Ancient Greek Novels*, 170–71).

41. Often in the novels the author narrates how both protagonists are instantly infatuated when they first see each other. This is not the case in Achilles Tatius's novel. Initially only Leucippe's passion is narrated. On the love-at-first-sight trope in the novels see Apuleius's *Metam.* 5.22; Chariton, *Callirhoe* 1.1.5–10; Xenophon, *Anthia and Habrocomes*, 1.3.1.

42. *Chaereas and Callirhoe* is one of the earliest novels, typically dated to the mid-first century CE (Tomas Hägg, *The Novel in Antiquity* [Berkeley: University of California Press, 1983], 5–6; B. P. Reardon, introduction to Chaereas and Callirhoe in *Collected Ancient Greek Novels*, 17; Ronald F. Hock, "The Greek Novel," in *Greco-Roman Literature and the New Testament*, ed. David E. Aune [Atlanta: Scholars Press, 1988], 128; Goold, LCL.

Dionysius doesn't want anyone else to see the letter from Chaereas because they would then know that his wife has a previous husband who is still living. Only Dionysius knows this information; the banqueters do not. This is because Dionysius's eyes alone saw the words "I am alive," written by Chaereas, even though other individuals were present.[43] Upon *seeing* (εἶδεν) the words, not reading the words, Dionysius faints. If all reading was vocalized in antiquity, then the banqueters surrounding Dionysius would have heard the words and known what caused Dionysius to faint because he would have involuntarily spoken them aloud.[44] Instead, they presume that he had some kind of apoplectic attack (ἀποπληξίας αὐτοὺς ἔσχε). The logic of the scene depends on a character's ability to read a text silently.

Josephus reports a situation in *Life* 216–27 that resembles Dionysius's reading in *Chaereas and Callirhoe*. In this section of his autobiography, the Jewish historian is reporting the ruse of John of Gischala, who wanted Josephus either to be deposed of his role as governor of Galilee or to be dead. John, in conjunction with the high priest in Jerusalem, Ananus, sends an embassy from Jerusalem to Chabolo of Galilee where Josephus is residing. The purpose of the envoy is to capture Josephus without having to attack the infantry that resided with him. To do so, the conspirators send a letter to Josephus via a single soldier requesting that Josephus come to them.

Once the soldier arrives with the letter, he requests that Josephus quickly read it and write his response because the letter deliverer was in a hurry to return to the envoy. If the soldier sees Josephus read the letter, he will be pressured into writing his response immediately. Josephus delays and reads the letter both stealthily and silently. When no one was looking he "opened the letter, took in at a glance the writers' design and sealed it up again" (τὴν ἐπιστολὴν ἀναπτύξας μηδενὸς ἐμβλέποντος κἀξ αὐτῆς ταχὺ συνεὶς τὴν τῶν γεγραμμένων ἐπίνοιαν, πάλιν αὐτὴν ἐσημηνάμην) (Josephus, *Life* 222–24 [Thackeray, LCL]). He then pretends not to have read it (ὡς μὴ προανεγνωκώς).

Initially the verb "read" is not used with respect to Josephus's activity. He quickly "takes in" the intention of the writers by furtively glancing at the letter. The scene not only presumes that Josephus possesses non-vocalized reading

---

43. As the narrative progresses Dionysius rereads the letter when he is by himself (καθ' ἑαυτὸν γενόμενος) and then again with another person, namely his friend Pharnaces.

44. Taken to its extreme the doctrine that all reading was vocalized in antiquity is revealed to be absurd. When someone who was literate happened to see written words they did not uncontrollably and unwittingly speak them.

abilities, but also that he can silently skim the text, an action he refers to as reading.

The New Testament provides no unambiguous evidence to silent reading in antiquity. However, Luke 4:16–20, the passage in which Jesus reads from the Isaiah scroll in his hometown synagogue, implies that Jesus can scan through a scroll quickly and silently, as Josephus does his conspirators' letter. Jesus's scanning purposes are different from Josephus's. He is locating a particular passage.

Luke's Jesus proves himself adept at both utilizing and navigating a scroll. He unrolls it (ἀναπτύξας), finds a specific text (εὗρεν τὸν τόπον), reads it, and then rolls the scroll back up (καὶ πτύξας τὸ βιβλίον). For anyone who was literate in antiquity and regularly read from scrolls or bookrolls, handling and finding a passage will not have been a remarkable skill. Nonetheless, it was an ability that one possessed only through practice. According to Luke, Jesus had no problem handling the technology and publicly reading the text. This is the only passage in the New Testament wherein Jesus physically touches a written text. Chris Keith argues that Luke, in distinction from its Synoptic counterparts, clearly presents Jesus as a scribally literate teacher.[45] Not only can Jesus handle the scroll, but his ability to read it aloud also implies advanced learning.

Our concern here is not with Jesus's act of reading Jewish Scripture aloud, though this does represent a common reading event in early Jewish and Christian circles. These will be addressed at greater length in the following chapters. More relevant is Jesus's ability to find the passage in the Isaiah scroll before he reads it aloud. The ability to scan a scroll for a particular section of text presumes that one can read silently and possesses advanced reading skills. A passage from Galen highlights how one might roll from passage to passage, scanning for portions to declaim aloud.[46] Herein the doctor-philosopher addresses his reader with the second-person singular pronoun "you," instructing them how to demonstrate that Galen's own thinking on the pulse is not a novelty, but is earlier attested in Archigenes:

---

45. Chris Keith, *Jesus' Literacy: Scribal Culture and the Teacher from Galilee*, LNTS 413 (New York: T&T Clark, 2011), 142–45; Chris Keith, *Jesus against the Scribal Elite: The Origins of the Conflict* (Grand Rapids: Baker Academic, 2014), 59–62. Keith argues that in Luke 4:16–30 Jesus is presented as a "legitimate scribal-literate authority" on five counts. The third is most relevant here: Jesus's ability to unroll, read, and reroll the scroll assumes scribal-literate skills that a carpenter would not have possessed (*Jesus against the Scribal Elite*, 61).

46. I am dependent on W. Johnson for this reference, though he quotes it for another purpose: to show how intellectual reading communities competed with one another (*Readers and Reading Culture*, 95).

But you, so that you do not get confused, take up the book of Archigenes and read it to them [λαβὼν ἀνάγνωθι τὸ τοῦ Ἀρχιγένους βιβλίον αὐτοῖς], first the part having this title [ἐπίγραμμα] for the chapter heading [κεφαλαίου], *On the Size of the Heart Beat*.... Next, rolling the book up a bit [μικρὸν ἐπειλίξας τὸ βιβλίον], read again the section *On Intensity* [of the heartbeat].... Now roll the book up a little [more] and read the beginning of the section *On Fullness* [of blood in the arteries] [ἐπειλίξας τὸ βιβλίον ὀλίγον τὴν ἀρχὴν ἀνάγνωθι τοῦ περὶ τῆς πληρότητος λόγου]. Then, halting the argument [λόγος] for a moment, that is, halting your reading of the book [τὴν ἀνάγνωσιν τοῦ βιβλίου], say to them that I am saying nothing new, but what Archigenes has said too.[47]

The hypothetical reading event that Galen describes is not a perfect analogue to the event that Luke 4 depicts. It does, however, testify to the practice of rolling to discrete passages, finding them on the basis of their opening words, and then reading them aloud.[48] Galen, like Luke, presumes that the reader possesses the ability to scan the text and find certain passages without reading it continuously. The respective texts that Galen's interlocutor and Jesus read possess symbolic value in and of themselves. The text is authoritative, and the reader mediates it to those gathered.

Returning to Luke with Galen's testimony to rolling and scanning in mind, what is most significant is that Jesus found a specific place (εὗρεν τὸν τόπον) in the Isaiah scroll. As François Bovon notes, per synagogue practice, Jesus might have selected the Isaianic passage himself, it might have been the prescribed reading, or it could have been chosen by lot.[49] Whatever the case, Jesus "found" (εὗρεν) the text in the scroll. Particularly if the scroll were a complete copy of Isaiah like 1QIsaᵃ, as Joseph Fitzmyer suggests the author has in mind, then Luke depicts Jesus looking for the passage by rolling through the scroll,

---

47. Galen, *Differences of Pulses* 591–92K; trans., W. Johnson, *Readers and Reading Culture*, 95. Greek text, Kühn, *Claudii Galeni opera omnia*, 8:591–92.

48. Similarly, Seneca the Elder mentions a reading event wherein a certain Labienus "rolled up a good deal of the book" (magnam partem illum libri convolvisse et dixisse) to pass over portions (*Contr.* 10.pref.8; Winterbottom, vol. 2, LCL). It is erroneous to suppose that scrolling through a text was more difficult for literate persons in Greco-Roman antiquity than it is for moderns.

49. François Bovon, *Luke 1: A Commentary on the Gospel of Luke 1:1–9:50*, trans. Christine M. Thomas, Hermeneia (Minneapolis: Fortress, 2002), 153.

akin to the instructions Galen provides his reader.[50] Under the "all-reading-is-vocalized" hypothesis, we have to imagine that Jesus and Galen's interlocutor are reading aloud or mumbling to themselves as they look for the particular passages to be read publicly. The far more likely scenario is that Luke imagines Jesus to be able to scan the Isaiah scroll silently and find the passage that he is looking for. Not only does this make better narrative sense, but it amplifies Jesus's literary capacities that Keith suggests Luke is promoting. This presentation of Jesus as a scribally literate teacher continues as Jesus "sits down" in Luke 4:20, taking the posture of a pedagogue, and then tells those present that the text had been fulfilled in their hearing.[51] The passage serves as our lone example from the New Testament wherein the ability to read a text silently is presumed.

At the risk of belaboring the point, I have extensively reproduced and addressed evidence to silent reading. Much of this primary source testimony is well remarked upon by classicists.[52] The interested reader will find A. K. Gavrilov's list of twenty-four textual instances wherein "silent reading is more or less certainly implied" to be of great value.[53] To press the risk a bit further, I offer brief excerpts from the following eight texts that also imply or directly attest to silent reading:

- Discussing how persons with certain physical disabilities can still participate in literary activities, Cicero contrasts reading and hearing in *Tusc.* 5.40. He states that persons who are deaf ought to remember that "far greater pleasure can be derived from reading verse than hearing it" (deinde multo maiorem percipi posse legendis his quam audiendis voluptatem) (Cicero, *Tusc.* 5.40 [King, LCL]).[54]

---

50. Joseph A. Fitzmyer, *The Gospel according to Luke I–IX* (New York: Doubleday, 1981), 531.
51. John Nolland, *Luke 1–9:20* (Dallas: Word Books, 1989), 198.
52. W. Johnson writes, "Without hesitation we can now assert that there was no cognitive difficulty when fully literate ancient readers wished to read silently to themselves, and that the cognitive act of silent reading was neither extraordinary nor noticeably unusual in antiquity" ("Toward a Sociology of Reading," 594).
53. Gavrilov, "Techniques of Reading," 70–71. Likewise, Burfeind addresses many of the same texts as Gavrilov and marshals others in "Wen hörte Phillipus?" 139–41.
54. W. P. Clark called attention to this passage in 1931 ("Ancient Reading," *CJ* 26 [1931]: 698–700), and Knox similarly cites it to make his case that silent reading was not atypical in antiquity ("Silent Reading in Antiquity," 427). Cicero's statement flies in the face of the

24 • *Reading*

- In his biography of Nero, Suetonius writes that when the emperor was considering judicial cases he had his advisers write up their opinions, which he would read "silently and in private" (tacitus ac secreto legens), before rendering his decision (Suetonius, *Nero* 15.1 [Rolfe, LCL]).
- Plutarch reports that at the height of the Catiline conspiracy, Caesar received a "little note" (γραμματιδίου μικροῦ) from Servilia while Cato was present. Supposing that the note was from the enemy, Cato was indignant when Caesar read it silently (τὸν μὲν ἀναγινώσκειν σιωπῇ). Caesar then handed the note to Cato, who, upon reading it, finds it is a sultry letter (ἀκόλαστον ἐπιστόλιον) (Plutarch, *Brut.*, 5.2–3 [986] [Perrin, LCL]).
- Plutarch also reports an occasion when Alexander was reading a letter from his mother "silently to himself" (καὶ σιωπῇ πρὸς ἑαυτὸν ἀναγιγνώσκοντος) while another individual, Hephaestion, was present (Plutarch, *Alex. fort.* 7 [340A] [Babbitt, LCL].
- In *Spec. Laws* 1.214, Philo writes of those who read the Holy writings with their mind rather than just with their eyes (τῶν διανοίᾳ μᾶλλον ἢ ὀφθαλμοῖς ταῖς ἱεραῖς γραφαῖς ἐντυγχανόντων, Philo, *Spec. Laws* 1.214). Similarly in *Leg.* 1.83 he proverbially asks how the ascetic "could read without eyes" (πῶς ἀναγνώσεται χωρὶς ὀμμάτων ὁ ἀσκητής, Philo, *Leg.* 1.83). If the association between reading and vocalization is as strong as some would have it, then Philo would naturally think of reading as a labial affair, not an ocular one.[55]
- Writing to Valerius Paulinus to assure him that oratory is revered among the masses, Pliny the Younger draws a distinction between auditory and visual appreciation of a text. He writes, "Some people listen (*audiant*) and others read (*legant*); let's create something worthy of the ears (*auribus*) and the papyri (*chartis*)" (Pliny the Younger, *Ep.* 4.16 [Radice, LCL]).[56]
- Quintilian argues that literary vocabulary is built not by memorizing lists, but by both "reading and hearing" (legendo atque audiendo) the best literature.

---

assumption that Latin poetry was meant to be heard in public performance rather than read silently. In due course, we will address the social contexts in which different kinds of discourses were experienced, as well as how they were experienced. But it is worth foregrounding here the claim that, contrary to much popular assumption, the destination for poetry was not public recitation, but rather private, individualized reading, as Holt N. Parker has argued ("Books and Reading Latin Poetry," in *Ancient Literacies: The Culture of Reading in Greece and Rome*, ed. William A. Johnson and Holt N. Parker [Oxford: Oxford University Press, 2009], 187–88).

55. See also Philo, *On the Preliminary Studies* 20.

56. English trans, McCutcheon, "Silent Reading," 13, which I am dependent on for this reference.

While emphasizing the importance of prosody in speech, Quintilian offers stage actors as a prime example, since "they add so much charm to the greatest poets that their productions give us infinitely more pleasure when heard than when read" (nos infinito magis eadem illa audita quam lecta delectent) (Quintilian, *Inst.* 10.1.8 [Russell, LCL]).[57]

- There is a folktale wherein Acontius tricks Cydippe into reading words written on an apple that bind her in a marriage oath to him.[58] In Ovid's *Heroides*, which is written from Cydippe's perspective of the event, Cydippe begins by stating that she read a letter from Acontius "without so much as a murmur, lest my tongue unwittingly might swear by some divinity" (scriptumque tuum sine murmure legi, iuraret ne quos inscia lingua deos) (Ovid, *Her.* 21.1–2 [Showerman, LCL]).

Across several genres of literature over several centuries in different places and traditions, silent reading was not rare or extraordinary. It was well known. Literate persons could read both aloud and silently. Antiquity does know of the silent, solitary reader. But this is not to claim that antiquity is ignorant of the solitary, vocalizing reader. Ancient reading practices are not a zero-sum game. Like silent reading, vocalized reading in various settings is well attested in Greco-Roman antiquity, including when persons were alone. The number of texts that attest to private vocalized reading in antiquity approximates those that attest to silent reading.[59]

Vocalized Reading

As a result of the default assumption that ancient reading was vocalized, a "confirmation bias" often leads both classical and biblical scholars to suppose that recorded instances of solitary reading are vocalized even when a text does not state this to be the case.[60] Reading is assumed to involve vocalization even if no hints of it are present. Since silent reading was well known in antiquity, we ought not to assume that every reference to "reading" implies vocalization.

---

57. I am dependent on McCutcheon ("Silent Reading," 13) for this reference.
58. The tale is relayed in Aristaenetus (Rudolf Hercher and Jean François Boissonade, eds., *Epistolographi Graeci* [Paris: Didot, 1873], 140–42).
59. Gavrilov, "Techniques of Reading," 69–73; McCutcheon, "Silent Reading," 14.
60. I borrow the phrase "confirmation bias" from McCutcheon who employs it with respect to classical studies on silent and vocalized reading ("Silent Reading," 14).

Ambiguous Cases of Reading Aloud

To demonstrate this confirmation bias and to move toward examples of solitary vocalized reading in antiquity, we will examine five cases wherein the method of reading, whether silent or aloud, is not stated. These are ambiguous cases that might imply solitary, vocalized reading, but the situation does not demand it. The balance of evidence in only one of these five cases implies vocalized reading. The other four are ambiguous, and I make no claim as to which mode their authors have in mind.

The first three ambiguous cases come from three different letter writers: Pliny the Younger, Cicero, and Fronto. All three are personal letters written to individuals. While there is some debate as to how "authentic" and "personal" these letters are, especially in Pliny's case, there is no reason to doubt that they accurately reflect the media dynamics of their authors.[61] Each is participating in a known trope, remarking on their own literary routines or the literary routines of others. These descriptions offer insight into literary practices in antiquity.

In his published letters, Pliny the Younger leaves behind unique and substantial evidence to everyday life in the Roman empire.[62] He writes of politics, leisure, love, income, Christians, friendship, and much more. Pliny provides a snapshot of Roman antiquity's literate media culture.[63] He writes about education, composition practices, publication norms, private and public speeches and reading events, the book trade, and the copying and excerpting of texts. While Pliny the Younger ran in very different social circles than most early Christians, he offers a basis for understanding a host of media in the gospels' cultural context and we shall frequently return to his letters in subsequent chapters.

Pliny himself curated and published his letter collection in nine installments.[64] These nine books contained letters written to over 100 correspondents

---

61. The authenticity of Pliny's letters is surveyed in Rex Winsbury, *Pliny the Younger: A Life in Roman Letters* (London: T&T Clark, 2014), 16–18.

62. Winsbury, *Pliny the Younger*, 3.

63. Winsbury notes that at least fifty-five of Pliny's letters address literary life in Rome, and that he, more than any other writer, "shows us how the literary scene worked in his day and in the century or so straddling his lifetime" (*Pliny the Younger*, 159).

64. That Pliny's letters were published in such a manner suggests that publication was not primarily, and certainly not solely, the public recitation of a text. Publication is addressed at greater length in part 3 of this book. It is possible that Pliny offered readings of selected letters, but this will have made for an odd sort of reading event. More likely, Pliny simply released the letters for distribution among friends, colleagues, and libraries (Winsbury, *Pliny the Younger*, 15).

and were likely released over a series of years before they were collected.[65] The nine-book volume contains 247 letters written between the years 97 and 112 CE.[66] At some later point a tenth book was added, probably not by Pliny himself and perhaps long after his death, which contained 121 letters of correspondence between Pliny and the emperor Trajan.[67]

The collection itself is an anomaly as literature goes, making it difficult to classify. While they contain autobiographical details, Pliny's letters are not themselves an autobiography.[68] Nor, writes Pliny, are they a history (Pliny the Younger, *Ep.* 1.1). They have been likened to a kaleidoscope, offering different glimpses into Pliny's life and world as one reads and rereads them.[69] The letters, as Roy K. Gibson and Ruth Morello note, offer their reader "an almost infinite number of configurations and connections."[70] Pliny himself writes, in the collection's first letter, that their compilation is incomplete and haphazard (Pliny the Younger, *Ep.* 1.1).[71] The letters provide us tantalizing insights, but not always complete pictures of media practices in antiquity.

With respect to solitary reading, Pliny offers one such snapshot in a letter to Pomponius Bassus. Pliny congratulates Bassus on his retirement and remarks on the ideal location he has chosen to do so. He writes, "You live in a lovely spot, you can take exercise on the shore and in the sea, and have no lack of conversation or books to read and have read to you [multum audire multum lectitare], so that although you know so much, every day you can add something new" (Pliny the Younger, *Ep.* 4.23 [Radice, LCL]).

Bassus's villa had an extensive library and no shortage of slaves to read or tell stories to him. When Pliny mentions Bassus's reading, there is nothing that strongly suggests one particular mode of reading, whether it be silent or vocalized, over the other. Pliny does, however, make a distinction between hearing and reading. Despite Radice's translation reproduced above, which

---

65. Winsbury, *Pliny the Younger*, 15.

66. P. G. Walsh, trans., introduction to *Pliny the Younger, Complete Letters*, Oxford World's Classics (Oxford: Oxford University Press, 2009), ix.

67. Winsbury, *Pliny the Younger*, 15.

68. Roy K. Gibson and Ruth Morello, *Reading the Letters of Pliny the Younger: An Introduction* (Cambridge: Cambridge University Press, 2012), 10–15.

69. John Henderson, *Pliny's Statue: The Letters, Self-Portraiture and Classical Art* (Exeter: Liverpool University Press, 2002), 195n5.

70. Gibson and Morello, *Reading the Letters*, 1.

71. The fact that Pliny self-reflects on the haphazard nature of his curation suggests that it is not actually so haphazard.

presumes that Bassus both listens to and reads "books," texts are not directly mentioned in the passage. More literally, Bassus will have "much to hear, much to read." When Pliny states that Bassus will have much "to hear," he likely has in mind conversations, gossip, oral stories, and texts read to him. When he writes that Bassus will have much "to read," he presumes that texts are involved and probably not another person. Pliny implies a solitary reading event. And while hearing and reading are contrasted in the letter, there is no strong indication as to whether Pliny assumes Bassus reads aloud or silently.

The second ambiguous case of private reading is likewise a personal letter that addresses one's daily routine. In this letter, the author describes his own practices rather than another's. Cicero writes to his friend, Paetus, apprising him of his daily literary routine.[72] As part of the *salutatio* ritual, Cicero received his clients first thing in the morning. Once the stream of visitors stopped, Cicero began to engage his literary work, either writing or reading (*litteris me involvo; aut scribo aut lego*). He states that some of his visitors stuck around to listen to him (*me audiunt*) (Cicero, *Amic.* 193 [Shackleton Bailey, LCL]).

It is unclear whether the "listening" (audiunt) refers to the first activity mentioned, namely the receiving of callers, or to Cicero's "writing and reading" (aut scribo aut lego). If it is the former, then this is no explicit case of vocalized reading. The visitors are not listening to Cicero engage in literary endeavors but are conversing with him as part of the clientship ritual.

If it is the latter, the loiterers hope to overhear Cicero at work. A confirmation bias might lead us to assume Cicero reads and writes aloud. While it is certainly plausible that Cicero's callers hang about to listen to him write and read, the notion is romanticized. The question is whether it has been romanticized by modern myths about ancient reading and writing practices or by Cicero himself. Do we falsely suppose that listeners gather around Cicero's door in hopes of hearing him declaim a text or write one? Or does Cicero hubristically present this as the case? Under the confirmation bias of vocalized reading, the latter is a real option, but the text itself does not demand the conclusion. The case is ambiguous, and the evidence does not seem to favor either vocalized or silent reading.

---

72. Busch and McCutcheon both cite this text as evidence for vocalized reading in antiquity (Busch, "Lautes und leises Lesen," 9–11; McCutcheon, "Silent Reading," 10–11). The former does so to suggest that vocalized reading was more common than silent reading in antiquity, while the latter does so in service of the argument that both modes were practiced.

Like Pliny's friend Bassus, Marcus Aurelius had an ideal place for repose. His was Alsium, known in antiquity as a favorite vacation destination of emperors. Responding to a previous letter wherein Marcus was taciturn about his holiday activities at Alsium, his mentor, Fronto, imagines the emperor's routine: "Lying around in the midday sun, submitting to the urge to take a nap, then calling Niger, and telling him to bring your books. Then, when the desire to read strikes you, you might refine your thoughts with some Plautus, or satisfy your appetite with Accius, or soothe yourself with Lucretius, or set yourself aflame with Ennius ... if someone came to you with stories, you would listen to them" (Fronto, *De Fer. Als.* 3).[73] Both hearing and reading are mentioned, though they are not directly paired as in Pliny's letter. Fronto speculates that Marcus would listen (*audires*) to stories (Fronto, *De Fer. Als.* 3 [Haines, LCL]). This is a different activity than the reading (*legendi*) of books (*libros*) that Niger brings to Marcus. It is unclear whether Fronto imagines that Niger merely delivers the books to Marcus or whether he imagines Niger to be the one who does the reading of Plautus, Accius, Lucretius, and Ennius. If the latter is the case, then this is evidence of vocalized reading, but not by an individual to himself. Rather, it represents another common method of reading addressed at greater length below: a slave reading a text aloud to an individual or small group. If it is the former, however, we, with Fronto, might imagine Marcus reading the texts to himself either aloud or silently. Neither option is implied by the letter.

Our fourth case comes from a passage previously addressed with respect to the eye-voice span. In *The Ignorant Book Collector* 2, Lucian satirizes the person who fancies himself learned because he has purchased deluxe volumes.[74]

---

73. Trans. *Fronto: Selected Letters*, ed. Caillan Davenport and Jennifer Manley (New York: Bloomsbury, 2014), 135–36.

74. Balogh and Hendrickson, both following Christoph Martin Wieland, presume that Lucian is here accusing the ignorant book collector of reading poorly (Balogh, "*Voces Paginarum*," 84–85, 228; Hendrickson, "Ancient Reading," 192–93; Wieland, *Lucians von Samosata Sämtliche Werke* [Leipzig: Im Verlag der Weidmannischen Buchhandlung, 1788], Sechster Teil, 35n3). Knox shows that, according to Wieland and Hendrickson, the problem with the collector's reading is that it is not slow and enunciated, negatively affected by silently reading portions. For Balogh, Lucian disparages the reading because eyes and mouth are not aligned (Knox, "Silent Reading in Antiquity," 424–26). Knox further argues that Lucian is making a concession about the collector's reading, and not an accusation ("Silent Reading in Antiquity," 424–26). This makes much better sense of the passage, as Lucian's real accusation is that the ignorant book collector does not possess adequate knowledge of his books' contents.

According to Lucian, the true literati are more concerned with the message than they are with the medium. The ability to traffic in the content of literature matters more than anything else.

Amid his calumny, Lucian grants that the ignorant book collector has the capacity to declaim texts: "To be sure you look at your books with your eyes open and quite as much as you like, and you read some of them aloud with great fluency, keeping your eyes in advance of your lips [καὶ ἀναγιγνώσκεις ἔνια πάνυ ἐπιτρέχων, φθάνοντος τοῦ ὀφθαλμοῦ τὸ στόμα]" (Lucian, *Ind.* [Harmon, LCL]). He assumes that books were read aloud. It is not clear what kind of reading event Lucian is addressing here, however. Those who have previously remarked on this passage presume that Lucian has in mind the book collector reading privately. If this is the case, then the passage surely attests to the vocalized, solitary reading of texts. There is another possibility: Lucian might have in mind the public declamation of books. His hypothetical interlocutor might be offering a reading from one of his prized volumes. In this case, Lucian admits that the collector is a fine reader, but lambastes his insufficient knowledge of the texts themselves. He is, per Lucian under this take, not any better off than a slave who is able to read a discourse at a dinner party.

The final ambiguous case of private vocalized reading in antiquity is an early Christian text: the Shepherd of Hermas. Reading, writing, and sharing texts figure prominently throughout the Visions of Hermas, but especially in the first two.[75] In Hermas's first vision the audience is introduced to an elderly woman who is described as "having a document in her hands" (ἔχουσα βιβλίον εἰς τὰς χεῖρας) (Herm. Vis. 1.2.2 [2.2]).[76] The woman reads aloud from this document after asking Hermas if he wishes to hear her read (θέλεις ἀκοῦσαί μου ἀναγινωσκούσης) (1.3.3 [3.3]). After she reads, Hermas tells the audience that he did not have the strength to remember the great and marvelous things that he heard in the first part of the text, but that he could remember the last words, which he reproduces (1.3.4 [3.4]).

It is in Hermas's second vision that we find an ambiguous case of solitary, vocalized reading. One year after his first visionary encounter of the elderly

---

75. The Similitudes and Mandates are themselves presented, per Herm. Vis. 5.1.5–7 (25.5–7), as dictated from the Shepherd. See Carolyn Osiek, *Shepherd of Hermas: A Commentary*, Hermeneia (Minneapolis: Fortress, 1999), 102.

76. Text, Michael W. Holmes, ed., *The Apostolic Fathers: Greek Texts and English Translations*, 3rd ed. (Grand Rapids: Baker Academic, 2007). Unless otherwise noted, translations of Hermas are my own.

woman, Hermas sees her again, this time "walking and reading a little book" (περιπατοῦσαν καὶ ἀναγινώκουσαν βιβλαρίδιον) (2.1.3 [5.3]).[77] The longer document (βιβλίον) from the first vision has become a short document (βιβλαρίδιον), perhaps a "heavenly letter."[78] Unlike in the first vision, the woman's reading to Hermas is not narrated. She simply asks Hermas if he is able "to announce these things to God's elect." Hermas replies that he cannot remember them, but that he can copy the document.[79]

How does Hermas know that he cannot remember the message? Is it that he heard the little book read aloud and knows that there is simply too much material to repeat from memory? This is possible. The contents of the little book are later embedded in the text and total just over five hundred words, perhaps too many for Hermas to memorize (Herm. Vis. 2.2.2–3.4 [6.2–7.4]). This interpretation assumes, first, that the woman's "reading" (ἀναγινώκουσαν) was vocalized and, second, that Hermas's statement τοσαῦτα μνημονεῦσαι οὐ δύναμαι ought to be translated "I cannot remember *so many things*," as in Michael W. Holmes's rendering.[80] Hermas is remarking on the quantity of the words, not their quality.

Or is that Hermas *sees* rather than hears the document that the woman is silently reading and knows that there is too much in it to announce from memory? He can already assess, on the basis of the document's size, that there is just too much there. This interpretation likewise privileges the number of words in the document. Whatever the case, the narrator is not explicit about whether the text was read aloud or silently. Given that both modes were known, either is conceivable.

A different interpretation of Hermas's inability to remember the message tilts the evidence in favor of vocalized reading in this ambiguous case. Rather than translating τοσαῦτα μνημονεῦσαι οὐ δύναμαι as "I cannot remember so

---

77. The woman is capable of walking and handling the text at the same time. Ancient readers could multitask while engaging texts.

78. Osiek, *Shepherd of Hermas*, 52.

79. It is presumed that Hermas has basic literary skills in both writing and reading. He is able to transcribe documents (Herm. Vis. 2.1.3 [5.3]; 2.4.5 [8.3]), take down dictation (Herm. Vis. 5.1.5–7 [25.5–7]), read privately (Herm. Vis. 5.1.5 [25.5]), and read publicly (Herm. Vis. 2.4.3 [8.3]). The author's depiction of Hermas's literacy is addressed at greater length in Jonathan E. Soyars, *The Shepherd of Hermas and the Pauline Legacy*, NovTSup 176 (Leiden: Brill, 2019), 32–38. Soyars concludes that Hermas is presented as at least semi-literate.

80. Holmes, *Apostolic Fathers*, 463.

many things," I suggest that the demonstrative τοσαῦτα is better rendered as emphasizing the quality of the message: "I cannot remember *such great things*."[81]

There are three reasons for this. First, there is a wordplay in which Hermas escalates the woman's preceding question. She asks, "Can you announce these things (ταῦτα)?" to which Hermas makes his reply with τοσαῦτα rather than ταῦτα. While they might be just "things" to the heavenly being, they are much more to the earthly Hermas. Second, elements of Hermas's second vision parallel those of the first. In the first vision, the woman reads aloud from the larger book. The reading event is narrated. After his experience of the first reading, Hermas tells his own readers that he did not have the strength to remember the great and marvelous things that he heard. There is a parallel between Hermas's statements in the first and second vision, and he uses the same inflected form of the verb "to remember" (μνημονεύω) in each: [82]

ἤκουσα μεγάλως καὶ θαυμαστῶς ὃ οὐκ ἴσχυσα μνημονεῦσαι.

I heard great and marvelous things which I was not strong enough to remember. (Herm. Vis. 1.4.3 [4.3])

τοσαῦτα μνημονεῦσαι οὐ δύναμαι.

I am not able to remember such great things. (Herm. Vis. 2.1.3 [5.3])

Third, the trope of incomprehension upon the initial experience of a divine message continues throughout the Visions of Hermas. Whenever Hermas sees a vision, its knowledge or meaning must be revealed. The visions are apocalyptic, after all. This is why Hermas cannot initially make out the syllables in the little book (Herm. Vis. 2.1.4 [5.4]). The knowledge of the writing (ἡ γνῶσις τῆς γραφῆς) must be apocalyptically revealed (ἀπεκαλύφθη) to him, which happens after Hermas has fasted and beseeched the Lord for fifteen days (Herm. Vis. 2.2.1 [6.1]).

The problem is not that the visions are too lengthy for Hermas to remember; it is that they are too heavenly. They cannot be understood apart from

---

81. This is one of the primary glosses for the pronoun. See BDAG, LSJ s.v. "τοσοῦτος."
82. My translation follows that of Osiek (*Shepherd of Hermas*, 48) who notes that the adverbial forms μεγάλως and θαυμαστῶς are corrupt in Sinaiticus and that the adjectives refer either to what Hermas hears or to the glories of God mentioned in the text's previous sentence (*Shepherd of Hermas*, 50).

divine revelation. When Hermas sees the elderly woman walking and reading, he has an experience of the divine message read in the little book (Herm. Vis. 2.1.3 [5.3]). The implication is that the woman was reading the text aloud as she walked. Hermas hears the text, but he knows that outside of his ecstatic state he will not be able to remember its content. The words he has heard will be nonsensical to him without divine revelation.[83] Even when Hermas does "copy" (μεταγράφω) the text, its words and meaning remain incomprehensible until they are revealed (ἀπεκαλύφθη) (Herm. Vis. 2.2.1 [6.1]).[84]

All five of these cases are nondescript when it comes to the reading mode narrated in the text. All of them assume private reading events, but none of them unequivocally state whether the reading was done aloud or silently. Influenced by the myth that all reading was vocalized and the confirmation bias that it engenders, it is easy to assume that in each case the author implies vocalized reading. This need not be the default assumption. In most cases, we simply cannot determine that an author has one specific mode of reading in mind.

Upon further investigation of one of them, namely the Shepherd of Hermas, it was determined that a solitary, vocalized reading event was assumed. While it required some interpretive lifting to reach this conclusion, there are other cases in which vocalized private reading is presented less ambiguously.

Unambiguous Cases of Reading Aloud

In a letter to Fuscus Salinator, Pliny the Younger describes his literary habits during his summers in Tuscany. The text attests to both Pliny's writing habits and his reading habits. He mentions reading twice. First, he states that after a nap and a walk he reads "a Greek or Latin speech [orationem Graecam Latinamve] aloud and with emphasis [clare et intente lego]," as a digestive aid (Pliny the Younger, *Ep.* 9.36 [Radice, LCL]). Shortly after this statement, Pliny notes that during dinner, if he is dining with his wife or friends a book is read (*liber legitur*).

With respect to the first time Pliny mentions reading aloud in the letter, he gives no indication that others are present as he reads. The purpose of vocalizing is its supposed health benefit. The salubrious advantages of vocalized reading were celebrated in literate circles in Greco-Roman antiquity. The amateur

---

83. Soyars, *Shepherd of Hermas*, 36.
84. Hence the divine passive here.

physician Celsus prescribes reading aloud (*legere clare*) as the best activity to strengthen a weak stomach (Celsus, *De Medicina* 1.8 [Spencer, LCL]).

Pliny states that he made a regular practice of reading aloud even when he was alone. He read aloud and in private for his own benefit. This is not to state that Pliny *always* read vocally, but that he did so regularly.[85] Vocalized private reading was a known practice among the literati.

In his funeral oration for Julian, Libanius addresses Julian's busy days (Libanius, *Oration* 18.175). Even when he was relaxing, Julian was engaged in literary activities. After breakfast and having completed his state affairs, Libanius writes of Julian's reading habits. "Not to be outdone by the cicadas, he would make for his piles of books and read aloud until, in the evening, his care for the empire recalled him to his task" (Libanius, *Oration* 18.175 [Norman, LCL]). The implication is twofold. First, Julian's reading was vocalized since he was not to be outdone by cicadas. And second, his reading was melodious, since the songs of cicadas were proverbial for being sweet.

The final explicit case of private, vocalized reading is from the New Testament itself. Whereas there are no examples in the New Testament of a person reading silently to themselves, there is a case of an individual reading aloud to himself. This is the Ethiopian eunuch in Acts 8:26–40. In the passage, the eunuch is riding in his chariot and reading the prophet Isaiah (ἀνεγίνωσκεν τὸν προφήτην Ἡσαΐαν). There are questions related to the episode's realism: how does Philip, who is on foot, overtake a chariot? How loudly must the eunuch have been reading for Philip to overhear him over the noise of the horse and cart? Was the chariot driver listening to the reading event? What language was the text the eunuch was reading? These are of little interest to the author. Relevant is that Philip overhears a God-fearer from the far stretches of the world reading a prophetic text and recognizes it as Isaianic (ὁ Φίλιππος ἤκουσεν αὐτοῦ ἀναγινώσκοντος Ἡσαΐαν τὸν προφήτην).

There are three things noteworthy about reading in the passage. First, the eunuch possesses his own copy of an Isaiah scroll, which he reads to himself.[86] Personal possession of Jewish Scripture was known to Luke and Luke's

---

85. Pliny specifies this salubrious mode of reading as "reading aloud" (legere clare). If Pliny knew reading always to be vocalized there would be no need to specify.

86. Commentators frequently note that owning a scroll suggests the eunuch is of some means (Darrell L. Bock, *Acts*, BECNT [Grand Rapids: Baker Academic, 2007], 518; Keener, *Acts 3:1–14:28*, 1580).

audience.[87] Furthermore, personal reading of Jewish Scripture must also have been known, since that is precisely what Philip comes upon.

Second, the Ethiopian has no issue navigating a scroll as he travels on a chariot. Once we recognize that scrolls were not as cumbersome to navigate as is sometimes claimed, we see that persons could read to themselves in a variety of settings, including while they traveled.[88] There is no need to posit, as Craig S. Keener does, that the Ethiopian might have had a servant with him to help roll and unroll the scroll.[89]

Third, that Philip heard (ἤκουσεν) the man reading implies that the eunuch is reading aloud.[90] The logic of the episode presumes that the audience of Acts knows that vocalized reading was common, even when an individual

---

87. In Josephus's *Antiquities* 20.44 the God-fearing Adiabene king Izates is reading Torah to himself when a certain Eleazar comes in and convinces the king that he ought to have himself circumcised. This passage will be discussed at greater length in the next chapter, but it is worth forwarding that Josephus narrates private reading of a personal copy of Jewish Scripture. Like the Ethiopian eunuch, king Izates is a God-fearer. Neither Luke nor Josephus suggests that there was any difficulty for a God-fearer to acquire a personal copy of Jewish Scripture. Fourth Macc. 18:10–18 suggests that devout Jewish families also engaged Jewish Scripture privately. A variety of verbs are used with respect to different genres of Jewish Scripture. Most notably, in 4 Macc. 18:11 the righteous mother tells her children that their father used to "read" (ἀνεγίνωσκεν) them the slaying of Abel by Cain (τὸν ἀναιρεθέντα Αβελ ὑπὸ Κάιν), as well as the sacrifice of Isaac (καὶ τὸν ὁλοκαρπούμενον Ισαάκ) and the account of Joseph's imprisonment (καὶ τὸν ἐν φυλακῇ Ιωσήφ).

88. Though there is much testimony that *lectores* were often used for reading when one traveled. Burfeind takes the primary source evidence for traveling *lectores* to indicate that the Ethiopian was not actually reading aloud himself, but rather that someone was reading aloud to him ("Wen hören Philippus?" 142–44). Given the multiple ways texts were read, it is not impossible that the author or audience imagined this kind of reading event, but the narrative sense of the passage does not demand it. The pericope indicates that the Ethiopian is reading to himself since the interaction in the pericope is between Philip and the Ethiopian, not Philip, the Ethiopian, and a *lector*. Moreover, Philip asks the Ethiopian, "Do you know what you are reading?" (γινώσκεις ἃ ἀναγινώσκεις;). Both verbs are in the second-person singular. Luke very well could have posed the question with a passive: "Do you know what is being read?" (γινώσκεις ἃ ἀναγινώσκεται;).

89. Keener, *Acts 3:1–14:28*, 1584.

90. Commentators frequently note this, often also citing various myths about ancient reading habits. For example, F. F. Bruce suggests that modern print better facilitates learning how to read silently than does "ancient handwriting" (*The Book of Acts*, NICNT [Grand Rapids: Eerdmans, 1988], 175). Keener claims that reading aloud was the normal practice because it allowed the reader better "to catch the flow of thought" presented in a continuous script (*Acts 3:1–14:28*, 1583). Luke implies that the eunuch was reading aloud, but to suggest this is because of typography is a *non sequitur*.

was reading alone. If vocalized reading were not known, the audience would be left wondering how Philip knew that the eunuch was reading from Jewish Scripture and how he recognized the text as Isaianic. Just as the logic of many passages assumed knowledge of silent reading, this passage assumes that the audience of Acts knows of private, vocalized reading.

Conclusion

The foregoing evidence to both silent and vocalized reading should not be pressed to state that vocalized reading was the norm over and against silent reading, or vice-versa. Reading aloud does not preclude silent reading; silent reading does not preclude vocalized reading. If silent reading was unremarkable, then it is no surprise that authors do not remark on it. The ability to read silently is assumed. The lack of ubiquitous testimony to reading in this manner cannot be taken as evidence that it was less common than vocalized reading. Persons could and did read silently in Greco-Roman antiquity.

The evidence also suggests that vocalized reading was known, even when one read in solitude. But this is not to claim that it was a common practice at the expense of silent reading. Vocalized reading was a more common mode of engaging texts in Greco-Roman antiquity than it is in Western modernity. Our reading cultures do in fact differ from the reading cultures of antiquity. Understanding these reading cultures while not exoticizing them as wholly different from our own equips the interpreter as she engages it. One aim of this chapter is to de-exoticize ancient reading practices and to demonstrate how they are both similar to and different from our own. Because we are dealing with a culture of reading, the foregoing analysis about modes of Greco-Roman reading is not and cannot be exhaustive.[91] By exploring these practices, we are better able to understand the reading cultures, systems, and practices of Greco-Roman antiquity, Second Temple Judaism, and early Christianity.

Both silent and vocalized reading occurred in these cultures. Having established that persons in antiquity read *both* aloud and silently, we move to a related topic: types of reading events in antiquity. There were multiple kinds of reading events. Because reading is not simply an individual act, but a sociocultural system, these events differ on the basis of a number of factors,

---

91. W. Johnson notes that trying to understand a cultural system is asymptotic: the aim is to better understand the system, even if its complexity defeats final analysis ("Toward a Sociology of Reading," 606).

including the kind of text engaged, where it is engaged, who engages it with whom, when they engage it, why they engage it, and the private or public space in which it is engaged.

The evidence reveals a variety of reading events. Persons read individually, they read in pairs and small groups, and they read in larger groups. There were different kinds of "readings" in different spaces. Some readings were wholly public, and anyone could attend, but private readings were more common.

CHAPTER 2

Solitary and Communal Reading

Media Myth: Texts were always or usually engaged in communal reading events.

Media Reality: Reading was both a communal and solitary affair. Individuals read texts to themselves, both aloud and silently. Communal reading events were diverse. Small groups read and engaged texts together. Texts were publicly read to large gatherings of people. Antiquity was characterized by a variety of reading events, constituted by different numbers of persons in participation of the event. A given text could be read in different ways and in different social contexts.

◆ ◆ ◆

Reading methods were diverse. Persons read both silently and aloud. A corollary to the myth of vocalized reading is the myth that reading was always or usually communal in antiquity. Under the influence of the vocalized reading myth and the communal reading myth, the logic is that when individuals did read to themselves, they did so in preparation for or imitation of public reading. There is no place for solitary, personal reading.

Brian J. Wright claims, "It would be no exaggeration to state that virtually all literature during this time period was composed to be read communally."[1] For Wright, not only were all texts meant for communal reception, but they were also composed with it in mind. Wright's statement echoes Paul J. Achtemeier's assertion that all texts in antiquity were organized for the ear, not the eye.[2] The myth has perhaps exerted its greatest influence among biblical performance critics.[3] For example, David Rhoads writes, "Simply put, the

---

1. Brian J. Wright, *Communal Reading in the Time of Jesus: A Window into Early Christian Reading Practices* (Minneapolis: Fortress, 2017), 59.
2. Paul J. Achtemeier, "*Omne Verbum Sonat:* The New Testament and the Oral Environment of Late Western Antiquity," *JBL* 109 (1990): 18. Achtemeier is explicit: "All material in antiquity was intended to be heard" ("*Omne Verbum Sonat,*" 18).
3. Performance criticism has helped to disabuse biblical scholarship of its textual and post-Gutenberg biases. For some performance critics, however, the pendulum has swung far in the opposite direction and functions of orality are emphasized at the expense of textuality.

writings we have in the New Testament are examples of 'performance literature,' that is, literature that was meant for performance—like music or theater or ancient poetry."[4] For Wright, Achtemeier, and Rhoads, texts in antiquity, and especially the New Testament documents, were composed exclusively for communal reception.

The textual evidence suggests otherwise. It is an exaggeration to state that "virtually all literature" was produced with an eye to communal reception.[5] The media cultures of Greco-Roman antiquity, Second Temple Judaism, and early Christianity were all characterized by a diversity of reading events. Reading could be solitary or communal, private or public. Communal readings did take place, but this was not the exclusive way that texts were experienced.

The primary source testimony to reading events in antiquity is considerable. Descriptions of such events reveal the normalcy of reading in various contexts. Reading was not an exotic act. Persons casually read to their children at home. They read to pass the time or avoid socializing with other persons. They read and researched when their lives were in imminent danger. They read in service of and preparation for worship. They read privately to dispute theological claims and entire movements. They read themselves to sleep. They continued reading casually when peers came calling. There was no one setting, purpose, experience, or method of reading.

There are several different ways that the evidence to diverse reading events in antiquity might be assembled. It can be presented chronologically. Alternatively, it might be grouped by social provenance: Greco-Roman, Second Temple Jewish, early Christian, and otherwise. I have chosen to present the evidence in two broad categories: texts implying that an individual is reading alone and texts indicating that several people engage the discourse together. The latter category is expansive since groups participating in a reading event

---

This is Larry W. Hurtado's pointed critique in "Oral Fixation and New Testament Studies? 'Orality,' 'Performance' and Reading Texts in Early Christianity," *NTS* 60 [2014]: 323–24). But see also the response from Kelly R. Iverson ("Oral Fixation or Oral Corrective? A Response to Larry Hurtado," *NTS* 62 [2016]: 183–200).

4. David Rhoads, "Performance Events in Early Christianity: New Testament Writings in an Oral Context," in *The Interface of Orality and Writing: Speaking, Seeing, Writing in the Shaping of New Genres*, ed. Annette Weissenrieder and Robert B. Coote, WUNT 260 (Tübingen: Mohr Siebeck, 2010), 169. Whitney Taylor Shiner's take is similar: "First-century works were almost always heard in a communal setting rather than read silently by individuals" (*Proclaiming the Gospel: First-Century Performance of Mark* [Harrisburg, PA: Trinity Press International, 2003], 1).

5. Wright, *Communal Reading*, 59.

can vary in size from two persons to any number of persons. This second, broad category I call "communal reading," which can be further divided into subcategories based on the number of people involved in the reading event.

Both "communal reading" and "public reading" have been used in New Testament scholarship to refer to any event in which more than one person participates, regardless of the space in which that event takes place.[6] A public or communal reading, per these parameters, might consist of two persons reading a text in a private residence. I aim to be more nuanced than this, differentiating between the terms "solitary," "communal," "small group," "moderately sized group," "large group," "public," and "private."[7] Communal reading is an umbrella category for any reading event in which more than one person participates. Small-group and large-group reading events fall under this umbrella. When I write of a small group, I mean between two and ten people. A moderately sized group is between ten and fifty persons, and a large group consists of fifty or more people. Solitary reading is when one person reads a text to oneself.

Public reading, as I use the phrase, is an event wherein a text is directly read from in a space where a group of persons can be present without much difficulty.[8] A private reading, in contrast, is an event in which a text is directly read from, but the event is not easily accessible to anyone and everyone. For example, a private reading might take place in an individual's residence.

---

6. Dan Nässelqvist prefers the phrase "public reading" but explicitly notes that this kind of reading event "exists in both public and private settings" (*Public Reading in Early Christianity: Lectors, Manuscripts, and Sound in the Oral Delivery of John 1–4*, NovTSup 163 [Leiden: Brill, 2016], 15). For him, "public" simply means that multiple persons are present. Wright, in contrast, prefers the phrase "communal reading" to "public reading." Communal reading is any event "in which two or more persons are involved" (*Communal Reading*, 12). This sets the parameters for what constitutes a communal reading event wide. Wright considers Luke 1:63, wherein Zechariah writes the four words "his name is John" (Ἰωάννης ἐστὶν ὄνομα αὐτοῦ) on a writing tablet and a small group reads them to be a communal reading event (*Communal Reading*, 128). The loose definition thus flattens reading events into a single category with little nuance. The reading of four words on a writing tablet is as communal as reading the entirety of Torah to all gathered Jerusalem (*Communal Reading*, 128 and 106–7, respectively).

7. With Wright, I consider "communal reading" to be any event in which a text is read, and more than one person is present (*Communal Reading*, 12). However, I attempt to avoid the phrase because it lacks specificity with respect to the public or private nature of the reading event.

8. A reading at a private residence to persons who are invited is not a public reading event. Similarly, a public event where a text is utilized, but not directly read from, under this definition is not a public reading event.

I make these distinctions because there is not a one-to-one correlation between communal and public reading. A communal reading event can be either public or private. A private reading event can consist of any number of persons and does not necessarily entail a small group. The terms "public" and "private" refer to the sociality of the event, whereas "communal," "small group," and "large group" refer to the number of people present at a given event.

Before turning to the evidence for various kinds of communal reading events in antiquity, we look to cases in which individuals read alone. This evidence cuts across the myth that reading was always or usually communal. There is no question that communal reading events were common, but solitary reading events were as well.

Solitary Roman Reading

We have already encountered many occasions in which individuals read alone. We found Ambrose reading silently to himself when his students came calling. In the Greek novels, Cleitophon feigned reading while snooping on his newfound love, and Dionysius read to himself in the presence of many others at a banquet. Josephus similarly read a letter to himself while others were present in *Life* 222–24. From the letters of the Greco-Roman literati, we learn that Bassus, Cicero, Pliny the Younger, and Marcus Aurelius all read while alone. We encountered the woman in Hermas's second apocalyptic vision, walking and reading to herself. The Ethiopian eunuch in Acts 8 was reading aloud to himself when Philip overheard the words from Isaiah. The central question when we addressed these accounts was not whether solitary reading occurred. That was given. The question was if the reading was silent or vocalized.

There is no shortage of other texts that attest to individuals reading alone, especially among Roman literates of high social status. Holt N. Parker writes, "First, the Romans read to themselves; second, the Romans read to each other. Because the first fact oddly enough seems to be in danger of being forgotten or ignored, it needs to be pointed out that Romans did in fact read books while alone. We discover people reading all the time, with no need for, or mention of, company."[9]

---

9. Holt N. Parker, "Books and Reading Latin Poetry," in *Ancient Literacies: The Culture of Reading in Greece and Rome*, ed. William A. Johnson and Holt N. Parker (Oxford: Oxford University Press, 2009), 196.

If the danger of forgetting that Romans read to themselves is acute in classical studies, the danger of forgetting that early Jews and Christians read to themselves is acute in biblical studies. With respect to solitary Roman reading, Parker offers the following evidence to individuals reading alone:[10]

- Cicero finds Cato at Lucullus's villa surrounded by books of Stoic philosophers, reading them all by himself (Cicero, *Fin.* 3.7–10).
- Cato reads to himself before committing suicide (Plutarch, *Cat. Min.* 68–70 [792–94], Appian, *Bell. civ.* 2.98–99, Dio Cassius, *His. rom.* 43.11.2–5).
- Horace reads and writes by himself (Horace, *Sat.* 1.6.122–23).
- Seneca reads and writes alone early in the day (Seneca, *Ep.* 65.1).
- Martial frequently embeds jokes in the *Epigrams* that are experienced between author and reader alone (Martial, *Epigr.* 3.68.11–12; 3.86.1–2; 11.16.9–10). For example, in *Epigr.* 3.86 Martial writes, "I told you beforehand, warned you, virtuous lady, not to read part of my frolicsome little book; nonetheless, look, you are reading it" (Ne legeres partem lascivi, casta, libelli, praedixi et monui: tu tamen, ecce, legis) (Shackleton Bailey, LCL).
- Severus read Martial's poetry to himself while at parties or the theatre because he preferred it to the entertainment happening in those venues (Martial, *Epigr.* 2.6).
- Pliny the Younger went on reading and making extracts as Vesuvius erupted (Pliny the Younger, *Ep.* 6.16; 6.20).

This last case illustrates that reading was a banal activity for those who were literate. Pliny was in such a habit of reading that he did it when his life was in imminent danger. Reading is not an exotic, public act.

The same is true when persons read to calm their minds or to fall asleep. The somniferous effect of reading is a topic addressed by Greco-Roman, Jewish, and early Christian authors. In the third century CE, Plotinus marshals reading as the prime example of an activity that one does without being self-conscious that she is doing it (Plotinus, *Ennead* 1.4.10).[11] It is an exercise that settles the mind. Augustine writes of an experience common to all readers, ancient or modern: reading a page of text, forgetting what was just read, and having to reread it (Augustine, *Trin.* 11.8.15).[12] Six centuries before either Augustine or

---

10. Parker, "Books and Reading," 196–98.
11. Cited in M. F. Burnyeat, "Postscript on Silent Reading," *ClQ* 47 (1997): 76.
12. Cited in Burnyeat, "Postscript on Silent Reading," 76.

Plotinus, Aristotle posed the following question about the sleep-inducing effect of reading: "Why is it that in some people, if they begin to read, sleep overtakes them when they don't want it to, whereas others, who want to sleep, are made to be awake when they take up a book?" (Aristotle, *Probl.* 18.1.1 [Mayhew, LCL]).

Reading is soporific when it is private and silent, not when it is public and vocalized.[13] In a very different context from Aristotle, Enoch enters an apocalyptic, visionary sleep as he reads the petition that he transcribed for the Watchers (1 En. 13:7–10). Reading in antiquity was known to slow down the mind and induce sleep, just as it does today. Reading has this effect only under certain conditions. Chief among them is that it is private and solitary.

There is a surfeit of evidence that demonstrates that private reading was well known, especially among the literati. Reading in literate Roman circles was not always public. Texts were not always written with the intention that they would be read publicly. But is the same true in early Jewish and Christian circles? Is there evidence that Jewish individuals and Christian individuals read Jewish and Christian texts while they were alone?

It is mistaken to assume that Jewish and Christian reading practices diverged from Greco-Roman practices. Why should Jews and Christians have different reading practices than their non-Jewish and non-Christian contemporaries? They did not. Like their literate Greco-Roman counterparts, literate Jews and Christians participated in a variety of reading events, including reading texts to themselves.

Solitary Jewish and Christian Reading

In *On the Special Laws*, Philo addresses why Deut. 17:18 requires that the king write out a copy of the book of the law with his own hand (Philo, *Spec. Laws* 4.160–67). The short answer, for Philo, is that writing slows down one's train of thought. "For while one is reading [ἀναγινώσκοντος] fleeting thoughts glide

---

13. Interestingly, though immaterial to the ancient context, certain electronic media can erode reading's soporific effect. Reading from an electronic tablet, specifically an iPad, has been shown to impinge on sleepiness in comparison to reading from a physical, printed book (Anne-Marie Chang et al., "Evening Use of Light-Emitting eReaders Negatively Affects Sleep, Circadian Timing, and Next-Morning Alertness," *Proceedings of the National Academy of Sciences of the United States of America* 112 [2015]: 1232–37; Janne Grønli et al., "Reading from an iPad or from a Book in Bed: The Impact on Human Sleep. A Randomized Controlled Crossover Trial," *Sleep Medicine* 21 [2016]: 86–92).

away in the torrent, but in writing [τῷ δὲ γράφοντι] they are engraved and established at leisure."[14] To know the law is to write it by hand.

But writing one's own copy of the law is not enough. Having written the contents of the law, Philo encourages the king "to try to study and to read [it] everyday" (πειράσθω καθ᾽ ἑκάστην ἡμέραν ἐντυγχάνειν καὶ ἀναγινώσκειν). As he looks back on those words written in his own hand daily, the king will remember why: "I wrote this from its beginning. Did I use one of my myriads of servants? Or to fill up a book as the hired writers do? Or as those who train their eyes and their hands for sharp sight or quick writing do? Is this why? No. It was so that these things written in a book [αὐτὰ ἐν βιβλίῳ γράφων], the divine and unfading marks, might immediately be copied and impressed into my mind [μεταγράφω καὶ ἐναπομάττωμαι τῇ διανοίᾳ]" (Philo, *Spec. Laws* 4.163).[15] The king's best practice, according to Philo, is to have his personal copy of the law written in his own hand so that he might read it daily and engrave its words upon his mind. Elsewhere in *On the Special Laws*, Philo suggests that it is better to study the holy writings with one's mind rather than just with one's eyes. The best way to do this is not simply to read privately, which Philo presumes that people do with their eyes, but to read it privately in one's own handwriting (Philo, *Spec. Laws* 1.214; 4.163; *Embassy* 1.83).

Whereas Philo offers hypothetical best practices for a king's copying the Mosaic law, reading it, and impressing it upon his mind, Josephus offers a historical account of a king's interaction with the law. *Jewish Antiquities* 20.17–53 relays the history of the God-fearers Helena, Queen of Abiadene, and her son, King Izates. The latter reads Torah privately.

The ruler of the Parthian client kingdom has resolved to embrace Jewish customs entirely but supposes that he cannot "truly be a Judean" (μὴ ἂν εἶναι βεβαίως Ιουδαῖος) unless he is circumcised. Izates is determined to undergo the procedure, though his mother and Ananias, a man of Judean ancestry who taught him to worship God, have discouraged him, as they suppose it will bring him into political conflict with his non-Judean subjects. Izates agonizes over the decision until he is finally convinced by a Galilean named Eleazar to have himself circumcised. Josephus narrates the turning point in *Ant.* 20.43–45:

> When [Eleazar] entered to greet [Izates], he found him reading the law of Moses [Μωυσέος νόμον ἀναγινώσκοντα]. He said, "Without knowing it, king,

---

14. Trans. my own.
15. Trans. my own.

you transgress the great laws and God also. For you ought not only to read [ἀναγινώσκειν] them, but most of all to do what they command. How long will you remain uncircumcised? But if you haven't yet read the law concerning this [εἰ μήπω τὸν περὶ τούτου νόμον ἀνέγνως], in order that you might see what impiety is, read it now [νῦν ἀνάγνωθι]!" Hearing these things the king delayed the deed no longer: entering in another room, he called in the physician and carried out what was commanded. Then sending for his mother and Ananias he informed them that the deed had been done. (Josephus, *Ant.* 20.43–45)[16]

As with the Ethiopian eunuch in Acts 8, here a God-fearer privately reads Jewish Scripture to himself. One of the necessary implications in both texts is that the reader possesses their own personal copy of authoritative texts. In the case of the eunuch, it is an Isaianic text; in the case of Izates, it is the law of Moses (Μωυσέος νόμον).

Josephus gives no indication that Izates was participating in a communal reading event when Eleazar came upon him. Their interaction makes it certain that the king was reading to himself. Twice Ananias uses second-person singular forms of "to read" (ἀναγινώσκω). On the first occasion, Eleazar proposes, with a bit of cheek, that perhaps Izates has "not yet" (μήπω) read that little part in the law about circumcision and therefore he has not yet undergone the procedure.[17] Eleazar's clever comment implies that the individualized, serial reading of texts was known. That is, perhaps Izates has not yet reached in his reading that part of Torah wherein circumcision is commanded.

The second instance of a second-person singular form of "read" is Eleazar's imperative, "read it now!" (νῦν ἀνάγνωθι). This entails finding a specific text in the scroll and reading that discrete passage. That is, Josephus, by way of Eleazar, assumes that finding a specific passage in a roll was not inconvenient, as is sometimes assumed. Eleazar's second-person singular command supposes not only that Izates could read the law to and by himself, but that he was previously doing so when Eleazar came upon him.

16. Trans. my own.
17. The statement is like Jesus's repeated question to scribal authorities in the canonical gospels, "Have you not read?" Usually, the question is in the second-person plural form, ἀνέγνωτε, and expects a positive answer, as the question is posed with the negative particle οὐ (Matt. 12:3, 5; 19:4; 21:16, 42; 22:31; Mark 2:25; 12:10; Luke 6:3). Though on one occasion, Luke 10:26, Jesus asks an individual how he reads the law (πῶς ἀναγινώσκεις).

46 • *Reading*

When we turn to early Christian circles, we find once again that private and solitary reading of texts was known. As with Izates and the Ethiopian eunuch, Christian individuals possessed personal copies of biblical texts and read them in private settings. Along with texts of Jewish Scripture, which later also became Christian Scripture, we find that Christian individuals possessed personal copies of gospels and other New Testament texts.

The evidence comes in two forms: manuscript and literary. First, the physical format of many early Christian documents suggests that they were personal texts. Second, early Christian writers testify to the personal possession and reading of texts. These early Christian writers do not suppose that personal access to Scriptural texts and the private reading of them is extraordinary. Their statements indicate that private possession and reading were well known, and manuscript evidence supports their supposition.

The private ownership of texts is especially well attested in manuscript evidence starting in the third century CE.[18] "Miniature" Christian codices from this period imply personal reading.[19] The physical forms of most manuscripts in Christian antiquity provide little evidence to reading practices and events, whether public or personal, but these small codices are an exception. The size of these texts made reading from them publicly arduous if not impossible. *P.Lond.Lit.* 204, a third-century Psalms codex, for example, measures 2.5 inches by 2.9 inches.[20] Other New Testament manuscripts of similar size from this period, including a 2 inch by 1.1 inch text of Jude and a 3.5 inch by 3.9 inch text of 2 John, strongly suggest that they were produced for personal, not public, reading.[21] For comparison, modern Gideon Bibles, which are certainly intended and better suited for personal, individualized use than public reading, are about three inches by five inches.

Along with texts that are now deemed canonical, apocryphal texts are attested in this miniature form. The manuscript evidence indicates that these texts were more likely to exist in miniature than were their now-canonical counterparts.[22] Personal reading of these texts became ubiquitous and so by the

---

18. Harry Y. Gamble, *Books and Readers in the Early Church: A History of Early Christian Texts* (New Haven: Yale University Press, 1995), 231–37.

19. Gamble, *Books and Readers*, 235–36; Larry W. Hurtado, *The Earliest Christian Artifacts: Manuscripts and Christian Origins* (Grand Rapids: Eerdmans, 2006), 160–61.

20. Hurtado, *Earliest Christian Artifacts*, 160.

21. Hurtado, *Earliest Christian Artifacts*, 160–61. See also Hurtado's catalogue of early Christian literary texts in the second and third centuries (*Earliest Christian Artifacts*, 209–29).

22. Gamble, *Books and Readers*, 160.

mid-fourth century Christian leaders attempted to regulate what was and was not read privately.[23] The Muratorian Fragment suggests that *The Shepherd of Hermas* should be read, but not publicly, and Cyril of Jerusalem promoted the strict guideline, "What is not read in the church should not be read privately" (Cyril, *Catech.* 4.36).[24] Cyril's statement presumes at least two kinds of reading events for the same texts, one communal and one private.

Literary evidence to the private possession and reading of Christian texts is pervasive in the third and fourth centuries.[25] We can push the chronological needle back even further. We will begin with the explicit literary testimony to private reading of Christian texts in the fourth century and work backward.

With respect to the fourth century CE, John Chrysostom's eleventh homily on the Gospel of John assumes private possession of the Fourth Gospel and encourages the personal reading and study of it.[26] He begins this sermon on John 1:14 by making a request of his hearers. He asks that beginning on the first day of the week they read privately "the section of the Gospel to be read" (τὴν μέλλουσαν ἐν ὑμῖν ἀναγνωσθήσεσθαι τῶν Εὐαγγελίων περικοπὴν) (John Chrysostom, *Hom. Jo.* 11.1 [PG 59:77]).[27] He specifies that each person should "take it with their own hands in their home, and read it in its entirety" (μετὰ χεῖρας λαμβάνων ἕκαστος οἴκοι καθήμενος ἀναγινωσκέτω συνεχῶς). It is likely that not all of Chrysostom's auditors were literate and possessed a personal copy of the Fourth Gospel. However, enough of them must have had the capacity for private reading for Chrysostom to encourage the individualized study of a particular gospel and to indicate that his request is neither "heavy or difficult" (βαρύ τι καὶ ἐπαχθές).

Like Chrysostom in the fourth century, Origen encourages the private study of biblical texts in the third century. In his eleventh homily on Genesis, Origen states that a Christian who wishes to dwell "by the well of vision" must not neglect, but rather be occupied with, the word of God "at home" (*domi*)

---

23. Gamble, *Books and Readers*, 234–35. For Gamble, Athanasius's 39th Festal Letter is exhibit A for this regulation. He argues that Athanasius's list must not be primarily concerned with texts that are improper for public reading since "by this time the likelihood that a heretical book would be publicly (that is, liturgically) read is very small" (*Books and Readers*, 235).
24. Quoted in Gamble, *Books and Readers*, 235.
25. Gamble, *Books and Readers*, 231–37.
26. I am dependent on Gamble for this reference (*Books and Readers*, 233).
27. Trans. my own.

(Origen, *Hom. in Gen.* 11.3).[28] But she must also enter the church frequently to "hear the word of God" (ecclesiam ad audiendum verbum Dei frequenter ingrediar). Gamble notes that there are several other homilies in which Origen "speaks of the importance of reading the Scriptures at home, recommending it as a daily exercise of at least a few hours."[29]

To Origen's testimony to private ownership and reading of biblical texts in the third century, we can add *The Apostolic Tradition*, which is attributed to Hippolytus, and Clement of Alexandria.[30] *The Apostolic Tradition* 41 provides instructions for what Christians ought to do on days when there is no teaching at a Christian gathering.[31] It counsels, "When each one is at his house, let him take a holy book and read in it sufficiently as it seems to him that it is profitable" (Hippolytus, *Trad. Ap.* 41.4).[32] In *Strom.* 7.7, Clement counsels that best Christian practice is to read Scriptures before meals at home.[33]

---

28. Text, Carol Heinric Eduard Lommatzsch, ed., *Origenis opera omnia*, vol. 8 (Berlin: Sumtibus Haude et Spener, 1838), 231.

29. Gamble, *Books and Readers*, 232. See Origen, *Hom. in Gen.* 10.1; 12.5; *Hom. in Ex.* 12.2, 27; *Hom. in Lev.* 11.7; *Hom. in Num.* 2.1.

30. The dating of the various materials that make up the *Apostolic Tradition* is fraught, and it is common to consider the text(s) "living literature," rather than the work of a single author or even a single editor (Jean Magne, *Tradition apostolique sur les charismes et Diataxeis des saints Apôtres*, Origines chrétiennes 1 [Paris: Magne, 1975], 76–77; Alexandre Faivre, "La documentation canonico-liturgique de l'Eglise ancienne," *RevScRel* 54 [1980]: 286; Allen Brent, *Hippolytus and the Roman Church in the Third Century: Communities in Tension before the Emergence of a Monarch-Bishop*, VCSup 31 [Leiden: Brill, 1995], 195–96; Paul F. Bradshaw, Maxwell E. Johnson, and L. Edward Phillips, *Apostolic Tradition*, Hermeneia [Minneapolis: Fortress, 2002], 13–14). A composition date ranging from the mid-second to the early third century CE is generally accepted (Alistair Stewart-Sykes, *Hippolytus: On the Apostolic Tradition: An English Version with Introduction and Commentary* [Crestwood, NY: St. Vladimir's Seminary, 2001], 12; Bradshaw et al., *Apostolic Tradition*, 14).

31. I am dependent on Gamble, *Books and Readers*, 232 for this reference.

32. Trans. Bradshaw et al., *Apostolic Tradition*, 196. The translation here is of the Sahidic text. Bradshaw, Johnson, and Phillips's modus operandi is to present four different witnesses to the *Apostolic Tradition* rather than merge the discrete witnesses into a single text. There is a lacuna in the Latin for this specific passage. Notably, the Arabic and Ethiopic both correspond to the Sahidic. Both instruct "everyone" to read a/the holy book "in his house" and read it (Bradshaw et al., *Apostolic Tradition*, 196).

33. In this section Clement is reflecting on the "private affairs" of the ideal Christian who prays, praises and reads before meals, sings during meals and before bed, and awakes during the night to pray.

To summarize: Chrysostom, Origen, *The Apostolic Tradition*, and Clement of Alexandria all testify to private ownership and reading of Scripture in the third and fourth centuries. Some of these authors explicitly encourage private reading, while others simply assume it as a practice. Most of these texts expect that Christians will experience Scripture not just privately, but also in communal events.

Tatian, Tertullian, and Justin Martyr all indicate that private, personal reading was also known in the second century.[34] Around 160 CE Tatian narrated his conversion to Christianity in *Or. Graec.* 29.[35] Having completed a religio-philosophical tour of the mystery rites, as well as having experienced the worship of both Jupiter and Artemis, Tatian was dissatisfied. He found these traditions and practices wanting. At this point he "happened upon" Judeo-Christian texts that would ultimately prompt his conversion. "Retiring by myself I considered in what sort of course I might find the truth. While reflecting on weighty matters, I happened to come across certain barbaric writings, older than the decrees of the Greeks and more divine than their erroneous way" (Tatian, *Or. Graec.* 29).[36] These ancient "barbaric" writings were Jewish scripture. Tatian does not state what texts he came upon but given his comparison of Homer and Moses two chapters later in *Or. Graec.* 31, it is likely to have been a Septuagintal text of Torah or some portion of it.[37]

Tatian's account is representative of two different second-century Christian tropes. The first is that Jewish and Christian texts, either studied privately or in accompaniment with instruction by a pedagogue, were catalysts for conversion

---

34. Adolf von Harnack likewise argued that the private use of Christian and Jewish texts was known in the second century and earlier (*Bible Reading in the Early Church*, trans. J. R. Wilkinson, Crown Theological Library 36 [London: Williams and Norgate, 1912], 32–47). Some of the passages addressed below are likewise discussed, usually briefly, by Harnack.

35. On the dating of *Or. Graec.* see L. W. Barnard, "The Heresy of Tatian—Once Again," *JEH* 19 (1968): 1–3.

36. Text, Jörg Trelenberg, *Tatianos, Oratio Ad Graecos Rede an Die Griechen*, BHT 165 (Tübingen: Mohr Siebeck, 2012), 160; trans. my own.

37. That Tatian became a Christian after reading a Septuagintal text implies one of two things. Either his chance encounter with these writings was accompanied by subsequent Christian instruction or, as Ian N. Mills suggests, "These writings came to him as Christian books" ("Pagan Readers of Christian Scripture: The Role of Books in Early Autobiographical Conversion Narratives," *VC* 73 [2019]: 488). If the latter is the case, then the Septuagintal text was "accompanied by something of the gospel traditions" (Mills, "Pagan Readers," 489). The accompanying written Jesus material will have served as the Christian interpretation of the old, divine "barbaric" writings under this proposal.

to nascent Christianity.[38] The second is that pagans could examine Scriptures on their own to judge the merits of Christianity. They did not have to experience Scripture via a communal reading event.

Tertullian also participates in this second trope at the end of the second century. He encourages those who believe that Christians care nothing about Caesar's health to "examine the words of God, our books, which we don't keep back and on many occasions copy for outsiders" (inspice dei voces, litteras nostras, quas neque ipsi supprimimus et plerique casus ad extraneos transferunt) (Tertullian, *Apol.* 31).[39] Not only does Tertullian assume that Christian texts are available for inspection, but, if they are not, he notes that Christians are willing to make them accessible.

About fifty years before Tertullian's claim that Christians make their texts available for investigation, Justin Martyr assumes that interested and antagonistic outsiders are able personally to examine Christian writings. He indicates as much in all three of his surviving works: the *First Apology*, *Second Apology*, and the *Dialogue with Trypho*.

In *1 Apol.* 28 Justin tells his purportedly pagan readers that they can find that the Christian names for the prince of the evil spirits are "serpent, Satan, and devil."[40] He writes, "Inquiring of our writings you are able to learn this" (ὡς καὶ ἐκ τῶν ἡμετέρων συγγραμμάτων ἐρευνήσαντες μαθεῖν δύνασθε). The point that Justin is making about the names of the archfiend is minor. He offers this statement about acquiring information from "our writings" (τῶν ἡμετέρων συγγραμμάτων) offhand, implying that personal investigation of Christian texts was well known.[41] He presumes that an interested outsider can access the text or texts and corroborate the minor point that he has made.

---

38. Mills ("Pagan Readers") demonstrates that Christian books played a role in the conversion of six prominent pagans to Christianity: Tatian (*Oratio ad Graecos* 29–30), Theophilus of Antioch (*Autol.* 1.14), Commodian (*Instructiones* 1), Dionysius of Alexandria (*apud* Eusebius, *Hist. eccl.* 7.7), Justin Martyr (*Dial.* 7–8), and Clement of Alexandria (*Strom.* 1.1.11).

39. Trans. my own.

40. Trans. my own. The *First Apology* is addressed to the Roman imperial court, but it is doubtful that Justin was writing to the emperor himself. This was most likely a literary conceit (Charles Munier, "A propos des Apologies de Justin," *RevScRel* 61 [1987]: 177–86; P. Lorraine Buck, "Justin Martyr's Apologies: Their Number, Destination, and Form," *JTS* 54 [2003]: 45–59).

41. What "writings" Justin has in mind in *1 Apol.* 28 is difficult to determine. There are at least two possibilities. First, it might be that Justin is thinking of collective Christian writings, whatever such a "collection" of Scripture might have consisted of for him in the middle of the second century. If this is the case, then Justin does not have a specific text in mind and

In *2 Apol.* 3 and on two occasions in the *Dialogue with Trypho*, Justin again takes for granted that outsiders to Christianity can personally investigate Christian texts. On these occasions, he has written Jesus traditions in mind. In the former, *2 Apol.* 3, Justin claims that the cynic Crescens deems Christians "atheists and impious" for one of three reasons: (1) he hasn't studied the teachings of Christ; (2) he has studied the teachings but does not understand their greatness; (3) he has studied and understood the teachings of Christ but acts as he does so that others will not suspect Crescens of being a Christian. In all three of Justin's hypothetical situations, he assumes that an outsider to Christianity has access to "the teachings of Christ" (τοῦ Χριστοῦ διδάγμασι), even if that outsider has not actually read them.

Whereas in the *Second Apology* Justin assumes a Gentile outsider can personally read written Jesus traditions, twice over in the *Dialogue with Trypho*, Justin indicates that his Jewish interlocutor, Trypho, has in fact read and studied gospel material. First, in *Dial.* 10, Trypho himself praises the Christian conduct that is commanded in the "so-called gospel" (ἐν τῷ λεγομένῳ Εὐαγγελίῳ) because he has "examined them closely" (ἐμοὶ γὰρ ἐμέλησεν ἐντυχεῖν αὐτοῖς). Then again in *Dial.* 18 Justin reminds Trypho that Trypho himself "has read [ἀνέγνως] the things taught by our savior."[42] Here Justin uses the second-person singular form of the verb "to read," ἀνέγνως. In the previous passage, *Dial.* 10, Trypho uses a similar verb, ἐντυγχάνω in the infinitive with the first-person pronoun, ἐμοί. In both cases, Trypho individually reads and investigates Christian textual materials, and specifically written Jesus traditions.[43]

---

presumes that these names can generally be found in Christian scripture. The second possibility is that Justin is alluding to Rev. 12:9, wherein the "ancient serpent" (ὁ ὄφις ὁ ἀρχαῖος) is "the one called the devil and Satan" (ὁ καλούμενος διάβολος καὶ ὁ σατανᾶς). If this is the case, then Justin presumes that his readers can find the Christian names for the prince of evil spirits in a specific Christian text, namely Revelation.

42. Trans. my own.

43. It would make things simple if Trypho was in fact a historical individual whose words were preserved accurately or verbatim in the *Dialogue*. Were this to be the case, we would then possess explicit evidence that someone who did not identify with the Christian movement, and specifically a Jewish individual who rejected Christian claims, was able to access and read a gospel text in the middle of the second century. However, that Trypho is a "real" interlocutor with whom Justin engaged is a matter of debate. There are a variety of takes on the figure and function of Trypho in the *Dialogue*. For a survey of the various positions, see Timothy J. Horner, *Listening to Trypho: Justin Martyr's Dialogue Revisited*, CBET 28 (Leuven: Peeters, 2001), 15–32. My position is that Trypho was not in fact Justin's historical interlocutor but represents the kinds of persons with whom Justin was engaged in debate. The evidence from the *Dialogue*

Justin can imagine a Jewish interlocutor reading written gospel material. If the only way to experience gospel writings in the middle of the second century was in communal reading events, then Justin's statements about Trypho's reading would be nonsensical to his own reading audience and they would be difficult for him to imagine in the first place. At minimum, Justin knows of the possibility of Jewish individuals personally reading and studying written Jesus traditions, as Trypho does, and, at maximum, he knows of this practice taking place in actuality.

In the second century, there are three writers who indicate that Scripture was read privately by outsiders to Christianity. Their testimony is of varying sorts. Tatian's is personal. He indicates that he, when he was not yet a Christian, personally read a Christian text. Tertullian informs us of the Christian habit of making Christian texts available to outsiders. And Justin, chronologically before Tertullian, assumes that his interlocutors, whether real or hypothetical, had access to Christian writings, specifically texts about Jesus. They do not have to attend a communal reading event to experience Christian Scripture. These texts are freely accessible to investigate privately and individually.

If Christian texts were available to literate non-Christians for private use in the second century, then they must have also been available to literate Christians. They certainly were to the Christians Tatian, Tertullian, and Justin, who all read and studied Christian texts privately. Two additional writers, Ignatius of Antioch and Bishop Melito of Sardis, confirm that in the second century Christians read Scriptures privately.

In his letter *To the Philadelphians*, written in the first half of the second century CE, Ignatius identifies a source of contention that he has encountered. He writes, "I heard some people say, 'If I don't find it in the archives, I do not believe it in the gospel'" (Ignatius, *Phld.* 8:2).[44] Notably, both the verbs "find" (εὕρω) and "believe" (πιστεύω) are in the first-person form. This presumes that both "the archives" (τὰ ἀρχεῖα) and "the gospel" (τὸ εὐαγγέλιον) are things that can be scrutinized by an individual.[45]

---

does not unambiguously depict historical events in which a Jewish opponent to Christianity read one or more written discourses about Jesus, but it imagines it.

44. Trans., Holmes, *Apostolic Fathers*, 243.

45. It is a matter of debate whether "the archives" and "the gospel" refer to written materials for Ignatius. Jan A. Dus surveys the various options and the variant texts in "Papers or Principles? Ignatius of Antioch on the Authority of the Old Testament," in *The Process of Authority: The Dynamics in Transmission and Reception of Canonical Texts*, ed. Jan Dušek and Jan Roskovec, DCLS 27 (Berlin: de Gruyter, 2016), 155–59. "Archives" almost certainly suggests written Scriptures, since Ignatius's immediate retort to his opponents' objection is "it is written," a single

While Ignatius implies the textual comparison of antecedent Scriptural texts with written Jesus traditions, Melito of Sardis produced a written document that would facilitate just such a comparison. In *Hist. eccl.* 4.26.13–14, Eusebius preserves the preface to a lost book of extracts by Melito, who wrote around 180 CE. In the text quoted by Eusebius, Melito lists "the books of the Old Testament" (τὰ τῆς παλαιᾶς διαθήκης βιβλία).[46] Before Melito offers this list, he provides the reason that he drew it up in the first place. A certain Onesimus had desired not only to know the "accurate facts about the ancient writings," which Melito's list addresses, but also "to have extracts from the Law and the Prophets concerning the Savior and concerning all our faith" (Lake, LCL). Eusebius states that Melito's list precedes the extracts that Melito made for Onesimus, a copy of which Eusebius presumably possessed. Melito creates the list so that Onesimus might know not only "accurate facts about the ancient writings," but also the texts from which the extracts are drawn. Melito writes as much in the concluding words of the preface: "From these I have made extracts and compiled them into six books" (ἐξ ὧν καὶ τὰς ἐκλογὰς ἐποιησάμην, εἰς ἓξ βιβλία διελών) (Lake, LCL). Melito's extracts are produced for an individual to facilitate personal reading and comparison of a particular set of texts in the second century CE.

Conclusion to Solitary Reading

In the third and fourth centuries CE there is straightforward evidence to the private reading of biblical texts, including the gospels. This practice was also known in the second century, as outsiders to Christianity had personal access to Christian texts that they read individually. Christians did the same, as evidenced by Ignatius and Melito. In chapter 3, I will argue that the solitary reading of at least one gospel, namely Luke, can be pressed back into the first century. And while the Gospel of Luke provides the only evidence from the early Jesus movement to the personal reading of written gospel material in the first century CE, Greco-Roman and Jewish texts both contemporaneous

---

word in Greek: γέγραπται (Dus, "Papers or Principles?" 160). "It is written" is a stock phrase for citing Scripture in the New Testament and Ignatius employs it elsewhere when he himself cites written texts (Ignatius, *Eph.* 5:3; *Magn.* 12:1).

46. According to Melito these are "Genesis, Exodus, Numbers, Leviticus, Deuteronomy, Joshua the son of Nun, Judges, Ruth, four books of Kingdoms, two books of Chronicles, the Psalms of David, the Proverbs of Solomon and his Wisdom, Ecclesiastes, the Songs of Songs, Job, the prophets Isaiah, Jeremiah, the Twelve in a single book, Daniel, Ezekiel, Ezra" (Melito *apud* Eusebius, *Hist. eccl.* 4.26.14 [Lake, LCL]).

with and antecedent to the gospels demonstrate that solitary reading was one way that texts were experienced. It is erroneous to suppose that early literate Christians diverged from Greco-Roman and Jewish reading habits in the first century only to fall back in line with those habits in the second, third, and fourth centuries. Christian texts were read both personally and communally from their outset.

Before turning to the gospels themselves to assess the reading events for which they were made in the first century, we survey communal reading events in Greco-Roman antiquity, Second Temple Judaism, and early Christianity. The purpose of this survey is to establish that there were different kinds of communal reading events in these contexts.

Communal Reading

Greco-Roman, Second Temple Jewish, and early Christian texts all indicate that smaller-scale readings were more common than reading to a critical mass of persons. The latter kind of event is known and described on occasion, but these events are usually considered to be extraordinary. More common is the reading of a discourse to a relatively modest gathering of persons in a non-public setting. While the primary sources rarely indicate the precise number of persons present at reading events, most seem to presume less than fifty persons present.

GRECO-ROMAN LARGE-GROUP READING

Lucian begins *Herodotus* by relaying how the historian gained his fame. He did so not by slowly gathering it in, but through one brazen reading event (Lucian, *Herodotus* 1–3).[47] Lucian writes that Herodotus disguised himself as an Olympic competitor and "waited for a packed audience to assemble, one containing the most eminent men from all Greece." Once his stage was set, Herodotus "recited his histories, bewitching his audience that his books were called after the Muses" (ᾄδων τὰς ἱστορίας καὶ κηλῶν τοὺς παρόντας, ἄχρι τοῦ καὶ Μούσας κληθῆναι τὰς βίβλους αὐτοῦ) (Kilburn, LCL).

This public reading stunt won Herodotus instant acclaim. The story traveled and Herodotus became better known than the Olympic athletes themselves. Others began to take this bypass to glory, giving their own recitations before large assemblies. Lucian tells his reader that he himself took

---

47. I am dependent on Nässelqvist for this reference (*Public Reading*, 71).

the Herodotean shortcut. When he wanted to gain fame in Macedonia, he did not travel to each city but lectured in front of Macedonia's finest to gain their approval (Lucian, *Herodotus* 7–8).

Lucian presumes that recitations to large groups occurred not only in the fifth century BCE with Herodotus but also in his own second-century CE context. Aulus Gellius likewise attests to the large-scale reading of a text in the second century, though the reading was of Ennius's *Annals*, written some three centuries earlier. In *Att. Noc.* 18.5 Gellius writes of news being brought to the rhetorician Antonius Julianus that a lector (*anagnosten*) was reading the *Annals* aloud "to the people in the theater in a very refined and musical voice" (voce admodum scita et canora Ennii annales legere ad populum in theatro) (Gellius, *Att. Noc.* 18.5 [Rolfe, LCL]). Julianus decides to go to the public event, and when he arrived the lector was reading book 7 of the *Annals* to great applause.

The purpose of the anecdote for Gellius is not to highlight the fact that persons read to large groups in the public space of the theater. Rather, it is to set up Julianus's grammatical and textual commentary on a particular phrase.[48] As with the novelists who presumed that silent and personal reading was known to their own readers, so also does Gellius employ a large-group, public reading event in the theater as a narrative element that will have been known to his own audience.

Staging readings in the public space of the theater was apparently also an antic for which Nero was well known. According to Suetonius, the emperor read his poems both at home and in the theater. The latter setting was to the delight of all (*non modo domi sed et in theatro, tanta universorum laetitia*) (Suetonius, *Nero* 10.2 [Rolfe, LCL]). Dio has a different opinion of Nero's (in)famous readings. He tells of an occasion when Nero read (ἀνέγνω) in the theater some Trojan lays of his own making during a popular festival and characterizes the event as one of the many "ridiculous things" (γελοῖα) that Nero did (Dio Cassius, *Hist. rom.* 62.29.1 [Cary, LCL]).

---

48. Julianus calls attention to the fact that this lector had read the phrase *quadrupes equus* rather than the more ancient, enigmatic, and, in his estimation, correct *quadrupes eques*. The former was apparently a commonplace variant since many of those gathered to Julianus indicated they had always read *quadrupes equus* in their schooling. Julianus is proved correct about the antiquity of *quadrupes eques*, as Apollinaris consults a copy of the *Annals* of "heavy and vulnerable antiquity" (librum summae atque reverendae vetustatis) that reads such.

For Dio, Nero's theater readings were but one symptom of his insanity. Similarly, Pliny, in a letter to Catius Lepidus, tells of the absurdity of his archrival Marcus Aquilius Regulus who fully displayed his immodesty by staging large-scale reading events (Pliny the Younger, *Ep.* 4.7).[49] After the death of his son, Regulus attempted to immortalize him in writing, readings, statues, and portraits. Regulus declaimed a biography of his son to a "huge audience" (ingenti auditorio) and circulated a thousand copies of the work throughout the empire, requesting that councilors in each place appoint skilled persons to read the biography "before the citizens" (qui legeret eum populo) (Pliny the Younger, *Ep.* 4.7 [Radice, LCL]).

Pliny has little sympathy for Regulus's loss, and his letter is scathing.[50] He opines that writing and circulating such a eulogy for a "mere boy" is a mark of Regulus's shamelessness. In closing the letter, Pliny asks Lepidus if he knows anyone who has been forced publicly to read "this woeful book of Regulus" (hunc luctuosum Reguli librum).[51] In his disparaging letter, Pliny implies not only that an author might read their own work to a large audience, but that they might also arrange large-group reading events from afar.[52]

These cases indicate that public reading to a large group was known to the Greco-Roman literati, but each one of them is exceptional. Herodotus strays from normal recitation practices to gain fame. Gellius uses the large-group setting to emphasize his overarching point about a common mistake in the textual tradition of Ennius's *Annals*. Nero's actions border on the absurd. Pliny presents Regulus's readings as a mark of his immoderation. The reading

---

49. On Regulus's immoderate life according to Pliny, see William A. Johnson, *Readers and Reading Culture in the High Roman Empire: A Study of Elite Communities* (Oxford: Oxford University Press, 2010), 47–48.

50. Among other calumnies, Pliny writes that Regulus "has weak lungs, clouded utterance, a hesitant tongue, the dullest imagination, and a non-existent memory—in short, nothing but the brain of a madman" (P. G. Walsh, trans., *Pliny the Younger, Complete Letters*, Oxford World's Classics [Oxford: Oxford University Press, 2009], 86).

51. Walsh, *Pliny the Younger*, 86.

52. This is an excellent example of Jan Assmann's "extended situation" (*Religion and Cultural Memory: Ten Studies*, trans. Rodney Livingstone [Stanford, CA: Stanford University Press, 2006], 103–5). The possibility of the "extended situation" is opened when a discourse enters the written medium. It can be experienced across time and space. Chris Keith has argued that one of the Gospel of Mark's innovations is creating an "extended situation" by textualizing previously non-textual Jesus traditions (*The Gospel as Manuscript: An Early History of the Jesus Tradition as Material Artifact* [Oxford: Oxford University Press, 2020], 89–99).

of texts to large groups of people in a public space was known in these circles but was not commonplace.

GRECO-ROMAN READING SMALL-GROUP READING

More common than public, large-group readings among the Greco-Roman literati was the private reading of texts to groups that were small or moderate in size, usually by a lector. A caveat needs to be made here. Lectors did not replace personal, private reading. They supplemented it. For those who were literate, having a text read to them was a separate and additional way to experience a written discourse. For most literate persons, this practice did not stand in place of reading a text for oneself.[53] Rather, persons read to themselves, and they had lectors read to them for a variety of reasons.

In *Ep.* 7.21, Pliny the Younger attests to both practices. Reading to himself is his default mode, at least when he is engaged in study, as he offers the reason that he is presently having texts read to him: he must abstain from both writing and reading and study with "ears alone" (solisque auribus studeo) because of his current eye problem (*infirmati oculorum*).[54] At the end of the letter he playfully writes that his eyes work well enough to see that the chicken that the letter's recipient had sent him was "quite plump." But they were not working well enough to read texts. Pliny's lector thus served as his eyeglasses.[55]

Pliny also used lectors as a convenience. He had texts read to him when his eyes were infirmed and when his hands were occupied. Pliny speaks to this convenience in *Ep.* 9.36. There he details his daily routine during his summers in Tuscany. Shortly after informing his reader, Fuscus, that he regularly reads texts aloud to himself to exercise his voice, Pliny notes that at dinner he has a text read aloud to him if he is with his wife or a few friends (*si cum uxore vel paucis*) (Pliny, *Ep.* 9.36 [Radice, LCL]).[56] When Pliny details the routine of his uncle, he notes that the Elder Pliny likewise had texts read to him while he ate, as well as when he sunbathed and washed (Pliny the Younger, *Ep.* 3.5). Pliny's

---

53. Parker, "Books and Reading," 200.
54. Cited in Parker, "Books and Reading," 200; text, Radice, LCL.
55. This was one of the functions of Roman *lectores* according to Raymond J. Starr ("Reading Aloud: Lectores and Roman Reading," *CJ* 86 [1991]: 343). Nicholas Horsfall argues that one of the reasons that lectors and scribes were essential in Roman antiquity is that ophthalmia was so common in this context ("Rome without Spectacles," *Greece & Rome* 42 [1995]: 49–56).
56. Presumably if more than a few friends are present then the entertainment would be more extravagant than reading (Walsh, *Pliny the Younger*, 360).

elder colleague Spurinna had books read to him if he was "alone" on his daily three-mile walk and also during his pre-dinner rest (Pliny the Younger, *Ep.* 3.1).[57]

Here we must acknowledge how slavery underpinned Greco-Roman literary endeavors and particularly small-group reading events. When Pliny writes of having a text read to him because of his eye trouble and when small groups listened to a reading over dinner, there was always another human being doing that reading. That human was most often an enslaved person.[58] Greco-Roman literary culture was infused with slavery. Though they normally remain nameless in the sources, persons who were enslaved "were the indispensable enabling infrastructure of Roman literary life, as of written exchanges of all kinds."[59] The writing, reading, and circulation of texts did not happen apart from the forced labor of these individuals.[60]

While Pliny and his contemporaries had texts read to them by enslaved lectors, they themselves also read their authored texts to one another in small groups. In a letter to Terentius Scaurus, Pliny writes about reading one of his own speeches to his friends: "I invited some friends to hear me read a short speech which I am thinking of publishing, just enough of an audience to make me nervous, but not a large one, as I wanted to hear the truth" (Pliny the Younger, *Ep.* 5.12 [Radice, LCL]). Pliny does not state how many persons attended this reading event, but the group was not large. This was his normal practice: reading a discourse to a handful of friends with the express purpose of receiving pre-publication feedback on it.

In *Ep.* 7.17 Pliny outlines his process: "I myself seek praise not while reciting, but when I am read, so there is no form of correction which I disregard. Initially I scrutinize alone what I have written. Next I read it with two or three others. After that I pass it over to others to annotate, and if I am in doubt about them, I ponder their comments again with one or other of my friends. Finally, I read out the speech to a number of people, and it is then, believe me, that I make the most incisive corrections."[61] It is only toward the end of his editorial process that Pliny read his discourses to a "number of people"

---

57. Spurinna is not actually alone in these cases since someone is reading the text to him.

58. Or a freedman (Rex Winsbury, *The Roman Book: Books, Publishing and Performance in Classical Rome* [London: Bloomsbury, 2009], 82).

59. Winsbury, *Roman Book*, 81.

60. Lest we find ourselves on a chronistic moral high horse, we ought to be reminded of the extent to which many of the electronic media devices that hold digital texts and by which many texts are composed are manufactured using unjust labor practices that exploit human beings.

61. Walsh, *Pliny the Younger*, 173.

(*pluribus*). On occasion a recitation might involve a group of more than ten, but the more usual practice was to read to a small group of trusted friends.[62] If a single author was reading their own work or having their work read by a lector, they did so in a private space, usually the writer's villa.[63] The persons that attended such events came by invitation, and an author needed to be judicious about whom they invited.

Pliny states this unequivocally: "Anyone giving a reading must beware of eccentricity either in himself or in the audience he invites" (Pliny the Younger, *Ep.* 6.15 [Radice, LCL]). The statement concludes a letter in which Pliny relays banter between an author and an audience member who interrupted the reading event. In *Ep.* 6.17, Pliny relays another type of disrespect he observed at a reading event: a handful of wise guys did not interact with the reading whatsoever. They did not speak, stand, or sign for their "dearest friend" (amicissimum) whom they had come to hear. Pliny tells the letter's recipient that Pliny himself does not invite the "general public" (populum) to his recitations, "but a select and limited [certos electosque] audience of persons whom I admire and trust, whom I observe individually and fear as a whole" (Pliny the Younger, *Ep.* 6.15 [Radice, LCL]). By choosing his invitees from a pool of friends he reveres, Pliny lowers the risk of a chilly reception.

Pliny's letters raise several important issues related to reading discourses to small groups in Roman literary circles. First, Pliny's communal readings were not a form of "publication." These events preceded the written version's distribution. The oral declamation of select passages from the discourse was not itself its release.[64] Even recitations were a "penultimate draft."[65] In his letters, Pliny frequently writes about getting feedback, both oral and written,

---

62. On the private nature of recitations, see Peter White, *Promised Verse: Poets in the Society of Augustan Rome* (Cambridge: Harvard University Press, 1993), 293; W. Johnson, *Readers and Reading Culture*, 47; Florence Dupont, "*Recitatio* and the Reorganization of the Space of Public Discourse," in *The Roman Cultural Revolution*, ed. Thomas Habinek and Alessandro Schiesaro (Cambridge: Cambridge University Press, 1997), 45–47.

63. White, *Promised Verse*, 293n65. White cites the following texts in which recitations take place in a "great man's" (*vir magnus*) mansion: Seneca, *Suas.* 6.27; Tacitus, *Ann.* 3.49.1; *Dial.* 9.3; Martial, *Epigr.* 4.6.4–5; Pliny the Younger, *Ep.* 8.12.2; Juvenal, *Sat.* 1.12; 7.40. Johnson adds the following letters from Pliny in which Pliny read in his own home or the home of a friend: *Ep.* 2.19; 4.19; 5.3, 12; 6.6; 8.21; 9.34.

64. Parker has debunked the myth that publication took the form of recitation ("Books and Reading," 206–17). He also shows that readings to small groups and recitations consisted of only portions of the author's work, not the whole discourse.

65. Parker, "Books and Reading," 210.

60 • *Reading*

on his various texts and incorporating it into the respective discourse before it goes public in writing.[66] Second, communal readings were not always accompanied by pomp and circumstance, especially when the reading was only for a small group of friends. Corollary to this is that readings were not necessarily enjoyable; there were bad readings and bad readers.[67]

Exhibit A is Pliny's letter to Suetonius in which he seeks advice about an informal reading of verse that he has written (Pliny the Younger, *Ep*. 9.34). This is the so-called pantomime letter.[68] Pliny recognizes that his public reading abilities are second-rate, at least when it comes to reading verse.[69] When he is organizing an informal reading of some poetry he has written to a small group, Pliny plans to use one of the freedmen in his service to do the reading for him. He asks Suetonius if he should just sit as a spectator or "accompany [the reader's] words with low voice, eye, and gesture" (Pliny the Younger, *Ep*. 9.34 [Radice, LCL]). Pliny must have been quite unsure of his ability to read verse aloud since the reader that he has chosen to read for him is not particularly skilled himself.

The account shatters the notion that a learned individual must be a masterful public reader. There is not a one-to-one correlation between oral skills and literary prowess. One might write well but not be able to read well the text that they have written, even if it is only to a small, informal gathering of colleagues.[70] That persons were more to less skilled at reading certain kinds of

---

66. Also in *Ep*. 5.12, Pliny requests that Scaurus himself provide written feedback on the written speech. This was apparently a regular practice of Pliny. He similarly asks for written feedback on another speech from Maturus Arrianus (*Ep*. 1.2), and states that he has marked a text for Cornelius Tacitus in *Ep*. 7.20. In the same letter, Pliny states that he is awaiting similar feedback from Tacitus, as they had traded their texts with one another.

67. A modern analogue is the romanticized notion of the academic conference. For those who have not attended such a (reading) event, it is often assumed that the readings that take place are exciting, cutting-edge, and well done. Anyone who regularly attends such meetings, however, knows that there is no shortage of bad readers and readings at them.

68. Winsbury, *Pliny the Younger*, 160–61.

69. Pliny states that he can manage speeches just fine. It is reading poetry that poses a problem.

70. One might even earn the reputation of being a skilled orator when one was a poor public reader and a poor writer. In *Ep*. 4.7, in which Pliny lambastes Regulus, he states that his rival only won "the popular reputation of an orator" because he is bold and brash (Radice, LCL). Not only is Regulus a wretched reader, according to Pliny, but he is also a poor writer. Pliny states that "you would think [Regulus's speech was] written by a boy rather than about one" (Radice, LCL). Regulus was probably much more adept than Pliny admits, but it is pertinent

discourses returns us to lectors and another reason that one might privately utilize one in a small-group setting: to hear a text read eloquently. In *Oration* 18, Dio Chrysostom suggests that comedies and tragedies ought to be read "through others" (δι' ἑτέρων) (Cohoon, LCL).

In the oration, Dio is addressing the statesman who is just beginning his instruction in public eloquence. He compares rhetorical training to physical: just as the physically unfit person starts with light exercise, the person untrained in eloquence starts his literate training plan with "light" texts, namely Menander and Euripides. He must first experience the eloquence of the poets and the best way to do so is to hear someone else read them who knows how to do it well.[71] Not just any reader will do. The statesman-in-training ought to hire or purchase someone who is well trained in reading the poets, or else attend an event wherein they are read.[72]

Dio's counsel is that well-written texts should be read well. In *Ep.* 3.15, Pliny writes to another possibility: that a text might be read well but not written well.[73] The letter is addressed to Silius Proculus, who has requested that Pliny read some of his poetry and provide his judgment on its suitability for publication. Pliny writes his response after he has heard Proculus give a reading of some of the verse, but before he has had the opportunity to read critically Proculus's texts. Given their oral declamation, Pliny judges that "it is a splendid work and ought not to remain unpublished" (Pliny, *Ep.* 3.15 [Radice, LCL]).

Pliny recognizes that Proculus's reading style possesses "great charm and skill." Pliny admits that Proculus's ability to read well might influence his judgment of the text's worth. "The pleasures of the ear" might dull Pliny's "critical powers" of reading the text with his eyes (Pliny, *Ep.* 3.15 [Radice, LCL]).

---

that he imagines and presents Regulus as an unskilled reader and writer. Literarily deficient figures must have been known for Pliny's presentation to have any relevance.

71. Wright marshals this passage to suggest that, for Dio, "reading works to oneself is a careless way of reading" (*Communal Reading*, 84). This, however, misunderstands Dio's point. He is recommending a certain manner of reading for a certain kind of text, not offering a principle about the best way to experience all discourses.

72. Parker contends that there is evidence for the private performance of the ancient poets by professionals at banquets, but that there is no evidence for their public recitation ("Books and Reading," 210).

73. Or one might be a brilliant orator without the use of a text at all. In *Ep.* 2.3, Pliny offers effusive praise of Isaeus: "He has a remarkably eloquent style, rich in variety, and though he always speaks extempore his speeches sound as though he had spent time on preparing them" (Radice, LCL).

Perhaps Proculus can offer a skilled reading in a small-group setting but is less skilled as a writer.[74] If this were the case, then the verses would be less worthy of publication, despite the captivating reading event for which they were made.

Marcus likewise describes a successful reading in a letter to his tutor, Fronto. Three people were involved. One was the writer of the text, one the reader of the text, and one the hearer of the text. Marcus declaimed a portion of one of Fronto's written speeches to his father. So pleased was Marcus's father that he claimed the words were "Worthy of the writer himself!" (Marcus Aurelius, *Ad M. Caes.* 1.6).[75]

Marcus does not state whether he is performing Fronto's speech from a script or from memory.[76] What is clear is that he is using a text written by someone else during a reading event that consisted of only two people. He reads part of his tutor's speech to his father. While the primary point is that persons read communally in small groups, it is also worth noting that Marcus's reading is a substitute for Fronto's actual performance of the speech at a different time and in a different place. The discourse can be experienced in one way at one time and place and in a different way at a different time and place. In response to the news of the welcome reception of Marcus's reading by his father, Fronto writes back to Marcus, "Samples of my speech, which I had picked out for you, you read [*rectasti*] to your father yourself, and took the pains to declaim them, wherein you lent me your eyes, your voice, your gestures, and above all, your mind for my service."[77]

What do we conclude from Marcus's correspondence with Fronto, Dio's oration, and Pliny's letters surveyed here? First, communal reading events did not constitute the publication of a respective discourse. Oral proclamation and publication were not the same thing. Discourses were judged not only by the communal, vocalized reading event for which they were made but also by

---

74. There is similar testimony from Seneca in *Ep.* 1.46.3. After spending an entire letter praising Lucilius's new writing, Seneca states that he will address the book at greater length after he reads it again, writing that his judgment is unsettled "as if I had heard it read aloud, and not read it myself" (tamquam audierim illa, non legerim; Gummere, LCL). Seneca's statement is nearly proverbial: be aware that one can misjudge a discourse by hearing it and not having read it.

75. Trans. Caillan Davenport and Jennifer Manley, eds., *Fronto: Selected Letters*, Classical Studies Series (New York: Bloomsbury, 2014), 75.

76. The speech in question was part of the arbitration process in a will that had yet to be opened (Davenport and Manley, *Fronto*, 78; Edward Champlin, *Fronto and Antonine Rome* [Cambridge: Harvard University Press, 1980], 61–62).

77. Marcus Aurelius, *Ad M. Caes.* 1.7 (Haines, LCL).

how they were received privately. They were evaluated by both ears and eyes. Second, not all communal readings, whether to large or small groups, were enjoyable and not everyone who had the ability to read did so well. Third, persons regularly participated in various kinds of communal reading events. Communal reading in small groups was not uncommon for the Greco-Roman literati. Persons read to themselves, they read in pairs, they read in small- and medium-sized groups, and texts were publicly read to the masses. The balance of evidence indicates that in Greco-Roman literary circles, the first three kinds of reading events were most common. This is mirrored in the reading cultures of Second Temple Judaism and early Christianity.

EARLY JEWISH AND CHRISTIAN LARGE-GROUP READING

The first major Jewish event to take place in reconstructed Jerusalem after the reconstitution of the temple, according to Neh. 8:1, is a public reading of the "book of the law of Moses" (סֵפֶר תּוֹרַת מֹשֶׁה). The event is accompanied by pomp and circumstance.[78] The entire body of restored Israel is present: "both men, women, and all who could hear with understanding" (Neh 8:2 NRSV, הַקָּהָל מֵאִישׁ וְעַד־אִשָּׁה וְכֹל מֵבִין לִשְׁמֹעַ). The setting of the reading, "facing the square, before the Water Gate" (8:1 NRSV) is accessible to all.[79] The revered scribe Ezra, accompanied by six persons on his right and seven on his left, reads the law all morning atop a platform specially crafted for the occasion. The gathered multitude stands and listens with rapt attention.

The entire event is exceptional. It is, after all, a historic occasion. The author's intention is not merely to describe a public reading event, but to emphasize that Torah and allegiance to it is the foundation on which renewed Jerusalem is built.[80] Nehemiah goes to great lengths to emphasize that the

---

78. G. J. Venema suggests that the event is the "conclusion and the climax" of the restoration of Jerusalem and the temple in Ezra-Nehemiah (*Reading Scripture in the Old Testament: Deuteronomy 9–10, 31, 2 Kings 22–23, Jeremiah 36, Nehemiah 8*, OtSt 48 [Leiden: Brill, 2004], 163).

79. Trans. my own. Venema notes that the event is accessible to all precisely because its setting is not the temple (*Reading Scripture*, 163). First Esdras 9:38, in contrast to Neh 8:1, reports the event took place in the "area before the east gate of the temple" (τὸ εὐρύχωρον τοῦ πρὸς ἀνατολὰς τοῦ ἱεροῦ πυλῶνος).

80. Venema, *Reading Scripture*, 172.

reading was accompanied by interpretation and teaching so that the gathered masses could understand the law.[81]

The whole event echoes two formative occasions in Israel's history: Moses's public reading of the law before the people in Deut 31 and Josiah's reading the rediscovered "book of the law" in 2 Chr 34 and 2 Kgs 22, which prompted Israel to reform their idolatrous ways and renew the covenant.[82] We will take these texts in reverse order. I suggest that Neh 8 echoes both.

Several ideological and linguistic parallels indicate that Neh 8 evokes the circumstances of Josiah's reforms narrated in both 2 Chr 34 and 2 Kgs 22. In 2 Chr 34:14 (NRSV), the textual object rediscovered is "the book of the law of the LORD given through Moses" (סֵפֶר תּוֹרַת־יְהוָה בְּיַד־מֹשֶׁה). In 2 Kgs 22:8 it is simply the "book of the Law" (סֵפֶר הַתּוֹרָה). In both narratives, the book is first read to Josiah and subsequently to "all the people" (2 Kgs 23:2; 2 Chr 34:30, כָּל־הָעָם). Both texts emphasize the all-inclusive nature of the event. Second Kings 23:2 notes that "all the people of Judah, all the inhabitants of Jerusalem, the priests, the prophets, and all the people, both small and great" (כָּל־אִישׁ יְהוּדָה וְכָל־יֹשְׁבֵי יְרוּשָׁלַם אִתּוֹ וְהַכֹּהֲנִים וְהַנְּבִיאִים וְכָל־הָעָם לְמִקָּטֹן וְעַד־גָּדוֹל) were gathered. And 2 Chr 34:30 is nearly identical: "all the people of Judah, the inhabitants of Jerusalem, the priests and the Levites, all the people both great and small" (כָּל־אִישׁ יְהוּדָה וְיֹשְׁבֵי יְרוּשָׁלַם וְהַכֹּהֲנִים וְהַלְוִיִּם וְכָל־הָעָם מִגָּדוֹל וְעַד־קָטָן) constitute the multitude.

Similarly in Neh 8, Ezra brings out the "book of the law of Moses, which the LORD had given to Israel" (סֵפֶר תּוֹרַת מֹשֶׁה אֲשֶׁר־צִוָּה יְהוָה אֶת־יִשְׂרָאֵל), presumably from the newly restored temple, and reads it before "all the people" (כָּל־הָעָם).[83] The thrust of the parallels to 2 Kgs 22 and 2 Chr 34 is that Ezra's reading event is momentous not only because it follows upon the rebuilding of the temple and the reconstitution of Jerusalem, but also because it is, like Josiah's reading event that preceded it, part of the ceremony of the covenant's renewal. The precedent for such covenant-renewal reading was first set in Deut 31:10–13.

Having proclaimed the decrees and laws that will offer either life or death to Israel in Deut 4–30, Moses himself sets standards for the regular, public

---

81. Neh 8:2–3 (NRSV) twice states that those who were present "could hear with understanding." In vv. 7–8 the author writes that thirteen Levites "helped the people to understand the law" (מְבִינִים אֶת־הָעָם לַתּוֹרָה), which was read "with interpretation" (וְשׂוֹם שֶׂכֶל).

82. Venema, *Reading Scripture*, 138–81.

83. The phrase כָּל־הָעָם ("all the people") is repeated eleven times in the chapter, emphasizing not only the public nature of the event, but the fact that all regathered Israel heard the law read (Venema, *Reading Scripture*, 163–64).

reading of the law in Deut 31:10–13. All Israel is to gather every seventh year during the festival of booths to hear the law read.

While "all the people" (כָּל־הָעָם), the phrase that formed a linguistic link between Neh 8 and 2 Kgs 22 and 2 Chron 34, does not appear in Deut 31, "all of Israel" (כָּל־יִשְׂרָאֵל) does on two occasions (Deut 31:7, 11). "The people" (הָעָם) mentioned in v. 12 (NRSV) consist of "men, women, and children, as well as the aliens residing in your towns." Everyone is present at the reading. The most significant parallel between Deut 31:10–13 and Neh 8 is the festival at which the reading to the masses takes place: *sukkoth* ("booths").

The prescription in Deut. 31:10 is that every seventh *sukkoth* the entirety of the law is to be read to all the people. The purpose of the reading is that the people might be reminded of their covenantal commitment and thus "live in the land." It is no coincidence that in Neh 8 it is precisely this festival that is enacted in vv. 16–18. The text thus recasts Ezra as a "new Moses" at a historic moment. As G. J. Venema puts it, "Moses' reading from the 'book of the *torah*' to Israel, in view of and immediately before the entry into the Land, is echoed by Ezra's reading after the return from exile."[84] The point is that public reading of the law to the entire people is no ordinary occurrence.[85]

This historic reading event initiates the Second Temple period, at least according to the author of Nehemiah, and events similar to it continue to be narrated throughout the period. Both the Letter of Aristeas and 1QSa envision such events in which a discourse is read to a massive group.

In the Letter of Aristeas, which tells the tale of the Septuagint's origins, the discourse read is the Greek translation of the Law. The legend goes that at the request of the Egyptian King Ptolemy II seventy-two Jewish translators were sent from Jerusalem to Alexandria to prepare a Greek translation of Torah for the great library there. Upon the project's completion, which happened to take exactly seventy-two days, the Greek text was publicly read aloud to the city's entire Jewish community.[86]

---

84. Venema *Reading Scripture*, 181.

85. Rather, it happens every seven years, if the command in Deut. 31:10 was enacted, and at momentous points in Israelite history. M. Yoma 7:1 indicates that portions of the Law were read by the high priest on the Day of Atonement. Because the reading relates to Temple rituals, the text must presume a large gathering. This would make reading of Torah to a gathered mass a yearly occasion, but the text specifically indicates that only select portions of Leviticus are read.

86. Letter of Aristeas 308–9. Text and translation in the following are from L. Michael White and G. Anthony Keddie, eds., *Jewish Fictional Letters from Hellenistic Egypt: The Epistle of Aristeas and Related Literature* (Atlanta: SBL Press, 2018) 166–67.

Like the event in Neh 8, this reading is accompanied by much pomp precisely because it is historic. It takes place in the very same place where the miraculous translation occurred. The translators themselves are present at the reading event and are accompanied by "the Jewish people" (τὸ πλῆθος τῶν Ἰουδαίων), presumably the entire Alexandrian Jewish demographic. Per Letter of Aristeas 310–11, the translation was accepted with no revisions and a curse was uttered against anyone who might alter the text so that "it should be protected always and remain ever unchanged" (ἵνα διὰ παντὸς ἀέννααα καὶ μένοντα φυλάσσηται).[87] King Ptolemy II received the translation happily, considered all of the translators his dear friends, and lavished them richly with his wealth.

The circumstances in Aristeas are exaggerated, including the reading of the Greek Mosaic law to the entire population of Alexandrian Jews. Nonetheless, it suggests that the author of Aristeas can imagine such a large-scale reading event, even if it was extraordinary.

As an appendix to the Community Rule, 1QSa offers future prescriptions for how the community is to operate, specifically militarily, in the "final days." The text imagines that all Israel will recognize their error and finally join the *Yahad*. In 1QSa 1:4–5 the author describes what must happen when the newcomers join the community: "When they come, they shall assemble all those who come, including children and women, and they shall read into [their] ea[rs] [a]ll the precepts of the covenant, and shall instruct them in all their regulations, so that they do not stray in [the]ir e[rrors]."[88] The passage imagines a future, eschatological reading event. It is unclear in the text whether or not this reading and instruction is to take place at regular intervals as the newcomers flow into the community or whether it takes place at one time after the influx has ceased. Given the precedent for reading the law to all of gathered Israel, women and children included, at historical moments in Deut 31, 2 Chr 34, 2 Kgs 22, and Neh 8, the latter seems more likely. The first act of reconstituted, eschatological Israel is, per 1QSa, a large-group reading event in which all the people, even the women and children (מטף עד נשים) hear "all the statutes of the covenant" (כ[ו]ל חוקי הברית).

Whereas the Letter of Aristeas and 1QSa present extraordinary large-group reading events that likely did not occur in actuality, an account relayed by Josephus in *Life* 236–61 presumes to offer a more historical reading event.

---

87. White and Keddie, *Jewish Fictional Letters*, 168–69.
88. Florentino García Martínez and Eibert J. C. Tigchelaar, trans., *The Dead Sea Scrolls: Study Edition*, 2 vols. (Grand Rapids: Eerdmans, 1998), 101.

Herein John of Gischala is enacting one of his many plots to have Josephus removed from his governorship over Galilee. In this ruse, John's brother Jonathan designed "to write to all of the cities and villages in Galilee" (γράφειν πρὸς πάσας τὰς ἐν τῇ Γαλιλαίᾳ πόλεις καὶ κώμας), as well as to Jerusalem, in order to incite rebellion against Josephus (Josephus, *Life* 236).[89] Catching wind of the scheme, Josephus dispatched several regiments to intercept Jonathan's men and the letters that they carried. He also ordered a large group of armed Galileans to protect him at Gabaroth, which they happily obliged filling "the whole plain in front of the village" (πᾶν τὸ πεδίον τὸ πρὸ τῆς κώμης) with soldiers.

After some of the slanderous letters had been intercepted, Jonathan and his companions entered the plain that was full of Josephus's protectors in an unsuccessful effort to stir up foment. It is at this point that Josephus takes the opportunity to address Jonathan before the gathered multitude. He reads aloud (παρανεγίνωσκον) two of the intercepted letters, which greatly agitated his mass of supporters against Jonathan (Josephus, *Life* 260). Josephus employs the vocalized, large-group reading of these texts to dismantle his rival's machination.[90]

In conclusion, all these instances indicate that reading a discourse to a gathered mass had precedent in Second Temple Judaism. Especially with respect to reading Scripture, the large-group event is extraordinary and happens at unique and historic points. This kind of reading event must have occurred on occasion. Texts were read to massive groups of people. But this was a rare occurrence and should not be considered the norm. More common was reading texts, and particularly Scripture, to a moderately sized group. This was the case in both Second Temple Jewish and early Christian reading cultures.

JEWISH AND CHRISTIAN READING IN MODERATELY-SIZED GROUPS

In the Book of the Watchers, specifically 1 En. 13, the righteous scribe Enoch writes up a "memorandum of petition" (ὑπόμνημα τῆς ἐρωτήσεως) for the fallen angels, which they request he read to the Most High. Having transcribed the text, Enoch proceeds to sit by the waters of Dan and read the petition to God. The author, writing in the first person from Enoch's perspective, states,

---

89. Text, Thackeray, LCL. Trans. my own.

90. Compare to *Life* 216–17, wherein Josephus leverages private, silent reading to overturn one of Jonathan's ploys.

"I recited (to God) the memorandum of their petition until I fell asleep" (ἀνεγίγνωσκον τὸ ὑπόμνημα τῶν δεήσεων αὐτῶν ὡς ἐκοιμήθην).[91] Enoch reads the Watchers' petition "before the face of" (ἐνώπιον/לפני/פדום) God.[92] The phrase has a cultic connotation, and the reading event serves as Enoch's intercession for the Watchers. The event might be classified in one of two different ways. It can be considered an example of personal reading to oneself, insofar as only one human being is present in the narrative and engaging the written text. Alternatively, it might be classified as reading in a small group because two entities are present: one human, namely Enoch, and one divine. In either case, what is described is not a "historical" reading event and so what matters is the author's ability to imagine a reading event wherein two parties engage a text in a certain manner. In this case, the author of 1 Enoch is familiar with reading events in which one person reads a written petition aloud to another individual.

The case is similar at the conclusion of the Letter of Aristeas. In the previous section we saw that the Greek translation of Torah was read aloud to all the Jews in Alexandria. Immediately following its warm reception in that reading event, the translation was read privately to King Ptolemy II: "Everything was also read to him, and he was greatly amazed at the mind of the lawgiver" (παρανεγνώσθη δὲ αὐτῷ καὶ πάντα, καὶ λίαν ἐξεθαύμασε τὴν τοῦ νομοθέτου διάνοιαν).[93]

The Greek text made for two different kinds of reading events that occurred in succession: an initial public reading to a large group followed by private reading to an individual. As with Josephus's account of King Izates, Aristeas can imagine a Gentile king experiencing Jewish Scripture in a private space. In this case, the text is read to the king and the king does not read himself. Not only does the verb παραγινώσκω suggest reading aloud or publicly, it is here in the passive with "everything" (πάντα) as its subject and the pronoun as its indirect object.[94] At least two people are involved, one as reader and one as hearer.[95]

---

91. George W. E. Nickelsburg and James C. VanderKam, *1 Enoch: The Hermeneia Translation* (Minneapolis: Fortress, 2012), 32. Greek text: Matthew Black and Albert Marie Denis, eds., *Apocalypsis Henochi Graece*, PVTG 3 (Leiden: Brill, 1970), 27.

92. George W. E. Nickelsburg, *1 Enoch*, Hermeneia (Minneapolis: Fortress, 2001), 238.

93. White and Keddie, *Jewish Fictional Letters*, 168–69.

94. LSJ, s.v. παραγινώσκω. See also 2 Macc 8:23; 3 Macc 1:12; Philo, *Flaccus* 100.

95. In Josephus's account of the events in *Ant.* 12.110 it is also clear that the laws are read aloud to the king. In this case, the phrase is a genitive absolute and "the laws" are the subject of

Like Aristeas, Philo can envision the reading of Torah privately in small groups, even if an actual event is not described. While commenting on Lev 22:27, which requires that a calf, sheep, or goat be left with its mother for seven days after its birth, Philo rails against the practices of infanticide and exposure (Philo, *Virtues* 131–33).[96] He sardonically writes: "Read this law, you good and highly prized parents, and hide your faces for shame, you who ever breathe slaughter against your infants, who mount your wicked watch over them as they leave the womb, waiting to cast them away, you deadly enemies of the whole human race" (Colson, LCL).

Essential for our purposes is the relationship between the participial phrase "read this law" (τοῦτον ἀναγνόντες τὸν νόμον) and the finite, imperative verb "cover your faces" (ἐγκαλύψασθε).[97] Philo firmly has his tongue in his cheek as he calls those who would expose infants "good and highly prized parents" before raising his calumny against them in a bout of name-calling. Philo is also bitingly cheeky when he tells the "deadly enemies of the human race" to cover their faces. The verb is playing on the act of reading indicated in the participle. Not only does "cover up" (ἐγκαλύπτω) carry the connotation of veiling, but also of shame.[98] Philo is thus suggesting that those parents who expose their infants cover their eyes as they read this law, since they ignore it, and by doing so they veil themselves in shame. The verbal pun works because Philo assumes here, as elsewhere, that reading is an ocular affair.[99]

Philo also intimates that parents read the law together. It is possible that the "parents" (γονεῖς) addressed by Philo are collective. That is, Philo could be addressing any parent who might expose their child. More likely Philo has in mind parents participating in familial reading of Torah. Philo can and does imagine a situation in which parents read the law from Leviticus and ignore it altogether and bring shame upon themselves in the act of communal reading.

---

the passive participle: μάλιστα δὲ τῶν νόμων ἀναγνωσθέντων αὐτῷ καὶ τὴν διάνοιαν καὶ τὴν σοφίαν ἐξεπλάγη τοῦ νομοθέτου ("Moreover, when the laws were read to him he was likewise amazed at the mind and wisdom of the lawgiver"). Text, Marcus, LCL; trans. my own.

96. Philo likewise has choice words about the practices in *Spec. Laws* 3.110–14.

97. There are several different ways that the first line might be translated. Colson, reproduced above, takes both the finite verb ἐγκαλύψασθε and the participle ἀναγνόντες as carrying an imperatival force. C. D. Yonge translates the sentence as a question: "Do you then, you excellent and most admirable parents, read this law and hide your faces [...]?" (*The Works of Philo* [Peabody, MA: Hendrickson, 1993], 653).

98. LSJ, s.v. ἐγκαλύπτω.

99. See also Philo, *Spec. Laws* 1.214; *Embassy* 1.83; *Prelim. Studies* 20. In all these texts Philo assumes that reading primarily happens with eyes, not ears.

The familial act of engaging Scriptural traditions is also attested in 4 Macc 18:7–18. In this text the martyred mother recounts how her husband, the father of the seven martyred sons, regularly engaged Scriptural tradition with their sons. The author depicts a variety of different events in which Jewish Scripture was engaged in a familial setting. In many of these cases, a text need not be present for the traditions to be experienced. Some of the verbs in the passage indicate that the father read to his family from physical texts, while others suggest something oral and memorial. The father "taught" (ἐδίδασκεν) his sons the law and the prophets (τὸν νόμον καὶ τοὺς προφήτας). He "read" (ἀνεγίνωσκεν) the tales of Cain and Abel, Isaac, and Joseph. He "spoke" (ἔλεγεν) of Phineas, "taught" (ἐδίδασκεν) of Hananiah, Azariah, and Mishael. He "glorified" (ἐδόξαζεν) Daniel's endurance in the lions' den. The father "reminded" (ὑπεμίμνησκεν) his sons of an Isaianic passage, "sang" (ἐμελῴδει) a Psalm of David, and "recited" (ἐπαροιμίαζεν) one of Solomon's proverbs, "affirmed" (ἐπιστοποιεῖτο) the words of Ezekiel, and "did not forget" (οὐκ ἐπελάθετο) a specific song that Moses taught (ᾠδὴν μὲν γάρ ἦν ἐδίδαξεν Μωσῆς).

The passage supports Philo's assumption that parents and families read Scripture together. It also reveals that Scripture was engaged in different kinds of ways and consisted of different media. Various texts and traditions made for various events. Some of these involved reading from a physical text and others did not.

Finally, at least one text from Qumran attests to communal reading events in which a modest number of persons were in attendance. The Community Rule, 1QS 6:6–8, provides regulations for two different kinds of reading events. The first appears to be individualized and the second is communal. In the broader context of 1QS 6:1–8, stipulations are outlined for local gatherings of the *Yahad* or "community." The text states that if ten or more members of the community are gathered "wherever they dwell" (בכול מגוריהם) two things must happen: first, a priest must be present and, second, someone must be studying the law at all times (איש דורש בתורה יומם ולילה). This is the individual reading event that 1QS 6 requires.

Immediately following is a requirement for regular, communal reading. The Community Rule provides instructions for these events in 1QS 6:7b–8: "And the Many [הרבים] shall be on watch together for a third of each night of the year in order to read the book, explain the regulation, and bless together."[100]

---

100. García Martínez and Tigchelaar, *Dead Sea Scrolls*, 1:83. "The book" likely refers to the law as well as other authoritative writings, such as Jubilees. See Shem Miller, *Dead Sea Media: Orality, Textuality, and Memory in the Scrolls from the Judean Desert* (Leiden: Brill, 2019), 51n55.

Since this particular requirement mentions "the Many" (or "general membership") (הרבים) and immediately follows regulations for gatherings of the *Yahad* outside of Qumran, it might apply to the "community" (יהד) in a narrow or a broad sense. The "Many" in 1QS 6:7b might refer only to those dwelling at Qumran or it might be inclusive of any place where the ten-person quorum is met.[101] Whichever is the case, communal reading takes place. If the regulation applies to outlying communities, then the size of those readings is ten or more. If the stipulation applies to the Qumran dwellers, then the size of the reading event is larger.

Regular, scheduled reading of authoritative texts was not unique to the Qumran community or to the *Yahad* diaspora. Scripture reading in the Second Temple period was also a fixture of synagogue practice. As Anders Runesson puts it, "One liturgical activity stands out among the rest in the sources and characterises the 'synagogue' more than anything else: the public reading, expounding and teaching of the torah."[102] While reading also took place in synagogues on non-Sabbath days, "the seventh day was dedicated to communal reading and studying."[103]

Both Philo and Josephus offer portraits of reading events in various synagogue gatherings. Philo vividly describes what the Essenes do in their synagogues on the Sabbath: "Then one takes the books and reads aloud [ἀναγινώσκει] and another of especial proficiency comes forward and expounds [ἀναδιδάσκει] what is not understood" (Philo, *Good Person* 82–83 [Colson, LCL]). But it is not just the Essenes who read, interpret, teach on the Sabbath according to Philo. This was widespread Jewish practice.

In *On Dreams*, Philo tells of a man he knew of very high rank who was a prefect and governor of Egypt who wanted to change Jewish customs (τὰ

---

101. The positions are summarized in Miller, *Dead Sea Media*, 49–50, from which the phrase "outlying communities" also comes. See also Sarianna Metso, "Whom Does the Term Yahad Identify?," in *Defining Identities: We, You, and the Other in the Dead Sea Scrolls*, STDJ 70 (Leiden: Brill, 2008), 73–77.

102. Anders Runesson, *The Origins of the Synagogue: A Socio-Historical Study*, ConBNT 37 (Stockholm: Almqvist & Wiksell, 2001), 191. Runesson lists the following texts in which the reading, teaching, or presence of Torah scrolls is mentioned: Philo, *Dreams* 2.127; *Creation* 128; *Hypothetica* 7.11–13; *Embassy* 156–57, 311–13; *Moses* 2.215–16; *Spec. Laws* 2.60–62; *Contempl. Life* 30–31; *Good Person* 80–83; Josephus, *J.W.* 2.289–92; *Ant.* 16.43–45, 164; *Ag. Ap.* 2.175; Mark 1:21, 39; 6:2; Matt 4:23; 9:35; 13:54; Luke 4:15, 16–30, 31–33, 44; 6:6; 13:10; Acts 9:20; 13:5, 14–16; 14:1; 15:21; 17:2–3, 10–11, 17; 18:4–6, 26; 19:8; John 6:59; 18:20 (*Origins of the Synagogue*, 191–92n91).

103. Runesson, *Origins of the Synagogue*, 192.

πάτρια), particularly concerning the Sabbath (Philo, *Dreams* 2.127). He asks if there was a natural disaster on the Sabbath if Jews would remain tranquil in their homes (μεθ' ἡσυχίας πάσης οἴκοι διατρίψετε). The man continues the line of questioning and as he does so he describes synagogue activity on the Sabbath: "And will you sit in your conventicles and assemble your regular company and read in security your holy books, expounding any obscure point and in leisurely comfort discussing at length your ancestral philosophy?" (Philo, *Dreams* 2.127 [Colson and Whitaker, LCL]).

Philo similarly describes communal reading in *Hypothetica* 7.11–13 and *Contempl. Life* 30–31. For Philo communal reading in a synagogue is not an end itself. Its purpose is advancement in knowledge of ancestral traditions, philosophy, and virtue. Moreover, there are several texts in which Philo writes concerning Sabbath synagogue practice and how it advances virtue and philosophy but communal reading of Scripture is not mentioned (Philo, *Creation* 128; *Embassy* 156–57, 312–13; *Moses* 2.215–16; *Spec. Laws* 2.60–62).

For Philo, the purpose of hearing the law on the Sabbath is to promote development and certain kinds of action. The same is true for Josephus in *Ag. Ap.* 2.173–75. Here he praises Moses for joining together two different modes of teaching: verbal instruction and actual practice. Because practice comes from instruction, Moses commanded "that every week men should desert their occupations and assemble to listen to the Law and to obtain a thorough and accurate knowledge of it" (Thackeray, LCL). Per *Ag. Ap.* 2.175, what distinguishes Jews is that they actually know their laws and ancestral customs because they hear and study them on a weekly basis.

Several texts from the New Testament confirm the picture of weekly synagogue Scripture reading presented by Philo and Josephus. In Luke 4:16–30, Jesus reads communally from an Isaiah scroll and then offers brief words of instruction on the basis of that text on a Sabbath day. In Acts 13:14–41, Paul and Barnabas enter the synagogue in Antioch on the Sabbath (τῇ ἡμέρᾳ τῶν σαββάτων) and, after the reading of the law and the prophets (μετὰ δὲ τὴν ἀνάγνωσιν τοῦ νόμου καὶ τῶν προφητῶν), the synagogue leaders ask if they would like to speak a "word of exhortation to the people" (λόγος παρακλήσεως πρὸς τὸν λαόν), to which Paul obliges in Acts 13:16–41.[104] The pair is then urged by the people to speak on the same topic "on the following Sabbath" (τὸ μεταξὺ σάββατον). And at the Jerusalem council in Acts 15:21 James summarily states

---

104. Trans. my own.

that from generations past "[Moses] has been read in the synagogues every Sabbath" (ἐν ταῖς συναγωγαῖς κατὰ πᾶν σάββατον ἀναγινωσκόμενος).

Communal Jewish synagogue reading appears to have set a precedent for one form of early Christian communal reading. In an oft-cited passage, Justin Martyr details early Christian Sabbath activities (Justin Martyr, *1 Apol* 67). On Sundays, all who live in the cities or the country gather and "the memoirs of the apostles or the writings of the prophets are read" (καὶ τὰ ἀπομνημονεύματα τῶν ἀποστόλων, ἢ τὰ συγγράμματα τῶν προφητῶν ἀναγινώσκεται).[105] Like the Jewish synagogue reading practices detailed by Philo and Josephus, early Christian reading on Sunday, according to Justin, is one social activity among many in which the gathered group engages. Moreover, the reading of different kinds of discourses, whether they be the "memoirs of the apostles" or the "prophets," serves as a springboard for the president's "verbal instruction" (διὰ λόγου). The reading of the gospel material, presuming that this is what the "memoirs of the apostles" (τὰ ἀπομνημονεύματα τῶν ἀποστόλων) is referencing, is not the central activity of the gathering.[106] In fact, it does not appear that any one of the five activities detailed is more significant than the others.[107]

Justin's account of Sabbath reading practices is significant as it provides explicit evidence to communal reading of Christian texts in the mid-second century CE. The size of the Christian group appears to be medium or large, since Justin writes that all who live in the cities and the country gather in one place.

While the passage from Justin is frequently cited with respect to early Christian reading, liturgical, and ritual practices, the Acts of Peter explicitly narrates the reading of a gospel text.[108] The narrative is commonly dated to the end of the second century CE. It relays a scene in which Peter comes upon

---

105. Trans. my own.

106. Graham Stanton argues that the "memoirs of the apostles" refer to multiple different gospels in Justin (*Jesus and Gospel* [Cambridge: Cambridge University Press, 2004], 100–101).

107. The activities are: (1) reading, (2) interpretation and exhortation, (3) communal prayer, (4) presidential prayer, and (5) distribution of bread and wine.

108. Following Averil Cameron, we should remember that religious storytelling was just as formative as, if not more formative than, the technical writing of the apologists that necessarily reached only a limited audience (*Christianity and the Rhetoric of Empire: The Development of Christian Discourse* [Berkeley: University of California Press, 1994], 112–19). The apocryphal gospels and acts ought not be marginalized for the information that they present about early Christian realities and practices simply because they are narrative in form.

a reading of "the Gospel" (*euangelium*).[109] Marcellus, who has recently taken Peter's side in his rivalry with Simon, has invited Peter into his home so that they might together pray with the widows and elders. Peter enters the dining room (*triclinio*), sees that the gospel was being read, rolls it up, and begins to speak (*et uidit euangelium legi. inuolues eum dixit*).[110]

Peter then offers a lengthy exposition that begins with his personal reflection on the transfiguration. The implication is that Peter interrupted a reading of this account from some gospel text. This is confirmed by what follows in the narrative. In Acts of Peter 21, those gathered at the reading encounter events that echo elements of the transfiguration in the gospels. The dining room (*triclinium*) they are gathered in becomes "as bright as lightning, such as in the clouds," and all present are surrounded by "light such as no man can describe."[111] As a result, everyone is prostrated except for the blind widows who stand up and see three different figures, which results in their regained sight.

The passage is of particular interest since it is the earliest narrative text that depicts a reading of a gospel. While Justin reports that Christians communally read gospel material, the Acts of Peter provides a narrativized account of what one such reading event might have been like, even if highly imaginative.

The narrative imagines several noteworthy things about this reading event. First, it occurred in the "dining room" (*in triclinio*) in Marcellus's private residence.[112] Second, it is a small to medium gathering of persons. It is difficult

---

109. Acts of Peter 20. On dating in the late second century see Carl Schmidt, "Zur Datierung der alten Petrusakten," *ZNW* 29 (1930): 150–55; J. K. Elliott, ed., *The Apocryphal New Testament: A Collection of Apocryphal Christian Literature in an English Translation* (Oxford: Oxford University Press, 1993), 396; Jan N. Bremmer, "Aspects of the Acts of Peter: Women, Magic, Place and Date," in *Apocryphal Acts of Peter: Magic, Miracles and Gnosticism*, ed. Jan N. Bremmer (Leuven: Peeters, 1998), 17–18; Hans-Josef Klauck, *The Apocryphal Acts of the Apostles: An Introduction*, trans. Brian McNeil (Waco, TX: Baylor University Press, 2008), 84.

110. R. A. Lipsius and M. Bonnet, eds., *Acta Apostolorum Apocrypha*, 2 vols. (Leipzig: H. Mendelssohn, 1891), 1:66–67. Following Lipsius and Bonnet, I have not emended the Latin orthography. Thus we find "b"s for "p"s, "u"s for "v"s, and other such spellings. Trans. Elliott, *Apocryphal New Testament*, 413.

111. Elliott, *Apocryphal New Testament*, 414.

112. Nässelqvist takes this location to suggest that early Christian readings were "situated in a meal setting" and that this particular reading specifically happened "in the context of a communal meal" (*Public Reading*, 102). I see no reason to generalize from this passage that reading was always or even usually accompanied by eating. Rather, communally reading a gospel text in the dining room of a private residence, perhaps while or after hearers dined, is one setting in which a Christian reading event could take place.

to venture a guess about exactly how many persons are meant to be envisaged, since *triclinia* varied in size. The fact that the reading takes place at a residence to which specific persons had been invited implies that the event is not "public." The event described is communal but private. Third, the content of the reading is a gospel (*euangelium*) and its physical form is a scroll that Peter "rolls up" (*inuolues eum*). It might be surprising that the author of a late-second-century text imagines that a gospel text is written on such a medium.[113] However, we ought not assume singularity of practice when it comes to the material form of gospel. The medium in this case elevates the document's contents, which Peter calls "holy scripture of our Lord." Fourth, the author of the Acts of Peter presumes that the apostle had some role in writing Scripture and perhaps also this particular text. Peter uses the first person plural, "what we have written" (*scribsimus*), in reference to the phrase "holy scripture" (*sancta scribtura*).[114] If the author has in mind the association of Peter with the Gospel of Mark, then the Acts of Peter is another text that attests to the tradition that the apostle's voice stands behind Mark in some way and may presume a reading of that particular text.[115] However, no discrete gospel text is named.[116] It is simply "the gospel" (*euangelium*) that is read.

The passage describes a reading event that involved a physical manuscript followed by a teaching event related to that reading. Gospel material is read and subsequently explained within a social context. Both activities are oral and aural. The first involves direct textual mediation (i.e., reading) to a group;

---

113. Bremmer takes the passage to suggest that scrolls continued to be used in some early Christian circles ("Aspects of the Acts of Peter," 4–5).

114. The syntax here is taken in several different ways, but it is clear that Peter includes himself among those who write. The Greek of the passage is quoted in Isidore and reads ἃ ἐχωρήσαμεν, ἐγράψαμεν (PG 78:544a).

115. The claim that Mark served as Peter's amanuensis for the writing of the Gospel of Mark is common in early ecclesial tradition. See Papias *apud* Eusebius, *Hist. eccl.* 3.39.15; Clement *apud* Eusebius, *Hist. eccl.* 2.15.1–2; *Hist. eccl.* 6.14.6–7; Irenaeus, *Adv. Haer.* 3.1.1; Jerome, *De vir.* 8; Jerome, *Comm. on Matt.*; Tertullian, *Adv. Marc.* 4.1.1; 2.1–2; 3.4; 5.3–4; Eusebius, *Hist. eccl.* 2.16. On these texts and others, see C. Clifton Black, *Mark: Images of an Apostolic Interpreter*, Studies on Personalities of the New Testament (Columbia: University of South Carolina Press, 1994), 125–26; Nicholas A. Elder, *The Media Matrix of Early Jewish and Christian Narrative*, LNTS 612 (London: T&T Clark, 2019), 48–50.

116. Nor should we expect one to be named. As Matthew D. C. Larsen argues, in the first and second century specific gospel texts were largely considered to be specific instantiations of an overarching gospel tradition (*Gospels before the Book* [Oxford: Oxford University Press, 2018], 99–120).

the second does not. The account lines up well with the oft-cited passage from Justin Martyr (*1 Apol.* 67) in which he describes what takes place during Christian gatherings, namely reading, instruction, prayer, and a eucharistic meal.

The evidence from Second Temple Judaism and early Christianity reflects what was found with respect to Greco-Roman reading cultures. Public, large-group reading to a mass of people is a relatively rare event in all of these social contexts. When such events are relayed in texts, they are remarkable for one reason or another. The more common setting for communal reading is small and medium-sized groups.

These small to medium-sized reading events usually take place in a private setting. It is a romanticized notion of ancient reading to presume that public, communal readings were more normal than private readings. It is not as though one could meander the streets of first-century Rome, Jerusalem, or Ephesus and expect to come upon a reading event that was wholly public on any day of the week. Because reading is a social act, it usually happens in the private spaces wherein social networks are being established and realized.

Reading is a mechanism by which social bonds are established and strengthened. For the Greco-Roman literati, reading one's own writings in a variety of private or public settings was a way to establish one's literary network and to promote oneself socially. Jewish and Christian reading events likewise established and reinforced social bonds. But they did so specifically in the context of worship and formation of the individual and the group's religious identity. Reading in these circles appears to have both a horizontal, social component and a vertical, religious component.

Conclusion

Reading events in Greco-Roman, Second Temple Jewish, and early Christian antiquity were multiple. There was no single type, purpose, setting, or occasion for reading. Rather, reading took place in private and in public by both individuals and groups. The same discourse could be read in different ways and in different settings at different times by different persons.

Most of the texts treated in this chapter do not explicitly state the number of people that were present at a given reading event. This being the case the divisions between a small group, a moderately-sized group, and a large group are porous. For this reason, it is better to think about a spectrum or matrix of reading events that consist of various numbers of people and are more or less private.

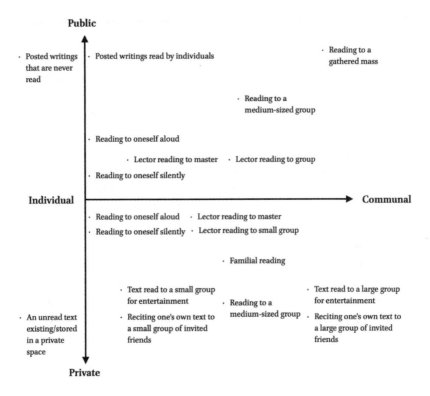

Figure 1. Spectrum of Reading Events

Most of the kinds of reading events on this matrix were addressed in the chapter. There are a few that were not. At the top of the public-private axis I have indicated that "posted writings read by individuals" are highly public though also individualized. Signs, notices, or graffiti, to all of which there is abundant literary and material evidence from antiquity, fall into this category. The written notice of Jesus's charge in Matt 27:37, Luke 23:38, and John 19:19–20 is an example of this type of text from the gospels.[117]

Some public postings might have gone completely unread, however. This category is set to the left of the matrix altogether, as such texts had no readers. In this category are other kinds of texts that are unread and public, such as

---

117. The medium of the written notice is variously described in the gospels. Matthew calls it "the written accusation" (τὴν αἰτίαν αὐτοῦ γεγραμμένην). In Luke it is "an inscription upon him" (ἐπιγραφὴ ἐπ' αὐτῷ). And John calls it a "title" (τίτλον). Trans. my own.

Tefillin. These are leather cases that hold "worn texts."[118] The texts themselves are usually inaccessible and unread either because the script is so small or because the casing itself is stitched closed with the writing inside. *Mezuzot*, containers holding Scripture and placed on the gates and doorposts of houses, would fall into the "unread text existing/stored in a private space" category. These are texts that serve a symbolic function in a private space.

The gospels should not be funneled into the same category on this matrix. Different kinds of texts were read different ways. The same gospel might have made for different reading events at different points in time and in different settings. A discourse can be used and received in different ways. There is literary evidence to the law of Moses being read by an individual in private, by an individual in public, by small groups in private, by small groups in public, and by large groups both in private and in public. By the second century CE a similar dynamic was at work with the gospels: they were experienced in a variety of social settings. Turning to the first century and the canonical gospels themselves, we find that this is not a new development. The gospels indicate that they are different kinds of texts from one another that made for various kinds of reading events.

---

118. See Stephen Reed, "Physical Features of Excerpted Torah Texts," in *Jewish and Christian Scripture as Artifact and Canon*, ed. Craig A. Evans and H. Daniel Zacharias, Library of Second Temple Studies 70 (London: T&T Clark, 2011), 86–97.

CHAPTER 3

Reading the Gospels

Media Myth: Each gospel was written to be experienced the same way.
Media Reality: Each gospel expresses its textuality differently, indicating that the gospels are different kinds of texts that made for different kinds of reading events.

◆ ◆ ◆

Texts in Greco-Roman antiquity, Second Temple Judaism, and early Christianity were read both silently and aloud and with varying numbers of people involved in any given reading event. There was no one way to engage a discourse in these contexts. Ancient reading practices were diverse. The gospels are not an exception. There was no one way to experience them. At times they were read by individuals silently or aloud. At other times they were read in groups of varying sizes. This chapter turns to the canonical gospels themselves to assess the reading events for which they might have been made in the first century. The gospels indicate that they were written for differing modes of reception. Invoking Chris Keith's recent work on the gospels' textual self-consciousness and Gérard Genette's paratextual theory, I contend that each gospel is self-conscious about its textuality and its textual medium.[1]

The gospels are not all conscious about their medium in the same way. They express that they were different kinds of texts made for different kinds of reading events. The Gospel of Mark implies that it still has a foot in the oral lifeworld, as it is "good news" (εὐαγγέλιον). Proclamation is its native mode of reception. Matthew designates itself a "book" (βίβλος), a label with which it sets itself on the same level as authoritative Scripture. It was to be read and studied at synagogue gatherings. The preface to Luke indicates that the Third Gospel was written for an individual reader, Theophilus, and was first experienced in a solitary reading event. John 20:30 labels itself a "document" (βιβλίον) that is but one writing in a sea of Jesus traditions, written and otherwise.

---

1. Chris Keith, *The Gospel as Manuscript: An Early History of the Jesus Tradition as Material Artifact* (Oxford: Oxford University Press, 2020); Gérard Genette, *Paratexts: Thresholds of Interpretation*, trans. J. E. Lewin, Lecture, Culture, Theory 20 (Cambridge: Cambridge University Press, 1997).

The Extended Situation, Textual Self-Consciousness, and Paratexts

In *The Gospel as Manuscript*, Chris Keith argues that the public reading of written Jesus traditions was one way that early Christians put gospel texts on display.[2] By reading the gospels in communal settings, they not only "imbue[d] these texts with special significance" but also forged an identity that was simultaneously indebted to and distinct from Judaism and its attendant synagogue reading practices.[3] Reading the gospels communally and liturgically "served as a distinct identity marker."[4]

Foundational to Keith's argument is that the gospels were read communally in pre-Constantinian Christianity.[5] He marshals seven texts in support of this claim: Mark 13:14, Matt 24:15, Justin Martyr's *First Apology*, Irenaeus's *Adv. Haer.* 2.27.1, the Muratorian Fragment, Eusebius's *Hist. eccl.* 6.12.1–4, and the Acts of Peter 19–20. Many of these texts were addressed in the previous chapters of this book to argue that Christian communal reading events were diverse, as were their Jewish and Greco-Roman counterparts.

Two of the texts Keith cites, Mark 13:14 and Matt 24:15, were not addressed in the previous chapter. With these references, Keith pushes communal reading of the gospels back into the first century CE and into the gospels themselves. Both texts refer to "the reader" (ὁ ἀναγινώσκων). Keith, with several other commentators, understands this reference to indicate a literate person who reads the gospel to a group.[6] The authors of Mark and Matthew intend their gospels to be read aloud from the moment of writing.[7]

Two other claims undergird Keith's argument. First, he maintains that reading aloud was the norm in Greco-Roman antiquity, even though silent

---

2. Keith, *Gospel as Manuscript*, 161–232.

3. Quotation from Keith, *Gospel as Manuscript*, 174; pp. 163–200 address the public reading of gospel manuscripts and pp. 201–232 argue for the role the public reading of gospel manuscripts played in forming early Christian identity.

4. Keith, *Gospel as Manuscript*, 203.

5. Keith, *Gospel as Manuscript*, 176–200.

6. Keith, *Gospel as Manuscript*, 177–80; Mary Ann Beavis, *Mark*, Paideia (Grand Rapids: Baker Academic, 2011), 197; Adela Yarbro Collins, *Mark: A Commentary*, Hermeneia (Minneapolis: Fortress, 2007), 597–98; R. T. France, *The Gospel of Mark*, NIGTC (Grand Rapids: Eerdmans, 2002), 52–53; Robert H. Gundry, *Mark: A Commentary on His Apology for the Cross* (Grand Rapids: Eerdmans, 1993), 742–43.

7. Keith does not go so far to suggest that the reference implies that these authors have "liturgical" reading in mind, though he states that such a manner of reading did occur shortly thereafter (*Gospel as Manuscript*, 180–82).

reading was known.[8] This is in service of his assertion, following William A. Johnson, that public reading is a social event. Second, he demonstrates that the canonical gospels are all "textually self-conscious."[9] Each promotes itself as a text.[10]

Keith's argument that the public reading of the gospels imbued them with authority and shaped early Christian identity is compelling. I work under the same premise, following Johnson, that reading is a social act and reading events are "intricate parts of socially constructed communities."[11] The premise can be advanced by assessing how *different* kinds of early Christian reading events were socially effective in *different* kinds of ways.

The gospels were read communally, and such reading events had social effects. Not all communal reading events were equal and communal reading was not the only way that texts were engaged. As Johnson puts it, "The reading of a given text in different contexts results in different reading events."[12] The gospels are not textually self-conscious in the same ways. They express their textuality differently. Mark refers to the "reader" in 13:14 but also labels itself "good news" (εὐαγγέλιον) from its outset. Matthew describes itself as a "book" (βίβλος) at its beginning, whereas John uses a related term, "document" (βιβλίον) at its end. Luke is self-conscious about its written-ness, but nowhere designates itself as "good news" or a "book" as its predecessors do. Luke indicates its medium with a literary preface.

These differing textual expressions indicate that the gospels are not identical with respect to their medium. Johnson's foundational claim about different

---

8. Keith, *Gospel as Manuscript*, 19, 172. Keith is more nuanced in his discussion of silent and vocalized reading than most. He recognizes that persons in antiquity could read silently and cites Frank D. Gilliard's important and overlooked response to Paul Achtemeier's influential article (Gilliard, "More Silent Reading in Antiquity: *Non Omne Verbum Sonabat*," *JBL* 112 [1993]: 689–96; Achtemeier, "*Omne Verbum Sonat*: The New Testament and the Oral Environment of Late Western Antiquity," *JBL* 109 [1990]: 3–27), as well as A. K. Gavrilov's "Techniques of Reading in Classical Antiquity," *ClQ* 47 (1997): 56–73.

9. Keith, *Gospel as Manuscript*, 103–35.

10. This textual self-consciousness is on display in several places: the references to "the reader" in Mark 13:14 and Matt 24:15; Matt 1:1, which labels the narrative a "book" (βίβλος); the Lukan prologue that puts the gospel in competition with its written predecessors; John 20:30, which identifies itself as a "document" (βιβλίον) and the statements of John's written-ness in 21:24–25.

11. Keith, *Gospel as Manuscript*, 20.

12. William A. Johnson, *Readers and Reading Culture in the High Roman Empire: A Study of Elite Communities* (Oxford: Oxford University Press, 2010), 11.

kinds of texts and their attendant reading events can be applied to the gospels.[13] Gérard Genette's paratextual theory helps to assess the kinds of texts that the gospels are and the reading events for which they were first made.[14]

According to Genette, texts are "rarely presented in an unadorned state."[15] They are accompanied by several features that surround them. These are what he calls "paratexts." With respect to modern books, these features include covers, the name of the author, prefaces, dedications, tables of contents, and illustrations. These are not quite the text itself, yet they are directly and physically (or electronically) attached to it. Paratexts are heterogeneous in form but united in function: they present, literally "make present," the text in the world.[16]

As "thresholds" and "vestibules," paratexts facilitate a reader's experiences of the discourses to which they are attached.[17] Paratextual norms differ in various contexts, but "a text without a paratext does not exist and never has existed."[18] This dovetails with the so-called material turn in biblical studies, which emphasizes the materiality of manuscripts as objects.[19] Brent Nongbri calls for "greater attention to the books themselves as artifacts, to the archaeology of early Christian manuscripts."[20] That is, how texts are *presented* in their manuscript form.

---

13. W. Johnson, *Readers and Reading Culture*, 11.

14. Genette, *Paratexts*. David Aune has also applied Genette's work on paratexts to the Synoptic Gospels to assess Mark and Matthew's genre ("Genre Theory and the Genre-Function of Mark and Matthew," in *Mark and Matthew I*, ed. Eve-Marie Becker and Anders Runesson, WUNT 271 [Tübingen: Mohr Siebeck, 2011], 145–75). Aune argues that Matthew is a biography proper and that Mark is a parody of the same genre. I have previously employed Genette's paratextual theory with respect to the beginnings of the Synoptics in "The Synoptic Gospels as Mixed Media," *Biblical Research* 64 (2019): 45.

15. Genette, *Paratexts*, 1.

16. Genette, *Paratexts*, 1.

17. Genette, *Paratexts*, 2. Genette further differentiates between "epitextual" and "peritextual" paratexts. Epitexts are not physically attached to the text but are exterior to it. Author interviews, commentary on a text, or a conversation about it are all examples. Peritexts, in contrast, are around the text itself though at varying degrees of distance. With respect to the gospels, titles, prefaces, and prologues are all peritexts and patristic commentary on the gospels themselves are epitexts.

18. Genette, *Paratexts*, 3. Though, as Genette notes, paratexts without texts do exist, such as when texts lost to history are known only by their titles.

19. For a review of the "material turn," see Keith, *Gospel as Manuscript*, 36–39.

20. Brent Nongbri, *God's Library: The Archaeology of the Earliest Christian Manuscripts* (New Haven: Yale University Press, 2018), 11.

Each gospel remarks on its medium at its edges, at the borderland, vestibule, or threshold between text and reader. The gospels' media-conscious expressions occur at their beginnings or endings. Like other paratexts, these expressions would not exist apart from the text to which they are attached. Mark 1:1, Matt 1:1, and Luke 1:1–4's raisons d'être is the discourse that follows it. John 20:30 and 21:24–25's raisons d'être is the discourse that precedes it.

Paratexts have illocutionary force.[21] One of their primary functions is to indicate what kind of text is at hand and how it ought to be received without directly stating that information. The paratexts to this book, *Gospel Media*, do not explicitly declare "this is an academic book in the field of biblical studies that most readers will read to themselves in service of their own understanding." Though, in their own way, they communicate that information.

To summarize and move toward the gospels themselves: from Keith we take the claim that the gospels are textually self-conscious but amend it to specify that the gospels are textually self-conscious about their medium. Each gospel's paratext, which is a theoretical concept from Genette, designates the narrative to which it is attached with a media term. Mark 1:1 calls itself "good news" (εὐαγγέλιον). Matthew 1:1 labels itself "a book" (βίβλος). The Lukan preface suggests that what follows is "an account" (διήγησις). And John 20:30 states that what preceded it is "a document" (βιβλίον). If each gospel is a different kind of text and different kinds of texts make for different kinds of reading events, then we should not expect that the gospels were read or experienced the exact same way.[22]

Mark

The Gospel of Mark commences with the phrase "The beginning of the gospel of Jesus Christ" (ἀρχὴ τοῦ εὐαγγελίου Ἰησοῦ Χριστοῦ). Mark 1:1 is frequently taken as the title for the narrative that follows.[23] The words label the entire

---

21. Genette, *Paratexts*, 10–12.
22. This illocutionary force did not require that each gospel be received as it was intended. Because the gospels were objects with permanence, they were used in different ways, even shortly after they were written. By writing of the "intended use" of the gospels, I mean the kind of early reading event we can best surmise based on the gospels' peritexts, their content, and comparison with other discourses and the reading events for which those discourses made.
23. This is the case in Allen Wikgren, "ΑΡΧΗ ΤΟΥ ΕΥΑΓΓΕΛΙΟΥ," *JBL* 61 (1942): 11–20, esp. 15–17; Rudolf Pesch, *Das Markusevangelium: Einleitung und Kommentar zu Kap. 1,1–8,26*, 4th ed., 2 vols., Herders theologischer Kommentar zum Neuen Testament (Freiburg: Herder,

narrative.[24] It is a peritextual vestibule that moves the reader into the discourse. The phrase also demonstrates a media consciousness with the word "gospel" (εὐαγγέλιον). The narrative is not self-conscious about its textuality, but about its orality.

The term "gospel" would not connote a written genre of literature until the middle of the second century CE.[25] In the first century and earlier the word "gospel" (εὐαγγέλιον) and its verbal counterpart, "to proclaim good news" (εὐαγγελίζομαι), carried oral freight. This is the case in other New Testament writings, the Septuagint, Greco-Roman literature, and Second Temple Jewish texts.[26] Mark's use of the term to designate something that exists in written, manuscript form is unprecedented.

This presents a quandary: how can a written text be "orally proclaimed news"? Marshall McLuhan proposes a "Russian nesting dolls" model of media, wherein "the 'content' of any medium is always another medium."[27] For McLuhan, the content of writing is speech itself. Speech, when put into

---

1984), 74–75; M. Eugene Boring, "Mark 1:1–15 and the Beginning of the Gospel," Semeia 52 (1990): 43–81; France, *Gospel of Mark*, 50–51; John R. Donahue and Daniel J. Harrington, *The Gospel of Mark*, SP 2 (Collegeville, MN: Liturgical Press, 2002), 60; M. Eugene Boring, *Mark: A Commentary*, NTL (Louisville: Westminster John Knox, 2006), 29; Collins, *Mark*, 87; Joel Marcus, *Mark 1–8: A New Translation with Introduction and Commentary*, AB 27 (New York: Doubleday, 2008), 143–46.

24. Three aspects of Mark 1:1 suggest that it introduces the entire narrative. First, the phrase is a verbless nominative absolute, a construction that often occurs in introductory materials. Second, Jewish texts in the Second Temple Period frequently began with an "independent titular sentence" (W. D. Davies and Dale C. Allison, *Matthew 1–7*, ICC [London: T&T Clark, 2004], 151). Third, Greco-Roman texts, and especially histories, often indicate their content in their opening words (Loveday Alexander, *The Preface to Luke's Gospel: Literary Convention and Social Context in Luke 1.1–4 and Acts 1.1*, SNTSMS 78 [Cambridge: Cambridge University Press, 1993], 29). For a more detailed discussion on Mark 1:1 as an introduction to the entire gospel, see Nicholas A. Elder, *The Media Matrix of Early Jewish and Christian Narrative*, LNTS 612 (London: T&T Clark, 2019), 157–58.

25. For an overview of the positions on how the term came to designate a written genre in the second century, see Elder, "Synoptic Gospels," 47n23.

26. For discussions of the various primary sources see John P. Dickson, "Gospel as News: Εὐαγγελ- from Aristophanes to the Apostle Paul," *NTS* 51 (2005): 212–30; Michael F. Bird, *The Gospel of the Lord: How the Early Church Wrote the Story of Jesus* (Grand Rapids: Eerdmans, 2014), 9–11; Elder, *Media Matrix*, 158–61; Elder, "Synoptic Gospels," 47–48.

27. Marshall McLuhan, *Understanding Media: The Extensions of Man* (Cambridge: MIT Press, 1994), 8.

the written modality, is necessarily affected by its new medium. The medium is the message.

This is Mark's innovation: the gospel textualizes antecedent oral Jesus traditions and is self-conscious about this from its outset. But why textualize a previously oral tradition? Numerous theories have been offered: the deaths or impending deaths of early gospel tradents or eyewitnesses; persecution and pogroms; the destruction of the Jerusalem temple; the killing of oral traditions; or a combination of two or more of these. Recently Keith has argued that, as a manuscript, the Gospel of Mark creates what Jan Assmann calls an "extended situation" (*zerdehnte Situation*).[28] The extended situation allows cultural memories to be experienced across time and space. One does not have to be physically co-present with a tradent to experience a discourse. The necessity of interpersonal communication is obliterated. The manuscript can be read by an individual or read to individuals who are miles and centuries removed from its author. For Keith, the visualization of the manuscript itself within the extended situation is formative. The presence of the text at a public reading imbued the gospel tradition with authority by its physicality.

Not all texts were used or experienced the same way, however. A discourse can exist in physical form and serve multiple functions. Texts like Mark are written documents that are employed in different oral and literary contexts. At times texts were directly read from, whether privately or publicly. At other times, these same texts served memorial functions. They were "memory aids" and re-oralized in performance or declamation. There is precedent for written documents simultaneously being influenced by both oral and textual modalities of communication and also for being received in different kinds of reading events.

Pliny the Younger twice states that his hendecasyllables are read, copied, and sung (*Ep.* 4.19; 7.4).[29] They are written texts that make for a variety of reading events by other persons. But it is not just his verse that is received various ways. In *Ep.* 1.20, he claims that he is of the unpopular opinion that the best-delivered speeches are identical to their written counterparts. The written version is "the model and prototype for the spoken version" (Pliny the Younger, *Ep.* 1.20 [Radice, LCL]). Pliny presumes that the oral speech is

---

28. Keith, *Gospel as Manuscript*, 29–32, 89–92; Jan Assmann, *Religion and Cultural Memory: Ten Studies*, trans. Rodney Livingstone (Stanford, CA: Stanford University Press, 2006), 103–8.

29. In *Ep.* 4.19 he claims that his wife sings his verses to the accompaniment of her lyre and in *Ep.* 7.4 he claims that Greeks who have learned Latin sing them set to a cithara or lyre.

prepared beforehand in writing but is not read from directly. The text is not present when the speech is given, even though the speech ought not stray from the written text.

Pliny writes of his reluctance to give a "reading" (*recitem*) of a speech in *Ep.* 2.19. The entire passage is worth quoting, as it demonstrates how the reading of the same text in different contexts makes for different events. Pliny considers the differences between "speeches" and "readings":

> You urge me to give a reading of my speech to a group of friends. I will since you ask it, but with many misgivings. I know very well that speeches when read lose all their warmth and spirit, almost their entire character, since their fire is always fed from the atmosphere of court: the bench of magistrates and throng of advocates, the suspense of the awaited verdict, reputation of the different speakers, and the divided enthusiasm of the public; and they gain too from the gestures of the speaker as he strides to and fro, the movements of his body corresponding to his changing passions. (Hence the loss to anyone who delivers his speech sitting down—he is at a real disadvantage by the mere fact of being seated, though he may be as gifted generally as the speakers who stand.) Moreover, a man who is giving a reading has the two chief aids to his delivery (eyes and hands) taken up with his text, so it is not surprising if the attention of his audience wavers when there is no adventitious attraction to hold it nor stimulus to keep it aroused. (Pliny the Younger, *Ep.* 2.19 [Radice, LCL])

The social circumstances of a speech give it something special. A reading, in contrast to a speech, takes away the reader's eyes and hands since they are occupied with the roll. The audience is not held captive by a reading of a speech the same way the audience is held captive by the speech itself. The text's physical presence hinders the discourse's reception. Since Pliny's court speeches are pre-written, the same text can be used in different ways. On the one hand, the speech exists physically in textual form but is not employed for its "spoken version." On the other hand, the written speech can be read aloud with the text present, but doing so, per Pliny, diminishes its performative value.

A written speech can also later be read or performed by a person who did not write it. Pliny argues that longer books and speeches are better than shorter ones, not least because "when published they look better and more impressive in a good-sized volume" (Pliny the Younger, *Ep.* 1.20.5 [Radice, LCL]). He cites several examples of published speeches that are long and well known.[30] Pliny

---

30. Pliny includes Demosthenes, Aeschines, Hyperides, Pollio, Caesar, Caelius, and Cicero.

not only has read published speeches but he also circulates his own speeches so that others might read them. Speeches could also be declaimed by persons who did not write them. In *Ad M. Caes.* 1.6, Marcus Aurelius tells his tutor that he declaimed one of Fronto's speeches to his father. While it was warmly received, Marcus concedes that the words "ought to have been spoken by their own author."[31] In *Ad Verum Imp.* 2.1, Fronto similarly indicates that emperors frequently used ghostwriters for various types of discourses, including speeches.

The relationship between orality and textuality with respect to speeches is complex. A "speech" (*oratio*), which is by its etymology something oral, is initially written and, according to Pliny, the written version should be closely followed when the speech is declaimed. However, it is best that the text itself is not present during the speaking event. After the oral event, the written speech can be experienced in several different ways with or without the text present. Even this is to project too much of a linear order onto the process, however. Pliny notes in *Ep.* 1.20 that some speeches "were published without being delivered" (Pliny the Younger, *Ep.* 1.20.10 [Radice, LCL]). However received, court speeches began life textually and then are put to various uses.

With Galen, the relationship between orality, textuality, reading, and circulation is just as complex as it is with Pliny. For Pliny, texts were often used in the service of oral events. On several occasions in Galen's writings, the script is flipped. An oral discourse became textualized. Galen tells his readers that oral events were the genesis for several, though certainly not all, of his texts.

At times Galen recognizes the antecedent orality of his writings in the respective texts themselves, usually in their opening peritexts. He begins *Thrasybulus* with a preface to its eponymous reader stating that nothing that he composes (συγγράψασθαι) therein is different from that which he has spoken on the topic (Galen, *Thrasybulus* 1).[32] The content of the writing is identical to what one would have encountered in Galen's oral speeches, demonstrations, or debates. The preface to *The Affections and Errors of the Soul* is similar: "You want a written version of the answer I gave you orally, regarding Antonius the Epicurean's book on *The control of the individual affections*; I shall now make you one, and this is its beginning (τὴν ἀρχήν)."[33] P. N. Singer notes that there

---

31. Caillan Davenport and Jennifer Manley, eds., *Fronto: Selected Letters*, Classical Studies Series (New York: Bloomsbury, 2014), 75.

32. Text Johnston LCL. See also Karl Gottlob Kühn, ed., *Claudii Galeni opera omnia*, 22 vols. (Leipzig: Car. Cnoblochii, 1821), 5:806.

33. P. N. Singer, trans., *Galen: Selected Works*, The World's Classics (Oxford: Oxford University Press, 1997), 100; text Kühn, *Claudii Galeni opera omnia*, 5:1.

is a "double orality" to *Affections and Errors*: its background was an extemporaneous speech and it was subsequently dictated.[34] It is an "oral exposition, of which our text is a more or less accurate transcription."[35]

Galen indicates in the peritextual prefaces of both *Thrasybulus* and *Affections and Errors* that the texts that follow are ὑπομνήματα, a term that is variously translated "notes," "memory aids," and "reminders." In these cases, the "reminders" are of what Galen has previously said on the respective topics. I flag this here because we will return to the topic of ὑπομνήματα and its applicability to the gospels in chapter 8.

While in these two texts Galen offers information about their origins, he more systematically remarks on the backgrounds and purposes of his texts in *On My Own Books* and *On the Order of My Own Books*. Not only does Galen indicate the different audiences and reasons for which his texts were written, but he also remarks on what texts or events stand behind them.

At times Galen created a text from an oral event and intended to circulate it. He was not surprised when the discourse reached a wide audience. This is the case with *Thrasybulus* and *Affections and Errors*, which had their genesis in an oral-instructional setting. Galen states in *On My Own Books* 17 and 21–22 that *Empiricism in Medicine* and *Lycus's Ignorance in Anatomy* had their genesis in another kind of oral event: a debate.

On other occasions, texts created from various oral contexts reached a wider audience than Galen intended because they were plagiarized.[36] Galen writes at the beginning of *On My Own Books* that his discourses were commonly used by charlatans in their own anatomical demonstrations and published under other names. This happened because "they were given without inscription to peers or pupils."[37] The texts were never intended "for publication" (πρὸς ἔκδοσιν) but rather were textualized as a favor for friends who wanted "a written

---

34. P. N. Singer, general introduction to *Galen: Psychological Writings*, ed. P. N. Singer, Daniel Davies, and Vivian Nutton (Cambridge: Cambridge University Press, 2014), 15–16.

35. Singer, general introduction, 39.

36. On the phenomenon of plagiarism and "accidental publication," see especially Matthew D. C. Larsen, "Accidental Publication, Unfinished Texts and the Traditional Goals of New Testament Textual Criticism," *JSNT* 39 (2017): 362–87; Matthew D. C. Larsen, *Gospels before the Book* (Oxford: Oxford University Press, 2018), 37–58.

37. Galen, *On My Own Books* 10K; trans. Singer, *Galen*, 3. In addition to the Greek text from Kühn, *Claudii Galeni opera omnia*, vol. 19, there is Georg Helmreich, Johannes Marquardt, and Iwani Müller, *Claudii Galeni pergameni scripta minora*, vol. 3 (Leipzig: Teubner, 1891).

record of what they had heard" (ὧν ἤκουσαν ἔχειν ὑπομνήματα).[38] Many of these texts were returned to Galen. He corrected them, gave them titles, and properly published them.

Galen's textualized oral discourses were put to various uses. They were not all engaged the same way. Some were read by the individuals to whom they were given. Others were reused in subsequent oral contexts. This is the case with an untitled text that Galen discusses in *On My Own Books* 15. The text's origin was a speech that Galen delivered against one of his rivals, Martialus. A friend sent Galen "a person trained in shorthand writing" in order that he, Galen, might dictate the speech and Galen's friend might "be able to use it against Martialus during examinations of patients."[39] Like *Affections and Errors*, this discourse is doubly oral: its originative context was a debate, and it was dictated. We might even label it triply oral, as its recipient intended to use it in another oral context.[40]

In *On My Own Books* 17, Galen states that *The Motion of the Chest and Lungs* was likewise for a student's reuse during anatomical demonstrations. After the student died other people got a hold of the text and someone was audacious enough to append his own preface and attempt to publish it textually as his own. There are two afterlives of this text, one oral and one textual.

These Galenic discourses are written texts, but they have an oral pre-history to them. Once a discourse entered into the textual modality it could be put to various uses. The texts made for a variety of "extended situations." At times they were employed by the persons to whom they were written in subsequent oral events. At other times, they were read or performed by individuals who happened to get their hands on them. At still other times, they were textually edited and "published" by persons not named Galen.

How does this all relate to the Gospel of Mark? There are three results that I wish to highlight here. First, authors and readers in antiquity were not oblivious to the overlap between orality and textuality. In Mark's media context, not only were texts employed in service of oral events, but oral events also resulted in textualized discourses. The latter phenomenon is relevant to the Gospel of Mark, which begins by peritextually labeling itself a "gospel," or orally proclaimed news. Mark, like Galen's texts that were textualized from oral

---

38. Galen, *On My Own Books* 10K; trans. Singer, *Galen*, 3.
39. Singer, *Galen*, 6.
40. Singer notes the possibility of *Affections and Errors* being triply oral as well, though in a slightly different manner (general introduction, 16).

events, has a foot in both the oral and textual world. It is an oral exposition subsequently textualized, and it is self-conscious about this from its opening words. We will return to the orality of Mark in chapter 6 and press the case further. Not only does the gospel originate from an antecedent oral tradition, but it is also oral as to its mode of composition. It is doubly oral.

Second, the oral-predecessor model might affect the way that we date Mark. With respect to dating Galenic treatises that are written up from antecedent oral events, such as *Affections and Errors*, Singer notes that composition cannot be boiled down to a single date.[41] One must think in terms of at least two dates in the writing process: one for the originative oral events and another for the text resulting from the events. The first date concerns the discourse as delivered orally and the second date the discourse as reduced to writing. Sometimes years or decades intervene between these two dates for Galen. In Singer's model, the simultaneously oral and textual discourse is in process. Fixing one specific date to it is impossible. This model works well for dating the Gospel of Mark. The narrative was not authored in a single moment of creative, literary genius. Rather, it was a tradition or set of traditions that were in process. Orally told on previous occasions, they became textualized. The exigencies of its previous tellings and those of its textualized form imprint themselves on the narrative.

Third, like the textualization of Galen's discourses, the textualization of Mark opens it to various types of reception. One of these was communal reading, as the reference to "the reader" in Mark 13:14 implies.[42] But the gospel's reception should not be limited to communal reading. Another mode was the re-oralization of the tradition. Galen often intended his orally derived texts to be reappropriated as memory aids.

This is one way that early Christian writers imagined Mark to have been experienced. For example, Clement states that after Peter had preached the message of the kingdom of heaven (τὸ κήρυγμα τῆς τῶν οὐρανῶν βασιλείας εὐαγγελιζόμενος) his hearers requested that Mark leave them a written reminder (διὰ γραφῆς ὑπόμνημα) of the unwritten teaching of the divine proclamation (τῇ ἀγράφῳ τοῦ θείου κηρύγματος διδασκαλίᾳ).[43] The composition circumstances and the term "written reminder" (διὰ γραφῆς ὑπόμνημα) parallel Galen's texts that had their genesis in an oral event and were subsequently textualized.

41. Singer, general introduction, 34–41.
42. Keith, *Gospel as Manuscript*, 177–80.
43. Clement *apud* Eusebius *Hist. eccl.* 2.14.6–2.15.2; text, Lake, LCL.

Those who heard the spoken word desire to have a written version so that they can reuse it. Clement then claims that Peter approved the text for study (εἰς ἔντευξιν) in the Roman gatherings.[44]

Immediately following this account from Clement in *Ecclesiastical History*, Eusebius states that Mark was sent to Egypt "to proclaim the gospel that he had written" (τὸ Εὐαγγέλιον ὃ δὴ καὶ συνεγράψατο, κηρῦξαι) (Eusebius, *Hist. eccl.* 2.16.1). Eusebius does not imagine Mark to read the gospel that he has textualized, but uses a verb associated with the oral lifeworld: to proclaim (κηρῦξαι). Eusebius never uses this verb with respect to the reception or use of any other written gospel.[45]

This brings us full circle to Mark 1:1. If the narrative is "news" (εὐαγγέλιον) as its peritext indicates, then its native mode of reception was proclamation. This is suggested by some of the early ecclesiastical testimony concerning the gospel's reception, as well as the ancient precedent for a written text having its genesis in oral events and being put to oral and literary reuse. Mark is a discourse with an oral genesis that could be reused orally and textually.

Matthew

Mark's textualization of the oral Jesus tradition was an innovation. The innovation was not to create a gospel book. The author could have labeled their text a book (βίβλος), but instead chose a term that did not connote something literary and bookish. By peritextually indicating that the content of the written

---

44. The phrase "for study" does not point definitively to a certain mode of subsequent reception, as the word ἔντευξις has both oral and literary connotations. That is, it can mean "reading," "speech," "prayer," and "intercession" (LSJ and BDAG, s.v. ἔντευξις).

45. Eusebius uses other verbs with respect to Mark's reception: "is extant" (φέρεται, *Hist. eccl.* 2.15.1); "made publication of" (τὴν ἔκδοσιν πεποιημένων, *Hist. eccl.* 3.24.7); "made public the writing" (γεγραφότος ἐκτέθειται, *Hist. eccl.* 3.39.14); "handed over in writing" (ἐγγράφως ἡμῖν παραδέδωκε, *Hist. eccl.* 5.8.3); "distributed" (μεταδοῦναι, *Hist. eccl.* 6.14.6).

With respect to Matthew's gospel Eusebius uses several different verbs related to its reception: "handed over" (παραδούς, *Hist. eccl.* 3.24.6); "interpreted" (ἡρμήνευσε, *Hist. eccl.* 3.39.16); "published" (ἐξήνεγκεν, *Hist. eccl.* 5.8.2); "found" (ἐπεγνωκόσιν; *Hist. eccl.* 5.10.3); "left behind" (καταλεῖψαι, *Hist. eccl.* 5.10.3); "given out" (ἐκδεδωκότα, *Hist. eccl.* 6.25.3). Eusebius's verbs of reception regarding Luke include: "left behind in books" (καταλέλοιπε βιβλίοις, *Hist. eccl.* 3.4.6); "made publication of" (τὴν ἔκδοσιν πεποιημένων, *Hist. eccl.* 3.24.7); "handed over" (παρέδωκεν, *Hist. eccl.* 3.24.15). Finally, the following verbs are used with respect to John: "left behind" (καταλελοίπασιν, *Hist. eccl.* 3.24.5); "gave out" (ἐξέδωκε, *Hist. eccl.* 5.8.4); "left behind" (ἐξέδωκε, *Hist. eccl.* 6.25.9).

document is something proclaimed, Mark positions itself between oral and written modalities. The text is a bridge between its antecedent oral traditions and the tradition's subsequent textual instantiations.

Matthew's innovation was to present itself as a book. Matthew, in contrast to its predecessor, labeled itself as such from its first word.[46] The narrative presents itself as a different medium than Mark, one that is akin to formative written traditions from Judaism's past.

The argument of this section proceeds in four steps. First, I establish that "book" (βίβλος) refers to Matthew's narrative in its entirety. Second, I argue that Matt 1:1 echoes both Mark's title and Scripture. The narrative hitches its wagon to the emerging written Jesus tradition but also to the great written tradition of Israel's past. Third, I contend that internal features to Matthew indicate that it was intended for reading events that mirrored synagogue practices in Second Temple Judaism. Fourth, I conclude that Matthew's "competitive textualization" was largely successful.[47] Matthew outdid its predecessor with respect to the frequency that it was copied and cited.

Whereas Mark begins with the phrase "Beginning of the good news about Jesus Christ" (ἀρχὴ τοῦ εὐαγγελίου Ἰησοῦ Χριστοῦ), Matthew begins with "Book of the origin of Jesus Christ, son of David, son of Abraham" (βίβλος γενέσεως Ἰησοῦ Χριστοῦ υἱοῦ Δαυὶδ υἱοῦ Ἀβραάμ). From its first word, Matthew designates itself a "book" (βίβλος).

As is the case with Mark, I take the opening sentence of Matthew to be a peritextual title for the entire discourse. This is not the only way that Matthew's opening words have been interpreted. Others argue that the phrase refers only to the genealogy of Matt 1:2–17 or to the narrative's first two chapters.[48] Six reasons suggest that Matt 1:1 refers to the entire narrative.

First, opening peritexts are a common feature of books throughout history.[49] It is rare for any written narrative to present itself in a bare form. If Matt 1:1 refers only to the genealogy or chapters 1 and 2, then it does not possess a

---

46. I hold to Markan priority and consider Mark to have been a tradition in process from about 40 to 70 CE. Matthew and then Luke were written between 70 and 80 CE, after both Mark's textualization and the destruction of the temple in Jerusalem in 70 CE. John followed sometime thereafter, around 90 CE.

47. Competitive textualization is a concept from Keith, *Gospel as Manuscript*, 100–130, which will be discussed at greater length below.

48. On those who take each position, respectively, see Ulrich Luz, *Matthew 1–7*, trans. James E. Crouch, Hermeneia (Minneapolis: Fortress, 2007), 69.

49. Genette, *Paratexts*, 1–3.

peritext that begins the entire narrative. If this were the case, then Matthew would begin more abruptly than Mark.

Second, while "book" (βίβλος) can refer to a shorter document embedded in a more expansive discourse and be translated "document" or some other such, this does not usually happen at the beginning of a text. If "Book of the origin of Jesus Christ, son of David, son of Abraham" refers only to Matt 1:2–17 or to Matt 1–2, we would expect another peritext or textual material to precede it. In those instances where the term "book" (βίβλος) means "document" for Matthew's predecessors and contemporaries, the word does *not* begin the text.[50] This connotation of the word is also less common than the word's primary meaning, "book," in the New Testament and patristic periods.[51]

Third, the word "book" in both Greek (βίβλος) and Hebrew (ספר) frequently begins Jewish texts that are antecedent to and contemporary with Matthew.[52] In these instances, the word refers to the entire text that follows. There are several precedents for the term "book" beginning an entire document; there are no precedents for a narrative beginning with the word "book" and that word referring to only a section of the entire discourse that follows.

Fourth, as Loveday Alexander notes, Greek writers in a variety of fields use their first sentence to indicate the content of the text.[53]

Fifth, Mark contains a peritextual title. Since Matthew follows and utilizes Mark extensively, omitting a title altogether would be a departure from its predecessor. Matthew was inspired by Mark's title, though objected to it and emended it for reasons that will be detailed below.[54]

Sixth, the sentence makes best grammatical sense as a title. Like Mark, Matthew's first words are a verbless, nominative absolute clause. "Book" is anarthrous. Matthew 1:1 resembles Mark 1:1 but differs from Gen 2:4 and

---

50. Luz makes this same point while arguing that Matt 1:1 serves as a title for the narrative (*Matthew 1–7*, 69). He cites LXX Gen 2:4; 5:1; Deut 24:1, 3; 2 Sam 11:14–15; 1 Kgs 20:8–9; 2 Kgs 5:5–7; Jer 39:10–16, 44 as cases in which the term means "writing, document, or record." To Luz's texts we can add 1 En 14:1; Philo's *Abraham* 11.

51. Davies and Allison, *Matthew 1–7*, 151.

52. Davies and Allison (*Matthew 1–7*, 152) list Nah 1:1; Tob 1:1; Bar 1:1; T. Job 1:1; Apocalypse of Abraham; 2 Esd 1:1–3; Sepher Ha-Razim as texts that begin with the term "book." See also J. Andrew Doole, *What Was Mark for Matthew? An Examination of Matthew's Relationship and Attitude to His Primary Source*, WUNT II 344 (Tübingen: Mohr Siebeck, 2013), 182.

53. Alexander, *Preface to Luke's Gospel*, 29.

54. That Mark's title inspired Matthew's is also the position of Luz (*Matthew 1–7*, 69) and Aune ("Genre Theory," 172).

5:1, two texts that it echoes and to which it is often compared. It is helpful to juxtapose all four texts in Greek and literal translation:

ἀρχὴ τοῦ εὐαγγελίου Ἰησοῦ Χριστοῦ [υἱοῦ θεοῦ].

Beginning of the gospel of Jesus Christ [Son of God]. (Mark 1:1)

βίβλος γενέσεως Ἰησοῦ Χριστοῦ υἱοῦ Δαυὶδ υἱοῦ Ἀβραάμ.

Book of the origin of Jesus Christ Son of David, Son of Abraham. (Matt 1:1)

αὕτη ἡ βίβλος γενέσεως οὐρανοῦ καὶ γῆς . . .

This is the book of the origin of heaven and earth . . . (Gen 2:4)

αὕτη ἡ βίβλος γενέσεως ἀνθρώπων . . .

This is the book of the origin of humans . . . (Gen 5:1)

Both LXX Gen 2:4 and 5:1, as well as their Hebrew counterparts, make it clear that the "book of the origin" references the immediate content that follows. They do so with the demonstrative pronoun "this." If Matt 1:1 referred only to the genealogy that followed or to the infancy narrative, this same convention would have been followed.

Matthew departs from Gen 2:4 and 5:1 in this respect. These texts are echoed as all three contain the phrase "Book of the origin" (βίβλος γενέσεως) followed by a genitive object. But Matthew is closer to Mark with respect to its use of an anarthrous nominative absolute. There is neither a pronoun nor an article in Matthew or in Mark as there is in Gen 2:4 and 5:1. Like Mark, Matthew makes Jesus Christ the objective genitive and, if Matthew's text of Mark contained "Son of God," Matthew mimics this convention with "son of David, son of Abraham."[55]

---

55. Many early and important manuscripts contain the phrase "Son of God" though several, including Sinaiticus, do not. Joel Marcus notes that it is more likely that the phrase was inserted into Markan manuscripts than that it was omitted, since this would be a significant deletion or oversight given the weight of the title (*Mark 1–8*, 141). Whether or not "Son of God" was in the version of Mark that Matthew possessed, there is a relationship between Matthew and Mark with respect to sonship language. Either Mark influenced Matthew or Matthew influenced later scribes who inserted sonship language into Mark on the basis of similar language in Matthew's title.

From Gen 2:4 and 5:1, Matthew takes the phrase "book of the origin," establishing a significant link with those Scriptural texts.[56] Following both Mark and Genesis, Matthew employs an objective genitive in its title, indicating who the central subject of the discourse is. Like Mark and unlike Genesis, Jesus Christ is the subject. Finally, and most significantly, Matthew has removed the media designation "gospel" (εὐαγγελίου) from Mark and replaced it with "book" (βίβλος).

That Matthew has replaced "gospel" from Mark suggests that the author rejects the term as a designation for the text that they are writing. Gospel was not a literary genre when Matthew was written. It connoted orally proclaimed news. The author was not writing news; the author was writing a book.

Removing the gospel label was necessary to establish the link with Genesis. This link does more than allude to antecedent texts. It elevates Matthew as a discourse that is of the same caliber as this predecessor. At the beginning of *On the Life of Abraham*, Philo states that the first of the five holy books of the law was titled Genesis on the basis of the phrase "the origin of the world" (τῆς τοῦ κόσμου γενέσεως). Elsewhere, when quoting the first book of Torah, Philo identifies the text as "Genesis" (γένεσις), which it had apparently come to be called by the first century CE (Philo, *Posterity* 127; *Eternity* 19). By using the word "genesis" or "origin" and echoing the grammatical structure of Gen 2:4 and 5:1, Matthew presents itself as a new book of Genesis.[57] Matthew isn't a book about the origins of the world, however. It is a book about the origins of Jesus Christ, the son of David, the son of Abraham.

The primary connotation of the term "book" (βίβλος) for Matthew's contemporaries is something authoritative and Scriptural. This is on full display in the New Testament, Philo, and Josephus. The word (βίβλος) appears ten times in the New Testament. Five explicitly refer to a specific text considered authoritative Scripture. Each is modified by a genitive word or phrase that specifies the contents of the book, whether it be "of Moses" (τῇ βίβλῳ Μωϋσέως) in Mark 12:26, "of the words of Isaiah the prophet" (βίβλῳ λόγων Ἡσαΐου τοῦ προφήτου) in Luke 3:4, "of the Psalms" (βίβλῳ ψαλμῶν) in Luke

---

56. That the allusions to Genesis were unmistakable to Matthew's audience is argued by Davies and Allison, *Matthew 1–7*, 151; Craig A. Evans, "'The Book of the Genesis of Jesus Christ': The Purpose of Matthew in Light of the Incipit," in *Biblical Interpretation in Early Christian Gospels*, ed. Thomas R. Hatina, vol. 2, *The Gospel of Matthew*, LNTS 310 (New York: T&T Clark, 2008), 66.

57. Davies and Allison, Evans, and Doole all argue similarly (Davies and Allison, *Matthew 1–7*, 151; Evans, "'Book of the Genesis,'" 66–67; Doole, *What Was Mark for Matthew?*, 182).

20:42 and Acts 1:20, or "of the prophets" (βίβλῳ τῶν προφητῶν) in Acts 7:42. Like Matt 1:1, "book" lacks the article in four of these five uses. Three times the term "book" is used in the New Testament with reference to the "book of life" (ἡ βίβλος ζωῆς).[58] The final two occasions are Matt 1:1 and the account of the Ephesian magicians burning their books in Acts 19:19. The significance here is that in at least eight of the ten total times the term "book" is used in the New Testament it designates something authoritative, whether it be a discrete Scriptural text or a heavenly book.

The case is similar in Philo and Josephus, who regularly modify the term "book" (βίβλος) with the adjective "holy" (ἱερά). In Philonian texts, the adjective is typically positive in degree and in the attributive position. Such is the case in *Cherubim* 124: "which Moses wrote in the holy books" (οὓς ἐν ἱεραῖς βίβλοις Μωυσῆς ἀνέγραψεν).[59] Other times it is in the attributive position, though superlative in degree, as in *Moses* 2.45: "the most-holy books" (αἱ ἱερώταται βίβλοι).[60] Also noteworthy is that the noun frequently appears in conjunction with various verbs for writing.

The way that Josephus employs the word is similar to Philo. The Jewish historian introduces a quotation of Gen 1 with the following words: "I found these things written in the holy books. They run thusly" (ταῦτα δ᾿ ἐν ταῖς ἱεραῖς βίβλοις εὗρον ἀναγεγραμμένα. ἔχει δὲ οὕτως) (Josephus, *Ant.* 1.26).[61] The dative plural "in the holy books" is Josephus's most common turn of phrase for referring to authoritative written traditions.[62]

Philo and Josephus nearly always modify the word "book" with the adjective "holy" when said book refers to Israel's past. While the New Testament does not append the adjective, the term primarily connotes authoritative writings. Books in this context are Scriptural and meant to be revered. Matthew has high aspirations when it labels itself a book, alludes to two texts from Genesis, and immediately connects Jesus with two prominent figures from Israel's past: David and Abraham. These connections do not cease with Matt 1:1. Jesus is

---

58. Philippians 4:3; Rev 3:5; 20:15.

59. Also Philo, *Worse* 161; *Posterity* 158; *Drunkenness* 208; *Migration* 14; *Heir* 258; *Dreams* 2.127; *Abraham* 156, 177, 258; *Moses* 2.11, 36, 45, 59, 95; *Decalogue* 1, 154; *Special Laws* 2.150; 4.175; *Virtues* 34; *Eternity* 19.

60. Also Philo, *Sobriety* 17; *Virtues* 95.

61. Text, Thackeray, LCL; trans. my own.

62. It is also used in Josephus, *Ant.* 1.82, 139; 2.347; 3.81, 105; 4.326; 9.28, 46; 10.58. The attributive phrase "holy books" in non-dative cases is used in Josephus, *Ant.* 10.63; 16.164; 20.261; *J.W.* 3.352; *Ag. Ap.* 1.1.

recast in the mold of Jewish personages throughout the gospel. Immediately following the title, the connection with David is strengthened by the division of the genealogy into sets of fourteen generations, which is frequently taken as a reference *via gematria* to the famous king. The infancy narrative has Jesus and his family moving in and out of Egypt in a manner akin to Moses. And Jesus teaches in five large blocks, resembling the fivefold division of Torah.[63] In these ways, Matthew resembles and remixes the "holy books" that were authoritative for his contemporaries.[64] It presents itself as sacred writ in a way that its predecessor, Mark, does not.

The final consideration in this section is the kind of reading event for which Matthew's medium as a Scripture-like book might have been made. If the native mode of reception of Mark's "gospel" is proclamation and hearing, then the native mode of reception of a Scripture-like book is reading. One hears news and one reads a book.

There are multiple modes and settings for reading in Greco-Roman antiquity. One kind of reading event seems to be particularly appropriate for Matthew considering the gospel's peritextual self-presentation and its content: synagogue reading. This is not to suggest that Matthew was limited to this mode of reception. The text was read in various ways. But the author of Matthew wrote with synagogue reading practices in mind and attempted to craft a text that was better suited to this kind of reception than was its gospel forebearer, Mark.

In chapter 2, texts that attest to synagogue reading practices were surveyed in service of the argument that small and medium-sized private readings were more common in early Judaism and Christianity than were large, public events.[65] What was not emphasized in that chapter was the liturgical shape of

---

63. Evans, "'Book of the Genesis,'" 67–69.

64. I use the verb "remix" here following Jill Hicks-Keeton, *Arguing with Aseneth: Gentile Access to Israel's "Living God" in Jewish Antiquity* (Oxford: Oxford University Press, 2018), 41–66. Hicks-Keeton argues that the concept of "life" in Joseph and Aseneth is creatively remixed from the creation accounts in Genesis. Not only is the verb "remix" more accurate with respect to Matthew's relationship to antecedent Scriptural texts than others such as "allude" or "echo," but Hicks-Keeton's work on Joseph and Aseneth demonstrates that other authors were remixing Scripture, and particularly Genesis, in Matthew's context.

65. The texts addressed in chapter 2 were 1QS 6:6–8, Philo, *Good Person* 82–83, *Dreams* 2.127, Josephus, *Ag. Ap.* 2.173–75, several New Testament texts, Justin Martyr, 1 *Apol.* 67, and Acts of Peter 20.

synagogue reading.[66] Two observations about this shape inform how Matthew is particularly crafted for reading in these contexts.

First, the reading of Jewish Scripture, and especially Torah, was the principal activity of the synagogue.[67] Scriptural texts were read in synagogue because they had been ascribed authoritative status. These are "holy books" meant to be venerated. The act of communal, liturgical reading in the synagogue reinforces the text's authority. Reading Matthew in a synagogue setting, whether in conjunction with Jewish Scripture or in its place, will have ascribed it a similar authoritative status.[68] Not only is it in competition with Mark, but also with authoritative Jewish Scripture itself.

Second, the normal practice was to exposit the text after a discrete portion was read. Reading the text was not usually an end itself. According to the stipulations in 1QS 6:7b–8 reading is to be followed by an "explanation of the regulation and blessing."[69] Of the Essenes' gatherings, Philo writes that one person reads (ἀναγινώσκει) the text and then another expounds it (ἀναδιδάσκει) (Philo, *Good Person* 82–83). Per *Dreams* 2.127 and *Hypothetica* 7.13, this practice was not peculiar to the Essenes. The former states "reading the holy books" (τὰς ἱερὰς βίβλους ἀναγινώσκοντες) and "explaining the unclear parts" (εἴ τι μὴ τρανὲς εἴη διαπτύσσοντες) was common synagogue practice.[70] The latter suggests that a priest or elder reads the holy laws and serially exegetes each one (ἀναγινώσκει τοὺς ἱεροὺς νόμους αὐτοῖς καὶ καθ' ἕκαστον ἐξηγεῖται).

In these cases, as well as in the synagogue events depicted in *Ag. Ap.* 2.173–75, Luke 4:16–30, and Acts 13:14–41, the reading of a select portion of text is followed by teaching, exposition, or exhortation. There is no indication that the text was read in its entirety or continuously.[71] While they held authority,

---

66. I employ the term "liturgy" of synagogue reading following Keith, *Gospel as Manuscript*, 163–232.

67. Charles Perrot, "The Reading of the Bible in the Ancient Synagogue," in *The Literature of the Jewish People in the Period of the Second Temple and the Talmud*, vol. 1 *Mikra* (Leiden: Brill, 1988), 137; Lee I. Levine, *The Ancient Synagogue: The First Thousand Years*, 2nd ed. (New Haven: Yale University Press, 2005), 150; Anders Runesson, *The Origins of the Synagogue: A Socio-Historical Study*, ConBNT 37 (Stockholm: Almqvist & Wiksell, 2001), 191–92; Keith, *Gospel as Manuscript*, 203–4.

68. Keith, *Gospel as Manuscript*, 211.

69. Florentino García Martínez and Eibert J. C. Tigchelaar, trans., *The Dead Sea Scrolls: Study Edition*, 2 vols. (Grand Rapids: Eerdmans, 1998), 83.

70. Trans. my own.

71. This was also the case in Justin's *1 Apol.* 67 and the Acts of Peter 20. A portion of text is read and then explained.

scriptural texts also served as a springboard for other liturgical actions. If Matthew's author presents their text as a Scriptural book to be read in synagogue, then it is likely that the book was intended to be read not in its entirety in one sitting, but rather in piecemeal fashion. Four reasons suggest that Matthew is suited for piecemeal, liturgical reading events to a degree that Mark was not.

First, Matthew is approximately 40% longer than Mark.[72] Mark also reads much faster than Matthew. Joanna Dewey notes that an ancient performance of Mark will have lasted approximately an hour and a half to two hours, which she states was the "customary duration" for ancient performances of varying sorts.[73] This is the approximate length of modern tellings of Mark, which continue to find success in the performative medium in a way that the other canonical gospels do not. Matthew will have taken at least 40% more time to read than Mark, as it is 40% longer. Ulrich Luz, however, suggests a duration for Matthew that is double Dewey's for Mark: four hours.[74] He proposes that Matthew was not read in one sitting, but that sections, such as chapters 8–9 or 21–23, were read continuously. This aligns with the typical synagogue practice of reading discrete portions of text and then explaining them.

Second, while Matthew is longer than Mark, it abbreviates several of the first written gospel's episodes. This is especially the case with the miracle stories in Matt 8–9.[75] For Mark, the immersive experience of each episode and the narrative in its entirety is important. The gospel shows rather than

---

72. Per word counts in NA28. Mark is 11,138 words long and Matthew 18,363 words long. Luke, in turn, is 43% longer than Mark at 19,494 words.

73. Joanna Dewey, *The Oral Ethos of the Early Church: Speaking, Writing, and the Gospel of Mark*, Biblical Performance Criticism Series 8 (Eugene, OR: Cascade, 2013), 95. Dewey has long championed an oral/aural approach to Mark, arguing that the narrative is crafted to be received in performative events. Along with the above essay, see Joanna Dewey, "Mark as Interwoven Tapestry: Forecasts and Echoes for a Listening Audience," *CBQ* 53 (1991): 221–36; Joanna Dewey, "From Storytelling to Written Text: The Loss of Early Christian Women's Voices," *BTB* 26 (1996): 71–78; Joanna Dewey, "The Gospel of Mark as Oral Hermeneutic," in *Jesus, the Voice, and the Text: Beyond the Oral and the Written Gospels*, ed. Tom Thatcher (Waco, TX: Baylor University Press, 2008), 71–87.

74. Luz, *Matthew 1–7*, 8. However, Pieter Botha, based on his own experimentation, suggests that Matthew will have taken just over two hours to read aloud, compared to an hour and fifteen minutes for Mark ("'I Am Writing This with My Own Hand...': Writing in New Testament Times," *Verbum et Ecclesia* 30 [2009]: 121).

75. See the classic work by Heinz Joachim Held, "Matthew as Interpreter of the Miracle Stories," in *Tradition and Interpretation in Matthew*, ed. Günther Bornkamm, Gerhard Barth, and Heinz Joachim Held (London: SCM, 1963), 165–299.

tells. Matthew is keen to tell.[76] Heinz Joachim Held influentially argued that the reason Matthew abbreviates Markan episodes was doctrinal.[77] Matthew emphasizes the teaching about Christology, discipleship, and faith embedded in episodes. Matthew likes its stories to have a pedagogical point and the point is sharpened by removing extraneous narrative. The effect is that episodes in Matthew are often more poignant than they are in Mark, which suits them for teaching and explanation.

Third, rather than abbreviating Markan material in which Jesus teaches, as happens with Markan narrative material, Matthew extends and supplements Jesus's teaching from Mark. Mark's teaching material, which is not extensive, is regularly expanded in Matthew.[78] In addition, the majority of Matthew's supplemental material to Mark, whether from a source (i.e., Q) or of the author's own creation, is teaching that comes from Jesus's own mouth. Parables and other discourses were well suited for exposition in a synagogue setting.

Fourth, Matthew has a distinct interest in synagogues. As J. Andrew Overman has shown, the evangelist consistently appends a personal pronoun, usually "their" (αὐτῶν), to the word synagogue.[79] Mark and Luke do not. Matthew 10:17, 12:9, and 23:34 all indicate that a synagogue is an established space into which one may enter.[80] This suggests to Overman that formative Judaism, with which Matthew was at odds, "was organizing to the extent that it was developing its own identifiable places of meeting and worship and officials to

---

76. Matthew abbreviates significant portions of the following pericopes: the healing of the paralytic (Mark 2:1–12 // Matt 9:1–8); the Gerasene demoniac (Mark 5:1–20 // Matt 8:28–34); the account of Jairus's daughter and the woman with a flow of blood (Mark 5:21–43 // Matt 9:18–26); the death of John the Baptist (Mark 6:17–29 // Matt 14:3–12); the feeding of the five thousand (Mark 6:30–44 // Matt 14:13–21); the healing of a boy with a spirit (Mark 9:14–29 // Matt 17:14–21); the preparation for Passover (Mark 14:12–16 // Matt 26:17–19).

77. Held, "Matthew as Interpreter."

78. The following teaching discourses in Mark are expanded in Matthew: the teaching about a house divided (Mark 3:23–30 // Matt 12:25–37); the reason Jesus offers for speaking in parables (Mark 4:10–12 // Matt 13:10–15); the teaching on marriage and divorce (Mark 10:1–12 // Matt 19:1–12); the parable of the wicked tenants (Mark 12:1–12 // Matt 21:33–46); the denunciation of the scribes and Pharisees (Mark 12:39–40 // Matt 23:1–36); the prediction of coming persecution (Mark 13:9–13 // Matt 24:9–14); teaching on greatness (Mark 10:42–45 // Matt 20:25–28).

79. J. Andrew Overman, *Matthew's Gospel and Formative Judaism: The Social World of the Matthean Community* (Minneapolis: Fortress, 1990), 59–62. The word "synagogue" is modified by the personal pronoun "their" (αὐτῶν) in Matt 4:23; 9:35; 10:17; 12:9; 13:54.

80. Overman, *Matthew's Gospel*, 61.

go along with these modest structures."[81] Matthew assumes similar meeting places and structures for its audience. If there are "their gathering places," there are, by extension, "our gathering places" in which liturgical activities took place, including reading Jewish scripture and the book of the origins of Jesus Christ.[82]

By crafting a text that was suitable for liturgical reading events accompanied by exposition, Matthew both anticipated and precipitated the development of a Christian reading culture that grew out of its early Jewish counterpart. By the second century CE, one stream of the Jesus movement had become "bookish" with its own texts that supplemented Jewish Scripture. The testimony from Justin Martyr in *1 Apol.* 67 indicates that both the "memoirs of the apostles" and "the prophets" were read in early Christian gatherings as long as time permitted (μέχρις ἐγχωρεῖ). These reading events, per Justin, were followed by verbal instruction and exhortation.

In the second century, there were multiple Christian textual traditions contending for reading time alongside Jewish Scripture. Chris Keith calls this "competitive textualization."[83] A tradition that is textually competitive is aware of "other written traditions that it holds in its direct or peripheral vision, *by which* or *with which* it is vying for (authoritative) status."[84] Keith is clear that competitive textualization does not necessarily imply a polemical relationship with preceding written traditions. An author can create a text that vies for authority and reading time with or without disparaging the texts with which it is in competition.

Whether or not Matthew intended to replace Mark, the gospel's mimicry of Jewish scripture as to its medium positioned it well in the competitive textual environment. The author of Matthew attempted to write a discourse that would suit the kind of reading events that were popular in their social and religious context. They succeeded.[85] The number of early extant manuscripts and citations of Matthew indicate that in the first three centuries it was favored over Mark, which is less frequently cited and of which there are fewer extant

---

81. Overman, *Matthew's Gospel*, 62.
82. Luz, *Matthew 1–7*, 54.
83. Keith, *Gospel as Manuscript*, 100–130.
84. Keith, *Gospel as Manuscript*, 103; italics in original.
85. D. Moody Smith states that Matthew's popularity nearly drove Mark into oblivion (*John among the Gospels*, 2nd ed. [Columbia: University of South Carolina Press, 2001], 31). While the claim is sensationalized, it well highlights Matthew's success that was built on the back of its predecessor.

manuscripts.[86] As Larry W. Hurtado puts it, "There is no reason to think that Mark was regarded with disapproval, but the manuscript evidence suggests that Mark was considerably less frequently and less widely used."[87] This is not by accident. While Matthew's apostolic association surely played a significant role in its early popularity, it is also the case that the Gospel of Matthew made for a different kind of reading event than Mark. This kind of reading event was already well established in Second Temple Judaism and waxed in popularity in the wake of the destruction of the Temple and the emergence of Christianity. Mark's innovation was to put oral Jesus traditions into the written modality. Matthew's innovation was to improve the written tradition for a particular context: synagogue and ecclesial reading.

Luke

Unlike Mark and Matthew, Luke does not possess a title. Its opening peritext is a preface. Like Mark and Matthew, the Third Gospel's peritext indicates something about its medium and mode of reception.[88] Christians and non-Christians could and did read Scriptural and gospel texts individually as early as the second century CE. Luke 1:1–4 indicates that the text was first read by an individual before it was read communally. Parallel prefaces to Luke's from "scientific literature," and particularly prefaces and the accompanying texts written by Galen, indicate that the Third Gospel was written for an individual who was the gospel's first reader.

---

86. Matthew and John both surpass Mark and Luke in the number of times they are cited in the first three centuries and the number of extant manuscripts. See Stephen R. Llewelyn, *A Review of the Greek Inscriptions and Papyri Published in 1982–83*, New Documents Illustrating Early Christianity 7 (Sydney: The Ancient History Documentary Research Centre, Macquarie University, 1994), 257–62; Graham M. Stanton, *Jesus and Gospel* (Cambridge: Cambridge University Press, 2004), 197–204; Larry W. Hurtado, *The Earliest Christian Artifacts: Manuscripts and Christian Origins* (Grand Rapids: Eerdmans, 2006), 20, 30–31.
87. Hurtado, *Earliest Christian Artifacts*, 31.
88. Acts 1:1 also employs a media-designation with respect to the Gospel of Luke: τὸν πρῶτον λόγον ("the first work"). The author is simply referring to the first roll of a multi-volume work. Chariton and Xenophon use λόγος ("work") similarly. After describing the content of a discrete portion of *Callirhoe* and *Anabasis*, respectively, they state that those things "have been described in the previous work" (ἐν τῷ πρόσθεν λόγῳ δεδήλωται). See Chariton, *Callirhoe* 5.1.1; 8.1.1; Xenophon, *Anabasis* 2.1; 3.1; 4.1; 5.1; 7.1. For all these authors, "work" does not describe the discourse as a whole, but a portion of it contained in one particular document.

Luke's preface states that the narrative is written for Theophilus.[89] He is mentioned in Luke 1:3: "It occurred also to me ... to write for you [σοι γράψαι], most excellent Theophilus."[90] The second-person singular personal pronoun, σοι, uniquely addresses the gospel to an individual.[91] While Matthew and Mark offer no explicit statements about whether their addressees are singular or plural, the colophon in John 20:30–31 implies that the Fourth Gospel was written for multiple persons.

There are several interpretive questions relevant to Luke's preface and the identity of its dedicatee. Was Theophilus an actual person? If so, was he an insider to the Jesus Movement? Or an interested outsider? Was he familiar with other narratives about Jesus, whether oral or written? Was he Luke's publisher or patron? And, most relevant to our purposes, how did Theophilus experience the text that was dedicated to him?

The Lukan preface itself offers little by way of answers to these questions. This being the case, interpreters turn to ancient prefaces that resemble Luke's. Historiographical prefaces, and especially those found in Josephus, were once

---

89. The corresponding preface in Acts 1 likewise mentions Theophilus, creating a link with Luke 1:1–4. The strength of the literary link between the two texts is a matter of debate, as is the number of verses in Acts 1 that constitute the secondary preface. With respect to the former debate, both Henry J. Cadbury and Joseph A. Fitzmyer maintain that Luke 1:1–4 governs both narratives (Cadbury, "Commentary on the Preface of Luke," in *The Beginnings of Christianity: Part I, The Acts of the Apostles*, ed. F. J. Foakes-Jackson and Kirsopp Lake [New York: Macmillan, 1922], 489–510, especially 48–90; Joseph A. Fitzmyer, *The Gospel according to Luke I–IX*, AB 28 [New York: Doubleday, 1981], 287–302). In contrast, Alexander contends, though somewhat tentatively, that the preface in Luke 1:1–4 does not have such close ties to Acts. The result is that Acts can be read either as volume two of Luke or as a stand-alone text (Alexander, *Preface to Luke's Gospel*, 146). As to the debate about what constitutes the preface of Acts, opinions vary widely. Some argue that the preface extends all the way to Acts 1:15. On the other end of the spectrum, Joseph A. Fitzmyer has the prologue ending at Acts 1:2 (*The Acts of the Apostles: A New Commentary and Translation*, AB 31 [New York: Doubleday, 1998], 191). In between these two extremes I. Howard Marshall assigns vv. 1–5 to the preface and Luke Timothy Johnson vv. 1–11 (Marshall, *The Acts of the Apostles: An Introduction and Commentary*, Tyndale Commentary [Grand Rapids: Eerdmans, 1980], 55; Johnson, *The Acts of the Apostles*, SP 5 [Collegeville, MN: Liturgical Press, 1992], 23–32).

90. Trans. my own.

91. I have opted to translate σοι as a "dative of advantage" here (Smyth §1481). As we shall see below, prefaces indicate that their texts are written for the benefit of the individual mentioned in the preface.

thought to be the best *comparanda* for Luke 1:1–4.[92] Loveday Alexander has contested the claim that the Lukan preface's closest analogues are historiographical.[93] She convincingly argues that Luke 1:1–4 is related to prefaces in "scientific literature" and "technical prose" (*Fachprosa*).[94] The texts in this genre participate in and are themselves products of a living, teaching tradition. They instruct their readers about topics with which they are already familiar.

Alexander draws several conclusions about the individual for whom Luke is written.[95] She contends that Theophilus must have been a real person, as is the present consensus, but we cannot know for certain whether or not he was Luke's social superior.[96] Theophilus appears to have been Luke's patron and was not being introduced to Christianity for the first time by Luke's narrative.[97] Alexander further argues that Theophilus was not Luke's "publisher" in the modern sense, but that his patronage could have supported both the public reading of the narrative and its preservation in a communal library for personal studying and copying.[98]

Alexander does not address the reading events in which the dedicatee might have experienced the narrative.[99] The scientific prefaces paralleling Luke can throw interpretive light on the question of how Theophilus experienced Luke. Luke is as much a discourse that was intended for private, individual reading

---

92. Josephus, *J.W.* 1.17 and *Ag. Ap.* 1.1–18 are frequently offered as comparative texts (Nolland, *Luke 1:1–9:20*, WBC 35A [Dallas: Word Books, 1989]), 4–5; David E. Aune, *The New Testament in Its Literary Environment*, LEC 8 (Philadelphia: Westminster, 1987), 121.

93. Loveday Alexander, "Luke's Preface in the Context of Greek Preface-Writing," *NovT* 28 (1986): 48–74; Alexander, *Preface to Luke's Gospel*.

94. Alexander, *Preface to Luke's Gospel*, 102–42.

95. Alexander, *Preface to Luke's Gospel*, 187–200.

96. Alexander, *Preface to Luke's Gospel*, 188–90. The present consensus is that he was in fact a real person whom Luke knew and was not a symbolic name for a reader or hearer that "loves God" or is "dear to God" (Fitzmyer, *Luke I–IX*, 299; François Bovon, *Luke 1: A Commentary on the Gospel of Luke 1:1–9:50*, trans. Christine M. Thomas, Hermeneia [Minneapolis: Fortress, 2002], 22–23; Alexander, *Preface to Luke's Gospel*, 188). As Alexander notes, the proper adjective for these literary affects is θεοφιλής (*Preface to Luke's Gospel*, 188). Symbolic, imaginary readers are rare in Greco-Roman prefaces, especially in the scientific treatises (*Preface to Luke's Gospel*, 73–75, 133, 188).

97. Alexander, *Preface to Luke's Gospel*, 190–92. That Theophilus was an "insider" to the Jesus Movement is also the position of Fitzmyer (*Luke I–IX*, 300) and Nolland (*Luke 1:1–9:20*, 5).

98. Alexander, *Preface to Luke's Gospel*, 193–200.

99. Based on Alexander's arguments, F. Gerald Downing has imagined what such a reading might have been like ("Theophilus's First Reading of Luke–Acts" in *Luke's Literary Achievement: Collected Essays*, ed. C. M. Tuckett, JSNTSup 116 [Sheffield: Sheffield Academic, 1995], 91–109).

as one that was intended for communal reading. A communal experience of Luke proceeds from the individualized experience. Theophilus encountered Luke's Gospel in several different ways: he read it privately, in small groups, and in larger early ecclesial gatherings. We ought not to privilege one of these reading events as normative for our interpretation of Luke.

Recent scholarship does just that by emphasizing the "communal" nature of the gospel. The result is that commentators pass over the significance of Luke being written for an individual. They concede that the text is addressed to Theophilus, but then immediately claim that the narrative is ultimately meant for a wider audience. For example, F. Gerald Downing speculates that Theophilus experienced the narrative "aloud" in a one- or two-sitting performance of Luke-Acts at a "relaxed mealtime."[100] Both the all-reading-is-vocalized and the all-reading-is-communal myths are at work here. While the author of Luke might have intended their work for a "larger audience," they also intended the narrative for a specific individual, Theophilus. Given the abundant evidence to private and personal reading in antiquity, we ought to assume that a text addressed to an individual was first read by that individual.

This can be corroborated by prefaces that resemble Luke's, especially from Galen. Galen's texts with prefaces that are dedicated to individuals were intended to be read by the individuals addressed and then by a wider audience. The dedications to individuals in these texts are meaningful and they suggest something about how the author envisioned the text to be received initially.

For example, the dedicatee of Galen's short treatise, *On Exercise with a Small Ball*, is Epigenes. The physician begins his text as follows:

> How great a good for health exercises are, Epigenes [ὦ Ἐπίγενες], and that they must precede food, was adequately stated by men of earlier times—both the best philosophers and doctors. However, the extent to which exercises with the small ball are superior to the others has never been set out in sufficient detail by anyone previously. It is proper, then, for me to state those things I know, so they will be judged by you, a man best practiced of all in the art of these. If stated adequately, they will seem useful to you and will be also employed by others to whom you transmit this work [χρήσιμα δ', εἴπερ ἱκανῶς

---

100. Downing, "Theophilus's First Reading," 92–93. Similarly, Darrell L. Bock, *Luke 1:1–9:50*, BECNT (Grand Rapids: Baker, 1994), 1:64; Joel B. Green, *The Gospel of Luke*, NICNT (Grand Rapids: Eerdmans, 1997), 45.

εἰρῆσθαι δόξειε, καὶ τοῖς ἄλλοις, οἷς ἂν μεταδῷς τοῦ λόγου, γενησόμενα]. (Galen, *On Exercise with a Small Ball* 1 [Johnston, LCL])[101]

In the discourse that follows, Galen regularly addresses his reader in the second person singular, though Epigenes is never mentioned again by name. The "you" becomes generic after the preface, but this does not mean that the dedication to Epigenes is meaningless. As Galen himself states, Epigenes is the first judge of the text, and it only will prove useful to others (τοῖς ἄλλοις) if Epigenes deems the arguments compelling and transmits them to subsequent readers in textual form.

Epigenes is the first reader of *On Exercise with a Small Ball*. The fact that the reader is addressed in second-person singular forms throughout the discourse suggests that Galen intended Epigenes's first reading of the text to be solitary. A "you" is doing the reading, not a "y'all." Only after the initial readings will the text have reached a wider audience. There was a chance that *On Exercise with a Small Ball* would never reach more readers, should Epigenes have deemed it unworthy.[102]

Another Galenic preface, or, better, set of prefaces, indicates that the physician's dedications to individuals were meaningful. Hiero is the dedicatee of Galen's sprawling work *The Method of Medicine*. This preface particularly resembles Luke's, and for this reason I reproduce it in its entirety in both Greek and English translation:

Ἐπειδὴ καὶ σύ με πολλάκις, ὦ Ἱέρων φίλτατε, καὶ ἄλλοι τινὲς νῦν ἑταῖροι παρακαλοῦσι θεραπευτικὴν μέθοδον αὐτοῖς γράψαι, ἐγὼ δὲ μάλιστα μὲν καὶ ὑμῖν χαρίζεσθαι βουλόμενος, οὐχ ἥκιστα δὲ καὶ τοὺς μεθ' ἡμᾶς ἀνθρώπους ὠφελῆσαι καθ' ὅσον οἷός τέ εἰμι προαιρούμενος, ὅμως ὤκνουν τε καὶ ἀνεβαλλόμην ἑκάστοτε διὰ πολλὰς αἰτίας, ἄμεινον εἶναί μοι δοκεῖ καὶ νῦν αὐτὰς διελθεῖν, πρὶν ἄπξασθαι τῆς πραγματείας, ἔχουσι γάρ τι χρήσιμον εἰς τὰ μέλλοντα ῥηθήσεσθαι.

Since you, my dearest Hiero, [have called upon me] many times, and now also certain other colleagues are calling upon me to write a method of medicine for them, and since I especially wish to oblige you [all], and no less also made a choice to help those who will come after us, as far as I am able, but have,

---

101. See also Kühn, *Claudii Galeni opera omnia*, 5:899.
102. Galen was surely confident that the text would be transmitted to others, given how often his texts were plagiarized, as he notes extensively in *On My Own Books*.

however, been hesitating and delaying each time for many reasons, it seems to me better to go over these reasons now, before I begin the treatise, as they do have some relevance about what is going to be said. (Galen, *Method of Medicine* 1K [Johnston and Horsley, LCL])[103]

The parallels with Luke 1:1–4 are conspicuous: both texts begin with a form of ἐπειδή, address their dedicatee with a superlative, employ the same infinitival form of γράφω preceded by a dative pronoun, and provide a justification for being written.[104]

The text has multiple readers, but Hiero is first among them. Galen writes that he wishes to oblige "you all" (ὑμῖν). It is also significant that Hiero and others have requested, on multiple occasions, the sort of systematic text that Galen provides in *Method of Medicine*. Galen wrote this first preface in the early 170s, but the completion of the fourteen-book project was delayed some twenty years.[105] The work is divided into two parts: books 1–6 and books 7–14. Galen reflects on the work's delay in another preface that is written at the beginning of book 7. This preface is not written to Hiero, who has since passed away, but to Eugenianus, and begins part 2 of *Method of Medicine*:

> My dearest Eugenianus [ὦ Εὐγενιανὲ φίλτατε], a long time ago I began to write the *Method of Medicine* as a favor for Hiero [πάλαι μὲν ὑπηρξάμην γράφειν Ἱέρωνι χαριζόμενος]. Then suddenly he was forced to spend a long period abroad. Soon after, he was reported to have died, whereupon I abandoned the writing [ἐγκατέλιπον κἀγὼ τὴν γραφήν]. For you know that I wrote neither this nor any other treatise to advance my popular reputation. [I write] either for the gratification of friends or so that I might exercise myself as the most useful practice in the present matter and as a laying by of notes against the forgetfulness of old age (as Plato said). (Galen, *Method of Medicine* 456K (Johnston and Horsley, LCL)

---

103. See also Kühn, *Claudii Galeni opera omnia*, 10:1.

104. The parallels do not imply influence in one direction or another. Rather, both contain topics and trope that were standard in the scientific prefaces. Alexander (*Preface to Luke's Gospel*, 69) summarizes these as sevenfold: (1) the author's decision to write; (2) subject of the work; (3) second-person address to a dedicatee; (4) nature of the subject; (5) others who have written on the subject; (6) author's own credentials; (7) comments about methodology.

105. Books 1–6 were written in the 170s and books 7–14 were written in the 190s (Johnston and Horsley, introduction to *Method of Medicine*, LCL, lxx–i).

Galen informs Eugenianus that *Method of Medicine* was written as a favor for Hiero and that with Hiero no longer living, Galen found little reason to complete the project. He was motivated to write his tome for a select, individual reader, and his inspiration died with Hiero. This is likely an affectation on Galen's part, but it nonetheless suggests that the specific person mentioned in the preface was relevant to the text's production and reception.[106] Galen suggests the same at the beginning of *The Order of My Own Books*. Many texts were created for friends and "are geared purely towards their particular level" (Galen, *Order of My Own Books* 49K).[107]

Galen concludes the preface to book 7 of *Method of Medicine* by noting that he only continued writing the encyclopedic treatise many years later because his new dedicatee, Eugenianus, and many others among Galen's pupils wished to have their teacher's work in writing. While Galen expects that his fourteen-roll text will reach the hands, eyes, and ears of others besides those who requested it, he also makes it clear that he has them in mind as he composes the text. They are his first readers among many.[108]

This is amplified in the recently discovered treatise *Avoiding Distress*, more commonly referred to by its Latin title, *De indolentia*.[109] The text is a

---

106. P. N. Singer concedes that such dedications were for Galen "literary tropes," but this does not mean that the reality behind the claim is not historical ("New Light and Old Texts: Galen on His Own Books," in *Galen's Treatise Περὶ Ἀλυπίας (De Indolentia) in Context*, ed. Caroline Petit [Leiden: Brill, 2019], 106).

107. Singer, *Galen*, 23. In addition to the Greek text from Kühn, *Claudii Galeni opera omnia*, vol. 19, there is Helmreich, Marquardt, and Müller, *Claudii Galeni pergameni scripta minora*, vol. 3.

108. Singer argues similarly, stating that the "historical reality" behind the claims that certain texts were written for Galen's friends need not be denied, even if the works are also intended for wider circulation ("New Light and Old Texts," 106–7). Singer cites *Method of Medicine* and the dedications to Hiero and Eugenianus therein as examples of discourses that are simultaneously written for individuals and with intention for wider circulation.

109. The discourse was previously known by its title only, but was discovered in 2005 by then PhD student Antoine Pietrobelli in a monastery in Thessaloniki (Vivian Nutton, introduction to "Avoiding Distress" in P. N. Singer, Daniel Davies, and Vivian Nutton, eds., *Galen: Psychological Writings* (Cambridge: Cambridge University Press, 2014), 72. The *editio princeps* was published in 2007 by Pietrobelli's supervisor, Véronique Boudon-Millot ("Un traité perdu de Galien miraculeusement retrouvé, Le *Sur l'inutilité de se chagriner*: texte grec et traduction française," in *La science médicale antique: Nouveaux regards. Études réunites en l'honneur de Jacques Jouanna*, by Véronique Boudon-Millot, Alessia Guardasole, and Caroline Magdelaine [Paris: Beauchesne, 2007], 72–123). A revised critical edition of the text with commentary was published in 2010 (Véronique Boudon-Millot, Jacques Jouanna, and Antoine Pietrobelli,

private letter written to an unnamed friend with whom Galen has been closely acquainted for most of his life.[110] This friend asked Galen to explain how he avoided distress after losing much personal property, especially irreplaceable texts, in the great fire of the warehouses along the Sacred Way (Galen, *Avoiding Distress* 2).[111] Throughout *Avoiding Distress*, and especially in its first half, Galen refers to personal matters with which his addressee is familiar. He directly interacts with statements in his friend's letter using second-person singular forms.[112] This indicates that this friend was Galen's first and primary reader. At the end of the letter-turned-treatise, however, Galen makes a remark while once again directly addressing his friend: "In writing for others on avoiding distress I have given you some advice that is superfluous to you" (τὰ δ᾽ ἄλλα γεγραφὼς εἰς ἀλυπησίαν συνεβούλευσα περιττά σοι λέγειν) (Galen, *Avoiding Distress* 79b).[113]

Galien, *Œuvres, Tome IV: Ne pas se Chagriner* [Paris: Les Belles Lettres, 2010]). The italicized English title I use, *Avoiding Distress*, is from Nutton ("Avoiding Distress").

110. Nutton, introduction, 48–49. Galen notes in *Avoiding Distress* that this friend was brought up and educated alongside him.

111. When referring to this text, I follow the numbered sections in the 2010 critical edition by Boudon-Millot, Jouanna, and Pietrobelli, which is often abbreviated BJP. Citations of the Greek text are from this edition.

112. In *Avoiding Distress* 11 Galen notes that his friend was "correct to write" (γράψαι ἀληθῶς) that Galen was not overly distressed about his losses in the fire. He continues in §12b to list additional losses that had "escaped [his friend's] notice" (λέληθέ σε). As he enumerates further casualties of the fire in *Avoiding Distress* 16, Galen introduces them with phrases like "you will be particularly distressed to learn" (λυπήσει δέ σε). And as he begins to describe how he avoided distress despite such losses in *Avoiding Distress* 39, Galen tells his friend that one of the two antidotes should be familiar to him because "you often heard me telling stories such as the one of which I shall now begin to remind you" (τὴν μὲν ἑτέραν ὑπὲρ ἧς ἀναμνησθῆναί σε χρὴ πολλάκις ἀκηκοότα διερχομένου <ἐμοῦ> τοιούτους λόγους ὧν καὶ νῦν ἄρξομαι τῆς ἀναμνήσεως). In *Avoiding Distress* 51, Galen mentions a significant aspect of his relationship with the addressee: they were "brought up and educated together" (ὡς ἂν ἐξ ἀρχῆς συναναστραφεὶς καὶ συμπαιδευθεὶς ἡμῖν). Finally, in *Avoiding Distress* 54–55, Galen writes that he and his individual reader share a similar view of the emperor Commodus. Unless otherwise noted, translations are from Nutton, "Avoiding Distress."

113. Following Nutton, whose translation is reproduced here, I take τὰ ἄλλα to refer to other persons and not to other writings, as does the French translation in BJP and the English in Clare K. Rothschild and Trevor W. Thompson, eds., *Galen's De Indolentia: Essays on a Newly Discovered Letter*, Studien und Texte zu Antike und Christentum 88 (Tübingen: Mohr Siebeck, 2014), 35.

The line between the private and communal nature of the discourse becomes blurred. The text is written for an individual friend, but Galen also suggests that the discourse is written for others. *Avoiding Distress* was meant to be read by this individual and by a wider audience.[114] It is personal and public. As Clare K. Rothschild and Trevor W. Thompson put it, "Galen's letters were probably intentionally both public and private—written originally with a single individual in mind to address a question posed by that person, but eventually intended for a much wider readership."[115] Because of the blurred private-public lines, Rothschild and Thompson classify *Avoiding Distress* as a "letter-treatise."[116]

It is not only in Galen's letters that the division between private and public is indistinct. This was also the case with *Method of Medicine* and *On Exercise with a Small Ball*. These discourses have an air of formality about them that is curtailed in *Avoiding Distress*. The former are explicitly addressed to individuals, which suggests that these readers were of utmost importance to the writing of the discourse. But Galen's personal references fall out after the preface in these texts. This is not so with *Avoiding Distress*, throughout which Galen addresses his reader in the second person singular and makes personal comments about him.

There is a spectrum of formality when it comes to discourses that began life written for individuals but subsequently reached a wider audience. *Method of Medicine* and *On Exercise with a Small Ball* are personal-turned-public texts that are formal. *Avoiding Distress* is personal and turning public but bears the marks of its personal address to a greater extent than the former two treatises. Some Galenic texts would not fall on this spectrum at all because from their outset they were intended for a broad audience, indeed "for all" (πᾶσιν) and "for publication" (πρὸς ἔκδοσιν).[117]

---

114. Rothschild and Thompson note that a similar dynamic is at work in *Affections and Errors* wherein Galen is self-conscious that that tractate might fall into the hands of others (Rothschild and Thompson, *Galen's De Indolentia*, 13). Therein Galen likewise addresses his reader in the second-person singular.

115. Rothschild and Thompson, *Galen's De Indolentia*, 13.

116. Rothschild and Thompson, *Galen's De Indolentia*, 13.

117. Galen states that this is the case with *Matters of Health* in *On the Order of My Own Books* 2. I am dependent on Singer ("New Light and Old Texts," 126) for this reference. Singer also calls attention to *My Own Doctrines* 14, wherein Galen suggests two of his works on ethical philosophy are written for a wider audience.

On this spectrum, Luke is closer to Galen's *Method of Medicine* and *On Exercise with a Small Ball* than it is *Avoiding Distress*. The narrative is addressed to an individual, Theophilus, and personal remarks about that individual are made in the preface. Theophilus is Luke's first reader. The narrative is a gospel for *a* Christian initially, even if for *all* Christians subsequently.[118] That the narrative is written first for an individual has several implications for Luke generally and for the reading events in which Theophilus might have experienced the discourse.

First, Luke intended Theophilus to read the gospel himself. Given the surfeit of evidence to solitary reading, our default assumption ought to be that texts addressed to individuals were read by individuals. This is not to argue that the same text was not also read by other people or groups. Nor is it to suggest that the initial reader did not also participate in or stage communal events. Texts can be simultaneously intended for specific individuals and for a wider readership. That wider readership can be other people reading the text to themselves or it can be gathered groups hearing a reading of the text. An author might send the text to the addressed individual and to other individuals and groups.[119] We need not assume that an author distributed an addressed text *only* to the addressed individual. Texts could be distributed more widely by both their first readers and their authors. Circulation methods in antiquity were multiple and a given discourse could be distributed several ways simultaneously.

Second, if the author of Luke had a relationship with Theophilus that was like Galen's relationships with his dedicatees, then Theophilus must have been an "insider" to the Jesus movement and already had significant experiences with its traditions and practices. He was well known to Luke, as dedication copies were only ever presented to friends.[120] This makes sense considering Luke 1:4, wherein the author states that they write so that Theophilus might know the certainty concerning "the words with which [he] has been instructed" (περὶ ὧν κατηχήθης λόγων). When Galen writes for an individual, that person has some commitment to Galen's teaching. Galen knows the capacities and experiences

---

118. Should the pun not be clear: Richard Bauckham et al. have argued that the Gospels were not written for specific communities but for wider reception in Bauckham, ed., *The Gospels for All Christians: Rethinking the Gospel Audiences* (Grand Rapids: Eerdmans, 1998).

119. Galen, *Avoiding Distress* 8–9 is especially relevant in this respect, as Galen notes therein that multiple copies of works were made and were to be sent to varying destinations.

120. Raymond Starr writes, "We do not hear of a single author who sent a gift copy to a complete stranger" ("The Circulation of Literary Texts in the Roman World," *ClQ* 37 [1987]: 214).

specific to the friends and pupils for whom he writes. If this is also true of Luke's writing, then unique Lukan material and Lukan redactions might not only be a result of the evangelist's motivations, but might also result from the experiences, knowledge, and concerns of the individual for whom he writes.

Third, that Luke writes for the benefit of an individual reader is another way that the gospel's preface differs from Josephus's historiographical prefaces to which it is commonly compared.[121] Luke writes for an individual (σοι γράψαι) in order that they might know (ἐπιγνῷς) certain things. Josephus, at the beginning of *Jewish War*, *Jewish Antiquities*, and *Against Apion*, writes that these texts are intended for a wide readership. Because fraudulent accounts of the Jewish war were circulating, Josephus determined to translate his account of the war into Greek "for those living under the Roman government" (τοῖς κατὰ τὴν Ῥωμαίων ἡγεμονίαν) (Josephus, *J.W.* 1.3).[122] Josephus composes what he determines to be a bipartisan account "for the lovers of truth, not those who please themselves" (τοῖς γε τὴν ἀλήθειαν ἀγαπῶσιν ἀλλὰ μὴ πρὸς ἡδονὴν ἀνέγραψα) (Josephus, *J.W.* 1.30).[123] Josephus claims that the *Jewish Antiquities* were likewise written for a wide audience, namely "all the Greeks" (ἅπασι [...] τοῖς ἕλλησιν) who might find the discourse worthy of examining (Josephus, *Ant.* 1.5).[124] In the preface to *Against Apion*, Josephus implies that the *Jewish Antiquities* had indeed reached a wide audience. It established the ancient pedigree of the Jewish people to those who perused the text (τοῖς ἐντευξομένοις αὐτῇ). Some, however, were not convinced. They still considered the Jews to be of late stock because they found no mention of them among the Greek historiographers. Josephus thus writes *Against Apion* "to convict our detractors of malignity and deliberate falsehood, to correct the ignorance of others, and to instruct all who desire to know the truth concerning the antiquity of our race" (Josephus, *Ag. Ap.* pref. [Thackeray, LCL]). The difference between Josephus and Luke is subtle though significant. For Josephus, the wider audience is in

---

121. Contrary to the opinion of Christopher N. Mount, who writes, "The dialogue between author and reader in the preface to Lk-Acts suggests a social and literary context very similar to the one presupposed by the writings of Josephus" (*Pauline Christianity: Luke-Acts and the Legacy of Paul* [Leiden: Brill, 2002], 74).

122. Text, Thackeray, LCL; trans. my own.

123. Text, Thackeray, LCL; trans. my own.

124. Text, Thackeray, LCL; trans. my own. Josephus mentions Epaphroditus by name in *Ant.* 1.8–9 and suggests that he was a catalyst for the writing. However, Epaphroditus is but one of the many who desired to know Jewish history and exhorted Josephus to complete his ambitious project.

mind first, and an individual, when addressed, happens to be a part of that wider audience. For Luke, however, the individual is the primary addressee, and the wider circulation follows upon the individual experiencing the text.

Fourth, we should not pass over the reference to Theophilus as Luke's first reader. While Luke and his dedicatee likely transmitted the narrative to others in multiple ways, Luke also intended Theophilus first to experience the discourse himself. The prefaces that parallel Luke's imply that Theophilus read Luke's gospel before it was transmitted to others.

Fifth, and finally, Luke 21:20 removes the reference to the "desolating sacrilege" (τὸ βδέλυγμα τῆς ἐρημώσεως) from Mark 13:14 and Matt 24:15. Matthew 24:15 retains the enigmatic phrase from Mark and offers further clues as to what is meant by it, noting that Daniel the prophet spoke of the desolating sacrilege and that it will be standing in the holy place. Following the reference, both Mark and Matthew urge "the reader" to understand (ὁ ἀναγινώσκων νοείτω). Luke retains Jesus's temporal phrase "when you see" (ὅταν δὲ ἴδητε) but alters the object of sight. For Luke's Jesus, it is the imminent siege of Jerusalem that portends Judean flight to the mountains, not the recondite "desolating sacrilege."[125] With the "desolating sacrilege" Luke also removes the Markan and Matthean reference to "the reader." This is because Luke 21:20 is less cryptic than its predecessors. But it is also because addressing a generic "reader" makes little sense for Luke, who has a particular reader in mind, namely Theophilus. Luke emends the references to the "desolating sacrilege" and the "reader" not only to be more lucid than Mark and Matthew but also because the narrative is addressed first to an individual.

John

The Synoptic Gospels are all paratextually self-conscious about their medium in their opening lines. Matthew's first word, "book" (βίβλος) is a media-designation, as is Mark's third word, "gospel" (εὐαγγέλιον). The first four verses of Luke suggest what kind of text it is and that it was first read by

---

125. Commentators frequently mention that Luke has altered the "desolating sacrilege" only to leave the vestige in the mention of Jerusalem's "desolation" (ἡ ἐρήμωσις), usually noting that Luke is influenced by and making direct reference to the events of 70 CE (Joseph A. Fitzmyer, *The Gospel according to Luke X–XXIV*, AB 28A [New York: Doubleday, 1981], 1343; Luke Timothy Johnson, *The Gospel of Luke*, SP [Collegeville, MN: Liturgical Press, 1991], 323–26).

an individual. The Gospel of John is not textually self-conscious in its opening peritext, though it does have one.[126]

The Fourth Gospel's prologue (John 1:1–18) serves as a vestibule for entering the narrative world of the gospel. It also provides an interpretive frame for the discourse that follows, encouraging its audience to understand Jesus's identity from a certain vantage point. These first eighteen verses are part of the gospel, but they exist at the edge of the narrative and, like other peritexts, facilitate the audience's entrance into it.

John is paratextually self-conscious at its end. If introductory peritexts mediate a reader's entrance into the discourse, then closing peritexts mediate their exit from it. The Gospel of John has two such textually self-conscious concluding paratexts: the colophons at John 20:30–31 and John 21:24–25.[127] The Fourth Gospel is nondescript in its self-designation with the term βιβλίον, which ought to be translated as "document," rather than "book." The term appears in both colophons. The first, John 20:30–31, unequivocally labels the Fourth Gospel as this sort of text: "Now Jesus did many other signs before his disciples which are not written *in this document* [ἐν τῷ βιβλίῳ τούτῳ]." The second colophon, John 21:24–25, does not explicitly append the word to the narrative. In John 21:25, the author or editor writes of hypothetical written documents that the world could not contain if all of Jesus's deeds were textualized: "But there are many other things which Jesus did, and if each one were written I suppose the world itself would not be able to contain *the written documents* [τὰ γραφόμενα βιβλία]." The author or editor considers the Fourth Gospel to be one such written document.[128]

---

126. Though Christina Hoegen-Rohls makes a compelling argument that John 1:1's "in the beginning" is a transformation of Mark 1:1's "the beginning of the gospel" ("The Beginnings of Mark and John: What Exactly Should Be Compared? Some Hermeneutical Questions and Observations," in *John's Transformation of Mark*, ed. Eve-Marie Becker, Helen K. Bond, and Catrin Williams [London: Bloomsbury, 2021], 102–5).

127. The colophons and their role in the Fourth Gospel, especially with respect to John's posture toward the Synoptics, is addressed by Hans Windisch, *Johannes und die Synoptiker: Wollte der vierte Evangelist die älteren Evangelien ergänzen oder ersetzen?*, UNT 12 (Leipzig: Hinrich, 1926), 121–24; Smith, *John among the Gospels*, 28–29; Keith, *Gospel as Manuscript*, 131–54.

128. Whether or not John 21, and thus the second colophon, is "original" to the gospel remains an open question. That John 21 was not part of the "first edition" of the gospel was the position of Raymond E. Brown (*An Introduction to the Gospel of John*, ed. Francis J. Moloney, ABRL [New York: Doubleday, 2003], 199) and Martin Hengel (*The Johannine Question* [London: SCM, 1989], 84). More recently, Armin D. Baum makes a thorough argument that John 21:1–23 is a secondary appendix to the Fourth Gospel and vv. 24–25 are thus a later editorial

This word had a wider semantic range in the first century than did the closely related term, βίβλος ("book"), with which Matthew describes itself. In the New Testament, Philo, and Josephus βίβλος indicated authoritative, Scriptural texts. Occasionally βιβλίον carries a similar connotation.[129] More commonly, the term is generic, designating a "document" that may or may not be literature. This pattern holds not only for the New Testament, Philo, and Josephus but also for first-century texts more generally.

In the New Testament, βιβλίον refers to a text that would become Scripture in two passages, to a "certificate" in two, to a scroll or document in eight places, in the phrase "the book of life" on three occasions in Revelation, and is used as a media self-designation at the end of the Gospel of John and Revelation.[130] In Josephus, the word typically refers to written literary discourses, either Josephus's own or those authored by others, though on occasion it designates

---

epilogue ("The Original Epilogue [John 20:30–31], the Secondary Appendix [21:1–23], and the Editorial Epilogues [21:24–25] of John's Gospel," in *Earliest Christian History*, ed. Michael F. Bird and Jason Maston, WUNT 320 [Tübingen: Mohr Siebeck, 2012], 227–70). Several others have argued to the contrary, namely that John 21 and thus also the second colophon were not a later addition to John (Andreas J. Köstenberger, *John*, BECNT [Grand Rapids: Baker, 2004], 583–86; Hartwig Thyen, *Das Johannesevangelium*, HNT 6 [Tübingen: Mohr Siebeck, 2005], 794–95; Richard Bauckham, *Jesus and the Eyewitnesses: The Gospels as Eyewitness Testimony* [Grand Rapids: Eerdmans, 2013], 369–81; Keith, *Gospels as Manuscript*, 132–34). I am inclined to view John 21 as secondary to the gospel, since a single epilogue is a more common way to conclude ancient texts than are multiple epilogues. If the second colophon is from a later editor, that editor was still writing in near chronological proximity to the evangelist and is thus the first evidence to the reception of John as a βιβλίον ("document"). The second editor confirms the evangelist's media-designation in John 20:30. If the second colophon is from the evangelist, then the author twice over implies that the narrative is a βιβλίον ("document").

129. In the New Testament, the term is used for a text of Scripture in Luke 4:17, 20; Gal 3:10. Josephus uses the term with respect to Jeremiah's prophecy (*Ant.* 10.94), Daniel's prophecy (*Ant.* 10.210, 267), Isaiah's prophecies (*Ant.* 11.5), Solomon's odes and songs (*Ant.* 8.44), as well as Judaism's ancestral texts generally with plural forms of the word (*Ant.* 4.304; 8.159; 10.218; *Life* 418; *Ag. Ap.* 1.40).

130. The New Testament texts that use the term for something scriptural are Luke 4:17, 20; Gal 3:10. The term is used in the phrase "certificate of divorce" (βιβλίον ἀποστασίου) in Mark 10:4 and the parallel passage in Matt 19:7. The word carries the connotation of scroll or document in 2 Tim 4:13; Heb 9:19; 10:7; Rev 1:11; 5:1–9; 6:14; 10:8; 20:12. It is used in the phrase "the book of life" (τὸ βιβλίον τῆς ζωῆς) in Rev 13:8; 17:8; 21:27. The texts that self-designate as a βιβλίον are John 20:30; 21:25; Rev 22:18–19.

nonliterary texts.[131] Philo rarely uses the word and he does not appear to have one primary connotation for it.[132]

In other texts, the term has a similar range of meanings. For example, Plutarch refers to specific titled works with it.[133] But more than one titled work can also be collected in a single document (βιβλίον). This is the case in his preface to the Lives of Demetrius and Antony: "This document contains the Lives of Demetrius the City-besieger and Antony the Imperator" (Περιέξει δὴ τοῦτο τὸ βιβλίον τὸν Δημητρίου τοῦ Πολιορκητοῦ βίον καὶ Ἀντωνίου τοῦ αὐτοκράτορος).[134] The Lives are the kind of text; the document is their container. Plutarch uses βιβλίον to refer to brief documents of various sorts (Plutarch, *Cat. Min.* 28.1 [772]; *Lys.* 19.6–7 [444]). This range of the word is likewise reflected in authors roughly contemporaneous with Plutarch and John.[135]

The word with which the Gospel of John designates itself, βιβλίον, does not specify one kind of discourse or another, though it does have an expressly written connotation. It is an umbrella term that is employed with respect to a variety of written media and genres. A βιβλίον is a "document," and the document can be of varying sorts.

The Fourth Gospel's peritextual media designation indicates that the discourse is a written text, but beyond that, the label does not provide explicit information about what kind of written text it is or the reading event for which it might have made. In this way, it differs from the titular designations "orally

---

131. Josephus labels his own texts with the term in *Ag. Ap.* 1.320; 2.1, 296; *Ant.* 1.15; 20.267; *J.W.* 1.30; *Life* 361. He refers to literary discourses written by others with the word in *Ag. Ap.* 1.164, 176, 182; 2.183; *Ant.* 1.159. With respect to nonliterary texts, the word describes a letter in *Ag. Ap.* 1.101 and *Ant.* 16.256, and an order from Cyrus in *Ant.* 11.99.

132. In *Embassy* 1.19, Philo states that Moses calls the "word of God" (τὸν τοῦ θεοῦ λόγον) a "book" (βιβλίον). In *Planting* 1 and *Sacrifices* 51 the word refers to his own treatises. In *Dreams* 2.175 the word appears in a quotation of Deut 30:10, which self-designates as "the book of the law." And in *Spec. Laws* 4.163 it refers to a blank document that will be filled up with a discourse.

133. Plutarch, *Adv. Col.* 1 (1107d); 30 (1124e); *Suav. viv.* 1 (1086c); *Inim. util.* 1 (86c); *Luc.* 42.4 (519). Plutarch also designates a collection that contains two different discourses with the word βιβλίον (*Demetr.* 1.7 [889]).

134. Plutarch, *Demetr.* 1.7 (889); text and slightly modified translation from Perrin LCL. Similarly, in *Pericles* 2.4, Plutarch notes that the "tenth book" (τοῦτο τὸ βιβλίον) contains two different *Lives*. This is also the case with the preface to the "Lives of Alexander and Caesar."

135. The term designates literary, bookish discourses in Strabo, *Geography* 17.5 (C790); Epictetus, *Discourse* 1.4. It designates something nonliterary in *Epistle of Barnabas* 12, Appian, *Bell. civ.* 2.116; Apollonius of Tyana, *Testimonia* 258.

proclaimed news" (εὐαγγέλιον) and "book" (βίβλος) in Mark and Matthew, respectively. These provide information about the discourses that followed and the reading events for which they were made. To assess what kind of "document" (βιβλίον) John might be, we must look to texts that resemble the gospel's colophons, as we did with Luke's preface. Josephus's *Ag. Ap.* 2.296 and Plutarch's *Alex.* 1.1–3 are particularly illuminating *comparanda*. Each labels the text to which it is attached a βιβλίον ("document") and modifies the word with the nearer demonstrative "this" (τοῦτο), as does John 20:30.

Josephus's text, like John's colophons, concludes the document.

σοὶ δέ, Ἐπαφρόδιτε, μάλιστα τὴν ἀλήθειαν ἀγαπῶντι καὶ διὰ σὲ τοῖς ὁμοίως βουλησομένοις περὶ τοῦ γένους ἡμῶν εἰδέναι τοῦτό τε καὶ τὸ πρὸ αὐτοῦ γεγράφθω βιβλίον. (Josephus, *Ag. Ap.* 2.296)[136]

Let both this and the preceding document be written for you, Epaphroditus, lover of truth *par excellence*, and likewise, through you, for those who wish to know about our people.

There are two significant similarities shared between *Ag. Ap.* 2.296 and the Johannine colophons. First, the same word concludes both. Nothing follows the words quoted above in *Against Apion*. The last word of the discourse is a media designation, βιβλίον, the same word that concludes John. Second, "this document" (τοῦτο ... βιβλίον) and "the former document" (τὸ πρὸ [βιβλίον]) that Josephus references together make up the discourse as a whole. They are each one part of something more comprehensive. The individual "documents" are not *Against Apion*; *Against Apion* is the documents together. It exists only by being a combination of two parts. Each contributes to a discourse larger than itself.

This is the freight of the word we should bring to the Fourth Gospel's colophons. Not only is it in line with Josephus's comparable text, but it fits the wider use of the word in John's media context. "This document" in John 20:30 contains "these things" mentioned in v. 31. The author very well could have written, "But this document [τοῦτο τὸ βιβλίον] has been written so that you all might believe that Jesus is the Christ the Son of God." But they did not. The emphasis falls on the signs that are written in the document. The document

---

136. Text, Thackeray LCL; trans. my own.

contains the signs, and they are but some of the many that Jesus performed. John contributes to a tradition that is already unfolding.

This perspective aligns well with Plutarch's similar use of the term βιβλίον, which grammatically resembles John 20:30 to an even greater extent than *Ag. Ap.* 2.296 does. John and Plutarch both use the dative τῷ βιβλίῳ ("document") modified by the nearer demonstrative τούτῳ ("this").[137] In John 20:30 and *Alex.* 1.1, the phrase serves to particularize what is or is not contained within the respective document. For Plutarch, it is the Lives of Alexander and Caesar; for John, it is the "other signs" (ἄλλα σημεῖα) that are not written in the Fourth Gospel.

Plutarch indicates that two different discourses can be contained in one document (βιβλίον). The preface in *Alex.* 1.1–3 introduces both the Life of Alexander and the Life of Caesar. There is not a secondary preface for the latter. This is the opposite phenomenon of Josephus's *Ag. Ap.* 2.296. There, multiple documents make up one discourse, namely *Against Apion*. Here, multiple discourses, namely the Life of Alexander and the Life of Caesar, are contained in one document. In both cases, the document is not identical to the discourse.

Plutarch asks for his readers' forgiveness for not writing about all the famous actions of these well-known men and for being less than exhaustive with respect to the actions that he does write about. He knows readers will notice the omitted events. Plutarch justifies his condensed treatment, stating, "We are not writing Histories, but Lives" (οὔτε γὰρ ἱστορίας γράφομεν, ἀλλὰ βίους) (Plutarch, *Alex.* 1.2 [Perrin, LCL]). The medium, or in this case the "genre," is the message. Plutarch is interested in putting the character of both Alexander and Caesar on display, and writing in detail about their famous deeds is not the best way to accomplish this goal. Those can be found elsewhere. Plutarch wishes to disclose the "signs of the soul" (τὰ τῆς ψυχῆς σημεῖα) of these famous men through lesser-known deeds.

Plutarch expects that his audience will already be familiar with traditions about Alexander and Caesar. How could they not be? The Life of Alexander and the Life of Caesar both presume knowledge about these men and their great deeds. At the end of the preface, Plutarch states that he leaves it "to others" (ἑτέροις) to write the great deeds and conquests of Alexander and Caesar. He does not intend to supplant or replace other accounts. Plutarch's *Lives* accomplishes something different than do other written traditions about these men.

---

137. The only difference between the two is that John has the pronoun follow the noun, whereas Plutarch has it precede.

The case is similar with John. The Fourth Gospel complements Jesus's "many other signs" and "deeds." Just as Plutarch assumes deep wells of tradition about Alexander and Caesar, so also the author of John for Jesus. It is not that John is echoing a literary convention that is unique to Plutarch. Rather, both John and Plutarch understand themselves to be contributing to written traditions about figures that transcend the documents that they are writing. Plutarch's *Lives* is a drop in the bucket of traditions about Alexander and Caesar, and the Fourth Gospel is a drop in the Jesus bucket. The emphasis of both Johannine colophons is not just on what has been written in the text. It is also on what has not been written: the other deeds and signs that Jesus performed.

John anticipates that it will be experienced alongside other Jesus media in a manner that the Synoptics do not. The media self-designations in Mark, Matthew, and Luke do not imply that they were meant to be read alongside one another, even if they eventually were. While Luke's prologue references other written Jesus traditions, the author does not indicate that Theophilus has read or should read them. John presumes that its audience knows of other Jesus traditions and that subsequent ones might also be written. The gospel places itself within an expanding archive.

Does this suggest anything about the reading events for which John might have been made? In the previous sections on Mark, Matthew, and Luke we saw that their peritexts indicated certain modes of reception. John's self-designation as a "document" (βιβλίον) does not imply one kind of reading event or another. The term is generalized. What it does imply, however, is that early Christianity was continuing to develop a distinct reading culture, one that possessed several different kinds of texts that were engaged in a variety of ways.

This leads to the question: is John aware of other written Jesus documents, such as the Synoptic Gospels? The question will be addressed and answered affirmatively in chapter 8. There I shall argue that John is a literary metamorphosis of the Synoptic Gospels.

Conclusion

Each gospel is self-conscious about its textual medium. This self-consciousness is on display at the gospels' paratextual thresholds. The Synoptics' media-conscious paratexts appear at the beginning of their narratives, whereas the two in the Fourth Gospel are at the text's conclusion. The former are entrance thresholds, the latter exit thresholds. All indicate something about their respective text's medium, intended mode of reception, and how they participate in early Christian media culture.

The creation of the Gospel of Mark was a watershed event. Mark's innovation was to textualize oral narrative traditions about Jesus. As a discourse that was textualized from antecedent oral events, Mark existed at the borderland between orality and textuality and this is reflected in its self-designation as "orally proclaimed news" (εὐαγγέλιον). Once it existed in physical form, the narrativized Jesus tradition could be textually altered and developed by later authors.

Using the Markan text, Matthew created something more bookish, designating the text as such from its first word, βίβλος ("book"). Matthew developed the written Jesus narrative by imitating and presenting itself as other authoritative texts had. These books, like Matthew, are meant to be read and studied not only by individuals but in a communal, synagogue setting.

Luke likewise utilized Mark's innovative document to write something new and more literary. The Third Gospel's preface notes that other written Jesus traditions exist and that this new account (διήγησις) is in the same orbit as them. The existence of the preface establishes Luke as a different kind of text than its predecessors, which both possess titles. The preface presents the narrative that follows as a text written first for an individual. While dedicating a text to an individual is a literary affectation, this does not obscure the social reality behind it. Theophilus was intended as Luke's initial reader. Presenting a text as written for an individual does something different than does presenting it as a "book" or as "good news."

John is not as explicit about the existence of other written Jesus traditions as Luke is. The Fourth Gospel presents itself as one "document" (βιβλίον) amid other hypothetical written traditions about Jesus. It is a complement to Jesus traditions and texts that might be written in the future.

Recognizing that each gospel uniquely labels itself attunes us to the development of early Christian reading culture, which consisted of different kinds of texts that made for different kinds of reading events. The Gospel of Mark is news meant to be proclaimed. Matthew is a book that imitates and presents itself like other authoritative Scriptural texts. Luke is an account written to an individual but with an eye to wider reception. The Gospel of John promotes itself as another textual drop in a sea of Jesus traditions, written and otherwise.

The media diversity that characterizes the gospels also characterized the media environments of Greco-Roman literary culture and Second Temple

Judaism. This media diversity is reflected in reading practices from these overlapping environments. It no less characterized writing practices in these contexts. There were variegated methods, contexts, and purposes for reading in antiquity. There were also variegated methods, contexts, and purposes for writing. The gospels were not all read the same way, and they were not all written the same way.

PART 2

Writing

Just as myths about ancient reading practices exert influence in biblical scholarship, so also do myths about compositional practices. Consider this passage from Harry Y. Gamble's influential monograph, *Books and Readers in the Early Church*:

> In reading aloud the written was converted into the oral. Correspondingly, in the composition of a text the oral was converted to the written. In antiquity a text could be composed either by dictating to a scribe or by writing in one's own hand. Yet when an author did write out his own text, the words were spoken as they were being written, just as scribes in copying manuscripts practiced what is called self-dictation. In either case, then, the text was an inscription of the spoken word. Because authors wrote or dictated with an ear to the words and assumed that what they wrote would be audibly read, they wrote for the ear more than the eye. As a result, no ancient text is now read as it was intended to be unless it is also heard, that is, read aloud.[1]

Gamble moves seamlessly from a romanticized notion of reading in antiquity to a romanticized notion of writing. The myth that all reading was vocalized necessitates that all writing was vocalized, even if one wrote with their own hand. By claiming "the text was an inscription of the spoken word," Gamble excludes the complexity that exists between speaking and writing.[2] Writing in Greco-Roman antiquity is a way to capture orality in frozen form. Considering texts to be ossified oral discourses fails to recognize how different mechanics of writing alter the discourse itself. Inscribed objects are representations of thinking. Like reading, writing is a social act. It is a technology by which human thought is put into a communicable form. Different methods of writing organize and express thought differently. Composing on a smartphone

---

1. Harry Y. Gamble, *Books and Readers in the Early Church: A History of Early Christian Texts* (New Haven: Yale University Press, 1995), 204.
2. Similarly, Paul J. Achtemeier writes, "The normal mode of composition of any writing was to dictate it to a scribe" ("*Omne Verbum Sonat*: The New Testament and the Oral Environment of Late Western Antiquity," *JBL* 109 [1990]: 12).

is different from composing on an electronic tablet, which is different from typing on a computer, which is different from using a typewriter. These various modern technologies for composition leave their mark on the artifact itself. The medium into which a discourse is cast also impacts what is created. Writing a tweet on a computer is different from writing an academic monograph on a computer, even if the two compositions are written by the same author on the same topic using the same keyboard.

The principle is no less true in antiquity. Composing via dictation and composing by hand are different ways to organize and express human thought. These differing modes of composition affect the text that is produced. Dictation is given undue precedence and is misunderstood in reconstructions of how ancient texts were composed. It is common to suppose that all texts were created via dictation in Greco-Roman antiquity and that dictation was infused throughout the entire process of writing. Some imagine note-taking, preliminary drafts, presentation copies, and recopying all to have been accomplished via dictation. Composition is dictation all the way down. The primary sources present a more complex interplay between handwriting and composing by mouth.

The purposes of the three chapters in part 2 are to divulge the roles that both handwriting and dictation played in composition and then to assess the gospels accordingly. There was no standard model by which texts were produced. Ancient writing practices were diverse. They varied from genre to genre and author to author. This diversity is flattened under the all-texts-were-dictated myth. Some texts were created without the named author ever placing a writing implement on a surface.[3] Written discourses could be created by dictation alone. But the opposite is also the case: some texts were created without dictation playing any part whatsoever. Most common, especially for literary documents, was an interplay between handwriting and dictation in the act of composition. Both modes left their imprint on a written discourse.

The chapters address these different modes of composition, highlighting when and why they were utilized separately from and in concert with one another. Chapters 4 and 5 equip us with the tools, handwriting and dictation, respectively, with which we will assess the canonical gospels. Like Greco-Roman texts more broadly, the gospels demonstrate a complex interplay between writing by hand and writing by mouth. There is not a single model of composition for these texts. Each gospel bears the marks of handwriting and dictation in different ways.

---

3. Someone placed the writing implement on the surface, however. In Greco-Roman antiquity, this was often an enslaved person.

CHAPTER 4

Writing by Hand

Media Myth: Persons in antiquity did not often compose texts in their own hands.
Media Reality: Handwriting played an important role in the composition process of various kinds of texts, though how and why it was used varied on the basis of a text's genre and the author's social context, literacy, and compositional preferences.

◆ ◆ ◆

Persons of varying social levels wrote discourses in their own hands. This is not to suggest that persons did not dictate discourses in Greco-Roman antiquity. They did. We shall address dictation in the following chapter. This chapter surveys evidence for writing *sua manu* ("by one's own hand"). There were advantages to composing in such a manner and in certain situations it was expected that one would do so. This was especially the case with personal letters. There are three types of letters investigated in what follows: the correspondence between two sets of literary elites, fictional letters that are embedded in the romance novels, and personal papyri letters recovered from Egypt. Writing letters by hand was common in all three. Persons in antiquity sentimentalized their loved one's handwriting, just as we do today.

The gospels are not letters. Letter-writing conventions do not bear on how the gospels were written. That is not my argument in what follows. I survey these letters to demonstrate that writing by hand was common and to debunk two different notions: that writing in one's own hand was stigmatized and that only the literary elite at the top of the social ladder would have possessed the ability to write in their own hands.

After engaging handwritten letters, the chapter turns to the different roles that handwriting played in composing literary texts. Handwriting was used throughout the composition process: in research, note-taking, drafting, and creating a final, presentation copy. While different authors had different practices, handwriting was stereotyped as the careful way to compose.

Writing Literary Letters by Hand

In the correspondences between Cicero and Atticus and between Marcus and Fronto the normal practice was to handwrite letters. With respect to Cicero and Atticus, we possess only one side of the equation: Cicero's letters. What emerges is that it was not until their later correspondence that the two began to dictate letters or portions of letters to one another. The first time that Cicero broke the handwriting convention and dictated a letter to Atticus was in 59 BCE, when Cicero was nearly fifty years old. He begins *Att.* 43 as follows: "I believe you have never before read a letter of mine not in my own handwriting [nisi mea manu scriptam]. You may gather from that how desperately busy I am. Not having a minute to spare and being obliged to take a walk to refresh my poor voice, I am dictating this while walking [haec dictavi ambulans]" (Cicero, *Att.* 43 [Shackleton Bailey, LCL]). This letter apparently punctured the handwriting dam and Cicero began to dictate more frequently thereafter. In the next chapter, we will investigate several of the letters that Cicero dictated to Atticus and other individuals and the reason for which he did. Worth foregrounding here, however, is the fact that Cicero normally makes an excuse for dictating rather than writing by hand.[1] Cicero begins to flag whether he is dictating or handwriting in his later correspondence with Atticus. For example, in *Att.* 271 he begins with the words "I write this in my own hand" (Haec ad te mea manu) and in *Att.* 299.4 he calls attention to the shift into his hand with the words "this is my hand" (hoc manu mea).[2]

The same practice permeates the correspondence between Marcus and Fronto. In chapter 2, we briefly addressed one letter from the collated second-century correspondence between the two. In that letter, *De Fer. Als.* 3, Fronto imagined his pupil sunbathing and engaging in various literary activities. I suggested this was an ambiguous case of reading aloud. It was unclear whether Fronto imagined Marcus lounging about and reading texts to himself silently, aloud, or having texts read to him. When it comes to writing by hand in Marcus

---

1. In *Att.* 40 and 212, Cicero dictates so that if his letters are intercepted his handwriting will not be recognized. Cicero must have handwritten often if his handwriting was publicly known. In *Att.* 89, like in *Att.* 43, Cicero dictates because he is extraordinarily busy. In *Att.* 107 he dictates because he has not yet settled into a new space. In *Att.* 110 he dictates because he is traveling. Ophthalmia, inflammation of the eyes, is the reason he dictates *Att.* 137 and 162. In the former, he notes his letter would be longer if he were able to handwrite it. The fact of dictating results in a shorter letter.
2. Shackleton Bailey, LCL.

and Fronto's correspondence, there is no ambiguity: their standard practice was to handwrite letters to one another. Fronto expected autographed missives from his pupil; Marcus in turn expected the same from his teacher. On those occasions when letters or portions of letters were dictated, Marcus and Fronto, like Cicero, explained why the words were not handwritten.[3]

Fronto's preference that Marcus write to him by hand is most clearly expressed in a letter in which he asks Marcus for legal advice on a case that he is arguing (Fronto, *Ad M. Caes.* 3.3). Closing the letter, Fronto expresses his preference for autographs: "I, indeed, dote on the very characters of your writing: wherefore, whenever you write to me, I would have you write with your own hand" (Fronto, *Ad M. Caes.* 3.3 [Haines, LCL]).[4] Doting on the handwritten characters in personal missives is a theme that re-appears in the novels and in papyri letters. It is not simply the message of the letters that holds sentiment for Fronto and other recipients; so also does the way that the sender inscribes the characters on the page.

Most of the correspondence between Fronto and Marcus was handwritten. On occasion, one or the other apologizes or offers an excuse for not writing *sua manu* and dictating a text instead. Poor health is the most common reason for dictating. This is the case in a short letter whose sole purpose was to provide Marcus an update on Fronto's health (Fronto, *Ad M. Caes.* 4.9). In its entirety, it reads: "To my Lord. I have been troubled, my Lord, in the night with widespread pains in my shoulder and elbow and knee and ankle. In fact, I have not been able to convey this very news to you in my own writing [Denique id ipsum tibi mea manu scribere non potui.]" Marcus recognized immediately that the words were not written in Fronto's hand. Fronto is apologetic and brings it up again in a subsequent letter (also in *Ad M. Caes.* 4.9 [Haines, LCL]). Therein he states that he had to "employ another hand" for his previous letter, which was "contrary to our custom" (contra morem nostrum).

Fronto apologizes for other letters that he dictates. At the end of a long letter, Fronto pleads, "Do not be offended with me for not having answered your letter in my own hand, and that though the letter I had from you was

---

3. Annelise Freisenbruch, "Back to Fronto: Doctor and Patient in His Correspondence with an Emperor," in *Ancient Letters: Classical and Late Antique Epistolography*, ed. Ruth Morello and A. D. Morrison (Oxford: Oxford University Press, 2007), 251–54. Autographs aim "to convince the recipient (be it specified addressee or eavesdropping reader) of their 'authenticity,' or perhaps, 'sincerity'" (Freisenbruch, "Back to Fronto," 253).

4. *Ego vero etiam lierulas tuas disamo: quare cupiam, ubi quid ad me scribe, tua manu scribas.*

in yours" (*De Bello Parthico* 10 [Haines, LCL]). Fronto could not write by hand because the letter was extensive, Fronto's fingers were weak, and his right hand at that moment was "one of few letters." The case is similar in another long letter that Fronto dictated because of a cough and pain in his right hand (Fronto, *Ad Antoninum Imp.* 1.2).

In one of Marcus's letters, he handwrites despite illness and presumes that Fronto can gauge his health "by the shakiness of [his] handwriting" (quod haec precaria manu scribo) (Marcus Aurelius, *Ad M. Caes.* 4.8 [Haines, LCL]). On another occasion, Marcus's hand was shaking after his evening bath, and this is the reason that he opts not to write with it (Marcus Aurelius, *De Nepote Amisso* 1.2). The cold from exiting the bath has made it more difficult for Marcus to write with proper penmanship and so he opts to dictate.[5] Marcus apologizes for his penmanship in another letter that was apparently written as Fronto's letter carrier awaited Marcus's reply: "Maecianus was pressing, and it was right that your brother should return to you in good time. I beseech you, therefore, if you find any solecism or confusion of thought or shaky letter herein, put it down to haste" (Marcus Aurelius, *Ad M. Caes.* 4.2 [Haines, LCL]). Marcus feels obligated not only to write in his own hand but also to write well. The physical presentation of the letter mattered.

The usual practice for Marcus and Fronto, when it came to personal letters, was to write each other by hand. Under other social circumstances, dictating letters seems to have been Marcus's norm. In one letter, he tells Fronto that he cannot say anything because he just finished dictating thirty letters (Marcus Aurelius, *Ad M. Caes.* 5.47). Marcus writes to Fronto by hand after dictating these other letters. Social factors affect the mode of composition. When it came to business or official correspondence, Marcus dictated, presumably out of convenience and for the sake of time. Having composed those letters in one manner, Marcus turns to write to Fronto in another.[6]

Marcus and Fronto handwrote letters to one another because of their relationship and the nature of their personal correspondence. A certain kind of text written in the context of a certain social relationship called for a certain mode

---

5. Caillan Davenport and Jennifer Manley note, "The Roman bathing habit involved moving between hot and cold baths quite quickly, which would probably be enough to cause Marcus' hands to shake" (*Fronto: Selected Letters*, Classical Studies Series [New York: Bloomsbury, 2014], 200).

6. Similarly, in *De Fer. Als.* 4, Marcus dictates the beginning of a letter to Fronto while plagued by his official duties, but then, when he has more time, switches his mode of composition and finishes writing the letter in his own hand.

of composition. When personal letters were dictated, the mode of composition was explained and excused. Fronto's and Marcus's habit of writing *sua manu* was not exceptional. Other elite Romans handwrote to one another regularly. Those in the "middle ranks" of society did so as well, as demonstrated by the novels and personal papyri letters.

Writing Letters by Hand in the Novels

The novels are relevant for understanding media realities of antiquity not because they describe actual reading and writing events, but because they demonstrate how authors and readers imagined reading and writing to work. The logic of several scenes in the novels depended on certain reading practices, whether private or public, silent or vocalized. The authors of the novels also depict their characters writing personal letters by hand, suggesting that this was a common practice in their media context.

On several occasions in Chariton's novel, *Chaereas and Callirhoe*, writing and reading, and specifically writing and reading letters penned by the tale's protagonists, serve to advance the plot. We have already encountered one such occasion in chapter 1 of this book. In that scene, both Callirhoe and her second husband, Dionysius, suppose that the male protagonist, Chaereas, who is Callirhoe's true love and first husband, has died (Chariton, *Callirhoe* 4.5). Very much alive, Chaereas has written a letter to his wife, which Dionysius has intercepted and reads silently during a banquet.

Moving backward in the novel, we find the account of Chaereas writing this letter, not through a scribal intermediary but with his own hand (Chariton, *Callirhoe* 4.4.5–10). Mithridates, who had made it his business to reunite Chaereas with Callirhoe, suggests that Chaereas write to "try out the woman by letter" to see if she is willing to leave Dionysius. Mithridates then proposes, "Write her a letter: make her sad; make her happy; make her seek you; make her summon you" (Chariton, *Callirhoe* 4.4.5 [Goold, LCL]).

In solitude (μόνος ἐπ' ἐρημίας γενόμενος), Chaereas attempts to pen his letter but is initially hindered by a flood of tears and his trembling hand (ἀλλ' οὐκ ἠδύνατο, δακρύων ἐπιρρεόντων καὶ τῆς χειρὸς αὐτοῦ τρεμούσης). The narrator has no need to explain why Chaereas writes by hand or how he can do so. Readers of the novel assume that personal letters were often handwritten by their senders. Chaereas's handwriting added to the letter's emotional effect. When Callirhoe learns that Chaereas is alive, his own hand will provoke those emotions that Mithridates suggests to a greater extent than a dictated letter.

As the narrative progresses, Chaereas's handwriting in the letter stands at the center of a dramatic court scene in the novel's fifth book. Dionysius is convinced that Chaereas is dead and that Mithridates wrote the letter as part of a plot to take Callirhoe for himself. The two, Dionysius and Mithridates, are summoned to court before the Persian king Artaxerxes. Mithridates tells Chaereas that Dionysius's charge against him, Mithridates, is that "the letter which you wrote to your wife was written by me." The narrator similarly summarizes Dionysius's case: "Dionysius relied on the letter that Mithridates wrote to Callirhoe in the name of Chaereas (for of course he never imagined that Chaereas was alive)" (Goold, LCL). Mithridates secretly brings the very much alive Chaereas along to Persia and plans to produce him theatrically as the centerpiece for his case.

As the courtroom drama proceeds, Dionysius reads aloud the letter that he claims was forged in Chaereas's name and Mithridates responds. Before dramatically producing Chaereas to the court, and thus also to Callirhoe, he states that he did not write the letter as it is not written in his hand (οὐ γέγραφα· χεῖρα ἐμὴν οὐκ ἔχεις). The point about the letter's hand becomes moot, as Chaereas appears in court, dispelling Dionysius's claim that the letter was forged.

While Mithridates has no need to build his case on the fact that Dionysius "does not have his handwriting," he could have. Whether a text is authentically written in a respective individual's hand or is a forgery is a trope that extends far beyond this novel. It is also found in Suetonius, Cicero, Apuleius, Juvenal, Tacitus, Josephus, and Polybius.[7]

This is not the only scene in *Chaereas and Callirhoe* wherein handwriting figures prominently. It does once more after Callirhoe has been dramatically reunited with Chaereas. In the novel's final book, the eponymous female protagonist writes to inform Dionysius that she is now with Chaereas and to instruct him, Dionysius, to raise up their son without the aid of a stepmother. Toward the end of the letter, Callirhoe informs Dionysius that she has written in her own hand (ταῦτά σοι γέγραφα τῇ ἐμῇ χειρί) (Chariton, *Callirhoe* 8.4.6 [Goold, LCL]). Dionysius has no need of this notice. Before even opening the missive, he recognizes Callirhoe's letters (γνωρίσας τὰ Καλλιρόης γράμματα),

---

7. Suetonius, *Titus* 3; *Domitian* 12; *Gaius Caligula* 24; *Lives Augustus* 81; *Lives Caesar* 17; Cicero, *In Catilinam* 3.12.10–11; 4.3; *Phil.* 2.4.7–9; 2.7.16–17; *de Naturo Deorum* 3.30.74; Apuleius, *Apologia* 87.2; Juvenal, *Satire* 13; Tacitus, *Ann.* 30; Josephus, *J.W.* 1.3; *Ant.*, 14.4; 16.4; Polybius, *Histories* 30.8.4.

kisses the epistle, and holds it close as a substitute for his lost love's physical presence. The handwriting in the letter induces Dionysius's emotions.

There are several implications about the role of handwriting in *Chaereas and Callirhoe*. First, that Dionysius recognizes and weeps at Callirhoe's handwriting implies not only that he is familiar with her script but that it possesses sentimental value. For this narrative detail to have rhetorical effect, readers of the novel must know the experience of attaching sentiment to a loved one's handwriting. Second, when Callirhoe writes her letter, the narrator feels some need to make it clear that she is writing by hand. Not only does the narrator call attention to Callirhoe writing *sua manu* by stating that she herself took up the writing tablet with a feminine participle (λαβοῦσα) in 8.4.5, but also has her include the words "I write these things in my own hand" at the end of the letter. This, and the numerous other occasions in which ancient letter writers state that they are writing by hand, suggests that the practice of *not* writing in one's own hand was common. Though this is not to suggest that writing letters in one's own hand was not also common. It was. And this is the third implication of the role of autograph letters in *Chaereas and Callirhoe*: recipients often expected letters to be written in their sender's own hand. Social factors shape writing practices. It is not simply the contents of a letter's message that matters, but also its medium. A personal letter that was not written in the sender's own hand did not possess equal sentiment as one that was.

A similar case of handwriting is attested in Achilles Tatius's novel *Leucippe and Cleitophon*. In chapter 1 an instance of silent reading from this novel was evoked: the male protagonist, Cleitophon, pretends to read early in the novel to steal glances of Leucippe. Much later in the novel, after the protagonists have eloped but been separated from one another, an unfortunate series of events leads Cleitophon to presume that Leucippe is dead. This presumption is proven wrong, however, when he receives a letter from his wife. Narrating in the first person, Cleitophon states, "Even as I took it [the letter] from him, before I began to read it, I was thunder-struck; for I recognized Leucippe's writing! This was the tenor of it" (λαβὼν δέ, πρὶν ἀναγνῶναι, κατεπλάγην εὐθύς· ἐγνώρισα γὰρ Λευκίππης τὰ γράμματα) (Achilles Tatius, *Leucippe and Cleitophon* 5.18 [Gaselee, LCL]).

The letter writer's hand provokes an emotional response. Cleitophon narrates, "At this message I was moved with many emotions at once; I was flushed and pale, I was astonished and incredulous, I was full of joy and sorrow" (Achilles Tatius, *Leucippe and Cleitophon* 5.19 [Gaselee, LCL]). As he rereads the letter to himself, Cleitophon imagines that he can see Leucippe in it (καὶ ἅμα αὖθις ἐντυγχάνων τοῖς γράμμασιν, ὡς ἐκείνην δι᾽ αὐτῶν βλέπων καὶ ἀναγινώσκων). In his handwritten response to his wife, Cleitophon writes that while she is absent from him bodily, he sees her through her letters (ὅτι σὲ παρὼν παροῦσαν ὡς ἀποδημοῦσαν ὁρῶ διὰ γραμμάτων) (Achilles Tatius, *Leucippe and Cleitophon* 5.20 [Gaselee, LCL]). Like the letters in *Chaereas and Callirhoe*, letters in *Leucippe and Cleitophon* are written by hand by their senders. The handwriting of the sender possesses significant sentiment for the recipient. In both novels, it is not only the letter that stands in for the person's presence but also the handwriting itself.

Writing Letters by Hand in the Papyri

The novels imagine life and letter writing in antiquity. Papyri letters are tangible artifacts of them. They actualize the imagined sentimentalization of friends' and family members' handwriting. A second-century CE letter written to a certain Isidoros from his "brother" participates in the trope of seeing a person through their handwriting. The sender, whose name is lost in the letter's damaged opening, uses language that resembles Cleitophon's: "I received your letters, through which I seemed to behold you" (ἐκομι[σάμην σου] τὰ γράμματα δι᾽ ὧν ἔδοξά [σ]ε θεω[ρ]εῖν) (*SB* 14.11584).[8] Both here and in *Leucippe and Cleitophon*, it is the "letters" or "characters" (τὰ γράμματα), not the epistles, that the person is seen through.[9] While not explicit, it can be surmised that the letter writer is referring to their brother's handwriting.

In another personal letter, *BGU* 2.423, the sentimentalization of a family member's hand is expressly stated. This letter is remarkable for several reasons, foremost among them is that it is paired with another letter, *BGU* 2.632, that was sent by the same individual, though using different names, several years apart from one another. Both were discovered in the Fayûm and are paleographically dated to the second century CE. The pair provides a window into how life progressed for one Egyptian family nearly two thousand years ago.[10]

---

8. Text from the Duke Databank of Documentary Papyri (https://papyri.info/ddbdp/sb;14;11584).

9. "Letters" (τὰ γράμματα) can refer to the documents themselves. That is, the word can mean "epistles" and not the handwriting within them. However, later in the letter, the sender uses the term "epistle" (ἐπιστο[λήν]) to describe what Isidoros sends him. This being the case, I take the former term to mean "characters."

10. Adolf Deissmann imagines what happened "between the lines" of both letters, narrativizing the events of Apion and his family's life (*Light from the Ancient East: The New Testament*

Both are written by a recruit to the Roman army who is from Philadelphia. The first, *BGU* 2.423, was composed shortly after his arrival at Misenum, a major Roman port city. In it Apion informs his father, Epimachus, that he has arrived safely at the port, received pay for travel expenses, and taken the Roman name Antonius Maximus. Along with the letter, he sends his father a portrait of himself. Apion requests a written reply that will update him on his family's welfare and allow him to adore his father's handwriting (ἵνα προσκυνήσω τὴν χέραν).[11] Apion assumes the response will be written in his father's hand.

At least one of the two persons in this correspondence was expected to write their letters *sua manu*. The argument can be pressed further.[12] If Apion's expectation is for Epimachus to write by hand, then it stands to reason that Apion writes his letter in the same manner.[13] We have already seen in the novels that there is sentimental value attached to handwritten letters. This was also the case with Fronto and Marcus Aurelius's correspondence. They apologized and made excuses when letters were not written in their own hands. If Apion's father educated him well, as he states in the letter (με ἐπαίδευσας καλῶς), then writing and reading will likely have been an aspect of this education.[14] A grapho-literate and dutiful son would write to his father in his own hand. A handwritten letter nicely complements the other affectionate token that Apion sent: the sketch of himself.

But we need not speculate whether Apion wrote in his own hand based on social factors alone. A second letter recovered in the Fayûm, *BGU* 2.632, was also written by Apion, though under his new Roman name, Antonius Maximus. Years have passed since Apion reached Misenum and first wrote his

---

Illustrated by Recently Discovered Texts of the Graeco-Roman World, trans. Lionel Richard Mortimer Strachan [London: Hodder & Stoughton, 1910], 167–75).

11. Trans. my own. χεραν is an uncorrected form of χεῖρα.

12. In 1927, J. G. Winter suggested that we cannot know whether Apion wrote *sua manu* or dictated his first letter but that the latter is more likely the case ("In the Service of Rome: Letters from the Michigan Collection of Papyri," *CP* 22 [1927]: 239).

13. As Raffaella Cribiore also suggests (*Writing, Teachers, and Students in Graeco-Roman Egypt*, American Studies in Papyrology 36 [Atlanta: Scholars Press, 1996], 245–46).

14. Apion's education is betrayed in the letter itself, which is written in a clear script and adheres to ancient epistolary conventions. It follows them so closely that Hans-Josef Klauck and Daniel P. Bailey use it to introduce "standard letter components" in *Ancient Letters and the New Testament: A Guide to Context and Exegesis* (Waco, TX: Baylor University Press, 2006), 9–27. It is quite literally a textbook example of letter-writing etiquette.

father. There have been many developments in his life.[15] The writer now sports his Roman name, and no longer goes by Apion. He has a partner called Aufidia, two daughters, named Hope and Fortune, and a son named Maximus.[16] His sister Sabina, to whom he writes, likewise has a son named Maximus, presumably called such after his uncle.[17] In the second letter, Maximus prays to the local gods rather than to the Egyptian "Lord Sarapis" as in the first letter. The recipient's father, Epimachus, may have died in the time between the writing of the two letters, as he is not mentioned in the greetings.[18]

This letter appears to be written in the same hand as the first. This was the opinion of its first editor, Friedrich Krebs.[19] Given the time that has passed between the two letters and because the location of their writing has presumably changed, it would be extraordinarily unlikely that Apion used the same amanuensis to write them. If they are written in the same hand, it is assuredly Apion's.[20] Orthographic similarities confirm Kreb's original judgment that the hands are the same.[21]

In addition, the greeting, health wish, and conclusion in both letters are identical.[22] The result is that there are two uniform strings of words shared in the letters, one of eight words and one of three. While the greeting, health wish, and conclusion are stock elements of ancient letters, there were a vari-

---

15. Deissmann envisions these in poetic fashion, imagining that the sender's nephew, Maximus, who takes his name from his uncle, knows Maximus's face from the sketch that was sent to Epimachus years previously (*Light from the Ancient East*, 174–75).

16. As a parent of identical twin daughters with coordinating names, I imagine that Hope and Fortune were likewise twins.

17. Klauck and Bailey, *Ancient Letters*, 16.

18. This is the opinion of Deissmann (*Light from the Ancient East*, 172n2) and Klauck and Bailey (*Ancient Letters*, 16). Though it is worth noting that several lines of greetings are lost. A greeting to Epimachus might have been included in the lost lines.

19. His marginal note at the top of the reproduction of the letter in *BGU* 2.297 reads "Von derselben Hand wie No. 423."

20. Klauck and Bailey have recently expressed their doubt that the handwriting is the same, though they offer no comments about how the handwriting between the two letters differs (*Ancient Letters*, 16).

21. Notable at the level of individual letters are the similarities in the formation of the *phis*, *bētas*, and *sigma-epsilon* ligature. With respect to words and phrases, πλεῖστα χαίρειν, σε ὑγιαίνειν καί, and πρὸ μὲν πάντων appear in both letters and provide tangible points for comparing the hands. I am grateful to Susan Forshey, Paul Wheatley, and Timothy Mitchell for offering their critical eyes and comments on the hand of the letters.

22. The greeting in both is πλεῖστα χαίρειν followed immediately by the health wish πρὸ μὲν πάντων εὔχομαί σε ὑγιαίνειν.

ety of conventions and spellings one might have employed for all three.[23] If Apion was dictating and using different scribes to do so, there would be more variation in these conventional elements. For two different scribes to write these elements identically years apart from one another, Apion would have to be exacting in his dictation and the two scribes must not have taken any compositional liberties.

There are several reasons that Apion/Maximus might have written these letters in his own hand, and they are not exclusive to one another. For a grapho-literate individual, writing oneself can be more convenient than writing through an amanuensis. It is also the cheaper option. Even more significant is the social effect of handwritten letters. In his first letter, Apion explicitly states that he values his father's hand. A letter from his father updating him on his family's condition no doubt would have been welcomed by Apion, as would a handwritten letter from Apion to his loved ones back home.

The chance find of two letters written by the same person years apart is exceptional. Most extant papyri letters do not provide hints about their compositional mode. It is only in extraordinary cases that these conclusions can be drawn. One other such remarkable letter is P.Oxy. 1.119, a second- or third-century letter written by a young child to his father. The missive is infamous on account of the son's petulant tone. He chides his father for not bringing him along to Alexandria on business.

As Grenfell and Hunt note, "the letter is written in a rude uncial hand," and it is riddled with spelling and grammatical mistakes.[24] The author, Theon, wrote it himself by hand. This is what makes it so exceptional. But this is not the only letter that young Theon wrote his elder in his own hand. The boy threatens his father that, unless he takes him to Alexandria, he will not write him another letter (οὐ μὴ γράψω σε ἐπιστολήν). Theon must have written his father regularly, since he believes that the absence of a letter would cause as much emotional anguish as the cessation of other regular activities, such as conversing with him and wishing him well. He knows that his letters hold sentiment to his father, which is what gives the threat of not writing its sting.

---

23. Delphine Nachtergaele finds that there is much variety in these conventional elements in papyri letters ("Variation in Private Letters: The Papyri of the Apollonios *Strategos* Archive," *GRBS* 56 [2016]: 140–63).

24. Bernard P. Grenfell and Arthur S. Hunt, *Oxyrhynchus Papyri* (London: Egypt Exploration Society, 1898), 1:185.

The conclusion to draw from these three letters and those in the novels is that handwriting was not only valued at the highest tiers of society. It was not just the Ciceros, Frontos, and Marcus Aureliuses of the ancient world that sentimentalized their friends' and families' handwritten correspondence. The Apions, Epimachuses, Sabines, and Theons of antiquity did as well. That missives, especially when handwritten, were sentimentalized as a replacement for a loved one's presence is captured well by Palladas's fourth-century epigram: "Nature, loving the duties of friendship, invented instruments by which absent friends can converse: pens, paper, ink, handwriting [τὰ χαράγματα χειρός], tokens of the heart that mourns afar off" (Palladas in *Greek Anthology* 9.400 [Paton, LCL]).

Writing Literary Compositions by Hand

It was not just letters that were written by hand. Other kinds of discourses were as well, including literary compositions. Authors wrote in their own hands at various stages of a text's production. There were no standardized practices for when to write by hand and when to dictate. Some authors employed handwriting more extensively than others. Whereas one author might write all their extracts and notes by hand, another might prefer to dictate extracts. Rough and final drafts were handwritten by some and dictated by others. There is no one-size-fits-all model for ancient composition.

Because of the romanticized notion that texts were usually dictated, it might be surprising that the handwriting of eminent Romans was recognizable and remarked upon by various writers. Myles McDonnell marshals the following cases:[25]

- A friend of Pliny the Elder possessed two-hundred-year-old texts handwritten by Tiberius and Gaius Gracchus (*Nat.* 13.83).
- In the same passage, Pliny states that autograph versions of texts from Cicero, Vergil, and Augustus were very common in his day (*Nat.* 13.83).
- Quintilian also saw the handwriting of Cicero, Vergil, and Augustus with his own eyes and comments upon it (*Inst.* 1.7.20–22).
- Suetonius observed documents written in Augustus's and Nero's hands (*Aug.* 80.3; 87.1.3; 88; *Nero* 52.3).

---

25. Myles McDonnell, "Writing, Copying, and Autograph Manuscripts in Ancient Rome," *ClQ* 46 (1996): 473.

McDonnell claims that it was not uncommon to see autograph copies of texts written by distinguished Romans.[26] Persons at the very top of the social ladder, like Marcus and Fronto, had no shame about writing *sua manu*. The opposite is the case: they were ashamed when they dictated personal letters, as doing otherwise was "considered impolite."[27]

But it is not only personal letters that Marcus and Fronto wrote by hand. Throughout their correspondence, they hint at other texts that are handwritten. In a letter in which Marcus updates Fronto on his literary endeavors for the day, he states, "From half-past ten till now I have been writing and have also read a good deal of Cato, and I am writing this to you with the same pen" (Marcus Aurelius, *Ad M. Caes.* 2.4 [Haines, LCL]). Marcus was doing his own writing by hand before writing his mentor a letter in the same mode. In another letter, Marcus writes of taking his "pen in hand" (stilus in manus venit) when preparing to compose (Marcus Aurelius, *Ad M. Caes.* 2.10).

In these cases, Marcus closely associates composition with handwriting. Yet when he sent Fronto copies of his literary work to be corrected he had it reproduced by a scribe.[28] Marcus requests by letter that Fronto send him another writing promptly because he had finished his pedagogue's prior task (Marcus Aurelius, *Ad M. Caes.* 5.41). But Marcus does not send the completed work along with the letter because his scribe was not available to copy it for him. Marcus's practice was to keep his own copies of his handwritten work and send Fronto versions that were not written in his hand. His teacher would then usually correct the exercises *sua manu* (Marcus Aurelius, *Ad Amicos* 2.3). This highlights one of the chief ways that enslaved persons were used in the writing process: for making copies. Marcus might compose a text by hand, but he could not be troubled by the manual labor of copying it himself.

This helps to explain the curious case of a pair of letters, one from Marcus and another in response from Fronto (*Ad M. Caes.* 1.6 and 1.7). In the former, Marcus tells his pedagogue that he declaimed a portion of one of Fronto's speeches to his father, who could not be present at the speech when Fronto delivered it in court. With the letter Marcus included the speech that he, Marcus, had copied out in his own hand. In his letter of response Fronto gushes over this token of Marcus's affection: "For every letter of your letter I count myself to have gained a consulship, a victory, a triumph, a robe of

---

26. McDonnell, "Writing, Copying, and Autograph Manuscripts," 473.
27. McDonnell, "Writing, Copying, and Autograph Manuscripts," 474.
28. McDonnell, "Writing, Copying, and Autograph Manuscripts," 487.

honour" (Fronto, *Ad M. Caes.* 1.7.4 [Haines LCL]). Having his speech written in Marcus's handwriting makes it of inestimable worth.

But why is this gesture so touching to Fronto, if he regularly received handwritten letters from Marcus? It is because Marcus deigned to copy a document that he himself did not author. This was manual work he would have normally relegated to a slave. As McDonnell puts it, "Copying the work of another was a task inappropriate for an important and busy elite Roman."[29] Why Marcus copied the speech in his own hand is another question altogether. The most compelling answer is mnemonic purposes. Copying a text by hand improves one's memory of it in preparation for delivery.[30]

Marcus took up the stylus to write in his own hand for a variety of purposes: to compose personal letters, to complete rhetorical exercises, to write literature, and to memorize texts for oral declamation. Handwriting was a compositional mode authors utilized in varying stages of a literary text's production, including its "final" form. Plutarch writes that this was the case with Cato the Elder's History of Rome. In *Cat. Maj.* 20.4–5, he waxes poetic about Cato's paternal excellence. He was his son's pedagogue, athletic trainer, and schooled him on how to "swim lustily through the eddies and billows of the Tiber." Even more than all this, "His History of Rome, as he tells us himself, he wrote out with his own hand and in large characters [καὶ τὰς ἱστορίας δὲ συγγράψαι φησὶν αὐτὸς ἰδίᾳ χειρὶ καὶ μεγάλοις γράμμασιν], that his son might have in his own home an aid to acquaintance with his country's ancient traditions" (Plutarch, *Cat. Maj.* 20.4–5 [348] [Perrin, LCL]). Cato desired his son to read his history of Rome, and so wrote it out in his own hand with large, legible characters.

Plutarch's passing comment, "as he [Cato] himself tells us" (φησὶν αὐτός) suggests that Cato included this information in the "publication version" of his history with no shame. That Cato wrote an autograph copy of the *Origins* in a large, legible hand must have been proverbial for Plutarch and his readers. This act is impressive to Plutarch because Cato's history at seven books long was no small text.[31] To copy or write out a work of such length involved a significant investment of both time and physical energy, even more so when it is

29. McDonnell, "Writing, Copying, and Autograph Manuscripts," 489.
30. McDonnell, "Writing, Copying, and Autograph Manuscripts," 487–89.
31. While the *Origins* is not extant, information about its length and contents is offered by Cornelius Nepos in *Cato* 3.3.

done carefully and legibly.[32] It is the very definition of *manual* labor. Copying a final, presentation version of a text was a task delegated to slaves. That Cato would write such a copy in his own hand demonstrates his devotion to his son. The reason for writing it by hand is social.

Whereas Cato handwrote a presentation copy of a discourse for his son, Pliny the Elder often handwrote his notes and extracts. The younger Pliny provides a complete chronological bibliography of his late uncle's oeuvre, which consists of 109 volumes (Pliny the Younger, *Ep.* 3.5). He details how one person could produce so many texts in a single lifetime. The Elder Pliny worked under the pernicious principle that "any time not devoted to work was wasted" (*Ep.* 3.5.16).[33] He made extracts and notes of everything that he read or had read to him (Pliny the Younger, *Ep.* 3.5.10). The younger Pliny reports the various settings in which his uncle wrote these materials. His details make it clear that the elder Pliny was in the habit of handwriting notes and extracts. While he sunbathed or ate, a book was read aloud from which Pliny made extracts and notes. Rather than walk through Rome, he would be carried about in a chair so that he might continue to work by hand.

Pliny the Younger also indicates that the Elder dictated notes. Dictation is mentioned as one of his uncle's practices, but it may be as a concession. The only time notes are dictated, per this letter, is after Pliny had been immersed in the bath and "was being rubbed down and dried" (Pliny the Younger, *Ep.* 3.5.14 [Radice, LCL]).[34] In reality, Pliny the Elder probably made notes both in his own hand and via dictation.

The results of his manic devotion to productivity were his 109 volumes and 160 additional notebooks that were "written in a minute hand." At the end of the letter, Pliny estimates the extraordinary financial value of these notebooks to be at least 400,000 sesterces. Matthew D. C. Larsen notes that this is the same amount of money required to become a Roman knight and argues that the notebooks were valuable because they contained the Elder's "textual raw

---

32. Steve Reece emphasizes how laborious writing could be in antiquity (*Paul's Large Letters: Paul's Autographic Subscription in the Light of Ancient Epistolary Conventions*, LNTS 561 [New York: Bloomsbury, 2016], 12–16).

33. *Nam perire omne tempus arbitrabatur, quod studiis non impenderetur.* Text, Radice, LCL; trans. my own.

34. In the famous letter describing the eruption of Vesuvius, Pliny the Younger states that his uncle dictated everything that he was seeing. The Elder Pliny did dictate notes, but only in rare circumstances.

material."[35] The Younger Pliny differentiates between his uncle's published volumes (*volumina*) mentioned in the chronological bibliography and the 160 notebooks (*commentario*) he left behind upon his death. The latter were unfinished texts, extracts of other books and Pliny's own written thoughts on them. They are valuable because they are seedlings for new works.

The notes, both handwritten and dictated, could be fashioned into finished products. But this does not mean that there is a clear distinction between the notes and the volumes that they will become. Paul J. Achtemeier makes such a bifurcation when he suggests that notetaking was commonly done *sua manu* but the "normal mode of composition of any writing was to dictate it to a scribe."[36] Even if Pliny dictated his finished product, much of it was previously handwritten. It was not conceived in a transcriptive event.

The younger Pliny appears to have followed his uncle's example of mixing literary endeavors with recreation. He writes about one particularly successful hunting trip in which he caught three very fine boars (Pliny the Younger, *Ep.* 1.6). In the letter, Pliny outlines his hunting habits: he sits by the nets with his writing materials, namely stylus and notebooks (*stilus et pugillares*), and waits. If he goes home animal-less, at least he has "filled his notebooks." For Pliny, "being alone in the depths of the woods in the silence necessary for hunting is a positive stimulus for thought" (iam undique silvae et solitudo ipsumque illud silentium quod venationi datur) (Pliny the Younger, *Ep.* 1.6 [Radice, LCL]).[37] To maintain the silence necessary for hunting, Pliny must be writing notes himself and not dictating them.

Like Pliny, Horace mentions implements used for writing. He states that he has been caught up in the general public's "scribbling craze" (scribendi studio) (Horace, *Ep.* 2.1.108–117 [Fairclough, LCL]). Participating in the rise-early-and-write trope, Horace wakes before dawn and calls for "pen, paper, and writing-case" (calamum et chartas et scrinia). A similar notion is repeated in his proverbial statement, "Often you must flip your stylus to erase, if you hope to write something worth a second reading" (Saepe stilum vertas, iterum quae digna legi sint scripturus) (Horace, *Sat.* 1.10.72 [Fairclough (modified),

---

35. Matthew D. C. Larsen, *Gospels before the Book* (Oxford: Oxford University Press, 2018), 17–19.

36. Achtemeier, "*Omne Verbum Sonat*," 12–13.

37. Pliny suggests that Tacitus should follow his example: "So next time you hunt yourself, follow my examples and take your notebooks along with your lunch-basket and flask" (*Ep.* 1.6.3 [Radice, LCL]).

LCL]). Horace also objects to dictation because it produces a less-polished product (Horace, *Sat.* 1.4.9–13). In his imagination of how others write and his own writing, composition is a solitary affair that is carefully done by hand.

According to Porphyry, Plotinus also wrote his first drafts in his own hand. They were, however, far from "clean copies." Plotinus left the task of editing to others, especially Porphyry:

> When Plotinus had written anything he could never bear to go over it twice; even to read it through once was too much for him, as his eyesight did not serve him well for reading. In writing he did not form the letters with any regard to appearance or divide his syllables correctly, and he paid no attention to spelling. He was wholly concerned with thought; and, which surprised us all, he went on in this way right up to the end. He worked out his train of thought from beginning to end in his own mind, and then, when he wrote it down, since he had set it all in order in his mind, he wrote as continuously as if he was copying from a book. (Porphyry, *Vit. Plot.* 8.1–13 [Armstrong, LCL])

Plotinus's chief aim was to transfer his thought into the written medium and he did so by hand, just as one might copy a book by hand. He was not concerned with how the writing looked or even if words were spelled correctly, because others would polish the textual object for him. Similarly, when Suetonius claims to have seen poetry written in Nero's hand, he states that the texts were "worked out exactly as one writes when thinking and creating; so many instances were there of words erased or struck through and written above the lines" (Suetonius, *Nero* 52 [Rolfe, LCL]). Both Plotinus and Nero handwrote rough copies.

Their practice would have given fits to Quintilian, who champions elegant handwriting and careful initial composition.[38] In two different passages he emphasizes the importance of handsome penmanship. In the first, Quintilian proposes that training in handwriting ought to begin at the earliest stages of education (Quintilian, *Inst.* 1.1.27–29). Children should begin to develop their handwriting as soon as they can recognize the shapes of letters. They should do so not on a wax tablet, but on a board in which grooved letters have been cut. With a pen, students follow the grooves in the board for practice, which

---

38. In *Inst.* 10.3.17, Quintilian objects to the practice of drafting a whole subject "as rapidly as possible" (*velocissimo volunt*) and editing it subsequently.

strengthens the child's hand and eliminates the necessity of a pedagogue having to guide it.[39]

Quintilian offers the reason that early childhood training in handwriting is essential: not writing legibly results in the "wearisome task" of having to dictate "what we have written to a copyist." He recommends to handwrite legibly "at all times and in all places, and above all when we are writing private letters to our friends" (Quintilian, *Inst.* 1.1.27–29 [Butler, LCL]). Quintilian promotes well-written autographs as his standard and assumes that the "rough draft" of a text is normally handwritten, even if one's handwriting is sloppy.

Quintilian returns to the value of writing carefully by hand at the end of *The Orator's Education* (Quintilian, *Inst.* 10.3.1). He proverbially states, "The pen brings the most labor and the most profit." By "the pen" he means writing *sua manu*. Not only should one write often by hand, but one should frequently revise what has just been written (Quintilian, *Inst.* 10.3.6). Quintilian advises writing slowly and well, revising as one proceeds. Speed will come with time. He concludes with this maxim: "Write quickly and you will never write well, write well and you will soon write quickly" (Quintilian, *Inst.* 10.3.10 [Butler, LCL]). If one takes this route, Quintilian claims, material will not need to be written anew to create the final product, but merely chiseled into shape (Quintilian, *Inst.* 10.3.18).

Quintilian's thoughts on handwriting function as a springboard for his take on dictation, which he describes as "now so fashionable" (Quintilian, *Inst.* 10.3.19–27 [Butler, LCL]). The problems with composition by dictation are manifold. It causes one to rush their thoughts and forsake revision. It produces a crude, unpolished style that smacks of impromptu speaking. If the writer's amanuensis writes slowly then the flow of ideas is interrupted, producing annoyance on the part of the author dictating. Most detrimentally, dictation interrupts privacy, which, for Quintilian, is the fount of accomplished writing. Quintilian recommends handwriting alone and in silence.

---

39. This is remarkably similar to the Montessori method of learning to write using metal insets, which is meant to strengthen children's hands and to help them manage writing instruments (Maria Montessori, *Dr. Montessori's Own Handbook: A Short Guide to Her Ideas and Materials* [Cambridge, MA: Robert Bentley, 1964], 86–92). Quintilian's approval of having children play with ivory letters because "the sight, handling and naming of them is a pleasure" is also similar to the Montessori method of having children trace wooden and sandpaper letters, which, according to Montessori, "The child finds great pleasure in touching" (*Dr. Montessori's Own Handbook*, 93).

The conclusion to be drawn is not that writing by hand was the rule in antiquity. Rather, it was common and used to varying degrees and for varying purposes by varying authors. Quintilian believed that a text should be handwritten at every stage. Some texts in Greco-Roman antiquity were written without dictation playing any part. Others were written without the author ever picking up a pen. Both composition by hand and composition by mouth were normal practices. Some preferred the former, others the latter.

Conclusion

Handwriting played a significant role in composition. This did not encroach on the important role that dictation played. Composition by hand and composition by mouth were both utilized, often in concert with one another. Handwriting was utilized for composition for various reasons, kinds of discourses, and stages in the writing process. Elite letter writers preferred to write personal letters by hand. This was the case at the top of the social ladder, as demonstrated by the correspondence between Cicero and Atticus, as well as Marcus and Fronto. It was also true in the "middle rungs" of the ladder, as suggested by Apion/Maximus's letters, as well as young Theon's. The novels imagine letters being handwritten by their senders. Though Chaereas, Callirhoe, Leucippe, and Cleitophon only handwrite their letters in the narrative world, the authors of these two novels know well the practice and the sentiment attached to autographed missives in the real world. Actual practice informs the imagination.

Writing by hand was not a practice reserved only for composing letters. It was also utilized at various stages in the composition of different kinds of literary texts. Marcus composed speeches and rhetorical exercises in his own hand. The handwriting of many eminent writers was known and remarked upon by various authors, implying that the "final" forms of these discourses were written *sua manu*. This was also the case with Cato's *Origins*, which he handwrote for his son. The Plinys took notes in their own hands, often while engaged in other activities. Horace and Plotinus both took pen and stylus in hand for the initial stages of writing. Finally, Quintilian championed handwriting for every stage of the composition process. Various authors had different preferences for how to compose their texts. Their preferences changed depending on what kind of text they were writing. Some discourses were composed wholly by hand, some wholly by mouth, and some by a combination of the two compositional modes. There is not a clean bifurcation between oral and handwritten composition.

CHAPTER 5

Writing by Mouth

Media Myth: Composition always involved dictation, which was an act of freezing an oral discourse in written form.

Media Reality: Composition was an interplay between writing by hand and by mouth. Even when a text was dictated, the act of inscribing affected the spoken words. Not all forms of writing by mouth were equal and not all should be considered dictation.

◆ ◆ ◆

Plautus's comedy *Bacchides* vividly depicts a letter being composed via dictation. The slave Chrysalus is dictating to Mnesilochus who writes with his friend, Pistoclerus, present. With Chrysalus as ringleader, the group is hatching a plot to defraud Mnesilochus's father of a large sum of money. The scene runs as follows:

Chrysalus: You there (points to Mnesilochus), take the pen and those tablets quickly.
Mnesilochus: (taking them) What next?
Chrysalus: Write there what I'll tell you. I want you to write for the simple reason that your father may recognize your handwriting when he's reading it. Write—
Mnesilochus: (interrupting) What should I write?
Chrysalus:—a hearty greeting to your father in your own words. (Mnesilochus obeys)
Pistoclerus: What if he's writing a greeting of illness and death to him instead? That'll be more to the point.
Chrysalus: Stop interrupting.
Mnesilochus: What's been commanded is already in the wax.
Chrysalus: Tell me how.
Mnesilochus: "Mnesilochus heartily greets his father."
Chrysalus: Add to it quickly: "Chrysalus is reviling me all the time, father, because I returned the money to you and because I didn't cheat you." (Mnesilochus obeys)

Pistoclerus: Wait while he's writing.
Chrysalus: A lover's hand ought to be fast.
Pistoclerus: Faster at wasting money than at writing.
Mnesilochus: Speak. That's written.
Chrysalus: "Now, my father, you should be careful of him. He's coming up with tricks in order to take the money away from you. And he said that he really would take it." Write that down explicitly. (Mnesilochus complies)
Mnesilochus: Just tell me.
Chrysalus: "And he promises he'll give that gold to me so I can give it to prostitutes and eat it up and waste it in Greek style in brothels, father. But, father, mind he doesn't trick you today. Please be careful." (Mnesilochus keeps writing)
Mnesilochus: Speak further.
Chrysalus: Write down—
Mnesilochus: (interrupting) Just tell me what I should write.
Chrysalus: "But, father, I ask you to remember what you promised me: don't beat him. But do guard him at your place at home in fetters." (Mnesilochus finishes, Chrysalus turns to Pistoclerus) Give me the wax and thread immediately, you there. (passes the items on to Mnesilochus) Go on, fasten it and seal it quickly. (Plautus, *Bacchides* 724–55 [de Melo, LCL])

The fictive episode vividly portrays the practice of dictation. It offers rare insight into the process of writing a letter in this manner. The scene hinges on the custom of persons writing missives in their own hand. Mnesilochus is the character who takes Chrysalus's dictation because Mnesilochus's father will recognize his son's letters when he reads them (*pater cognoscat litteras quando legat*). The presumption of the characters and the audience is that Mnesilochus's father will know the letter is written from his son based on his handwriting.

The letter is composed by Mnesilochus. He is the one who puts the stylus to the wax. Though Chrysalus dictates, the "scribe" takes compositional liberties. For example, Mnesilochus writes a greeting in his own words (*salutem tuo patri uerbis tuis*). At points, Chrysalus is exacting in his dictation, commanding Mnesilochus to write the precise words that he speaks. Dictation was a collaborative process between the one dictating and the one taking dictation. At times, the written text reflects precisely what was spoken and at other times it does not.

The imprint of orality is not only left on a dictated text when the words are transcribed exactly as spoken. It is likewise left by the sociality of the event itself.

Writing through another person is a different social experience than writing by hand while alone. The thoughts that are translated into a communicable medium in the act of writing change based on who is present, the speed at which those thoughts are expressed, how they are expressed, how many brains are involved in the act of inscribing the text, and several other factors.

Chrysalus at times speeds up his thinking in the act of dictation, as Mnesilochus prods him to continue speaking. At other times, he slows down his thinking while he waits for his words to be textualized. At one point, Pistoclerus asks Chrysalus to stop speaking while Mnesilochus writes. Sometimes the written words are primarily Chrysalus's; sometimes they are Mnesilochus's. The social circumstances of the event affect what is expressed textually.

This principle is why Quintilian objects to "the luxury of dictation" (Quintilian, *Inst.* 10.3.19 [Russell, LCL]). Writing by hand slows down one's thinking.[1] When dictating, in contrast, the one who is taking dictation might either be "impatient," which results in the author's inability to slow down and carefully craft their words, or they might be a "slow writer or unreliable in understanding," which results in the author losing their train of thought because they are both delayed and annoyed. Quintilian then mentions physical habits of writing that stimulate thought but are embarrassing when another person is present: hand gestures, face contortions, nail biting, and others. The presence of another individual changes what is thought, written, and how it is written. Privacy, "which is lost when we dictate," is vital for accomplished writing, according to Quintilian (Quintilian, *Inst.* 10.3.19 [Russell, LCL]).

The dictation scene from Plautus envisions what composing a letter in this manner might have looked like in antiquity. The fictive account reflects actual composition practices, as the playwright's imagination is animated by reality. The scene, along with Quintilian's writing advice, demonstrates that the sociality of a writing event affects what is produced.

This chapter addresses how the social act of writing by mouth leaves its marks on a discourse. At times these marks are observable in texts themselves, either because the author calls attention to them or because some aspect of the writing reflects dynamics that are characteristic of speaking. The chapter then surveys the situations and purposes for which dictation was utilized. Dictation

---

1. Speaking is approximately ten times faster than writing by hand (Wallace L. Chafe, "Integration and Involvement in Speaking, Writing, and Oral Literature," in *Spoken and Written Language: Exploring Orality and Literacy*, ed. Deborah Tannen, Advances in Discourse Processes 9 [Norwood, NJ: Ablex, 1982], 37).

practices vary from author to author, genre to genre, and text to text. Writing is a complex set of social practices and there are no hard-and-fast rules about when, where, why, and how texts were dictated. But there are patterns as to what kind of discourse was dictated and the effects that dictation had on the written product. Mirroring the structure of the previous chapter, we begin with ancient letters, both from the literary elite and the papyri. We then proceed to other kinds of discourses that were written by mouth. In every case, composing by mouth is a complex interplay between writing and speaking, and the sociality of the writing or speaking event imprints itself on the written discourse that is produced.

Dictating Literary Letters

The previous chapter argued that writing personal letters by hand was common and even preferred if one had the ability to do so. Handwriting possessed sentimental value in antiquity just as it does today. Letter writers made excuses when they dictated. The following are cases of dictated letters that we have already encountered:

- Cicero was nearly fifty years old when he first wrote a non-handwritten letter to Atticus (*Att.* 43). He dictated because he was extraordinarily busy.
- In *De Nepote Amisso* 1.2, Marcus explains that he did not write this letter himself because he had just exited the bath and his hands were shaky.
- In *Ad M. Caes.* 4.9, Fronto updates Marcus on pain in his extremities that prevents him from writing in his own hand (*Denique id ipsum tibi mea manu scribere non potui*).
- Fronto likewise offers his poor health as an excuse for not writing in his own hand in *De Bello Parthico* 10 and *Ad Antoninum Imp.* 1.2.

These all demonstrate that for Cicero, Fronto, and Marcus, as for others who could write by hand, doing so was preferred when it came to this kind of text. They felt the need to excuse letters that were not autographed.

Even though it was preferred that personal missives be handwritten, this was not always the case in practice. Apologizing for and excusing dictation was a trope in letters written by elites. There were four common reasons for dictating letters rather than handwriting them: busyness, convenience, health, and secrecy.[2]

Cicero begins one letter to Atticus by excusing its dictation on account of his busyness: "The very fact that this letter is in a secretary's hand will show you how busy I am" (Cicero, *Att.* 89 [Shackleton Bailey, LCL]).[3] Dictating saved the sender time and so went together with a related excuse for the practice: convenience. In the first letter that Cicero ever dictated to Atticus, he tells Atticus that he dictated the letter while walking (*haec dictavi ambulans*) (Cicero, *Att.* 43 [Shackleton Bailey, LCL]).[4] Marcus likewise dictated while walking because, as he put it, "the wretched state of my body requires that exercise right now" (Marcus Aurelius, *Ad M. Caes.* 5.47 [Haines, LCL]). Dictating allowed the writer to multi-task.

Compromised health was another common reason for dictating a letter rather than writing it by hand. Fronto frequently used this as an excuse, especially as he aged. Ophthalmia, a condition of inflamed eyes that made both reading and writing difficult, was the most common ailment used to excuse dictation.[5] Letter recipients could make assumptions about the state of the sender's health based on whether their letter was handwritten or dictated. Cicero writes that when he received a packet of letters from Atticus, he particularly appreciated those in Atticus's own hand (*quae quidem erant tua manu*) (Cicero, *Att.* 125 [Shackleton Bailey, LCL]). He also welcomed having letters in Atticus's scribe's hand, which so resembled Atticus's own (*ad similitudinem*

---

2. Sometimes the honest excuse was best, as in Cicero, *Att.* 426: "You must not suppose it is out of laziness that I do not write in my own hand—and yet upon my word that is exactly what it is. I can't call it anything else" (text and trans. Shackleton Bailey, LCL).

3. In *Att.* 107, Cicero similarly states that Atticus cannot expect letters regularly to be written in his own hand until he is settled into his new residence and has more leisure time. In *Ep.* 8.9, Pliny the Younger writes to Cornelius Ursus that it has been a long time since he had a book or pen in his hand (*olim non librum in manus, non stilum sumpsi*) on account of being so consumed by his "friends' business" (text and trans, Haines, LCL).

4. He similarly dictates *Quint. fratr.* 23 while walking, informing his brother that he is so busy that he puts nearly everything into his "walking time" (*ambulationis tempus*). On another occasion, *Att.* 110, Cicero dictated a letter to Atticus while on a two-day journey in his carriage.

5. Nicholas Horsfall surveys the effects of ophthalmia on reading and writing practices among the literati in antiquity ("Rome without Spectacles," *Greece & Rome* 42 [1995]: 49–56). See Cicero, *Att.* 163; 206.

tuae), but he begrudged the implication of reading a dictated letter from Atticus. It meant that his friend was not well.[6]

Secrecy was a reason one might choose to dictate. On two occasions, Cicero addresses this phenomenon. He writes about his and Atticus's plan to change their names in confidential correspondence (Cicero, *Att.* 40). He reasons that he can continue to address Atticus as Atticus (and not Furius as previously suggested), but that he, Cicero, would dictate under the name Laelius. If the letter was particularly confidential and at risk of being intercepted, Cicero would neither write by hand nor use his seal. This must have been a relatively common practice, because elsewhere Cicero instructs Atticus to write letters to his friends for him (Cicero, *Att.* 212). If they question Atticus about the seal or handwriting, Cicero advises him to state that he "avoided these on account of the watch" (*Att.* 212 [Shackleton Bailey, LCL]).[7]

But confidentiality cut the other way. Something private might be handwritten rather than dictated so that the secretary would not learn the information the sender was conveying. Cicero stops dictating and handwrites a substantial portion of another letter to Atticus because of its confidential content. He states, "But here I go back to my own hand, for what follows is confidential" (Sed ad meam manum redeo; erunt enim haec occultius agenda) (Cicero, *Att.* 234 [Shackleton Bailey, LCL]). The change in hand and compositional mode is social. The information is for Atticus's eyes only.[8]

This brings up an often-overlooked fact of ancient letters and texts more generally: a single discourse could be composed partially by dictation and partially by hand. Several elite letters call attention to changes in and out of the sender's hand, demonstrating that writing this kind of text was often an interplay between handwriting and dictation.

---

6. The opposite is the case in *Att.* 123, wherein Cicero states that he is encouraged about Atticus's health because he wrote in his own hand.

7. On several occasions in *In Catilinam* (4, 10–11, 12), Cicero recounts how persons are convicted based on their letters, seals, and handwriting (*tabellae, signa, manus*). Similarly, Suetonius recounts how Caligula prostituted several of his sisters and then defamed them by making public their handwritten conspiracy letters. The trope of a person's handwriting convicting them was so ubiquitous that Juvenal can satirically write about the masses being convicted in courts on account of their handwriting (*Sat.* 13).

8. In *Amic.* 402, Brutus alludes to information he wrote to Cicero the previous day in *Amic.* 401. He doesn't mention what that information is, presumably because it is confidential: in the previous letter Brutus informed Cicero that a joke about assassinating Caesar had been attributed to Cicero.

Mass production was a common reason that a letter was not entirely written in a sender's own hand. If a letter was intended for several different recipients, then several copies of it needed to be made. Reproduction was a task relegated to slaves and secretaries. The writer of a letter created the first copy, either by handwriting it or dictating it, and passed it on to be reproduced by one or more persons who served as copiers in human form.

The practices of handwriting personal letters and relegating the copying of mass-produced letters to a secretary were so ubiquitous that Cicero could joke about them at Trebatius's expense. Cicero had received several letters from his friend and comments, "[They are] all very nice, except for one feature, which surprises me: is it not unusual to send several identical letters in one's own handwriting?" (Cicero, *Amic.* 3 [Shackleton Bailey, LCL]). Cicero jests that all the handwritten letters are so similar to one another in content that they look like secretary-made copies of the same letter. Because the relationship between sender and recipient is not at the fore when a letter is sent to multiple persons, it was not expected that such letters be handwritten.[9] If the relationship that the sender had with one or more of the recipients called for it, he or she might append a handwritten subscription to the mass-produced letter.

In a letter to Caelius Rufus, for example, Cicero remarks, "The last little page in your own hand gave me quite a jolt" (*extrema pagella pupugit me tuo chirographo*) (Cicero, *Amic.* 93.3 [Shackleton Bailey, LCL]). In it, Rufus had informed Cicero that the orator Curio, who was formerly a fierce opponent of Caesar, had come out in support of him. This information, not Rufus's handwriting itself, is what causes Cicero's jolt. What was written in Rufus's own hand had resonance to his relationship with Cicero.

Cicero's tone changes when he addresses the handwritten portion of Rufus's letter. Formerly in the letter, Cicero was formulaic and businesslike, but remarking on Rufus's handwritten subscription, he becomes sarcastic and playful: "You don't say so! Curio now standing up for Caesar? Who would have thought it?—except me! For upon my soul, I did think it. Powers above, how I should enjoy a laugh with you!" (Cicero, *Amic.* 93.3 [Shackleton Bailey, LCL]). Rufus's last page has a different social effect than do the previous pages that were presumably dictated and mass-produced. It is handwritten precisely for

---

9. This appears also to have been the case for bureaucratic correspondence. In *Ad M. Caes.* 4.8, Marcus tells Fronto that he just finished dictating thirty letters, presumably of official correspondence.

this reason. The mode of composition changed based on the content written. The mechanics of writing are tied to the sociality of writing.

In another letter to Atticus, Cicero writes about a letter he himself received from Pompey (Cicero, *Att.* 151). The letter contained mass-produced information about military endeavors in Picenum. At the end, Pompey wrote in his own hand to Cicero that he should come to Luceria, which Pompey believed to be the safest place for Cicero. The handwritten portion was information that was particular to Cicero, while what preceded was generalized.

These cases highlight the importance of conveying personal information in one's own hand. It was acceptable to send mass-produced letters or information in a secretary's hand, but it was not as acceptable to address an individual in the scribe's hand.

In these two letters from Cicero, we encounter discourses that were partially handwritten and partially dictated to or copied by a scribe. But we know this only because of Cicero's response to the practice in his own letters. The letters from Cicero are not themselves partially handwritten and partially dictated. They describe letters composed in that manner. There are also several letters that themselves call attention to a change in compositional mode, such as when Cicero handwrites confidential information (Cicero, *Att.* 234). Cicero likewise calls attention to the shift into his own hand for the final paragraph of another letter, using three words: "Hoc manu mea" (this is my hand) (Cicero, *Att.* 299 [Shackleton Bailey], LCL).

Cicero again calls attention to a change in hand in an extraordinarily long letter to his brother, Quintus. The letter was written over a period of approximately two weeks, which we know because he dates several different paragraphs (Cicero, *Quint. fratr.* 21).[10] Toward the end of the long letter, Cicero notes a change to Tiro's hand for a single paragraph (Cicero, *Quint. fratr.* 21.19). He states that he himself wrote the lines that immediately preceded but then dictated to Tiro the present paragraph. While Cicero mentions the change in hand only once, it is conceivable that more than one section of the letter was dictated to Tiro. It is easy to imagine Cicero starting it, walking away from it, having Tiro transcribe some, leaving it, and then coming back to it again.

A similar situation is depicted in a letter from Marcus to Fronto (Marcus Aurelius, *De Fer. Als.* 4). Amid his busyness, Marcus dictates an introductory

---

10. The first date mentioned in the letter is September 10th and the last is September 27th. Cicero himself notes that the letter was written over a long period and that its contents are varied in *Quint. fratr.* 21.23.

paragraph informing Fronto that his daughter has recovered. Marcus then reads a packet of letters from Fronto and addresses his tutor at greater length in his own hand. He mentions that the first paragraph was dictated but does not flag what must have been a change into his own hand in the second. Marcus is confident that Fronto will recognize his hand.

Those at the top of the social ladder knew and utilized mixed modes of composition, even within a single letter. Handwritten personal missives were preferred but reading a letter that was wholly or partially written in a hand that did not belong to the sender was common. Dictation was employed for a variety of reasons and had a social effect on both the writing and the reading of the letter. What is the case at the top of the social ladder is also reflected lower down it, as indicated by papyri letters.

Dictating Papyri Letters

The practice of mixing modes of composition in personal letters was not confined to the likes of Cicero and Pliny. The phenomenon appears in everyday papyri letters. There were three ways a letter might be composed:

1. wholly written in a sender's own hand,
2. wholly dictated to a scribe,
3. partially dictated to a scribe and partially written in the sender's own hand.

P.Brem. 61 contains two of these three modes on a single sheet.[11] It is part of a large cache of letters written to a certain Apollonios, who was a civil administrator in Hermopolis.[12] The document contains three different letters: one from an unnamed sister, one from Apollonios's friend Chairas, and one from his uncle Diskas. The bodies of the first two letters are written in the same hand because they were dictated to the same scribe. Both letters add a greeting in the sender's own hand. As a result, there are three different hands in the first two letters: one is the scribe's and the other two belong to their

---

11. For translation of and commentary on P.Brem. 61, see Roger S. Bagnall and Raffaella Cribiore, *Women's Letters from Ancient Egypt, 300 BC–AD 800* (Ann Arbor: University of Michigan Press, 2009), 142–43.

12. Bagnall and Cribiore, *Women's Letters*, 139. Apollonios and the contacts who wrote to him were upwardly mobile. That is, they were in the upper, though not elite, class.

respective sender. The entirety of the third letter is written in a fourth hand, that of Apollonios's uncle Diskas.[13]

We are left to wonder why Diskas composed in his own hand while Chairas and Apollonios's sister appended handwritten greetings. Based on their fluent hands in the subscriptions, each must have possessed the ability to handwrite their letters. Perhaps Diskas had time to spare and they did not. Whatever the reason for dictating the bulk of their correspondence, each added a personal touch to their dictated letter by appending handwritten well wishes. This is similar to the practice of supplementing a mass-produced letter with handwritten material. Though in these cases the letters are not mass-produced; they are sent to one person and the subscription is much shorter.

Penning handwritten final greetings was not a universal convention, but they do appear often in papyri letters. When there is a change in hand in a letter's final greeting, it can usually be presumed that the body was dictated, and the well-wishes were handwritten. From the same cache of correspondence that contains P.Brem. 61, there are several other examples of letters that are dictated with a handwritten greeting appended. There are also letters written entirely in the sender's hand. Apollonios's mother, Eudaimonis, is the person who composes the most letters in the cache, eleven in total.[14] Eight of her letters were dictated with appended handwritten greetings and three were written entirely in her own hand.[15]

Dictation can be detected when the hands in a letter are varied. If a letter is written in a single hand, it becomes more difficult to determine whether it was handwritten by the sender or dictated. A handsome hand does not always indicate that it is scribal. Handwritten subscriptions from senders are also elegantly written in papyri letters.[16]

---

13. Bagnall and Cribiore, *Women's Letters*, 142.

14. Nine to her son and two to her daughter-in-law, Aline (Bagnall and Cribiore, *Women's Letters*, 139).

15. Bagnall and Cribiore, *Women's Letters*, 139. Eudaimonis's handwritten letters are P.Giss. 22, 23, 24.

16. For example, *BGU* 2.423 and 623, the two letters from Apion/Maximus that I argued in the previous chapter were handwritten by their sender, are handsomely penned. The converse, however, sometimes suggests that the sender wrote themself. If a letter is written with some difficulty, it becomes more likely that it is penned by the sender and not a scribe. Though even in these cases the letter might have been dictated to a friend or family member who was not a fluent writer.

When several letters from a single sender in different hands are extant, it is possible to determine which are handwritten and which are dictated. This is the case with *BGU* 4.1204–1207. Before being used for mummy cartonnage, these four first-century BCE letters were glued side by side.[17] Some are dictated by the sender and some are handwritten. There is no change in hand in any of the individual letters.

All four are sent from Isidoira to her "brother" Asklas. The collection permits direct comparison of letters that were dictated and handwritten. Isidoira handwrote *BGU* 4.1205 and 1206, while 1204 and 1207 were dictated.[18] The content of all four letters is similar and they were written to the same individual in close chronological proximity to one another. Their differences can be pinned to their compositional mode.

Differences emerge from the first word of each letter. In the two handwritten by Isidoira she spells her name "Isidoira" ('Ισιδώιρα) and the recipient's name "Asklas" ('Ασκλᾶτι).[19] In the two letters that are dictated there is variation in the names. The recipient's name is spelled "Asklepiades" ('Ασκληπιάδηι) in both. In *BGU* 4.1207, Isidoira's name is spelled "Isidorai" ('Ισιδώραι), and in 1204 there is a small lacuna at the end of Isidoira's name, so that all that is extant is "Isido" ('Ισιδώ). It is possible that this scribe spelled Isidoira's name as she herself did, "Isidoira," but the lacuna appears to have space only for two letters and so the "proper" spelling of the name, "Isidora" ('Ισιδώρα) is probable.[20]

In the two handwritten letters, Isidoira's initial greetings are nearly identical to one another:

['Ι]σιδώιρα 'Ασκλᾶτι τῶι ἀδελφῶι [χαίρειν] καὶ διὰ παντὸς ὑγιαί[ν]ειν καθάπερ [ε]ὔχομαι. (*BGU* 4.1205)

Isidoira to Asklas her brother, [greetings] and always be well, just as I pray.

---

17. For translation and commentary on all four, see Bagnall and Cribiore, *Women's Letters*, 114–22.

18. This is the conclusion to which Bagnall and Cribiore come based on the letters' hands and styles. The hand in 1205 and 1206 is elegant, though labored. The general style and linguistic characteristics are also the same in both. P.Oxy. 1204 and 1207, in contrast, are written in a fast, business hand with only minor errors and the general air of being professionally composed (Bagnall and Cribiore, *Women's Letters*, 116–19).

19. Text for all four letters is from the Duke Database of Documentary Papyri. Translations are my own. Because I believe Isidoira best knows how to spell her name, I refer to her as such rather than the corrected "Isidora."

20. As indicated by the line immediately below, wherein the lacuna is filled with two letters: χαῖρε[ιν].

Ἰσιδώιρα Ἀσκλᾶτι τῶι ἀδελφῶι χαίρειν καὶ διὰ παντὸς ὑγειαι καθάπερ εὔχομαι.
(*BGU* 4.1206)

Isidoira to Asklas her brother, greetings and always be well, just as I pray.

The only difference between the two is the spelling of "be well" (ὑγιαί[ν]ειν, ὑγειαι). Immediately following the greeting, each handwritten letter confirms that Isidoira received letters from Asklas with the phrase "I have received what you have written" (κεκόμισμαι ἃ ἐγεγράφις).

The dictated letters are slightly different in their initial greetings:

Ἰσιδώ[ρα] Ἀσκληπιάδηι τῶι ἀδελφῶι χαίρε[ιν] κα[ὶ ὑ]γιαίνειν διὰ παντός.
(*BGU* 4.1204)

Isido[ra] to Asklepiades her brother, greetings and be well always.

Ἰσιδώραι Ἀσκληπιάδηι τῶι ἀδελφῶι χαίρειν καὶ ὑγιαίνειν [δι]ὰ παντ[ός]
(*BGU* 4.1207)

Isidorai to Asklepiades her brother, greetings and be well always.

Both move "always" (διὰ παντός) after "be well" (ὑγιαίνειν) so that the two infinitives, "greetings" (χαίρειν) and "be well" (ὑγιαίνειν), are directly paired. Both also remove "just as I pray" (καθάπερ εὔχομαι) from the greeting.[21] Like the handwritten letters, *BGU* 4.1207 confirms that Isidoira has received Asklas's letters immediately following the greeting, though in this case the words are minimally extant. What remains differs slightly from how Isidoira expressed the same information in her handwritten letters. "What you have written" is spelled with the second-person singular ending -εις (ἐγεγράφεις) rather than -ις (ἐγεγράφις) as in the handwritten letters. The verb "I have received" (κεκόμισμαι) also appears to follow the relative clause "what you have written" rather than precede it.[22]

In short, the beginnings of the letters that are handwritten by Isidoira show remarkable consistency with one another in wording and spelling. The same ideas are expressed in the dictated letters, which are stylistically consistent with one another but differ from Isidoira's handwritten letters.

21. The beginning of *BGU* 4.1204 thus reads: Ἰσιδώ[ρα] Ἀσκληπιάδηι τῶι ἀδελφῶι χαίρε[ιν] κα[ὶ ὑ]γιαίνειν διὰ παντός. And the beginning of *BGU* 4.1207 reads: Ἰσιδώραι Ἀσκληπιάδηι τῶι ἀδελφῶι χαίρειν καὶ ὑγιαίνειν [δι]ὰ παντ[ός...]

22. I write "appears" because only the first three letters, κεκ, are extant after ἐγεγράφεις.

This pattern continues in the letters' farewells. The handwritten letters are identical: "And take care of yourself so that you may be well. Goodbye." (καὶ σεατοῦ ἐπειμελοῦ, ἵν' ὑγιαίνης. ἔρρωσο.) The farewells in the dictated letters slightly vary from those of the handwritten letters and from one another. They read:

καὶ σεατοῦ [ἐπιμελοῦ ἵν'] ὑγιαίνης, ὃ δὴ μέγιστόν ἐστι. ἔρρω(σο). (*BGU* 4.1204)

And [take care] of yourself [in order that] you may be well, which is most important. Goodbye.

καὶ τἆλλα σατοῦ δὲ ἐπιμ[ελοῦ] ἵν' ὑ(γιαίνης). ἔρρωσο. (*BGU* 4.1207)

And otherwise, also take care of yourself in order that you might be well. Goodbye.

The stock elements of these letters, whether at their beginnings or their endings, are more consistent when they are handwritten by the sender. When Isidoira dictates these, they show greater variation, either because the scribe has introduced different words or because Isidoira has spoken different words than she wrote.

A similar phenomenon appears in another pair of wholly dictated papyri letters.[23] These letters were, like Apion's/Maximus's first letter addressed in the previous chapter, written from an Egyptian recruit at Misenum to a parent in Egypt. The letters were created on the same day by the same sender and addressed to the same recipient. However, they were written by two different scribes in two different locations. They permit direct comparison of two different persons writing a letter on behalf of another person.

The first letter is written from the Roman port at Ostia, before the recruit, Apollinarius, makes the trip to nearby Rome to receive his military assignment.[24] Apollinarius has written through an amanuensis, as it is written in two different hands. The change in hand does not occur at the final greetings, which we might expect if the sender were to personalize the letter. Rather, after

---

23. P.Mich. 8.490 and 491.
24. P.Mich. 8.490; text in what follows is from the Duke Database of Documentary Papyri (http://papyri.info/ddbdp/p.mich;8;490).

the letter was composed, Apollinarius learned his assignment was at Misenum and had someone append this information to the already-written letter.[25]

Apollinarius's second letter was written on the same day as the first. The letter is written in a different hand and differs from the first letter in style and spelling throughout.[26] Whereas the two handwritten letters from Apion/Maximus addressed in the previous chapter and those from Isidoira in this chapter demonstrate similarities in their use of letter-writing conventions, these dictated letters from Apollinarius vary markedly with respect to these conventions and the spelling of significant words.

The initial greeting (πολλὰ χαίρειν; many greetings) is identical in both letters, but the health wishes and thanksgivings that follow the greetings differ. The second letter follows standard conventions with the phrase "before all else I pray for your health" (πρὸ μὲν πάντων εὔχομαί σε ὑγειαίνειν). The first letter, in contrast, contains a non-standard sentence (πρὸ παντὸς ἔρρωσό μοι ὑγιαίνουσα). It is "an ungrammatical blending of the [standard] opening and closing wish."[27] The conventional conclusions of the two letters also differ from one another as well, the first ending with "farewell and good health" (ἔρρωσό μοι ὑγιαίνουσα) and the second with "I pray for your health" (ἐρρῶσθαί σε εὔχομαι).

Several names occur in both letters but are spelled differently, as was also the case with Isidoira's letters. The recipient's name, Taesis, ends with an omega in the first letter and a non-subscripted iota in the second (Ταησίῳ, Ταήσι). The second letter appends "lady" (κυρίᾳ) to the title mother, which is spelled differently in the two letters (μητρί, μητρεί). The writer greets Karalas and his children in both letters, but the name is spelled "Kalalas" in the first. Finally, Apollinarius makes a request for a letter about his mother's and siblings' health in the middle of both letters, but in wholly different words.

Two conclusions follow from Apollonarius's and Isidoira's dictated letters. First, the means of composition affects the written product. This can be for the better or the worse. In the case of Isidoira's letters, one might suggest that the dictated letters are "better written" because they contain fewer misspellings

25. It is possible that the second hand is Apollonarius's own. However, it is more likely that it is the hand of another scribe and that Apollonarius is grapho-illiterate. If he could write and appended this information himself, we might expect him also to handwrite a greeting to his mother in one or both of the letters.

26. Text in what follows is from the Duke Database of Documentary Papyri (http://papyri.info/ddbdp/p.mich;8;491). Trans. my own.

27. J. G. Winter, "In the Service of Rome: Letters from the Michigan Collection of Papyri," *CP* 22 (1927): 241.

and follow prescriptive grammar more closely than those that are handwritten. However, the handwritten letters appear to express Isidoira's thought in a less-mediated manner than do the dictated letters. The scribes who write Isidoira's and Apollonarius's letters introduce their own thought into the text. This is the result of two minds being involved in the composition process.

The second conclusion follows from this: composing via dictation, as a social act, does not freeze one's thoughts in written form or provide unmediated access to the speaker's words. The fact of another person being involved in the composition process means that a dictated text is mediated. This mediation comes in degrees. A dictated text can more or less represent the author's spoken words. There are occasions when a text is dictated and reflects the author's words nearly verbatim.

Two final papyri texts exemplify how a document can closely represent the words that the author spoke in the process of dictating: P.Oxy. 56.3860 and P.Oxy. 903.[28] A man named Alexandros penned the former, a long fourth-century letter, from the spoken words of a woman named Taesis. Alexandros's identity peeks through the letter in the final greetings, where he states, "I Alexandros wore myself out writing this letter" (καὶ ἀπεκάκησα ἐγὼ ὁ Ἀλέξανδρος γράφων σοι τὰς ἐπιστολάς).[29] This letter was dictated in its entirety, as there is no greeting appended in Taesis's own hand.[30]

Bagnall and Cribiore judge that the task of writing was so exhausting for Alexandros because he was not a fluent writer.[31] Both his comment and rugged hand suggest as much. As a slow writer, Alexandros was not able to take Taesis's dictation and alter her prose. The result is that we are "hearing Taesis almost unvarnished."[32] It is a rare case in which the text's dictation is confirmed and the scribal intervention was minimal.

---

28. Text from the Duke Database of Documentary Papyri (http://papyri.info/ddbdp/p.oxy;56;3860). For English translation and commentary, see Bagnall and Cribiore, *Women's Letters*, 378–79.

29. Trans. Bagnall and Cribiore, *Women's Letters*, 378.

30. It is rare for the identity of the writer to come through a dictated letter, but this does happen on occasion. Another case is P.Mich. 8.482, a second-century letter in which the sender states that Peteeus greets the recipient, his wife, and his horse named Bassos. Because the first five lines of the letter are missing, Bassos the horse and Peteeus the human are the only named individuals that appear in the letter as we have it.

31. Bagnall and Cribiore, *Women's Letters*, 379. Indeed, as they state, there are sixty-five errors in the 390-word letter.

32. Bagnall and Cribiore, *Women's Letters*, 379.

What characterizes the letter stylistically is of great interest: parataxis accomplished by frequent use of καί, the almost total absence of δέ, direct discourse following "that" (ὅτι), and unique vocabulary.[33] These features also characterize other unpolished dictated papyri letters in which the "secretaries were not able or did not care to alter significantly the words that they heard."[34] Letters of this sort are "tinged with the colors of everyday speech."[35]

But it is not only letters that could be characterized by everyday speech as a result of transcription. This is also the case with early drafts of some petitions. Benjamin Kelly offers a two-stage model of composition for these official documents in Roman Egypt.[36] The petitioner first offered an oral account to a scribe or group of scribes who then reduced the spoken version to a formal, written petition. Kelly notes deletion and interlinear additions in nonliterary papyri are revelatory of this process.[37]

A text of this sort that Kelly does not mention is P.Oxy. 903. This is an affidavit spoken by an unnamed wife against her abusive husband. It contains supralinear additions and reads as a breathless account of a woman who is rightly fed up with her abuser. Like Taesis's letter addressed immediately above, the petition is characterized by parataxis accomplished by καί, infrequency of δέ, short idea units, and direct discourse following ὅτι.

Taesis's letter and this woman's petition are instructive in a similar respect: they both offer the unique combination of being created from an oral event, possessing narrativity, and only lightly being modified in their written form. They provide samples of oral narrative transmitted in the textual mode. As we shall see in the next chapter, the linguistic features that these two texts share with one another are the very ones that characterize the Gospel of Mark.[38]

---

33. Bagnall and Cribiore, *Women's Letters*, 379.

34. Bagnall and Cribiore, *Women's Letters*, 61.

35. Bagnall and Cribiore, *Women's Letters*, 61–62. Bagnall and Cribiore note the following women's letters that fall into this category: P.Abinn. 34; P.Oxy. 6.932; P.Mert. 2.82; P.Yale 1.77; P. Mich. 8.473.

36. Benjamin Kelly, *Petitions, Litigation, and Social Control in Roman Egypt* (Oxford: Oxford University Press, 2011) 42–45.

37. Kelly, *Petitions*, 44n29. He specifically notes BGU 4.1139 and BL 8.42.

38. Worth forwarding here is the volume of "and" (καί) in the letter. It appears 41 times in the letter out of a total 380 words, which is 10.8% of the total words or once for every 9.3 words. This frequency is consistent with other paratactically structured texts and with what sociolinguists find is normal for spoken narrative.

Dictating Literary Compositions

Letters could be composed by hand, dictation, or a mixture of the two. How a letter was composed affected the textual product. For the elite, dictating a personal letter usually required an excuse. Busyness, convenience, poor health, and confidentiality were the most common. On several occasions, senders apologized not only because their letters were dictated and less personal, but also because they were shorter than usual on account of being dictated. In papyri letters, scribes introduce their own words and thoughts into a letter to varying degrees. Dictation was not an act of freezing spoken words in written form. There are occasions when the written text closely represents the words that are spoken. More often, the thoughts and words of the speaker are mixed with the thoughts and words of the writer. And while dictation was usually intentional, written discourses could also be unintentionally written by mouth. In these cases, an oral discourse was textualized, but the speaker lost authorial control over what was textualized.

As an advocate for careful composition and handsome penmanship, Quintilian disapproved of dictation. He disparages the practice twice in the *The Orator's Education*. The first time he recommends writing slowly and carefully. Failing to do so results in ill-formed writing that is unintelligible and "produces a second laborious stage of dictating what needs to be copied out" (unde sequitur alter dictandi quae transferenda sunt labor) (Quintilian, *Inst.* 1.1.28–29 [Russell, LCL]). Quintilian's objection to dictation is personal. He finds using dictation to edit and create a well-penned copy of a discourse to be laborious. His demurral reveals one of the primary purposes of dictation: to create a clean copy of a text. In this scenario the discourse is handwritten and then dictated. Writing by hand and by mouth are utilized in concert, but the latter can be avoided if one writes well and neatly from the beginning of the process.

The second time Quintilian disparages dictation his issue is not with it at the end of the composition process, but at its beginning (Quintilian, *Inst.* 10.3.19–21). Quintilian criticizes those who create an entire draft as quickly as possible, calling it their "raw material" (*silvam*) that they will revise.[39] His denunciation of this practice transitions into his take on composing via dictation, which he calls a "luxury" (*deliciis*). Because a scribe at times stymies one's flow of thought and at other times expedites it, "what pours out is not

---

39. The process is described by Porphyry in *Vit. Plot.* 8.1–13. He states that Plotinus wrote in precisely this manner.

only unpolished and casual, but sometimes off the point" (Quintilian, *Inst.* 10.3.20 [Russell, LCL]).

Horace held a similar position on composing via dictation, at least as the method was utilized by his satiric predecessor Lucilius: "Often in an hour, as though a great exploit, he would dictate two hundred lines while standing, as they say, on one foot. In his muddy stream there was much that you would like to remove. He was wordy, and too lazy to put up with the trouble of writing—of writing correctly, I mean; for as to quantity, I let that pass" (Horace, *Sat.* 1.4.5–13 [Fairclough, LCL]). Lucilius's dictation is careless. The number of lines he composed in a single hour and the hyperbolic statement that he dictated "standing on one foot" is lampoon. Horace is unimpressed by the quantity of Lucilius because of its poor quality.

Both Quintilian and Horace object to composing new material via dictation because it diminishes the style of the written product. Per Horace, Lucilius's hasty dictation created a "muddy" (*lutulentus*) product that should have been more thoroughly edited. Quintilian claims that composing via dictation created an unpolished, casual, and off point discourse (*udia tantum et fortuita, sed inpropria interim*).

Their objections to dictation reveal several things. First, composing via dictation could result in a particular style and that style was stigmatized. Composing in this manner didn't always result in an "oral style," however. One could dictate carefully and avoid such infelicities. Stylistic disfluencies were revised in the editorial process. Nonetheless, both Horace and Quintilian associate hasty dictation with an inelegant textual product.

Second, dictation was used in various stages of the writing process. It was both an editing and compositional tool. There was not one single purpose for dictation.

Third, authors composed and edited discourses via dictation. Quintilian's and Horace's preferences indicate that there were options when it came to creating and revising written discourses.

That writers other than Quintilian or Horace utilized dictation in the composition process is not to suggest that these authors did not also write by hand. Writing by hand and writing by mouth were not exclusive to one another. Both compositional modes could be utilized in the production of a single text. An author could at times compose a discourse by hand and at other times compose a different discourse by mouth. Authors had their preferred practices but were not bound to one method of composition each time they composed, and they had different compositional practices for different kinds of texts.

This is on display in Dio's eighteenth discourse, which is concerned with training for public speaking. The most relevant portion reads as follows:

> Writing, however, I do not advise you to engage in with your own hand, or only very rarely, but rather to dictate to a secretary. For, in the first place, the one who utters his thoughts aloud is more nearly in the mood of a man addressing an audience than is one who writes, and, in the second place, less labour is involved. Again, while it contributes less to effectiveness in delivery than writing does, it contributes more to your habit of readiness. But when you do write, I do not think it best for you to write these made-up school exercises; yet if you must write, take one of the speeches that you enjoy reading, preferably one of Xenophon's, and either oppose what he said, or advance the same arguments in a different way. (Dio Chrysostom, *Discourse* 18.19–20 [Cohoon, LCL])

The passage is sometimes taken as evidence that dictation was the normal compositional mode in antiquity.[40] However, Dio indicates that the statesperson-in-training had the ability either to dictate or write *sua manu* and did both. For Dio in this passage, dictation is preferable not in and of itself, but for training in public eloquence. It gets one "in the mood of a man addressing an audience" and is less laborious. Dictation is recommended for a particular purpose and kind of text.

Pliny the Younger also composed a certain kind of text via dictation. He implies that he writes his hendecasyllables orally in informal settings. He describes these as a set of disconnected passages. Their contents vary: "Here are my jokes and witticisms, my loves, sorrows, complaints and vexations; now my style is simple, now more elevated, and I try through variety to appeal to different tastes and produce a few things to please everyone" (Pliny the Younger, *Ep.* 4.14 [Radice, LCL]). The verses were characterized by frivolity and were created in spontaneous settings. Pliny writes that they are what he amuses himself with when he has spare time in his carriage, bath, or at dinner.

---

40. Paul J. Achtemeier, "*Omne Verbum Sonat*: The New Testament and the Oral Environment of Late Western Antiquity," *JBL* 109 (1990): 12–13; Yoon-Man Park, *Mark's Memory Resources and the Controversy Stories (Mark 2:1–3:6): An Application of the Frame Theory of Cognitive Science to the Markan Oral-Aural Narrative* (Leiden: Brill, 2010), 47.

That Pliny composes these while engaged in other activities suggests that they are dictated.[41]

Pliny remarks further on his hendecasyllables elsewhere, stating that they were composed "whenever [he] had time, especially when traveling." He offers information about the reading events that the hendecasyllables made for, claiming, "They are read and copied, they are even sung, and set to the cithara or lyre by Greeks who have learned Latin out of liking for my little book" (Pliny the Younger, *Ep.* 7.4 [Radice, LCL]). Different compositional scenarios were utilized for different kinds of texts that in turn made for different kinds of reading events.

In another frequently cited passage, Pliny details his literary routine during his summers in Tuscany (Pliny the Younger, *Ep.* 9.36). Dictation is again the compositional mode, but the setting is different than when he writes his hendecasyllables. The day begins with Pliny lying in the dark, privately working out his thoughts in his head. He then calls his secretary, opens the shutters to let light in, and dictates what has been formed mnemonically. In a second letter written to the same individual, Pliny confirms that his routine scarcely changes during his winters in Laurentum (Pliny the Younger, *Ep.* 9.40). The only modification is that after dinner he sometimes forgoes listening to comedy or music and instead revises what was dictated earlier in order to fix it in his memory. Pliny hints that court speeches are the kind of text dictated, which he works on "if [he has] an urgent case pending" (si agendi necessitas instat) (Radice, LCL).

For two different kinds of texts, dictation played a prominent role in Pliny's composition process. Pliny also handwrote notes and extracts. While he does not indicate that he revises his dictated texts by hand, this is likely since editing *sua manu* was common and memorially effective. Pliny utilized multiple methods of composition.

Several centuries later, Jerome indicates that some of his discourses were dictated. He reflects on two texts composed in this manner at their conclusions. These are rare occasions when an author states how a text was composed.

---

41. Similarly, when Horace remarks on the masses composing verse, he states that they do so while supping: "The fickle public has changed its taste and is fired throughout with a scribbling craze; sons and grave sires sup crowned with leaves and dictate their lines" (Horace, *Ep.* 2.1.108–9 [Fairclough, LCL]). Horace notes that he also composes verses, though he appears to begin the composition by hand. Before sunrise he calls for "pen, paper, and writing-case" (calamum et chartas et scrinia).

164 • *Writing*

Though they are written later than most of the texts addressed in this book, Jerome's letters reveal how composing via dictation can affect a text. They also suggest that composing wholly by dictation was not standard practice.

Concluding the first dictated letter, Jerome states:

> I dictated this letter, talking quickly, in the space of one short night, wishing to satisfy a friend's earnest request and to try my hand, as it were, upon a scholastic subject—for that same morning my visitor, who was on the point of departure, knocked at my door—and at the same time, wishing to show my detractors that I too can say the first thing that comes into my head. I therefore introduced few quotations from the Scriptures and did not interweave my discourse with its flowers, as I have done in my other books. I extemporized as I went, and by the light of one small lamp poured forth my words in such profusion, that my tongue outstripped my secretaries' pens and my volubility baffled the tricks of their shorthand. I say this that those who make no excuses for lack of ability may make some for lack of time. (Jerome, *Ep.* 117.12 [Wright, LCL])

The text was not simply dictated. It was dictated quickly and was minimally edited. By calling attention to how the letter was composed, Jerome indicates that this was not his normal way of writing. One result of his hasty dictation is that Scripture is sparingly quoted. This is confirmed in the letter itself, which quotes biblical texts on only four occasions and in short snippets of no more than a sentence.[42]

The second dictated letter is a biography of Marcella written to Principia. In the closing paragraph, Jerome states that he "dictated in the wakeful hours of one short night" and thus "used no charms of eloquence" (Jerome, *Ep.* 127.14 [Wright, LCL]). The compositional mode serves as an excuse should Principia find the text less than eloquent. With respect to Scriptural quotations, there are many more in this letter than in the former, though the quotations are typically short in both.[43]

---

42. Psalm 69:12 in *Ep.* 117.1; Prov 10:9 in *Ep.* 117.4; Rom 12:17 in *Ep.* 117.4; Jer 3:3 at *Ep.* 117.9. In *Ep.* 117.9 Jerome alludes to the stain that cannot be washed from Jer 2:22 but does not quote the text.

43. In *Ep.* 127.11 Jerome combines Ps 104:29 with Ps 146:4. It appears that in both *Ep.* 117 and 127 Jerome mnemonically recalls passages rather than engaging them with physical texts.

In conclusion, dictation played a role in ancient writing, but not the only role. It is mistaken to claim that all or most texts were composed via dictation. Dictation was one tool utilized in the composition process and there were no standardized practices for how, when, and why it was employed. Different authors had different preferences for different kinds of texts.

Texts Derived from Oral Events

In this chapter I have used the term "dictation." With dictation there is intention in the composition process. The primary purpose of dictating is to textualize a discourse. The sociality of these writing events bends toward creating a text. But there is another way that a text can be written by mouth. This is when an oral discourse happens to become textualized but the primary purpose of the oral event was not to create a text. In these cases, the sociality of the events bends toward oral communication.

In chapter 3 we observed occasions of oral events standing behind written texts. When this happens, the two can relate to each other in various ways. Sometimes the written document closely matches the content and wording of the event and other times it does not. An author had varying levels of control over texts that were composed from antecedent oral discourses. At times, the textual version is meant to be circulated by the person involved in the event. At other times, the text is "accidentally published" or attributed to a person who did not write its content.[44]

Galen notes that certain discourses were textualized from oral predecessors.[45] He draws attention to texts written in this manner both in their prefaces and in *On My Own Books* and *On the Order of My Own Books*. Galen's purpose

---

44. "Accidental publication" is a term I use following Matthew D. C. Larsen (*Gospels before the Book* [Oxford: Oxford University Press, 2018]. 37–57). Accidental publication can happen whether or not a text was composed from an oral event. Moreover, a text can be composed from an oral event without being accidentally published. The phenomenon and its applicability to the gospels are addressed at greater length in part 3 of this book.

45. We have already had several occasions to observe Galen's texts. I wish to offer the reminder that Galen's compositional practices were not necessarily normative. Not all texts in antiquity were composed as Galen's were. Nor did Galen compose all his texts the same way. Galen is quite clear that his different kinds of texts were composed, edited, published, and used in different kinds of ways. He states explicitly at the beginning of *The Order of My Own Books* that his texts "do not all have the same purpose, function, or subject matter" (P. N. Singer, trans., *Galen: Selected Works*, The World's Classics [Oxford: Oxford University Press], 1997, 49).

in *On My Own Books* is to catalog his works and describe their respective composition scenarios. He does so because his ideas were regularly plagiarized and his name was attributed to texts that he did not produce. Galen offers the reason that some of his texts were "published by many people under their own names" (Galen, *On My Own Books*, 10K).[46] He gave incomplete, uncorrected versions to friends and pupils. He had no intention of making them public, but they were leaked.

These texts were written up for individuals "who had desired a written record of lectures that they had attended" (Galen, *On My Own Books* 10K).[47] After the leaked versions were discovered, they were returned to Galen. He corrected them, gave them proper titles, and published them. Galen states this is how *Bones for Beginners, The Pulse for Beginners*, a text on veins and arteries and another on nerves, and the *Outline of Empiricism* were all produced.[48]

In *On My Own Books* 14–15, Galen offers a similar origin for an unnamed text. An agonistic speech against Martialius was textualized. Galen was speaking on a medical topic that was randomly chosen. He refuted many of Martialius's positions on the topic, and a friend who also opposed Martialius wanted a written version of the speech. Galen obliged and the friend sent a scribe trained in shorthand to textualize it. Galen knew that a text was being created, but he was not engaged in a writing project.

This is how many of Galen's other leaked discourses were produced. He writes in *On My Own Books* 11 that such texts were either "dictated to young men at the beginning of their studies, or in some cases presented to friends at their request."[49] Because these are not shaped by the writing process, Galen acknowledges that they were dogged by various inadequacies. Some were too

---

46. Trans. Singer, *Galen*, 3. In addition to the Greek text from Karl Gottlob Kühn, ed., *Claudii Galeni opera omnia*, vol. 19 (Leipzig: Car. Cnoblochii, 1830), there is Georg Helmreich, Johannes Marquardt, and Iwani Müller, *Claudii Galeni pergameni scripta minora*, vol. 3 (Leipzig: Teubner, 1891).

47. Trans. Singer, *Galen*, 3.

48. Galen remarks further on the origins of *Empiricism in Medicine* in *On My Own Books* 17K (Singer, *Galen*, 7). He states that the origin of the work was a two-day debate between two doctors, Pelops and Philip. Galen transcribed the arguments of both doctors as an exercise for himself. The text was meant for Galen's own private consumption, but somehow came to leave his possession. In this case, the genesis of the text is an oral event, but the thought that is textualized is not Galen's; it is Pelops's and Philip's. The case is similar with his Hippocratic commentaries, which he states were notes completed as an exercise for himself.

49. Trans., Singer, *Galen*, 4.

long; some were too short. Their content was incomplete and their style inferior. They were suitable for their purpose, which was to provide Galen's pupils textualized information, but they were not suitable for public consumption (Galen, *On My Own Books* 10–11K).

They were shaped more by the social context of speaking than the social context of writing. That was the root of their inadequacy. By speaking the discourses and not altering them textually, Galen lost control over the minutiae of their content and style. When the texts came back into his possession, he regained that control and was able to improve the written versions. For Galen, a book needs to be "properly completed" (τὸ τελέως ἐξειργάσθαι) to be ready for public release (Galen, *On My Own Books* 13K).[50] Discourses that happened to become textualized were not properly completed.

Composing a text from an antecedent oral event was not always a concession for Galen. There are occasions when a written text had its roots in an oral event and the discourse was properly completed. Such is the case with *Affections and Errors* and *Thrasybulus*. At the beginning of each Galen states that their genesis was oral.

Affections and Errors begins with a brief preface before jumping into the subject matter *in medias res:* "You ask to have in note form, too, the reply I made to the question you put to us regarding Antonius the Epicurean's book, *Control of One's Particular Affections*; I shall now make you one, and I put this as its beginning."[51] Galen specifically designates the text as in "note form" (ὑπομνήματα). This word can also be translated "reminders," "memory aids," or simply "notes." While it has a wide semantic range and can refer to a variety of kinds of texts, it is frequently used of discourses that have a foot in both the oral and the written lifeworld.[52] As P. N. Singer puts it, "Such notes may be taken to remind one of what was said, or to assist one when making a speech or demonstration in the future."[53] *Affections and Errors* is an example of the

50. Trans., Singer, *Galen*, 5.
51. P. N. Singer, "The Diagnosis and Treatment of the Affections and Errors Peculiar to Each Person's Soul," in P. N. Singer, Daniel Davies, and Vivian Nutton, eds., *Galen: Psychological Writings* (Cambridge: Cambridge University Press, 2014), 237.
52. The semantic range of the term ὑπομνήματα is addressed at greater length in Nicholas A. Elder, *The Media Matrix of Early Jewish and Christian Narrative*, LNTS 612 (London: T&T Clark, 2019), 43–47.
53. P. N. Singer, general introduction to *Galen: Psychological Writings*, ed. P. N. Singer, Daniel Davies, and Vivian Nutton (Cambridge: Cambridge University Press, 2014), 16.

former kind of "memory aid." It is a text written as a reminder of what was said during an oral event.

Thrasybulus has a preface that is similar to the one in *Affections and Errors*. Galen begins the work noting the continuity between what he has written in the treaty and what he has already told Thrasybulus orally: "My arguments in what follows, Thrasyboulos, will be exactly the same as those I gave verbally when you set me this question. As you will be aware, if the subject is the same my treatment of it is the same; and I never advance an argument without knowledge of—and practice in—the method relevant to that argument."[54] Neither *Affections and Errors* nor *Thrasybulus* is composed directly from the oral event on which they are based. Rather, they are written as a reflection of those events. Galen has distance from the events and a greater level of control over the texts produced.

Oral events stand behind Galen's written texts in varying ways. A text could be composed from Galen's spoken words. This was no problem if the texts were used for their intended purpose and audience. Issues arose when works composed in this manner reached a wide audience because Galen had not written them for public consumption. At other times, Galen composed a text on the basis of an antecedent oral event and was prepared to circulate it. At still other times, no event at all stood behind a text.

Like Galen, Quintilian experienced his ideas being prematurely released in written form. Also like Galen, the ideas that stood behind Quintilian's incomplete texts were first presented as oral lectures. In the dedication of *The Orator's Education*, Quintilian informs the work's dedicatee, Marcus Vitorius, that it is of utmost importance that he, Quintilian, carefully compose the text from its beginning through its ending. Given Quintilian's remarks on careful composition, it is likely that he handwrote and edited most of the text himself.

Careful composition is urgent because two books on the same topic were already circulating in Quintilian's name (Quintilian, *Inst.* 1.pref.7 [Russell, LCL]). These contain his ideas, but they were not prepared for publication. Oral lectures stand behind both books, which were textualized from the events. The first was a two-day lecture event that was transcribed by slaves. The second was offered over the course of several days, taken down by shorthand (*notando*), and rashly published by those who did so.

In both of the books, the ideas are Quintilian's but he had little control over how they were presented because he was not directly involved in the

---

54. Trans., Singer, *Galen*, 53.

writing process. Since the second book was written via shorthand, many of the words are likely Quintilian's, but they are his words as spoken in a certain social context and not as he would write them.

In its preface, Quintilian affirms that *The Orator's Education* has continuity with the two rashly published works and by extension the lecture events on which they were based. However, it also differs from these books. He writes, "In the present work, therefore, there will be some things the same, many things changed, and very many things added, and the whole will be better written and worked up to the best of my ability" (Quintilian, *Inst.* 1.pref.8 [Russell, LCL]). Regaining control over the written material, Quintilian is able to present it in its proper form.

Quintilian's first two books on rhetoric were written by mouth from an oral event, but they were neither dictated nor edited. Impoverished style and content resulted. By working with the texts physically, Quintilian improved them. Quintilian's own written version corresponds to the previously released books but is expanded and better written.

With both Galen and Quintilian an oral lecture is textualized and released apart from the author's authority. That both had such experiences on multiple occasions indicates such experiences were common. This is confirmed by Horace's satirical allusion to the phenomenon (Horace, *Sat.* 2.4).[55] In the text, the narrator encounters a certain Catius, who has just attended a lecture on best practices in food preparation. Catius is rushing home to write down the important gastronomical rules that he has just heard. The satire is laid on thick, as Catius supposes these principles will surpass both Pythagoras's and Plato's in importance (Horace, *Sat.* 2.4.3–4). Catius further notes that it will be difficult to hold the entire lecture in his memory because "it was a subtle theme handled in subtle style" (Horace, *Sat.* 2.4.3–4 [Fairclough, LCL]). When asked who it was that gave such an excellent lecture, Catius refuses to identify his "authority" (*auctor*). Rather, he recites the culinary rules from memory.

Matthew D. C. Larsen notes that for the parody to land, the reader must know several things about Horace's satirical imagination, including "the regularity of an enthusiastic student or lecture-auditor writing down entire lectures."[56] Horace's satire assumes the ubiquity of what Galen and Quintilian experienced. Oral events were textualized without the author's knowledge.

---

55. I am dependent on Larsen, *Gospels before the Book*, 43–45 for this reference.
56. Larsen, *Gospels before the Book*, 44.

Two other elements of Horace's satirical imagination are noteworthy. First, Catius is taciturn about the lecturer's identity. This could be because he wants to pass off the culinarian's principles as his own or because he wants to honor him with a written version of the lecture. Second, Catius attempts to hold the subtle topic and style in his memory. He intends to reproduce the oral event as precisely as he can. The written version is meant to match the corresponding oral lecture.

The details of Horace's encounter with Catius are secondary to the satire's purpose, which is to mock the unnamed culinary savant.[57] Much like the novels and comedies, Horace's satire depends on a real practice to establish a scene. The practice is an individual hearing a lecture and attempting to reproduce it textually either to bolster their own reputation or the lecturer's.

For Horace, Quintilian, and Galen, creating a text from an oral event, while not dictating it, was a regular occurrence. The speaker was not directly involved in physically inscribing the words, at least initially. The ideas and style contained in the written text reflected what was spoken to differing degrees. This does not mean that the text was prepared for public release. It usually meant the opposite: the discourse was not ready for publication because it bore the marks of its oral context rather than the marks of the composition process. The written version of the oral discourse could return to an author, be reworked, and properly completed. It could also continue to exist in its unfinished form.

Conclusion

Writing by mouth was neither a simple nor a singular practice. It was not used to the exclusion of handwriting. A text could be wholly handwritten, wholly dictated, partially dictated and partially handwritten, or written down as a more or less verbatim transcription of an antecedent oral event. The last of these is not the same as dictating a text. Writing by mouth was a complex set of practices that affected the written product in various ways.

To conclude this chapter, I offer nine different observations about writing by mouth that have resulted from it:

---

57. Based on *Sat.* 2.2, 2.4, and 2.6, Deena Berg identifies the gourmand as Nasidienus Rufus, who is ultimately critiqued as "a windbag, whose misguided philosophy, self-important style, and eagerness to impress elicit revulsion and teasing, instead of respect and friendship" ("The Mystery Gourmet of Horace's 'Satires 2,'" *CJ* 91 [1995]: 141–51).

1. Dictation was employed both in place of and in conjunction with writing by hand.
2. Writing by mouth introduces another person's thoughts, words, and style into a discourse.
3. Some writers objected to dictation altogether, especially when it was used to create new material.
4. Despite these objections, authors dictated during the writing process for various reasons.
5. One of the most common reasons was to create a final, clean copy of a text.
6. A text that is written by mouth may or may not represent the words that were spoken.
7. Dictation, especially when done hastily, could result in inelegant writing.
8. A dearth of quotations of antecedent texts could be excused by hasty dictation.
9. Texts that were written from an antecedent oral event and not emended by their speaker could be considered incomplete with respect to their content and style.

These are not criteria by which one can scientifically evaluate "oral influence" on a written text. It would be a misapplication to use these observations as a plug-and-play method for assessing a given text's compositional mode. Nonetheless, assessing compositional influences on a written discourse is productive. Because writing, including its mechanics, is a social affair, it is worthwhile to examine the circumstances that might stand behind a written text. At times, it can be concluded that a text was orally composed or written from a spoken event. Such conclusions are easier to draw when the author themself states as much.

For the majority of ancient literature, however, authors do not indicate how their texts were composed. This is the case with the canonical gospels. There are no direct statements in Matthew, Mark, Luke, or John about how they were written, whether by mouth, by hand, or by some combination of the two. But this does not mean that their compositional influences cannot be probed.

CHAPTER 6

Writing the Gospels

Media Myth: The gospels were all written using the same compositional practices.
Media Reality: The gospels were composed using a variety of compositional practices.

❖ ❖ ❖

Different authors composed different kinds of texts in different ways. The gospels are all different kinds of texts from one another. Matthew refers to itself as a "book," Mark as a "gospel," Luke as an "account," and John as a "document." We should not expect the canonical gospels to demonstrate identical compositional influences. This chapter argues that they do not.

Mark was composed by mouth from antecedent oral events. It is saturated with oral residues. The gospel underwent minimal literary correction. The later Synoptics betray different compositional influences than Mark. Matthew and Luke each reflect written psychodynamics, a style characteristic of written narrative in comparison to spoken. They were carefully composed literary documents. Handwriting and revision were involved in their compositional processes. They remove Mark's residual orality in their reuse of the text and do not contain a preponderance of oral characteristics in their shared and unique materials. John stylistically stands alone. It does not correspond to either the prominently oral style of Mark or the literary style of Matthew and Luke. The Fourth Gospel introduces new semantics for written Jesus traditions.

Mark

From its outset, the Gospel of Mark declares its relationship to oral Jesus traditions with the phrase "the gospel of Jesus Christ." The term "gospel" (εὐαγγέλιον) possessed expressly oral connotations until the author designated their written text with the word. The Gospel of Mark textualized Jesus traditions that were previously experienced as oral traditions.

Mark may not have been the first written Jesus tradition. Francis Watson writes, "It is often claimed that communication within the first-century

Greco-Roman world was overwhelmingly oral, that only an elite minority were able to engage with written texts, and that prior to Mark traditions about Jesus were handed down through exclusively oral media. Such claims are entirely misleading."[1] Watson then insists that there must have been an interplay between orality and textuality in Jesus traditions before the Gospel of Mark was textualized.[2] This may be the case, but we do not have any physical evidence of it, and especially not in narrativized form.[3] Mark is the first extant narrative text about Jesus to exhibit interplay between orality and textuality, and is self-conscious about it in Mark 1:1.

Claiming that Mark textualized oral traditions is not to argue that the gospel attempted to put an end to them.[4] Written and oral discourses exist side by side. Creation of a new media form does not necessitate the suppression of another. Mark's innovation was to open new textual vistas for previously oral traditions.

There were various ways that a given text's composition might or might not relate to antecedent oral events. There were also several ways that a text might be composed:

1. A text could be wholly handwritten with no antecedent oral event.
2. A text could be wholly dictated with no antecedent oral event.
3. A text could be partially handwritten and partially dictated with no antecedent oral event.
4. An oral event might occur and the speaker in that event becomes a writer, subsequently handwriting the text using content similar to what was presented in the oral event.

---

1. Francis Watson, *Gospel Writing: A Canonical Perspective* (Grand Rapids: Eerdmans, 2013), 608.
2. Watson, *Gospel Writing*, 609.
3. I do not think that either the Gospel of Thomas or Q pre-dates Mark, or that the latter necessarily existed. If either did precede Mark, then it would be the first Jesus text to demonstrate an interplay between textuality and orality. Mark would still demonstrate an interplay of a different, narrativized kind. On the position that Thomas pre-dates Mark, see Watson, *Gospel Writing*, 271–85. I find Mark Goodacre's case that Thomas is a derivative, de-narrativization of the Synoptics convincing (*Thomas and the Gospels: The Case for Thomas's Familiarity with the Synoptics* [Grand Rapids: Eerdmans, 2012]).
4. As Werner H. Kelber infamously argued in *The Oral and the Written Gospel: The Hermeneutics of Speaking and Writing in the Synoptic Tradition, Mark, Paul, and Q* (Bloomington: Indiana University Press, 1983), esp. 91–95.

5. An oral event might occur and the speaker in that event becomes a composer who dictates the text using content similar to what was presented in the oral event.
6. An oral event might occur and the speaker in that event becomes a writer and composer who writes part of the text and dictates part of the text using content similar to what was presented in the oral event.
7. An oral event might occur in which the speaker knew the content from the event was being textualized by someone else, but never edited the textualized version themself.
8. An oral event might occur in which the speaker knew the content from the event was being textualized by someone else and did edit the textualized version themself.
9. An oral event might occur in which the speaker is wholly ignorant that the content from the event was being textualized by someone else. The content of the event could be written as it was occurring or after it was completed.

My aim in this section is to press further the case about Mark's reception from chapter 3 and to narrow down the most likely scenarios for its composition. The argument in chapter 3 was that Mark was textualized from an antecedent oral event and was read and re-oralized in different ways. If one or more oral events stand behind the composition of Mark, then the first three options above are precluded.

The fifth, seventh, and ninth are the most probable options. These three all involve a "double orality." An oral event stands behind the text and the composition of the text was also oral. Options four, six, and eight all suggest a level of authorial and editorial control that I shall argue is contrary to Mark's "unpolished" style. Oral traditions stand behind the Gospel of Mark, the narrative was composed by mouth, and it was minimally edited. This position makes sense of Mark's style, imprecise quotations of other texts, and the way that it was edited by later gospel tradents.

ORAL FEATURES

It is frequently protested that detecting oral features in a written text is an impractical or impossible task.[5] The objection is a response to oversimplified

---

5. Rafael Rodríguez, *Oral Tradition and the New Testament: A Guide for the Perplexed* (London: Bloomsbury, 2014), 118; Eric Eve, *Writing the Gospels: Composition and Memory*

appeals to "residual orality" and the valorization of spoken discourse in antiquity. Those that consider Mark to be an "oral composition" usually leave the category undefined and the mechanics by which a text might be orally composed unaddressed. They understate the gospel's status as a written text and its interplay between writing and speaking.[6] Those who deny the possibility of detecting oral influence on a text likewise downplay this interplay, though in the opposite direction. The result is that there are, on the one hand, those who find Mark to be thoroughly oral in all respects, and, on the other hand, those who question whether "oral features" are indicative of the narrative's composition at all.

The approach taken here is to affirm that Mark is a written text and that it is influenced by the oral mode of communication. It bears the marks of textuality and orality. Questions then arise about how one might assess what an "oral characteristic" within a written text is and how a preponderance of such characteristics might make their way into the Gospel of Mark.

The preceding chapters have begun to answer the latter question. A text might exhibit oral characteristics as a result of its compositional mode and relationship to oral events.[7] To make my position on Mark's composition clear: in continuity with the patristic writers, I consider two people to have been involved in the composition of the gospel, one as speaker and one as writer.[8] Whether written after the fact or taken down "live" from a single teaching or dictation event, the writer has attempted to represent the spoken discourse without taking extensive editorial liberties. This is not to assert that it is an

---

(London: SPCK, 2016), 69; Helen K. Bond, *The First Biography of Jesus: Genre and Meaning in Mark's Gospel* (Grand Rapids: Eerdmans, 2020), 86–88.

6. For example, Joanna Dewey writes, "The gospel remains fundamentally on the oral side of the oral/written divide" ("The Gospel of Mark as Oral Hermeneutic," in *Jesus, the Voice, and the Text: Beyond the Oral and the Written Gospel*, ed. Tom Thatcher [Waco, TX: Baylor University Press, 2008], 86). For a list of others who claim Mark is "oral literature" or characterized by a preponderance of "residual orality," see Nicholas A. Elder, *The Media Matrix of Early Jewish and Christian Narrative*, LNTS 612 (London: T&T Clark, 2019), 3n10. For a similar critique of what he calls the "oral-preference perspective," see Chris Keith, *The Gospel as Manuscript: An Early History of the Jesus Tradition as Material Artifact* (Oxford: Oxford University Press, 2020), 82–85.

7. There are other explanations offered for Mark's "oral features": they are the result of inadequate education, the author being a poor writer, a Septuagintalizing agenda, or imitating an oral style in writing. I do not find any of these to be compelling explanations for all the features of Mark detailed below. Moreover, none of them necessitates a particular compositional mode.

8. I make no claim as to whether those two persons were named "Peter" and "Mark."

exact transcription of a speaking event, as writing always changes a discourse. It is to claim that Mark is a written text that represents one or more oral events and coheres with the content and style of them.

Not only is this writing scenario consistent with compositional practices in Mark's media context, but it also makes sense of the patristic testimony and the gospel's characteristic style. This leads to the other question posed above: how might we assess what an "oral characteristic" is in Mark? I propose two tools. The first is ancient texts themselves. The previous chapter observed documents that were orally composed. With respect to personal papyri letters, we found that composing via dictation did not necessarily correlate to presenting the speaker's words verbatim. Those letters that do closely cohere to the spoken words from which they were written, however, tend to possess certain "oral characteristics": parataxis, limited particles that are not "and," direct discourse signaled by "that" (ὅτι), and unique vocabulary.[9]

When ancient writers reflect on texts that were dictated or composed from oral events, they do not mention these stylistic features. But they do critique dictated texts as inelegant. Quintilian calls them "unpolished and casual" (rudia tantum et fortuita) (Quinitilian, *Inst.* 10.3.19–21 [Russell, LCL]). Horace characterizes Lucilius's dictated texts as a "muddy stream" (flueret lutulentus) (Horace, *Satire* 1.4.11 [Fairclough, LCL]).

Other ancient authors are less critical of dictation. Dio claims that it prepares one for giving speeches (Dio Chrysostom, *Discourse* 18.19–20). Pliny the Younger indicates that his hendecasyllables were spontaneously dictated (Pliny the Younger, *Ep.* 4.14, 7.4). His court speeches were initially written by mouth and subsequently revised (Pliny the Younger, *Ep.* 9.36, 9.40). Jerome twice states that he dictated a letter quickly. On one of these occasions, *Epistle* 117, he claims that Scripture is quoted sparingly because of his compositional mode. On the other, *Epistle* 127, he excuses the letter's inelegance on the same basis. Galen's texts that were composed from antecedent oral events were not properly completed until he literarily revised them himself.

Ancient authors recognize that oral composition affects the content and style of a written text. At times, they note that such texts resemble the words as they were spoken. At other times, they critique them as crude. These authors do not, however, pinpoint what stylistic aspects result from the oral mode of composition.

---

9. Roger S. Bagnall and Raffaella Cribiore, *Women's Letters from Ancient Egypt, 300 BC–AD 800* (Ann Arbor: University of Michigan Press, 2009), 379.

Here enters the second tool for assessing oral characteristics in Mark: sociolinguistic research on the differences between speaking and writing narratives. Many of the features that characterize spoken narrative, according to sociolinguists, are stylistically consistent with what ancient writers claim about orally composed texts and with what characterizes Mark.

Linguistic research that directly compares spoken narrative to written traces its origins to the 1980 collection *The Pear Stories*.[10] The basis for the study was the Pear Film, a six-minute video with no dialogue. The movie was shown to study participants whose native language was English, Japanese, German, Greek, Mayan, or Chinese. Shortly after watching the film participants were tape- or video-recorded retelling its events. The collected stories were then the object of linguistic studies with varying foci. In some studies, the spoken narratives were directly compared with written versions produced by the same viewers. The years following the publication of *The Pear Stories* saw an explosion of research that compared spoken to written narrative using similar methods.[11] These studies find that there are certain phenomena that typify spoken and written narrative, respectively.

10. Wallace L. Chafe, ed., *The Pear Stories: Cognitive, Cultural, and Linguistic Aspects of Narrative Production* (Norwood, NJ: Ablex, 1980). The comparison of written and spoken language outside of linguistics stretches back much further, as indicated by the history of scholarship detailed by Wallace Chafe and Deborah Tannen in "The Relation Between Written and Spoken Language," *Annual Review of Anthropology* 16 (1987): 383–407.

11. The literature is vast, but some of the most important studies are Wallace L. Chafe, *Discourse, Consciousness, and Time: The Flow and Displacement of Conscious Experience in Speaking and Writing* (Chicago: University of Chicago Press, 1994); Wallace L. Chafe, "Integration and Involvement in Speaking, Writing, and Oral Literature," in *Spoken and Written Language: Exploring Orality and Literacy*, ed. Deborah Tannen, Advances in Discourse Processes 9 (Norwood, NJ: Ablex, 1982), 35–53; Wallace L. Chafe, "Linguistic Differences Produced by Differences between Speaking and Writing," in *Literacy, Language, and Learning: The Nature and Consequences of Reading and Writing*, ed. David R. Olson, Nancy Torrance, and Angela Hildyard (Cambridge: Cambridge University Press, 1985), 105–23; Wallace L. Chafe, "Linking Intonation Units in Spoken English," in *Clause Combining in Grammar and Discourse*, ed. Sandra Thompson and John Haiman, Typological Studies in Language 18 (Philadelphia: John Benjamins, 1988), 1–27; Wallace Chafe and Jane Danielwicz, "Properties of Spoken and Written Language," in *Comprehending Oral and Written Language*, ed. Rosalind Horowitz and S. Jay Samuels (San Diego: Academic Press, 1987), 83–113; Deborah Tannen, ed., *Analyzing Discourse: Text and Talk* (Washington, D.C.: Georgetown University Press, 1982); Deborah Tannen, "Oral and Literate Strategies in Spoken and Written Narratives," *Language* 58 (1982): 1–21; Deborah Tannen, ed., *Spoken and Written Language: Exploring Orality and Literacy*, Advances in Discourse Processes 9 (Norwood, NJ: Ablex, 1982); Karen Beaman,

The Idea Unit and Parataxis

The most salient feature of orally produced narrative is what is called the "intonation" or "idea unit."[12] Idea units are short bursts of speech, usually between four and seven words, that are strung along in grammatically simple ways, most often with a language's basic coordinating conjunction (i.e., "and") or no connective at all. The result is that paratactic structuring is the norm in spoken narrative and the coordinating conjunction appears about twice as often in it as compared to written narrative.[13]

The reason for the prominence of idea units and parataxis in speaking is neurological. These units contain what the human brain can process at any given moment. Speakers move from idea to idea and do not utilize neurological energy placing ideas in complex grammatical relationship with one another.[14] Idea units are characteristic of spoken narrative across languages and time.

Much of what follows presents quantitative data. Tables that present this data are provided throughout and combined in the appendix. You might find it advantageous to peruse the appendix of tables to chapter 6 before engaging the following sections.

"Coordination and Subordination Revisited: Syntactic Complexity in Spoken and Written Narrative," in *Coherence in Spoken and Written Discourse*, ed. Deborah Tannen, Advances in Discourse Processes 12 (Norwood, NJ: Ablex, 1984), 45–80. For a more detailed engagement with sociolinguistic studies that compare spoken and written discourse than is offered here, see Elder, *Media Matrix*, 16–28.

12. Chafe, *Discourse, Consciousness, and Time*, 53–70; Chafe, "Linguistic Differences," 106–11; Egbert J. Bakker, "How Oral Is Oral Composition?" in *Signs of Orality: The Oral Tradition and Its Influence in the Greek and Roman World*, ed. Anne E. Mackay (Leiden: Brill, 1999), 39.

13. Beaman, "Coordination and Subordination Revisited," 60–61.

14. This is not to state that ideas are not in different kinds of relationships with one another in the act of speaking. They are, but the relationship between ideas is also developed by para-grammatical features, such as gestures and intonation (Beaman, "Coordination and Subordination Revisited," 60–61).

	καί alone	καί and δέ combined	δέ alone	δέ-καί ratio	Other conjunctions (not καί or δέ)
Mark	9.7% or 1 in 10.12 (1,078/11,138)	11.1% or 1 in 8.95 (1,244/11,138)	1.4% (157/11,138)	1:6.87	24.5% of Total Conjunctions (405/1,649)
P.Oxy. 56.3860	10.8% or 1 in 9.26 (41/380)	11.1% or 1 in 9.05 (42/380)	0.2% (1/380)	1:41	28.8 % (17/59)
P.Oxy 903	9.1 % or 1 in 10.97 (36/395)	10.6% or 1 in 9.40 (42/395)	1.5% (6/395)	1:6	32.3% (20/62)

Parataxis in Mark is often noted as a feature of the narrative's "vernacular" Greek.[15] Sociolinguistic considerations give the claim more weight, as does data from the gospel itself. Most clauses, sentences, and pericopes in Mark begin with "and" (καί).[16] The volume of the connective outstrips every other text in the New Testament, except for Revelation.[17] In Mark, καί makes up nearly 10% of the total words. This is comparable to its volume in the two papyri documents introduced in the previous chapter, P.Oxy. 56.3860 and P.Oxy. 903. These are near transcriptions of oral accounts. Καί makes up 10.8% of the total words in the former and 9.1% in the latter.

---

15. Ernest Best, "Mark's Narrative Technique," *JSNT* 37 (1989): 49; Antoinette Clark Wire, *The Case for Mark Composed in Performance*, Biblical Performance Criticism Series 3 (Eugene, OR: Cascade, 2011), 80–84; Joanna Dewey, "Oral Methods of Structuring Narrative in Mark," *Int* 43 (1989): 37–38; James D. G. Dunn, "Altering the Default Setting: Re-Envisaging the Early Transmission of the Jesus Tradition," in *The Oral Gospel Tradition*, ed. James D. G. Dunn (Grand Rapids: Eerdmans, 2013), 70.

16. At the clausal level, καί coordinates 591 independent clauses in the gospel (Elliott C. Maloney, *Semitic Interference in Marcan Syntax*, SBLDS 51 [Chico, CA: Scholars Press, 1980], 66). With respect to sentences, per Paul Ellingworth, the word begins 64.5% (376/583) of the sentences in Mark (P. Ellingworth, "The Dog in the Night: A Note on Mark's Non-Use of KAI," *BT* 46 [1995]: 125). Based on the divisions in NA28, καί appears at the beginning of 92% (114/145) of Mark's paragraphs. Wire tabulates the number of times the connective begins pericopes in the various Greek reconstructions of Mark (*Case for Mark*, 83).

17. Καί occurs 1,087 times in Mark's total 11,138 words. This is 9.7% of the total words in the gospel or 1 in every 10.12. For comparison, Revelation uses καί 1,128 times of 9,856 total words, which is 11.4% or once for every 8.64 words. Matthew and Luke both curb the volume of καί from their predecessor, as the connective is used 45% and 33% less frequently in each, respectively.

Corollary to Mark's heavy dependence on parataxis is the gospel's tampered use of other connectives. Mark employs καί nearly two times more often than all other connectives combined.[18] After καί, the second most common conjunction is δέ ("but," "now," "and"). It appears once for every 6.87 occasions of καί. In spoken English narratives, Wallace Chafe finds that "and" constitutes 50% of all connectives and that "but" occurs one-fifth as often as "and."[19]

While we ought to be cautious about drawing conclusions from these sociolinguistic findings in a different language and a very different context, it is remarkable how closely Chafe's quantitative research lines up with both Mark and P.Oxy. 903 in this respect. In the gospel, δέ and ἀλλά occur 202 times to the 1,078 instances of καί (1 for every 5.34). The ratio of καί to δέ and ἀλλά in P.Oxy. 903 is 36 to 7 (1 for every 5.14).[20]

Not only is δέ far less frequent than καί in Mark but it is also used differently than its coordinating counterpart. In the broad scope of the term, δέ does not always or usually imply contrast. One of its primary functions is to coordinate clauses, sentences, or entire sections of discourse. The coordinating function of δέ is more common in literarily conceived narratives than it is in orally conceived narratives, as we shall see in the next section. In Mark, the conjunction usually occurs after a pericope has begun to develop. Unlike καί and also unlike δέ in Matthew and Luke, δέ will not often stand at the beginning of a new section of text in Mark. Its presence presupposes narrative progress and as a result "now" and "but" are more common translations of it in Mark than in the later Synoptics.

The cumulative result is that Mark is infamous for its choppy style. The surfeit of καί is indicative of this, but the issue runs deeper than parataxis. When a Markan pericope or the entire gospel is broken down into sense or idea units, these units begin with καί about one-half of the time. Just as instructive is that Mark's sense units average approximately five words, which fits comfortably within the four-to-seven-word range linguists find typical of idea units in spoken narrative.[21]

---

18. In comparison to Mark's 1,100 occurrences of καί, the gospel uses other connectives a total of 649 times. For a full list of these connectives and the number of times each is used, see Elder, *Media Matrix*, 72n113.

19. Chafe, "Linking Intonation Units," 10–12.

20. The other orally conceived papyri text, P.Oxy. 56.3860, uses each of these words for "but" (δέ and ἀλλά) one time each. Thus, the ratio is much lower at 1 "but" for every 20.5 "ands."

21. In 1936, James A. Kleist presented the entirety of Mark in sense units (*The Gospel of Saint Mark Presented in Greek Thought-Units and Sense-Lines with a Commentary* [New York:

Parataxis and short idea units are the first and strongest hints that orality has left its imprint on Mark, but they are not the only ones. Two other stylistic features that characterize Mark likewise reflect what is native to spoken narrative: prominent use of the discourse marker εὐθύς and the historical present.

The Discourse Marker εὐθύς

The recurrence of εὐθύς, usually translated "immediately," is often claimed to endow Mark with an air of rapidity.[22] This, however, is to ignore the multifunctionality of the word in the gospel. There are occasions in Mark where the term does carry its true adverbial sense connoting immediacy.[23] But just as often the word sequences the narrative, and the translation "next," "then," or some other such is more appropriate than "immediately." This is the case in Mark 1:21:

καὶ εἰσπορεύονται εἰς Καφαρναούμ· καὶ εὐθὺς τοῖς σάββασιν εἰσελθὼν εἰς τὴν συναγωγὴν ἐδίδασκεν.

And they enter into Capernaum and then on the Sabbath having entered into the synagogue, he was teaching. (Mark 1:21)

The term moves the discourse forward and does not indicate that the first thing Jesus did when he arrived in Capernaum was enter the synagogue. This is also the case two verses later:

καὶ εὐθὺς ἦν ἐν τῇ συναγωγῇ ἄνθρωπος ἐν πνεύματι ἀκαθάρτῳ

And so there was in the synagogue a person with an unclean spirit. (Mark 1:23)

Here εὐθύς is not a time adverbial signaling how quickly a spirit-possessed person was present (ἦν) in the synagogue. Rather, it works with the connective. In both Mark 1:21 and 23, εὐθύς is more closely tied to "and" (καὶ) than

---

Bruce Publishing Company, 1936]). His sense lines average 4.69 words per line. Of course, how one demarcates a sense line is subjective. However, when I divide Markan pericopes into idea units, I consistently find that these range somewhere between four and five words per unit. For example, Mark 1:21–28 averages 4.43 words per idea unit and Mark 5:25–29 averages 4.86 (Elder, *Media Matrix*, 68–71).

22. The word appears fifty-one times in the New Testament. Forty-two of these occurrences are in Mark.

23. Mark 1:18, 42; 4:5, 15, 16, 17, 29; 5:29, 42; 6:25, 54; 9:20.

to the verbal form that it technically modifies.[24] These are not isolated cases. Throughout the gospel, εὐθύς frequently follows "and" and sequences material. Translations such as "and then" or "and so" better capture the sequencing sense of the term than does "and immediately."[25]

I suggest that the multifunctionality of the term εὐθύς in Mark is indicative of it being a discourse marker and not simply an adverb.[26] There are three other linguistic features of discourse markers that closely correspond to εὐθύς in Mark.[27] First, discourse markers are considered a subclass of adverbs. They have corresponding homonyms and homophones that are properly adverbs.[28] The discourse marker εὐθύς has an adverbial homonym (i.e., εὐθύς) and, with εὐθέως, a homophone used exclusively as an adverb. Second, discourse markers usually occur toward the beginning of a clause.[29] In Mark, εὐθύς nearly always precedes the verb it modifies and occurs at the beginning of a sentence.[30] Third, discourse markers are native to spoken discourse and are negatively evaluated in formal, written discourse.[31] This characteristically Markan word is regularly altered or removed altogether by the authors of Matthew and Luke.

---

24. George D. Kilpatrick claims that whenever εὐθύς appears at the beginning of a clause in Mark it functions as a connecting particle rather than as an adverb of time ("Some Notes on Markan Usage," in *The Language and Style of the Gospel of Mark: An Edition of C. H. Turener's "Notes on Marcan Usage" Together with Other Comparable Studies*, ed. J. K. Elliott, NovTSup 71 [Leiden: Brill, 1993], 168).

25. In many instances it is evident that εὐθύς is sequencing the discourse: Mark 1:20, 21, 23, 29, 30, 43; 2:8, 12; 6:45, 50; 7:25; 8:10; 14:43, 45; 15:1. In others, the line between immediacy and sequencing is not as clear: Mark 1:10, 12, 28; 3:6; 5:2, 30; 6:27; 9:15, 20; 10:52; 11:2, 3; 14:72.

26. Definitions of discourse markers vary, but Deborah Schiffrin's has proved to be influential: "Sequentially dependent elements which bracket units of talk" (*Discourse Markers*, Studies in Interactional Sociolinguistics 5 [Cambridge: Cambridge University Press, 1987], 31).

27. For a more detailed discussion of these four features as they relate to Mark, see Elder, *Media Matrix*, 80–84.

28. Bernd Heine, "On Discourse Markers: Grammaticalization, Pragmaticalization, or Something Else?" *Linguistics* 51 (2013): 1208.

29. Laurel J. Brinton, *Pragmatic Markers in English: Grammaticalization and Discourse Functions*, Topics in English Linguistics 19 (Berlin: de Gruyter, 1996), 34.

30. Rodney J. Decker finds that εὐθύς follows a Markan verb on only two occasions (Rodney J. Decker, "The Use of Εὐθύς ('immediately') in Mark," *Journal of Ministry and Theology* 1 [1997]: 93).

31. Brinton, *Pragmatic Markers*, 33; Jan-Ola Östman, "The Symbiotic Relationship Between Pragmatic Particles and Impromptu Speech," in *Impromptu Speech: A Symposium; Papers of a Symposium Held in Åbo, Nov. 20–22, 1981*, ed. Nils Erik Enkvist (Åbo: Åbo Akademi, 1982), 170.

The Historical Present

Like discourse markers, the historical present is more native to spoken narrative than it is to written.[32] This is neither to state that speakers always utilize the historical present, nor is it to claim that it is wholly absent from written narrative.[33] In spoken narrative the historical present is discretional.[34] Some speakers will use it frequently, while others will not use it at all. Mark uses it frequently. By volume, the historical present appears more often in Mark than any other New Testament text.[35]

But it is not just the frequency of the historical present in Mark that aligns with spoken norms; its placement in pericopes does as well. In Mark, the historical present appears toward the beginning of a section when a new character, action, or setting is introduced.[36] A historical present is never the last verb in a pericope. Linguists find that in spoken narrative most historical present tense

---

32. Nessa Wolfson, "A Feature of Performed Narrative: The Conversational Historical Present," *Language in Society* 7 (1978): 215–37; Monika Fludernik, "The Historical Present Tense in English Literature: An Oral Pattern and Its Literary Adaptation," *Language and Literature* 17 (1992): 77–107; Monika Fludernik, "The Historical Present Tense Yet Again: Tense Switching and Narrative Dynamics in Oral and Quasi-Oral Storytelling," *Text: An Interdisciplinary Journal for the Study of Discourse* 11 (1991): 365–97.

33. When the historical present does appear in written narrative, it is considered a holdover from spoken norms. Suzanne Fleischman writes that this is the case in several different languages and cites various studies for each (*Tense and Narrativity: From Medieval Performance to Modern Fiction* [Austin: University of Texas Press, 1990], 79).

34. Fludernik, "Historical Present Tense Yet Again," 387; Wolfson, "Feature of Performed Narrative," 223; Nessa Wolfson, *CHP: The Conversational Historical Present in American English Narrative*, Topics in Sociolinguistics (Dordrecht: Foris, 1982), 29; Fleischman, *Tense and Narrativity*, 76.

35. It occurs 150 times (John C. Hawkins, *Horae Synopticae: Contributions to the Study of the Synoptic Problem* [Oxford: Clarendon, 1909], 114–18; Frans Neirynck, Theo Hansen, and Frans van Segbroeck, eds., *The Minor Agreements of Matthew and Luke against Mark: With a Cumulative List*, BETL 37 [Leuven: University Press, 1974], 224–27). The historical present makes up 9.9% of the total indicative verbs in Mark.

36. Mark 1:21; 3:13, 20; 6:30; 7:1; 8:22; 9:2; 10:1, 35, 46; 11:1, 15, 27; 12:13, 18; 14:17, 32, 33, 66; 15:20; 16:2 are all instances when a historical present occurs at the beginning of a pericope. According to Hyeon Woo Shin, the historical present begins a new pericope in Mark on sixty-six occasions and introduces a new event within a pericope on thirty-six occasions ("The Historic Present as a Discourse Marker and Textual Criticism in Mark," *BT* 63 [2012]: 50).

verbs occur in "complicating action clauses" or "turns" in the discourse.[37] They are remarkably rare at the conclusion of a spoken episode.[38]

In these three respects, unique Markan features cohere with what linguists find to be characteristic of spoken narrative. Oral composition best explains the prominence of parataxis, εὐθύς, and the historical present in Mark. Other explanations have been offered for Mark's style, but they do not adequately account for all three of these phenomena in the gospel. For instance, parataxis is sometimes claimed to result from "Semitic influence."[39] In its most plausible form, the argument is that Markan parataxis is inspired by the Septuagint wherein paratactic καί abounds. However, neither εὐθύς nor the historical present is particularly Septuagintal. Mark's paratactic similarity to spoken papyri narratives, which are not influenced by the Greek translations of Hebrew Scriptures, suggests that the issue runs deeper than "Septuagintal" or "Semitic" influence. Matthew, which is often claimed also to bear Aramaic, Hebraic, Semitic, or Septuagintal influence, alters this feature of Mark.[40]

Another explanation for Mark's unique features is that the gospel feigns orality. The author writes in a way that mimics speaking. If this is the case, then the writer has done a remarkable job imitating speech patterns. Linguists do find that writers sometimes use "oral strategies" in written narratives.[41] But this is difficult to do well because the act of writing slows down one's thinking and alters how thought is communicated. And if one wanted to feign orality in writing, the best way to do so in Mark's media context is to dictate *viva voce*. The best explanation for Mark's oral style is that the gospel was composed by mouth and was not extensively corrected after the fact.

---

37. "Complicating action clause" is Schiffrin's preferred nomenclature, whereas Fludernik uses "turns" (Deborah Schiffrin, "Tense Variation in Narrative," *Language* 57 [1981]: 51; Fludernik, "Historical Present Tense," 86).

38. Schiffrin, "Tense Variation"; Fludernik, "Historical Present Tense," 76; Fludernik, "Historical Present Tense Yet Again," 375–76.

39. Armin D. Baum, "Mark's Paratactic Καί as a Secondary Syntactic Semitism," *NovT* 58 (2016): 1–26; Rodney J. Decker, "Markan Idiolect in the Study of the Greek of the New Testament," in *The Language of the New Testament: Context, History, and Development*, ed. Andrew W. Pitts and Stanley E. Porter, Linguistic Biblical Studies 6 (Leiden: Brill, 2013), 47–49; Maloney, *Semitic Interference*, 66–67.

40. On the Aramaic, Hebraic, and Semitic features of Matthew, see J. Engelbrecht, "The Language of the Gospel of Matthew," *Neot* 24 (1990): 203–5; on the Septuagintal features of Matthew, see Ulrich Luz, *Matthew 1–7*, trans. James E. Crouch, Hermeneia (Minneapolis: Fortress, 2007), 22.

41. Tannen, "Oral and Literate Strategies," 5–19.

Matthew and Luke

Matthew and Luke modulate Mark for a new mode of reception. Whereas Mark is suited for proclamation, Matthew is primed for liturgical reading events and Luke for an individual reader, Theophilus. As different kinds of texts written for different modes of reception, they were composed differently than Mark was. Mark was composed by mouth from antecedent oral events and bears the marks of oral composition in the text itself. Because they possess literary ambition, Matthew and Luke were carefully composed. Handwriting and revision played central roles in their creation.[42]

Ancient authors note that there are stylistic differences between texts written by mouth and those that have gone through a thorough composition process. Galen found it necessary properly to complete discourses that happened to be textualized from oral events before releasing them in their "final" versions that were ready for public consumption (Galen, *On My Own Books* 10–11K). Quintilian let the publication version of *The Orator's Education* mature, so that he could "go over [it] again, with a reader's eyes" (*diligentius repetitos tamquam lector perpenderem*) putting it into "as correct a form as possible" (*emendatissimi*) (Quintilian, *Inst.* pref.3 [Russell, LCL]). He remarks on the differences between versions that were prematurely released and the one presented in publication form. Quintilian could just as well be recounting the differences between the later Synoptics and Mark: "In the present work, therefore, there will be some things the same, many things changed, and very many things added, and the whole will be better written and worked up to the best of my ability" (Quintilian, *Inst.* 1.pref.8) (Russell, LCL).

The leaked pre-publication versions were, according to Quintilian, written from oral lectures. One was taken down over a period of two days by enslaved persons to whom the task was delegated. Quintilian's ambitious students reduced the other to shorthand from a longer lecture course (Quintilian, *Inst.* 1.pref.7). Like Quintilian and Galen, Matthew and Luke take a discourse that was written from antecedent oral traditions and recast it in literary form.

---

42. I do not rule out the possibility that dictation was utilized in the composition process of either Matthew or Luke. However, neither is characterized by spoken norms the way that Mark is. Dictation did not always, or even usually, result in a recognizable oral register. There are several reasons for this: those who utilized dictation regularly to create literary texts could dictate in a literary register; capable scribes could emend expressions to make them more appropriate for the written medium; and a dictated text could be edited both by the scribe and the individual who dictated.

Some things from Mark are the same, many things changed, very many things added, and the whole of both Matthew and Luke are better written.[43]

Before addressing their literaturization, we briefly return to Luke's preface. While Matthew intimates that it has higher literary ambitions than Mark with its first word, "book" (βίβλος), Luke emphasizes the carefulness used in the writing process. In the preface, Luke's account implies that its predecessors have not demonstrated the same literary care. These predecessors are mentioned from the outset of the narrative in Luke 1:1: "Many set their hand to draw up an account" (πολλοὶ ἐπεχείρησαν ἀνατάξασθαι διήγησιν). The verb "draw up" (ἀνατάξασθαι) has subliterary connotations.[44] If the author wished to indicate that others had created literary texts, the more natural verbs would have been "compose" (συντάσσομαι) or "write" (γράφω). Luke uses the latter with respect to its own project just two verses later. "Draw up," in contrast, implies that "[Luke's] predecessors have retold this story, possibly in the sense of a written adaption of an oral account."[45] If Luke has Mark in mind, the verb is fitting. The author of the Third Gospel undertakes a different project, one with literary discrimination. Three elements of Luke 1:3 suggest this.

First, the participle "investigating" (παρηκολουθηκότι) is a common historiographical term that connotes thorough scrutiny of written texts.[46] The object of the participle, "everything" (πᾶσιν) can be either masculine or neuter. If masculine, then Luke investigated the "eyewitnesses" and "servants of the word" mentioned in Luke 1:2. The term is more likely neuter, however, and refers to the various textual "accounts" that others have attempted to draw up.[47] Luke has done due diligence by thoroughly engaging antecedent written accounts.

---

43. Matthew and Luke are "better written" than Mark when all are judged as texts read privately by individuals. If the Synoptics were judged as texts read or performed in a single sitting, then I would consider Mark to be the best written.

44. François Bovon, *Luke 1: A Commentary on the Gospel of Luke 1:1–9:50*, trans. Christine M. Thomas, 3 vols., Hermeneia (Minneapolis: Fortress, 2002), 1:19; John Nolland, *Luke 1:1–9:20*, WBC 35A (Dallas: Word Books, 1989), 6.

45. Bovon, *Luke 1:1–9:50*, 19.

46. Henry J. Cadbury, "Commentary on the Preface of Luke," in *The Beginnings of Christianity: Part I, The Acts of the Apostles*, ed. F. J. Foakes-Jackson and Kirsopp Lake (New York: Macmillan, 1922), 501; Bovon, *Luke 1:1–9:50*, 21. This is the connotation of the term in Josephus, *Life* 357; *Ag. Ap.* 1.53; 1.218.

47. Bovon, *Luke 1:1–9:50*, 1:21. See especially the similar use of "investigate" (παρακλουθέω) with "accuracy" (ἀκρίβεια) in Josephus, *Ag. Ap.* 1.218.

Two adverbs are then used to express the author's own fastidiousness: "carefully" (ἀκριβῶς) and "in order" (καθεξῆς). The latter unambiguously modifies the verb "write," and implies that Luke's account is in proper historical order. The former adverb, "carefully" (ἀκριβῶς), can modify the participle "investigate," the infinitive "write," or both. The syntax favors "write," since adverbs normally precede the words that they modify. However, the general sense of the passage also suggests an accuracy concerning Luke's investigation. This leads several commentators to suggest that "carefully" modifies both the participle and the infinitive simultaneously.[48] In either case, the author of Luke takes pride in the careful writing.

Finally, the verb that Luke's account uses for itself differs from the one applied to its predecessors. Luke "writes" (γράψαι) whereas the others have "drawn up" (ἀνατάξασθαι). François Bovon notes that Luke's verb "describes the art of a writer, and is emphatic here."[49] By using the verb and introducing the text with a preface, Luke differentiates between the literary nature of this project and what has come before it. The Third Gospel presents itself as a well-researched and carefully written text.

REDACTING ORAL CHARACTERISTICS

Luke and Matthew betray their literary ambition in the manner that they emend Mark. If the idea unit accomplished by parataxis, the discourse marker εὐθύς, and the prominence of the historical present are indicative of Mark's compositional mode, then the redaction of these are indicative of Matthew's and Luke's. The later Synoptic authors systematically emend or remove these particularities from their predecessor.

With respect to parataxis, Matthew's and Luke's total volume of "and" (καί) is significantly decreased from their predecessor. They use the connective 40% and 33% less frequently, respectively.[50] Since the most prominent function of "and" is to link short idea units in spoken narrative, it is instructive to establish how often it appears in comparison with all other words. In Matthew, καί

---

48. Nolland, *Luke 1:1–9:20*, 9; Bovon, *Luke 1:1–9:50*, 22.

49. Bovon, *Luke 1:1–9:50*, 22.

50. In Mark, 9.9% (1,100/11,138) of the total words are "and" (καί), whereas 6.5% (1,194/18,363) and 7.6% (1,483/19,494) of the total words in Matthew and Luke, respectively, are "and" (καί). For a more detailed analysis of Matthean and Lukan redaction of Markan parataxis, see Elder, *Media Matrix*, 137–41.

occurs once for every 15.38 words, and in Luke once for every 13.14 words. In Mark the conjunction appears once for every 10.12 words.

Matthew and Luke depress the frequency of the coordinating conjunction in the triple-tradition. In Markan pericopes that are paralleled in Matthew and Luke, καί makes up 9.7% of the total words in each, or 1 in every 10.34 and 10.32 words, respectively.[51] In Matthean pericopes shared with Mark, the volume is suppressed to 7.4% of the total words (once for every 13.57 words) and in Lukan pericopes to 8.0% (once for every 12.50 words). "And" (καί) does not regularly connect entire episodes or sentences in Matthew and Luke as it does in Mark. The coordinating conjunction begins most sentences and paragraphs in Mark. This is not the case in the later gospels. "And" (καί) begins 65% of Mark's sentences and 92% of its paragraphs. In Matthew, both sentences and paragraphs start with καί 21% of the time. And in Luke 30% of the sentences begin with καί and 32% of its paragraphs.[52]

Matthew and Luke regularly replace a Markan καί with δέ. The cumulative result is that δέ occurs frequently at the beginning of a new pericope in Mark's inheritors and its total volume is increased. Whereas the δέ-to-καί ratio in Mark is 1 to 6.87, it is 1 to 2.42 and 2.72 in Matthew and Luke, respectively.[53] This trend is reflected in Matthew's and Luke's redaction in the triple tradition. Therein, the δέ-to-καί ratio is 1 to 2.65 for Matthean pericopes paralleled in Mark and 1 to 2.38 for Lukan pericopes.[54] Perhaps more surprising is that δέ appears at a somewhat higher rate in both Matthew's double-tradition pericopes and its unique materials as compared to Luke's.[55] Luke is more keen to write δέ when following Mark than when composing its own material or following whatever one understands the double-tradition document to be, whether Matthew or Q. Matthew, in contrast, utilizes δέ more frequently in its own composition than when following Mark. This is likewise the case in

---

51. Triple tradition pericopes are from Kurt Aland, *Synopsis Quattuor Evangeliorum*, 13th ed. (Stuttgart: Deutsche Bibelgesellschaft, 1985).

52. Per NA28 sentence and paragraph breaks.

53. In Mark, δέ occurs 157 times and καί 1,078. In Matthew and Luke, the former appears 494 and 542 times, respectively, and the latter 1,194 and 1,483.

54. Compared to 1 to 6.66 for Markan pericopes paralleled in Matthew and 1 to 6.84 for pericopes paralleled in Luke.

55. In Matthean double-tradition pericopes, δέ constitutes 2.9% of the words and is used at a ratio of 1 to 1.96 compared to καί. In the Lukan double tradition these figures are 1.8% and 1 to 3.9. In unique Matthean materials the numbers are 4.0% and 1 to 1.32. And in Lukan pericopes they are 2.5% and 1 to 3.32.

Matthew's double-tradition material, which might be a continuation of the author's compositional tendency, under the Farrer theory, or a redactional tendency, if one holds to the two-document hypothesis.

Aside from their compositional and redactional nuances, Matthew and Luke both significantly decrease καί from their predecessor and increase the frequency of δέ. As a result, their ratio of δέ to καί is more similar to other narratives that possess literary ambition than it is to Mark. A sampling of other narratives contemporaneous with the Synoptics shows this to be the case:

- Mark: 1 to 6.87
- Matthew: 1 to 2.42
- Luke: 1 to 2.74
- John: 1 to 4.08
- Philo, *On the Life of Moses*: 1 to 2.25
- Philo, *On the Life of Joseph*: 1 to 2.56
- Philo, *Against Flaccus*: 1 to 2.67
- 3 Maccabees: 1 to 2.14
- Letter of Aristeas: 1 to 1.6
- Josephus, *Jewish War*: 1 to 1.38
- Josephus, *The Life*: 1 to 1.25

Authors are consistent in their use of καί compared to δέ across unique texts. They are also consistent with other writers as to these ratios and to the total volume of καί and δέ, respectively. In all of these nongospel texts, the volume of καί is between about 4.5% and 6.5%, the volume of δέ between about 2% and 4%, and the ratio of δέ to καί from 1:1.25 on the low end to 1:2.67 on the high end. Mark stands well outside all these ranges, and the later Synoptics fall within or very close to them.

It is because Matthew and Luke are texts composed differently and for a different purpose that they emend this characteristic of their predecessor that smacks of spoken narrative. Their changes align with written norms as observed by sociolinguists. While "and" is still the most common conjunction in written narrative, writers are keen to write longer clauses and place them in varying types of relationships with one another by a variety of grammatical means.[56]

---

56. Tannen, "Oral and Literate Strategies," 8; Chafe, "Linguistic Differences," 111–12; Chafe, "Linking Intonation Units," 23; Chafe and Danielwicz, "Properties," 104; Beaman, "Coordination and Subordination Revisited," 76.

This is because, in contrast to speakers, writers have cognitive time and space to manipulate their words and craft more intricate and complex sentences.

Particularly illuminating for Matthew is the author's favorite adverb, "then" (τότε). Sociolinguists find that in spoken narrative "then" is rare without "and" directly preceding it. Writers, in contrast, will use "then" as a weighted connective without "and."[57] "Then" rarely occurs in sentence-initial or paragraph-initial position when a narrative is spoken. It is more common in written narrative. "Then" (τότε) appears six times in Mark. "And" directly precedes it five times. It occurs fifteen times in Luke. Three of these are preceded by "and" (καί), and seven times the adverb is in sentence-initial position. Matthew employs "then" (τότε) ninety times. A full seventy of them are in sentence-initial position. On only ten occasions is the adverb preceded by "and." Thus, τότε (then) begins a Matthean "paragraph" more often than καί (and) does by a narrow margin.[58]

In sum, Matthew and Luke contain a higher dose of hypotaxis than does Mark. This occurs with respect to individual clauses and sentences, but also larger units and entire narrative episodes. Because parataxis, when visualized in writing, is negatively evaluated as subliterary, it comes as no surprise that Matthew and Luke alter this feature of Mark.

	Historical Present to Total Indicative Verbs	Historical Present to Total Indicative Verbs in Non-Speech Margins	Historical Present to Total Indicative Verbs in Speech Margins	Historical Present in Non-speech Margins to Historical Present in Speech Margins	εὐθύς (Immediately)
Mark	150/1,520 (9.9%)	77/808 (9.5%)	73/1,712 (10.6%)	1.05:1	41
Matthew	94/2,245 (4.2%)	28/1,215 (2.3%)	66/1,030 (6.4%)	1:2.35	5
Luke	11/2,445 (0.4%)	3/1,257 (0.2%)	8/1,188 (0.6%)	1:2.7	1

---

57. Beaman, "Coordination and Subordination Revisited," 76–77; Chafe, "Linking Intonation Units," 13.

58. "Then" begins 30 paragraphs, per NA28, "and" begins 29 paragraphs.

Matthew and Luke redact two other Markan features that are native to spoken narrative: the historical present and the discourse marker εὐθύς. Luke avoids the historical present. There are only eleven occasions of it in the Third Gospel. Most of these, eight, are forms of "say" (λέγω). In both speaking and writing, the historical present is most common in "speech margins," which are verbs that report words spoken.[59] Matthew does not avoid the historical present to the extent that Luke does, but most of Matthew's historical presents are speech margins. In total, Matthew uses the historical present ninety-four times and sixty-six of these are speech margins. In non-speech margins, the historical present constitutes 2.3% of Matthew's indicative verbs, 0.2% of Luke's, and 9.5% of Mark's.[60] With respect to direct redaction of their predecessor, Matthew removes or alters 130 of Mark's 150 historical presents and retains twenty.[61] Luke removes or alters 89 and retains one.[62] The historical present is a holdover from oral storytelling that is negatively evaluated and avoided in writing. This explains its minimal appearance in the later Synoptics.

Like paratactic structure and the historical present, discourse markers occur with much higher frequency in spoken narrative than in written. They are stereotyped as informal and subliterary in writing.[63] When reproducing Markan material, Matthew and Luke remove or alter the discourse marker εὐθύς from their predecessor. Luke removes twenty-two occasions of εὐθύς

---

59. Schiffrin, "Tense Variation," 58; Chafe, *Discourse, Consciousness, and Time*, 223; Wolfson, *CHP*, 50–52.

60. For a full table of the use of the historical present in both speech and non-speech margins, see Nicholas A. Elder, "The Synoptic Gospels as Mixed Media," *Biblical Research* 64 (2019): 57.

61. Willoughby C. Allen, *A Critical and Exegetical Commentary on the Gospel according to Saint Matthew*, 3rd ed., ICC 26 (Edinburgh: T&T Clark, 1912), xx. In the table it is noted that Matthew contains 94 historical present verbs. Of these, 20 come from shared Markan material and 74, the majority of which are in speech margins, from the double tradition or Matthew's unique material.

62. Bovon, *Luke 1:1–9:50*, 397n12. The total number of times that Luke removes the historical present from Mark is lower as compared to Matthew because there are pericopes that Matthew reproduces from Mark that Luke does not. In the table it is noted that Luke contains 11 historical present verbs. Of these, 1 is retained from Mark and 10 are from the double tradition or Lukan material.

63. Östman, "Symbiotic Relationship," 169; Richard J. Watts, "Taking the Pitcher to the 'Well': Native Speakers' Perception of Their Use of Discourse Markers in Conversation," *Journal of Pragmatics: An Interdisciplinary Monthly of Language Studies* 13 (1989): 208; Brinton, *Pragmatic Markers*, 33.

from Mark altogether, and Matthew eighteen.[64] On another seven occasions each, Luke and Matthew substitute a Markan εὐθύς with a proper adverb that connotes immediacy, εὐθέως or παραχρῆμα.[65] As a subclass of adverbs, discourse markers normally have homophonous and nearly homophonous counterparts. Εὐθύς has each, as the word can function as an adverb itself just as its nearly homophonous counterpart, εὐθέως, does. When εὐθύς is retained from Mark, which happens on only five occasions, all in Matthew, the term functions as an adverb connoting immediacy.[66]

This information quantifies what is well known: Matthew and Luke improve Mark stylistically. They are better writers. But they are better writers only when their products are judged in a certain manner with a specific mode of reception in mind. The later authors follow prescriptive grammar and craft more complex sentences than their predecessor. The kinds of stylistic and grammatical changes that Matthew and Luke make to Mark require careful composition. The precision with which they write comes from visualizing their words in the act of redacting and writing anew. By using Mark, they are manipulating the written words of a physical text.

The question remains as to the mechanics by which Matthew and Luke altered their predecessor. There are two options. First, they might dictate their alterations to an enslaved person or secretary who wrote down the text. The process entails editing the source text during the act of composition by dictation. In this scenario, Matthew or Luke makes eye contact with Mark, and dictates using material from it, interweaving the now stylistically improved material into their own composition. The second option is that Matthew or Luke made eye contact with Mark and rewrote portions of the source text by hand, interweaving it with their own material. This could happen in the act of producing a presentation copy, but that was not the normal procedure. Emendations to a text usually entered when an author reduced it to notes or as they produced a rough draft. The rough copy was then rewritten in a clean version, either in the author's own hand or by dictation.

---

64. Neirynck, *Minor Agreements*, 274–75. The apparent discrepancy from the total number of times that εὐθύς is used as indicated in the table and the number of times that Matthew and Luke remove or alter εὐθύς from Mark results from the episodes that Matthew and Luke do not reproduce from Mark.

65. Luke prefers the latter, while Matthew the former. On six occasions Luke substitutes παραχρῆμα for a Markan εὐθύς and only once substitutes εὐθέως. Matthew always substitutes εὐθέως.

66. Matthew 3:16; 13:20, 21; 14:27; 21:3.

Given the kinds of changes that Matthew and Luke make to Mark and the consistency with which they do so, the second mode of redaction is more likely than the first.[67] In the gospels' media context the stylus was nearly proverbial for correction. Horace writes, "Often you must flip your stylus to erase, if you hope to write something worth a second reading" (Saepe stilum vertas, iterum quae digna legi sint scripturus) (Horace, *Sat.* 1.10.72 [(modified) Fairclough, LCL]). Quintilian, introducing correction as the "most useful" (utilissima) aspect of study, states, "It has been held, and not without reason, that the pen is as active as it ever is when it scratches something out" (neque enim sine causa creditum est stilum non minus agere cum delet) (Quintilian, *Inst.* 10.4.1 [Russell, LCL]). He further recommends using tablets for initial drafts and leaving one side blank for corrections and additions (Quintilian, *Inst.* 10.3.31–32).[68]

John Poirier argues that New Testament scholarship has overlooked the important role that wax tablets played in the composition process.[69] He shows that their use in the gospels' media environment was ubiquitous. He concludes, "The evangelists almost certainly would have composed their Gospels with the aid of these tablets. This would have allowed them to refine their structure, phrasing and word choice with nearly as much ease as writers in the twenty-first century enjoy."[70] Long before Poirier, Roberts and Skeat demonstrated that using parchment notebooks for rough drafts was well established.[71] Both wax and parchment were highly re-usable. Wax because it could be smoothed out and parchment because the ink could be washed off.

In either form, the use of notebooks for the creation of literary documents was customary. Notebooks offered physical space to visualize words and emend them to reflect written norms. Visualization is precisely what endows written narrative with stylistic sophistication, exactitude, and complexity. Matthew and Luke, as carefully crafted and edited narratives, were worked out in draft

---

67. Though we should not exclude the possibility that Matthew and Luke had different techniques for redacting their source texts.

68. Quintilian suggests that wax tablets are best because they allow an author to pour forth their thoughts without the interruption of dipping reed in ink. Parchment notebooks are second best and should be used as a concession if an individual has poor eyesight.

69. John C. Poirier, "The Roll, the Codex, the Wax Tablet and the Synoptic Problem," *JSNT* 35 (2012): 19–21.

70. Poirier, "Roll, the Codex, the Wax Tablet," 21.

71. C. H. Roberts and T. C. Skeat, *The Birth of the Codex* (London: Oxford University Press, 1983), 15–23.

form using notebooks. This was akin to Galen's process of "properly completing" texts that were taken down from oral events.

MATTHEW AND LUKE'S INTERTEXTS

That Matthew and Luke were carefully composed in draft form with the aid of notebooks also explains features of their intertextuality with Scripture as compared to Mark's. Eric Eve rightly recovers memory for the evocation of Scriptural traditions and texts.[72] He suggests that the default assumption ought to be that the gospel writers worked from memory while engaging these traditions. This does not mean that the evangelists never made eye contact with manuscripts during the composition process. When there is a "particularly high degree of verbatim agreement" the assumption must be modified.[73] Usually the gospel writers quoted, alluded to, and echoed Scripture from memory, but on occasion they made eye contact with source texts. Matthew and Luke made eye contact with physical manuscripts of Scriptural texts during the composition process more often than Mark. They are more prone to double-check their references, especially when the references come from Mark.

Jerome opted not to embed Scriptural intertexts in *Epistle* 117 because he dictated it in one night, extemporizing as he went (Jerome, *Ep.* 117.12). Similarly, at the end of *Epistle* 127 Jerome states that he dictated the text and thus "used no charms of eloquence" (Jerome, *Ep.* 127.14 [Wright, LCL]). On one occasion Galen remarks on the absence of direct references to antecedent texts in his Hippocratic commentaries: "I seldom made direct reference to commentators. To begin with I did not have their commentaries with me in Rome, as all the books in my possession had remained in Asia. If, then, I remembered some particularly gross error on the part of one of them, such that anyone who followed it would suffer a severe setback in his medical practice, I would indicate this; otherwise, I would confine myself to my own interpretation, without reference to the conflicting interpretations of others" (Galen, *On My Own Books* 34K).[74] The practical reason that Galen did not reference others

---

72. Eve, *Writing the Gospels*, 47–50.
73. Eve, *Writing the Gospels*, 50.
74. P. N. Singer, trans., *Galen: Selected Works* (Oxford: Oxford University Press, 1997), 15. In addition to the Greek text from Karl Gottlob Kühn, ed., *Claudii Galeni opera omnia*, vol. 19 (Leipzig: Car. Cnoblochii, 1830), there is Georg Helmreich, Johannes Marquardt, and Iwani Müller, *Claudii Galeni pergameni scripta minora*, vol. 3 (Leipzig: Teubner, 1891).

who had written similar commentaries on Hippocrates is that he did not have those texts in his possession. When he did recall them, he did so memorially. Notably, per the context immediately preceding this excerpt, these commentaries were not public facing. They were first written for Galen's own benefit, and, like so many of his other discourses, were given to friends when requested.

Galen states that his later Hippocratic commentaries were "composed with an eye to general publication, not just the attainments of that individual [who requested them]" (Galen, *On My Own Books* 34K).[75] While the first set of commentaries was written on Galen's first visit to Rome in absence of his library and for private purposes, the second set was written during his second stay in Rome with access to his library and was public facing.[76] The two kinds of commentaries can be directly compared to one another.

Galen's treatment is more robust in the second category than in the first.[77] He was less thorough in his former commentary because he knew the attainments of the friend to whom he gave the text. In the preface to the second commentary on the same Hippocratic text, he writes, "I will begin by writing those things which I had omitted to say at the start of *The Elements According to Hippocrates*, since I knew that my friend was already familiar with them."[78] Galen must provide in writing the information that he cannot presume his public audience possesses. Not only do the two commentaries differ with respect to their content, but also their method and structure.[79] The later commentary is exacting, commenting on *The Nature of Man* line by line.

The point is not that Galen doesn't excerpt *any* texts when he composes the first category of commentaries. It is that Galen's textual products differ based on their social destinations. Private texts are less complete, and public-facing texts have been composed with greater care. When both exist in Galen's oeuvre, the movement is always from the former to the latter.[80]

---

75. Singer, *Galen*, 16.

76. Jacques Jouanna, "Galen's Reading of the Hippocratic Treatise *The Nature of Man*: The Foundations of Hippocratism in Galen," in *Greek Medicine from Hippocrates to Galen: Selected Papers*, ed. Philip van der Eijk, trans. Neil Allies (Leiden: Brill, 2012), 317–18.

77. Jouanna, "Galen's Reading," 317–19.

78. As quoted in Jouanna, "Galen's Reading," 318.

79. Jouanna, "Galen's Reading," 319.

80. This is not to state that many texts were not composed carefully from their outset with public reception in mind. Rather, it is to claim that if a text begins life for private uses, it is typically expanded and made more exact in its later, public-facing instantiations.

This same dynamic is reflected in the intertextuality of the Synoptic Gospels. Mark's intertextuality is allusive. The evangelist knows and engages Scripture, even artfully.[81] But "artfully" and "precisely" are not synonyms. When Mark reproduces known versions of Scripture verbatim, it is only in short snippets.[82] It does not appear that Mark consults written versions of the texts that are engaged, even when they are quoted.[83] Exact reproduction is a hallmark of writing, and even more so of print. Mark's allusive manner of intertextuality and his citation "mistakes" result from memorial recall of texts.

Matthew and Luke likewise default to memorial reproduction. But they also engage Scripture textually. They make eye contact with a manuscript and excerpt a portion of text. On at least one occasion in Matthew and one in Luke, the writers correct a memorial "misquotation" from Mark with a more precise and extended quotation of the source text.

Mark infamously begins with a mixed quotation of Exod 23:20, Mal 3:1, and Isa 40:3. This is the "most complete and explicit citation in the Gospel of Mark."[84] The evangelist attributes the amalgamation to "Isaiah the prophet." As Christopher Bryan cheekily puts it, Mark "cites (more or less)" and "does not trouble to check the source of his allusions."[85] Mark 1:2–3's intertextuality is inexact. Matthew and Luke make it exact.[86]

Both emend the introduction to the quotation and then reproduce only the words that are from Isaiah, moving Mark's "behold, I send my messenger before your face, who will prepare your way," which comes from Exodus

---

81. As has been established by Joel Marcus (*The Way of the Lord: Christological Exegesis of the Old Testament in the Gospel of Mark* [Louisville: Westminster John Knox, 1992]) and Richard B. Hays (*Echoes of Scripture in the Gospels* [Waco, TX: Baylor University Press, 2016], 15–103).

82. The partial-Shema quotation in Mark 12:29–30 is the greatest exception. It is thirty-eight words and follows LXX Deut 6:4–5 closely, diverging only at the end of the quote. Even in this case, though, memorial recall is likely because the Shema was ostensibly recited twice daily (Adela Yarbro Collins, *Mark: A Commentary*, Hermeneia [Minneapolis: Fortress, 2007], 572–73).

83. Richard A. Horsley argues similarly ("Oral and Written Aspects of the Emergence of the Gospel of Mark as Scripture," *Oral Tradition* 25 [2010]: 98).

84. Collins, *Mark*, 136.

85. Christopher Bryan, *A Preface to Mark: Notes on the Gospel in Its Literary and Cultural Settings* (New York: Oxford University Press, 1993), 138.

86. Under the two-document hypothesis, Mark 1:2–3 overlaps with Q, and Marcus suggests that Matthew and Luke follow the latter here (Marcus, *Way of the Lord*, 15). Even if the later evangelists are dependent on Q, they have both decided to follow the more precise citation against Mark's imprecision.

and Malachi, to Matt 11 and Luke 7, respectively.[87] Matthew keeps only the fourteen words from Isaiah, and Luke extends the quotation, adding the next twenty-nine words of Isa 40:4–5. The result is the longest quotation in Luke's gospel by a full seventeen words.[88]

Matt 3:3	Mark 1:2–3	Luke 3:4–6
For this is the one Isaiah the prophet spoke about, saying, "The voice of one calling in the desert: 'Prepare the way of the Lord! Make his paths straight!'"	As it is written in Isaiah the prophet: "Behold, I am sending my messenger before your face, who will prepare your way; the voice of one calling out in the desert: 'Prepare the way of the Lord! Make his paths straight!'"	As it is written in the Book of the Words of Isaiah the Prophet: "The voice of one calling in the desert: 'Prepare the way of the Lord! Make his paths straight! Every valley will be filled and every mountain and hill will be made low, and the crooked will be straight, and the rough roads smooth; and all flesh will see the salvation of God.'"
οὗτος γάρ ἐστιν ὁ ῥηθεὶς διὰ Ἡσαΐου τοῦ προφήτου λέγοντος· φωνὴ βοῶντος ἐν τῇ ἐρήμῳ· ἑτοιμάσατε τὴν ὁδὸν κυρίου, εὐθείας ποιεῖτε τὰς τρίβους αὐτοῦ.	Καθὼς γέγραπται ἐν τῷ Ἡσαΐᾳ τῷ προφήτῃ· ἰδοὺ ἀποστέλλω τὸν ἄγγελόν μου πρὸ προσώπου σου, ὃς κατασκευάσει τὴν ὁδόν σου· φωνὴ βοῶντος ἐν τῇ ἐρήμῳ· ἑτοιμάσατε τὴν ὁδὸν κυρίου, εὐθείας ποιεῖτε τὰς τρίβους αὐτοῦ.	ὡς γέγραπται ἐν βίβλῳ λόγων Ἡσαΐου τοῦ προφήτου· φωνὴ βοῶντος ἐν τῇ ἐρήμῳ· ἑτοιμάσατε τὴν ὁδὸν κυρίου, εὐθείας ποιεῖτε τὰς τρίβους αὐτοῦ· πᾶσα φάραγξ πληρωθήσεται καὶ πᾶν ὄρος καὶ βουνὸς ταπεινωθήσεται, καὶ ἔσται τὰ σκολιὰ εἰς εὐθεῖαν καὶ αἱ τραχεῖαι εἰς ὁδοὺς λείας· καὶ ὄψεται πᾶσα σὰρξ τὸ σωτήριον τοῦ θεοῦ.

While Luke might recall these additional two verses from Isaiah from memory during the composition process, it is more likely that in the act of correcting Mark's intertextuality the author has made eye contact with a manuscript of the "Book of the Words of Isaiah the Prophet" (Luke 3:4). Not only is the quotation the longest in Luke, but it is also three times longer than Luke's average quotation.[89] At its end, Luke has omitted both Isa 40:5a and c, keeping only 40:5b, "and all flesh will see the salvation of God." This is

---

87. Matt 11:10; Luke 7:27. Each has Jesus speak the quotation and introduces it with the phrase, "This is about whom it has been written" (οὗτός ἐστιν περὶ οὗ γέγραπται).

88. The next longest quotations are in Luke 4:18–19 and 10:27, which are each twenty-six words. The former also comes from Isaiah and the latter is the Shema from Deut 6.

89. Based on UBS4's quotation list, the mean length of Luke's quotations is 13 words and the median 10 words.

not a case of misremembering. It is the author omitting two lines so that the quotation ends on the Lukan note of salvation.[90] Reproducing a text of forty or more words from memory with such exactitude is not impossible. However, the longer the quotation and the more precisely it reflects its source text, the more likely it is that there is eye contact with a physical version of it in the process of composition.

While Matt 3 does not extend the quotation from Isaiah as Luke 3 does, there is another occasion when Matthew corrects and expands an imprecise Markan quotation. In Mark 4:12, Jesus offers the reason that he speaks in parables: "In order that in the act of seeing they shall see and not perceive, and in the act of hearing they shall hear and not understand, lest perchance they might turn and it be forgiven them."[91] Jesus's explanation frustrates interpreters on two counts. First, he is intentionally obdurate. Why speak with confounding riddles deliberately to cloud understanding?[92] Second, and more relevant for our purposes, his "quotation" can be pinned to Isa 6:9–10, but not any single textual version of it. The vocabulary in Mark's adaptation is Septuagintal even where the Septuagint departs from the Masoretic Text.[93] But there are also drastic differences between the Markan verse and LXX Isa 6:9–10. Mark 4:12 exhibits notable similarities to the Aramaic Targum, especially in the final clause "and it be forgiven them."[94] But Mark differs from the Septuagint, Masoretic Text, and the Targum, as "seeing" precedes "hearing" in only the gospel. The result is that Mark 4:12 does not reproduce any known text of Isa 6:9–10. It is a paraphrase recalled from memory.

---

90. The omitted clause from Isa 40:5a reads "and the glory of the Lord shall appear." As Nolland notes, the omission is fitting because "glory does not characterize the public ministry of Jesus but is the outcome of his suffering and will mark his return" in Luke (*Luke 1:1–9:20*, 144).

91. My own literal translation.

92. There have been interpretive attempts to soften Jesus's intransigence. Most notably, T. W. Manson explains the difficulty away based on Mark's mistranslation of the Aramaic from the Isaiah Targum (*The Teaching of Jesus: Studies of the Form and Content* [Cambridge: Cambridge University Press, 1943], 77–79).

93. Craig A. Evans, *To See and Not Perceive: Isaiah 6.9–10 in Early Jewish and Christian Interpretation*, JSOTSup 64 (Sheffield: Sheffield Academic, 1989), 92; Joel Marcus, *Mark 1–8: A New Translation with Introduction and Commentary*, 2 vols., AB 27 (New York: Doubleday, 2008), 300.

94. The similarities with the Targum are presented by Manson (*Teaching of Jesus*, 77–79) and Evans (*To See and Not Perceive*, 92).

Both Matthew and Luke refine Mark's paraphrase, making it more poignant, though they do so by different editorial means:

Matt 13:13	Mark 4:12	Luke 8:10
"Because seeing they don't see and hearing they neither hear nor understand."	"In order that in the act of seeing they shall see and not perceive, and in the act of hearing they shall hear and not understand, lest perchance they might turn and it be forgiven them."	"In order that seeing they shall not see and hearing they shall not understand."
ὅτι βλέποντες οὐ βλέπουσιν καὶ ἀκούοντες οὐκ ἀκούουσιν οὐδὲ συνίουσιν.	ἵνα βλέποντες βλέπωσιν καὶ μὴ ἴδωσιν, καὶ ἀκούοντες ἀκούωσιν καὶ μὴ συνιῶσιν, μήποτε ἐπιστρέψωσιν καὶ ἀφεθῇ αὐτοῖς.	ἵνα βλέποντες μὴ βλέπωσιν καὶ ἀκούοντες μὴ συνιῶσιν.

Together Matthew and Luke remove the final clause in Mark that is shared with the Targum. They also eliminate Mark's redundant subjunctives that are paired with the participles. By paring down Mark's version, Matthew and Luke make it clear they are not attempting a quotation from the prophetic tradition. They also soften Jesus's intransigent purpose for speaking in parables.

While Luke retains Mark's obdurate ἵνα ("in order that"), Matthew reverses Jesus's logic for teaching in parables by altering it to a causal ὅτι ("because"). In Matthew, Jesus's teaching is not purposefully confounding. It is confounding because the outsiders are already intransigent. Matthew then continues the invective by properly quoting LXX Isa 6:9–10, introducing it with a fulfillment formula. The quotation is Matthew's second longest at forty-seven words.[95]

In an accordion-like intertextual move, Matthew has initially shortened the Markan paraphrase of Isa 6:9–10 to quote the text in full immediately thereafter. As was the case with Luke's extensive quotation of Isa 40, I contend Matthew has checked Mark's unfamiliar paraphrase and then reproduced more precisely a Septuagintal version of the text. This is a rare case in which Matthew's quotation matches the Septuagint nearly verbatim, diverging from it by only one word.[96]

---

95. Matthew's longest quotation is of Isa 42:1–4 in Matt 12:18–21.

96. Matt 13:15 omits "their" (αὐτῶν) after "ears" (ὠσίν) from Isa 6:10. The same text is quoted in Acts 28:26–27 and likewise diverges from the LXX by the same word. This may suggest that the author of Luke is familiar with Matthew's correction but has decided to place the extensive quotation elsewhere.

These instances of Matthean and Lukan expansions of Mark's imprecise intertextuality do not represent their normal procedure for quoting texts. In both Matt 13:14–15 and Luke 3:4–6, the protracted reproductions of Isa 6:9–10 and 40:4–5, respectively, are outliers. This is Luke's longest quotation and Matthew's second-longest. On no other occasion does Luke quote a text of more than thirty words and Matthew does so on only two other occasions.

Matthew and Luke found Mark's inaccurate visualization of a scriptural tradition objectionable. They set out to fix the miscitation of Isaiah in Mark 1:2–3 and the unfamiliar quotation from the same prophetic tradition in Mark 4:12. Doing so involved cross-checking the source text. These are the only occasions that Matthew and Luke extensively supplement a Markan mistake; they are not the only occasions they fix one, intertextual or otherwise.[97]

This is not to suggest that the later Synoptic authors are above intertextual tomfoolery or memorial mistakes. Matthew misattributes texts in a manner akin to Mark. Matthew 13:35, for instance, quotes Ps 78:2, but introduces the Psalmic text with the formula, "Thus was fulfilled what was spoken through *the prophet.*" Psalms are not prophets. Matthew 27:9-10 references Zech 11, but names "*Jeremiah* the prophet" in the fulfillment formula. Zechariah is not Jeremiah. In this case, the reference to the "potter's field" suggested Jeremiah, wherein the potter features prominently.[98]

It is unlikely that Matthew has consulted a physical manuscript to reproduce the intertext. The text is recalled memorially in the act of composition and is misattributed. Eric Eve's default assumption that the gospel writers cite Scripture from memory holds. However, there are occasions in which the later Synoptic authors are working from and making eye contact with physical texts. This is the case with their use of Mark itself and with Q if it existed, but also with the Isaianic texts they quote extensively. Matthew and Luke do reproduce traditions precisely. This involved making eye contact with a manuscript and either copying its words by hand or dictating the content exactly. Both acts are literary endeavors.

Matthew and Luke improve upon Mark intertextually and stylistically. Both kinds of improvement are indicative of their compositional mode. Extensively quoting an antecedent text after fixing the reference in their predecessor

---

97. Matthew, Luke, or both do so with Mark 2:26; 14:21; 14:27; 14:29. I address these at greater length in Elder, *Media Matrix*, 119–23.

98. Ulrich Luz, *Matthew 21–28*, trans. James E. Crouch (Minneapolis: Fortress, 2005), 473; Donald A. Hagner, *Matthew 14–28*, WBC 33B (Dallas: Thomas Nelson, 1995), 813.

involves manipulating a physical instantiation of the tradition. While memorial recall is not exclusive to composing a text by mouth, it is more native to that compositional mode than to crafting a written discourse by hand. Stylistic improvement involves the visualization and correction of the text.

John

Matthew and Luke present the opportunity to observe directly how they alter an antecedent text and to draw conclusions about their composition on that basis. This is not the case for John, whose relationship with the Synoptics differs from Matthew and Luke's reuse of Mark. Nonetheless, assessing John's stylistic features illumines its distinctiveness among the canonical gospels. The Fourth Gospel does not resemble either the style of Mark or the later Synoptics.

In some ways, John bears the hallmarks of a literarily, not orally, composed text to a greater extent than Matthew and Luke do.[99] In other ways, the narrative resembles stylistic features that are more characteristic of oral storytelling than written. The Fourth Gospel introduces a new semantics that does not stylistically correspond to Mark, Matthew, or Luke. We will look to three of the same linguistic features that we did with respect to the Synoptic Gospels: intertextuality, parataxis, and the historical present.

INTERTEXTS

John is not keen to reproduce and embed antecedent texts into the gospel. The narrative contains more citation formulas than it does quoted texts. On nineteen occasions, the Fourth Gospel indicates that a text is being referenced.[100] However, on two of these occasions nothing at all is quoted and on another two it is uncertain what discrete text is referenced. The results are that, at maximum, John contains seventeen quotations of Scripture and, at minimum, thirteen.[101] Even when the parameters are widened to include allusions, John's textual evocations are sparse. According to Richard B. Hays, Scripture is referenced

---

99. Contra Joanna Dewey (*The Oral Ethos of the Early Church: Speaking, Writing, and the Gospel of Mark*, Biblical Performance Criticism Series 8 [Eugene, OR: Cascade, 2013], 46–48).

100. John 1:23; 2:17; 6:31, 45; 7:38; 8:17; 10:34; 12:13, 15, 38, 39–40; 13:18; 15:25; 17:12; 19:24, 28, 36, 37. John uses several different citation formulae: "said" (εἶπεν), "says" (λέγει), "it is written" (γεγραμμένον ἐστίν), "it has been written" (γέγραπται), "these things were written" (ταῦτα ἦν γεγραμμένα), "to fulfill" (πληρωθῇ).

101. Hays, *Echoes of Scripture*, 284.

only 27 times in John, compared to 124 times in Matthew, 109 in Luke, and 70 in Mark.[102] When the Fourth Gospel does quote Scripture it is in short snippets, averaging eight words each.

The Fourth Gospel's longest quotation is nineteen words from LXX Isa 6:10 in John 12:39–40. This quotation is paralleled in the Synoptics and was addressed in the previous section. Mark's version of Isa 6:9–10 is inexact, and this was a result of memorial recall. Matthew and Luke each alter the Markan paraphrase and Matthew continues to reproduce the Septuagintal version.

It is possible that John's longest quotation was occasioned either by Mark's inexact allusion to the same Isaianic text or by Matthew's more exact and extended quotation of it. But I have no intention to press that argument here. Instead, I wish to call attention to a pattern with respect to the longer-than-average quotations in John: most of them have a parallel citation in the Synoptics. After John 12:40, the next longest quotation in the gospel is thirteen words from Zech 9:9, which appears just twenty-five verses earlier at John 12:15. This quotation is also paralleled in the Synoptics, and James W. Barker has made a compelling case that it is mediated to John by way of Matthew's Gospel.[103] In total, on only seven occasions does the Fourth Gospel quote a text of more than eight words, and five of these have parallel citations in one or more of the Synoptics.[104] The nine other occasions when John explicitly quotes material do not have Synoptic parallels, and each of these quotations is eight words or less.[105]

John's quotations overwhelmingly come from the Psalms and Isaiah. This is the case whether a Johannine citation possesses a Synoptic parallel or not. Twelve of John's fourteen quoted texts that are identifiable come from these two corpora.[106] The other two come from Zechariah, one apparently mediated by the Synoptics and the other a quotation of only four words.

I do not conclude from this data that John lacks access to scriptural texts or is unable to reproduce them. I take the Johannine reticence to engage texts directly, whether they be the Synoptics or Scripture, to be an extension of the author's agenda of literary metamorphosis. As Hays puts it, "John's manner of

---

102. Hays, *Echoes of Scripture*, 284.
103. James Barker, *John's Use of Matthew* (Minneapolis: Fortress Press, 2015), 63–92.
104. John's longest quotations are at John 1:23; 12:13, 15, 38, 39–40; 13:18; 19:24. Those that do not have a Synoptic parallel are John 12:38; 13:18.
105. John 2:17; 6:31, 45; 7:38; 8:17; 10:34; 15:25; 19:36, 37.
106. John 7:38; 17:12; 19:28 all contain quotation formulae, but nothing is quoted. John 8:17 contains a quotation formula, but it is difficult to ascertain what text is referenced.

alluding does not depend upon the citation of chains of words and phrases; instead it relies upon evoking *images* and *figures* from Israel's Scripture."[107] This is a departure from the Synoptics' manner of evoking intertexts.

Does John's intertextuality indicate anything about its composition, whether by hand, mouth, or a combination of the two? The method of evoking intertexts does not signal careful composition by hand. John's mode of memorial recall is at home in oral composition, but it is not exclusive to it. If it appeared alongside other predominately oral stylistic features, this method of evoking antecedent texts might be taken as evidence for oral composition. However, two characteristics of the Fourth Gospel, namely parataxis and the historical present, display written psychodynamics.

PARATAXIS

John is less dependent on καί ("and") than all the Synoptic Gospels. Mark defaults to paratactic structuring, which is a defining feature of oral storytelling.[108] Readers of Mark, including Matthew and Luke, consider this an element of literary disfluency. Matthew particularly depresses Mark's paratactic structure. But John employs καί even less frequently than does Matthew. The connective constitutes 5.5% of the Fourth Gospel's total words and 6.5% of the First Gospel's. When comparing John with the Matthean double tradition and unique Matthean pericopes, however, the volume of καί is nearly identical. The connective καί makes up 5.5% and 5.4% of the total words of each, respectively.

Turning to its position, καί begins only 11% of John's sentences. This compared to 65% of Mark's sentences, 21% of Matthew's, and 30% of Luke's. Similarly, καί begins 9% of John's paragraphs, compared to 92% of Mark's, 21% of Matthew's, and 32% of Luke's.[109] While Matthew's and Luke's use of καί is supplemented with δέ, John's use of the latter conjunction, like Mark's, is comparatively minimal, constituting 1.4% of the total words of both gospels compared to 2.7% and 2.8% of Matthew's and Luke's, respectively.

---

107. Hays, *Echoes of Scripture*, 284; italics in original.

108. Beaman, "Coordination and Subordination Revisited," 60–61; Paul Zumthor, *Oral Poetry: An Introduction*, trans. Kathy Murphy-Judy, Theory and History of Literature 70 (Minneapolis: University of Minnesota Press, 1990), 107.

109. In John, 14/155 paragraphs begin with καί, 114/145 in Mark, 29/237 in Matthew, 77/240 in Luke. With respect to sentences, 100/907 in John begin with καί, 376/583 in Mark, 202/979 in Matthew, and 309/1,017 in Luke. These all per the editorial decisions in NA28.

HISTORICAL PRESENT

At 165 occurrences, the historical present appears more often in the Fourth Gospel than any other. As to the percentage of the total number of indicative verbs it constitutes, however, John falls between Mark and Matthew.[110] In a manner akin to Matthew, John overwhelmingly employs the historical present with verbs of speaking. Of the 165 historical presents in the gospel, 125 of them are "speech margins."[111]

According to Mavis Leung, there are four common ways that John employs its forty historical presents outside of speech margins.[112] The following four categories are not mutually exclusive to one another. First, at twenty-two occurrences, the most common way the historical present functions outside of speech margins is to introduce new characters.[113] The second most common, at seventeen occurrences, is in near proximity to direct speech.[114] That is, direct speech triggers a shift into the historical present for these verbs that do not themselves introduce the speech but are in proximity to a verb that does.[115] The third and fourth most common uses of the historical present are to initiate a new pericope and to move a character into a new location, which happens on ten and eight occasions, respectively.[116]

Non-speech-margin historical presents in John primarily appear at the start of a new episode, when a new character enters the story, and when the story moves to a new location. This coheres well with sociolinguistic research, which finds that, especially in oral narrative, the historical present most frequently

---

110. Of Mark's indicative verbs, 9.9% (150/1,520) are historical presents, 6.4% of John's (165/2,556), and 4.2% of Matthew's (94/2,245). I follow Mavis Leung's tabulation for John's historical presents, which differs slightly from John J. O'Rourke's (Leung, "The Narrative Function and Verbal Aspect of the Historical Present in the Fourth Gospel," *JETS* 51 [2008]: 708; John J. O'Rourke, "The Historic Present in the Gospel of John," *JBL* 93 [1974]: 585–90).

111. Leung, "Narrative Function," 709.

112. Leung, "Narrative Function," 710.

113. John 1:29, 41, 43, 45; 2:9; 4:7; 6:19; 9:13; 12:22a, b; 13:6, 24, 26b, 26c; 18:3; 20:2a, b, 12, 14, 18, 26; 21:20.

114. John 1:15, 29, 41, 43, 45; 2:9; 4:7; 5:14; 12:23; 13:6, 26a, 38; 18:29; 20:2a, b, 26; 21:20.

115. On nine of these seventeen occasions, the verb introducing direct discourse is a historical present form of λέγω.

116. A historical present begins a pericope in John 1:43; 5:2, 14; 9:13; 11:38; 13:4a, b; 18:28; 20:1a, b and indicates movement into a new location in John 4:5; 11:38; 18:3, 28; 20:2a, b, 6a, 18.

appears at the beginning of an episode or when a new character or setting is introduced.[117]

This is not evidence that John was composed primarily by mouth in a manner akin to Mark. Two factors related to the historical present mitigate against such a conclusion. First, the historical present in John is rare when speech margins are excluded. Only 24% of John's historical presents are not verbs of speaking, compared to 30% of Matthew's and 51% of Mark's. Second, unlike Mark, the Gospel of John does employ the historical present to conclude a pericope on several occasions.[118] Monika Fludernik and Deborah Schiffrin each find that the historical present will not conclude a spoken episode.[119]

Whereas the Gospel of Mark closely follows linguistic norms for the historical present in spoken narrative, John does to a limited degree, while also diverging from them. This exemplifies Fludernik's description of the historical present in literature vis-à-vis oral storytelling: "There is a specific pattern of the use of the present tense within oral storytelling. Literary occurrences of the historical present tense only partly repeat this oral pattern, but can be explained as an extension and application of it to written narrative."[120]

The Fourth Gospel's consistent use of verbs that are imperfective in aspect does follow what is characteristic of spoken norms and resembles Mark. Sociolinguists find that the progressive tenses, which in Koine Greek are the imperfect and present, are more frequent in oral storytelling than written.[121] The imperfect and present tenses constitute 51% of John's total indicative verbs, compared to 54% of Mark's and 40% of both Matthew's and Luke's.[122] In unique Lukan and Matthean material, presents and imperfects make up 34% and 31% of the indicative verbs, respectively.

While John's style is often considered "simplistic," the analysis here demonstrates that it is not simplistic in a manner identical to Mark's. Two Markan

---

117. Fludernik, "Historical Present Tense," 202; Fludernik, "Historical Present Tense Yet Again," 375; Schiffrin, "Tense Variation," 51–52.

118. John 13:38; 20:18; 21:13a, b, c, per Leung "Narrative Function," 710.

119. Schiffrin, "Tense Variation, 51; Fludernik, "Historical Present Tense," 86; Fludernik, "Historical Present Tense Yet Again," 375–76.

120. Fludernik, "The Historical Present Tense Yet Again," 387.

121. Schiffrin, "Tense Variation," 58–59; Chafe, *Discourse, Consciousness, and Time*, 197–208.

122. In John, present and imperfect tenses constitute 1,314/2,556 total indicative forms, compared to 806/1,495 in Mark, 895/2,243 in Matthew, and 986/2,443 in Luke.

features that are especially illuminating with respect to Mark's compositional mode, parataxis and the historical present, are not mirrored in the Fourth Gospel. They are depressed even in comparison to Matthew and Luke, which consistently literaturize these oral residues from their predecessor. If John's composition scenario were like Mark's, parataxis would feature prominently, as it is a defining characteristic of spoken narrative.

Plotting the gospels on a spectrum of more to less oral or literary, John might be placed between Mark and the later Synoptics. In some ways, the Fourth Gospel reflects oral stylistic features to a greater extent than the later Synoptics do. In other respects, John's stylistic features manifest norms of written narrative to a greater extent than Matthew and Luke's do. This cautions against positioning John between the first and later Synoptics. The relationship between orality and literacy is not two-dimensional. John's style also prevents drawing firm conclusions about its compositional mode. The mixed stylistic features of John might imply that oral discourses have been literaturized and edited. They might equally suggest the gospel is a text that was dictated in literary mode and subsequently edited. Whatever the case, the Fourth Gospel differs from all three of its predecessors.

Conclusion

Just as the gospels were not all read the same way, so also they were not written the same way. There are a variety of methods and technologies for composing written discourses in any context. Certain kinds of texts are more likely to be composed utilizing certain processes. The reception of a text influences its composition.

A text that is informal or created for the purpose of re-oralization need not be literaturized in the same manner as one created to be read by individuals. Authors who do not expect their text to be scrutinized visually compose and edit differently than those who do.

Mark was reduced from an oral event for the purpose of re-oralization. The narrative's oral style reflects this and indicates that it was composed by mouth. When assessed literarily, Mark's style is substandard. When reactivated in oral mode, however, the gospel thrives. Matthew and Luke, as narratives written for different modes of reception, reflect different compositional influences. They emend Mark's oral stylistic features, crafting literaturized texts. When assessed literarily, they outmatch Mark. But the later Synoptics have a different effect when reactivated orally. Whereas Mark still works well as a discourse performed in its entirety, Matthew and Luke work best as texts read privately by individuals or aloud in sections. John cuts both ways. It succeeds as a discourse read not in its entirety, but in larger sections than Matthew or Luke. Just as the Fourth Gospel supplements the material from the Synoptics, so also does it complement the style and reading events for which they will have made.

PART 3

Circulating

Publication is a social construct. In the modern context, it is about making a work available for commercial distribution or sale. But in the etymological sense, "public-cation" is the process of making a discourse accessible to people. There are numerous ways that discourses can be made available. Publication constructs differ between social contexts and for different media forms. In our own context, monographs, textbooks, magazines, press releases, blog posts, emails, and Tweets are all written texts that are made public in differing ways. For some of these media, publication is an officious and finalized enterprise. For others, it is not. Some communication media are editable and retractable. Others are less so. The medium impacts the circulation of the message.

While publication practices in Greco-Roman antiquity differ from modern ones, overstating the dissimilarities in process neglects the similarities in their fundamental nature. In both contexts, publication is a social initiative by which a text becomes available to persons who did not produce it. Just as publication processes vary for modern media, so also did they vary for ancient and New Testament media.

The following two chapters survey social and material phenomena related to ancient distribution, circulation, and publication of texts. I use these three words differently. "Distribution" is an umbrella term. It connotes a discourse becoming available to one or more persons with whom it did not originate. "Circulation" involves the sharing of a text. A text can circulate in several ways. Circulation might be between an author and individuals to whom they make the text available. But a text can also reach individuals with whom the author has no social ties. "Publication" is the narrowest term of the three. It connotes a text making its way into the hands of a wide readership, usually intentionally.[1] Sociality unites distribution, circulation, and publication. All three are social initiatives by which texts are brokered between persons. Considering them as such allows us better to appreciate and evaluate their diverse forms.

---

1. The idea that "publication" makes a text available to anyone and everyone, in either the modern or ancient context, is a fiction. The accessibility of any written text is always limited by numerous factors, such as materiality, language, education, space, time, and social networks.

CHAPTER 7

Publication and Circulation

Media Myth: Texts were distributed following a "concentric circles" model in which the discourse gained more influence and readers as it went systematically through these different social circles.
Media Reality: Texts were distributed in a variety of different ways.

◆ ◆ ◆

Raymond J. Starr's model of circulating texts in Greco-Roman antiquity is celebrated in both classical and biblical studies. Starr proposes, "Romans circulated texts in a series of widening concentric circles determined primarily by friendship."[1] In figure 1, the innermost circles with solid lines represent the physical creation and distribution of texts, as well as making them known to friends through recitations. The notches in the line segment indicate a text's stops along the way to publication. After textualization, an indefinite number of these inner circles could have been added, depending on how thorough an author wished to be. The more feedback and revisions, the more circles.

In the first circle, a draft is sent to a single friend for feedback. The second circle widens as the author physically distributes and recites the discourse to additional confidants. The aims of circulation in these first two spheres are multiple: to strengthen social ties, to make friends aware of the text, and to improve it.

Several of Pliny's letters allude to sharing texts with colleagues in this manner. These letters are written to accompany or introduce a work that Pliny has included for review.[2] For instance, he sends a cover letter to Maturus Arrianus with a speech that accompanies it (Pliny the Younger, *Ep.* 1.2). In the opening lines of the letter, Pliny requests that Arrianus read and correct the speech, as he usually does. With feigned humility, Pliny informs him that its

---

1. Raymond J. Starr, "The Circulation of Literary Texts in the Roman World," *ClQ* 37 (1987): 213.
2. In addition to the letters addressed below, Pliny the Younger alludes to the practice in *Ep.* 2.5, 8; 3.15; 4.12; 4.14; 6.33; 9.35.

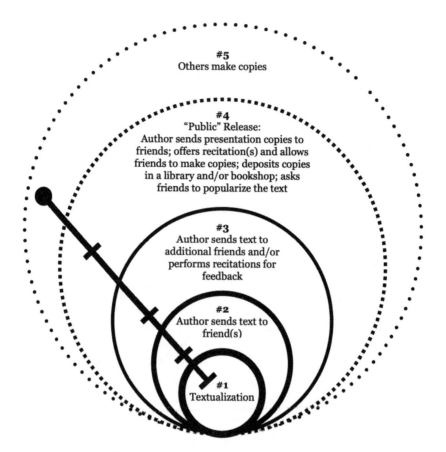

Figure 1. Concentric Circles Model

publication is dependent on his assessment of it: "My friends and I are thinking of publishing it, if only you cast your vote for the proposal, mistaken though it may be" (Pliny the Younger, *Ep.* 1.2 [Radice, LCL]). Pliny sends another letter as an attachment to comments he has made for Tacitus on either a book of the *Histories* or the *Dialogus*.[3] Pliny writes, "I have read your book, and marked as carefully as I could the passages which I think should be altered or removed" (Pliny the Younger, *Ep.* 7.20 [Radice, LCL]). Pliny then reminds Tacitus that he is still awaiting comments on one of his own works.

In both letters, feedback for the purpose of revision is a primary reason for exchanging texts. But there is also a social dimension to these exchanges.

---

3. See Radice, LCL 55:529n1.

This is on full display in the letter to Tacitus, wherein Pliny waxes poetic about being mentioned in the same breath as the historian. He writes, "There may be writers who are ranked higher than either of us, but if we are classed together our position does not matter; for me the highest position is the one nearest to you" (Pliny the Younger, *Ep.* 7.20 [Radice, LCL]). In another letter to Tacitus, Pliny gushes at the opportunity to remark on his writing (Pliny the Younger, *Ep.* 8.7). The flattery is a prelude to his confirmation that he will comment on Tacitus's pre-published work. The exchange of texts in the inner circles of Starr's model is not simply pragmatic. Individuals exchange their work not only to receive feedback on it, but also to form and strengthen social bonds.

The same was true of recitations. They strengthened social ties and sharpened a work. In *Ep.* 7.17, Pliny describes at length the entire process by which he revises texts. For Pliny, the initial delivery of the speech does not mark its publication. Publication is textual in nature. Pliny covets praise "not when a speech is first given, but when it is read by others upon its public release" (nec vero ego dum recito laudari, sed dum legor cupio). Consequently, he does not omit any mode of emendation when revising a speech for publication, describing the process as such: "First of all, I go through my work myself; next, I read it to two or three friends and send it to others for comment. If I have any doubts about their criticisms, I go over them again with one or two people, and finally I read the work to a larger audience; and that is the moment, believe me, when I make my severest corrections, for my anxiety makes me concentrate all the more carefully" (Pliny the Younger, *Ep.* 7.17.7–8 [Radice, LCL]). When Pliny reads to a larger audience, he specifies that it is not the "general public" (*populum*), but a "select and limited" group (*certos electosque*). He concludes the letter stating that his aim is to improve the text before it is put into the hands of the people (*dare . . . in manus hominum*), which happens at the fourth circle in Starr's model.

To get their work into the hands of the people, an author had several options that were not exclusive to one another. First, they could gift the text to friends in presentation copies. In addition, an author might offer recitations of the discourse, or portions of it, and make the text available for copying to those in attendance. They might also deposit the text in a library and bookshop, encouraging friends to spread the word about it. From these multiple places that the text was seeded, other persons could make copies of it, which is the outermost circle in Starr's model. There was no guarantee that the text would find any public traction. Starr writes, "If no one wanted to make a copy, no copies would ever be made except by the author himself for presentation to his friends."[4] If others did make a copy of the text, they did so at their own expense and the author was not compensated.

Upon public release, the author relinquished most control over their text. While they might attempt post-publication revisions, the task was more difficult after this point. The inner circles in Starr's model were characterized by feedback and fluidity and the outer circles by polish and finality.

Starr's concentric-circles model demonstrates how literary texts circulated through private channels in Greco-Roman antiquity. It works well as a descriptive representation and conveys the social nature of publication in elite reading communities. As is often the case with models, however, it is too tidy. Pliny's remarks and Starr's model both present ideal circumstances. There is no reason to doubt Pliny's description of his circulation and revision practices, but they should not be taken as prescriptive for every discourse that he made public nor for all authors in Greco-Roman antiquity.

The Complexity of Publication

Starr's model does not apply equally to every kind of text or reading community. Different media are circulated in different ways. Texts do not always move neatly outward in the concentric circles model. They relate to it in various ways. In what follows, Starr's model is complexified. It will be employed as a heuristic but will be modulated to reflect the diverse ways in which the circulation of texts did not reflect ideal publication practices.

"Accidental publication" is a term with which Matthew D. C. Larsen problematizes the "clean, idealized process of making a text public."[5] It is when "the author claims to have no knowledge of how a text became public and such publication was against his will."[6] The author wrote or dictated a preliminary version of the discourse but never released it publicly. The text somehow leaked.

Larsen offers several examples of accidental publication. The first comes from Cicero's remarks in a defamation oration he wrote.[7] He regrets that it became public, as he composed it in a fit of anger and its existence put him in a socially precarious position. Cicero never delivered the speech orally but

---

4. Starr, "Circulation," 215.
5. Matthew D. C. Larsen, *Gospels before the Book* (Oxford: Oxford University Press, 2018), 37–57, here 37.
6. Larsen, *Gospels before the Book*, 38.
7. Cicero comments on the speech in *Att.* 57 and 60.

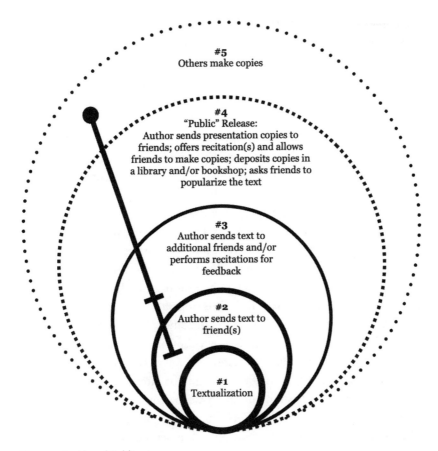

Figure 2. Accidental Publication

must have given a textual version to at least a few friends. He "suppressed it and never expected it to leak out" (sed ita compresseram ut numquam emanaturam putarem) (Cicero, *Att.* 57 [Shackleton Bailey, LCL]). It did, and portions are still extant.[8]

Larsen's second case of accidental publication comes at the end of Diodorus Siculus's massive forty-book project, *The Library of History*. Diodorus claims that his discourses were "pirated and published" (κλαπεῖσαι προεξεδόθησαν) before they were in their final form (Diodorus Siculus, *Library of History* 40.8 [Walton, LCL]). He does not disclose how the texts left his sphere of control,

---

8. For references, see Larsen, *Gospels before the Book*, 167n7.

but it presumably happened as portions of the project were offered to persons for feedback either physically or in recitations.

Cicero and Diodorus have different ways of handling their accidentally published texts. Because the existence of Cicero's calumny puts him in a delicate position, he proposes that it be passed off as a forgery (*puto ex se posse probari non esse meam*) (Cicero, *Att.* 57 [Shackleton Bailey, LCL]). This is possible, Cicero writes, because the speech "seems to be more carelessly written than [his] other compositions" (quia scripta mihi videtur neglegentius quam ceterae) (Cicero, *Att.* 57 [Shackleton Bailey, LCL]). Diodorus addresses the spurious publication head-on. He "publishes a statement that will expose any misconception" (τὸν ἐλέγχοντα λόγον τὴν ἄγνοιαν ἐκθέσθαι) (Diodorus Siculus, *Library of History* 40.8 [Walton, LCL]). This statement catalogues what is in the non-pirated, official version of *The Library of History*.

In both cases, the discourse is textualized by its author, but is never publicly released. Step four in Starr's model is skipped altogether. There is a jump from the second or third circle to the fifth. This trope repeats itself in several other authors. Arrian writes in the preface to Epictetus's *Discourses* that he textualized the teaching but did not know how it "spilled out to people" (ἐξέπεσεν εἰς ἀνθρώπους).[9] Galen frequently states in *On My Own Books* that he wrote texts for his students or himself that he did not intend to publish.[10] These were "private texts." Galen intentionally textualized the discourses, but he meant to circulate them only within his network. The introductions fell into other person's hands and were made public, sometimes in Galen's name and sometimes not.[11]

These examples not only call attention to accidental publication in antiquity, but also to the misattribution of texts. They presume plagiarism. There is ample evidence to various kinds of forgery in antiquity, including:

---

9. Trans. my own. I am dependent on Larsen, *Gospels before the Book*, 47–50 for this reference.

10. Galen, *On My Own Books*, 11–13K; 17K; 34–37K; 42K; 43K. The phenomenon is also mentioned often in *On the Order of My Own Books*. For an English translation see P. N. Singer, trans., *Galen: Selected Works*, The World's Classics (Oxford: Oxford University Press, 1997), 3–22. In addition to the Greek text from Karl Gottlob Kühn, ed., *Claudii Galeni opera omnia*, vol. 19 (Leipzig: Car. Cnoblochii, 1830), there is Georg Helmreich, Johannes Marquardt, and Iwani Müller, *Claudii Galeni pergameni scripta minora*, vol. 3 (Leipzig: Teubner, 1891).

11. For instance, Galen states that *The Motion of the Chest and Lungs* was written for a student, was leaked, and someone else attempted to pass off the text as their own after adding a preface (*On My Own Books* 17K).

1. A text being written in an author's name and containing ideas that were not that author's.
2. An author's textualized but unfinished ideas circulating in the author's name.
3. An author's textualized but unfinished ideas circulating in someone else's name.
4. An author's textualized and finished ideas circulating in someone else's name.
5. An author's untextualized ideas being textualized by someone else and circulating in the author's name.
6. An author's untextualized ideas being textualized by someone else and circulating in someone else's name.

Cicero assumes the first as a phenomenon, as he proposes passing off a text that he did write as this kind of forgery. Diodorus is not explicit, but it seems that he has the second plagiaristic phenomenon in mind with the pirated portions of *The Library of History*. Galen claims to have experienced the entire gamut of offenses. He begins *On My Own Books* with an anecdote about the first kind. While in a Roman bookshop he observed someone perusing a book titled "Galen the Doctor" (Γαληνὸς ἰατρός).[12] Another bystander looked at the text and immediately recognized it as a fake based on its style.

Galen then details the circumstances under which his discourses were "read by many under their own names" (τοῦ μὲν δὴ πολλοὺς ἀναγιγνώσκειν ὡς ἴδια).[13] These were texts not meant "for publication" (οὐδὲ πρὸς ἔκδοσιν) but were given "without title" (χωρὶς ἐπιγραφῆς) to pupils who wanted a "written record of what they heard" (ὧν ἤκουσαν ἔχειν ὑπομνήματα). Galen is clear that they are editorially incomplete. Passing them on to students in his inner circles, he lost authorial control. Many made their way back to him "for correction" (διορθώσεως ἕνεκεν) (Galen, *On My Own Books* 12K). He then properly completed them and gave them titles. In these cases, the discourse is written by its author, moves to the inner circles in Starr's model, jumps to the outer circle, is brought back into the inner circle, and again jumps to the outer circle with proper authorial attribution:

---

12. Text, Helmreich, Marquardt, and Müller, *Claudii Galeni pergameni scripta minora*, 3:91.
13. Text, Helmreich, Marquardt, and Müller, *Claudii Galeni pergameni scripta minora*, 3:91; trans. my own.

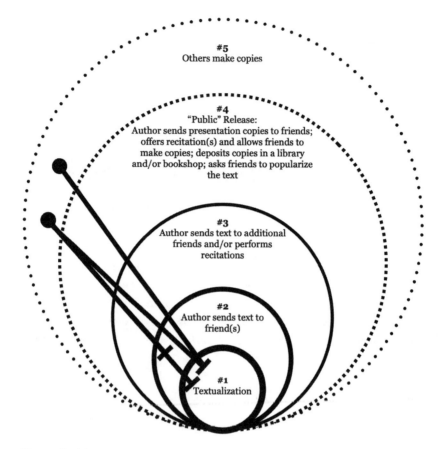

Figure 3. Revision

On other occasions, an author's speech was textualized but never brought back in for revisions. This resulted in the existence of unauthorized versions. These are occasions of "uncontrolled textualization" in which a text is created, but the author was not involved in the revision process.

This is addressed by Quintilian in *The Orator's Education*. He claims that there are speeches circulating in his name about whether a certain Naevius Arpinianus's wife committed suicide or was killed by her husband. These speeches have very little of him in them on account of "the negligence of the shorthand-writers who took them down to make money" (Quintilian, *Inst.* 7.2.24 [Russell, LCL]). Quintilian does not intend to supplant these unauthorized speeches with revised, authorized versions. The textualized

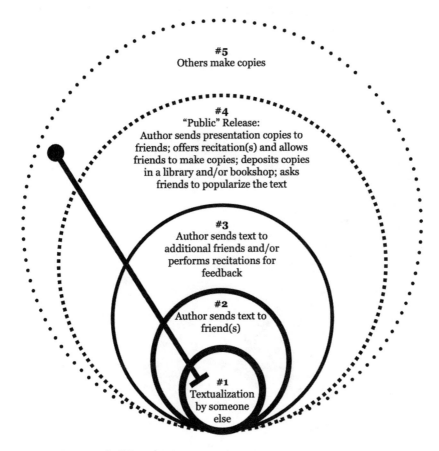

Figure 4. Uncontrolled Textualization

speeches reflect the thoughts and words of Quintilian, but they are unauthorized because they have not gone through their author's literary process.

The case is different with *The Orator's Education*. In its preface, Quintilian informs his dedicatee that two prepublication versions of his tome are circulating in his name (Quintilian, *Inst.* 1.pref.7). Both were textualized from oral events, but Quintilian was not in control of their revision or circulation. Quintilian intends to supplant the unauthorized versions. The result is that the discourse existed in multiple forms, even though each text had the same originating event. If an author subsequently textualized and published a discourse that was prematurely released, competing versions of it resulted.

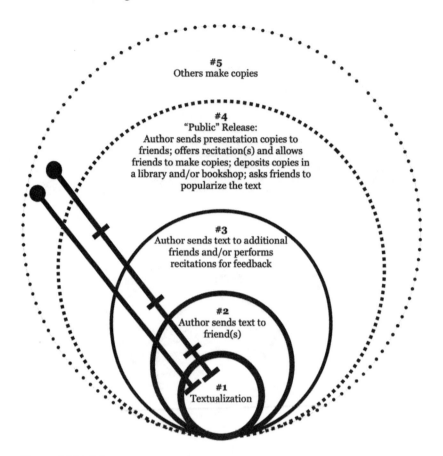

Figure 5. Multiplicity

This happened with Cicero's *Pro Milone*, which was composed in defense of Milo on the occasion of Clodius's death.[14] The speech as it was delivered was neither successful in its defense of Milo, nor in its eloquence, but it leaked and became textually available.[15] In his commentary on *Pro Milone*, Asconsius notes that two versions of the speech are extant. One is the version of the bumbling speech as Cicero delivered it. The other is "what [Cicero] composed

---

14. I am dependent on Timothy Mitchell for this reference ("Exposing Textual Corruption: Community as a Stabilizing Aspect in the Circulation of the New Testament Writings during the Greco-Roman Era," *JSNT* 43 [2020]: 11).

15. For comments on the speech's unsuccessful delivery, see Plutarch, *Cic.* 35 (878); Dio Cassius, *Roman History* 40.54.3–4.

in writing, and with such consummate skill that it may rightly be reckoned his finest" (Asconsius, *Commentary on Pro Milone* 42C).[16] The latter is the preferred, authorized version.

These instances fall into the fifth category of plagiarism and misattribution listed above. The left line represents the discourse as textualized by someone else but still circulating in the author's name. They move from the innermost circle to the outermost circle sans authorial revision. The right line represents the authorized version that may or may not have gone through each of the concentric circles in Starr's model.

In these examples, it is presumed that the textualized version of the discourse accurately represents the speaker's ideas. That was often the case. However, Origen describes two situations in which his words from a purported oral event were falsified. Both are relayed by Rufinus in *On the Falsification of the Books of Origen*.[17] Rufinus's agenda is to demonstrate how Origen's texts were regularly altered and interpolated. He reproduces a letter purportedly from Origen himself that describes one such situation. Origen writes that one of his debates with "a certain author of heresy" was textualized.[18] Origen's words from the debate were altered by this individual: "He added what he wanted to it, removed what he wanted, and changed what seemed good to him. Then he carried it around as if it were from me, pouring scorn conspicuously on the things that he himself had composed."[19] Origen claims that he had not "re-read or revised the work." He had no control over how his words and ideas from the debate were represented or altered. After recovering the text, Origen did not emend and republish it. Instead, he sent it along to the "brethren in Palestine" who were disturbed by the situation.

In this same letter, Origen tells of a different occasion in which his ideas were invented altogether in a fabricated debate. An individual who "was unwilling to meet and did not so much as open his mouth in [Origen's] presence" crafted a sham disputation between the two. This "certain heretic" then widely distributed the purported text of the debate. When confronted by Origen and

16. R. G. Lewis, trans., *Asconsius: Commentaries on Speeches of Cicero* (Oxford: Oxford University Press, 2006), 85.

17. I am dependent on Mitchell for this reference ("Exposing Textual Corruption," 17–18).

18. Translation of Origen's letter here and in what follows is from Thomas P. Scheck, trans., *Apology for Origen: With On the Falsification of the Books of Origen by Rufinus* (Washington, D.C.: The Catholic University of America Press, 2010), 128–30.

19. Trans., Scheck, *Apology for Origen*, 129.

asked to produce the text, the anonymous apostate cowered: "When without any shame he persisted in the impudent defense of his forgery, I demanded that the book be brought out in public, so that my style would be recognized by the brethren, who of course knew the things which I customarily discuss, and the kind of teaching I employ. When he did not dare to produce the work, he was convicted by everyone of forgery and was silenced."[20] As a physical artifact that can be both inspected and manipulated, the text can convict or acquit the individual accused of forgery.

Unpublished Material, Partial Release, Limited Circulation

An author ran the risk of losing control of their discourse whenever they placed a physical instantiation of it into the hands of another person. If a text leaked, it was normally from the inner circles in Starr's model. Authors often mention their reluctance to share their pre-published texts with others. This reluctance realizes itself in at least three ways: (1) holding back unpublished material altogether; (2) sharing only a portion of a written discourse; (3) circulating a discourse, or part of a discourse, only to select individuals.

Pliny writes a letter to persuade the reticent Octavius Rufus to publish his verses (*Ep.* 2.10).[21] He begins by asking him why he "withholds works of distinction for so long" (Pliny the Younger, *Ep.* 2.10 [Radice, LCL]). Pliny points out that some of Rufus's verses have already leaked and become "more widely known." He warns Rufus that he might lose control of them completely if he does not act. "Unless you recall [the leaked verses] to be incorporated in the whole, like runaway slaves they will find someone else to claim them." Outside the apparatus of publication, texts run the risk of being misattributed. Publication serves as a safeguard.

Pliny hopes that Rufus will publish his verses textually, but also writes that he will settle for hearing recitations. He is unequivocal that recitations are not themselves a form of publication. Offering a reading might make Rufus "feel more inclined to publish" (*magis libeat emittere*).[22] A reading serves

---

20. Trans., Scheck, *Apology for Origen*, 129.//
21. Pliny writes another letter, *Ep.* 1.7, to Octavius Rufus. Therein he also alludes to Rufus's reluctance to publish his verses, though it is not the primary topic of the letter as it is in *Ep.* 2.10.
22. In *Ep.* 3.15, Pliny the Younger states that he has heard recitations of Silius Proculus's poems and is confident that they will be suitable for publication, but that he cannot make specific comments until he has read the text itself.

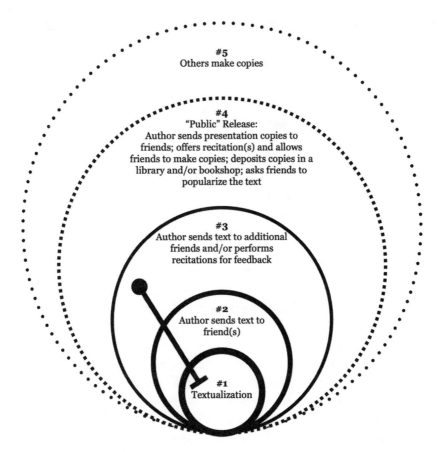

Figure 6. Limited Circulation

publication. Pliny hopes that his letter will provoke Rufus's "interminable hesitation," which Pliny warns might be reckoned as "idleness, indolence, or possibly timidity."

It appears from Pliny's letter that Rufus has shared prepublication material with others since some of his verses have leaked. However, Rufus has only circulated select portions of the verses in a limited manner. Pliny wishes Rufus to make the whole of the discourse public. This involves moving from stages two and three in the model to stage four. Pliny is explicit about this in another letter that encourages a colleague, none other than Suetonius, not to dally in publication. He writes that Suetonius's work is already perfect and that he wishes to see all his friends' books "being copied, read, and sold" (Pliny the Younger, *Ep.* 5.10.3 [Radice, LCL]).

Pliny writes at length concerning his own decision about partially releasing a discourse and limiting its circulation in a letter to Spurrina and his wife, Cottia, following the death of their son, Cottius.[23] Pliny wrote a panegyric for the couple's late son and offered recitations from it, but failed to mention the text or the reading to Spurinna. Spurinna learned of the recitation and requested a written version of what was read. Because several phenomena related to circulation are mentioned and are entwined with the social situation addressed in it, I reproduce the letter in its entirety:

> To Vestricius Spurinna and Cottia
> I refrained from mentioning when I was last with you that I had written something about your son, because, in the first place, I had not written it with the idea of telling you, but to give expression to my own feelings of love and grief, and then because I knew from what you had told me yourself that you, Spurinna, had heard that I had given a public reading, and I assumed that you had also heard what its subject was. I was anxious too not to upset you during a national holiday by reviving the memory of your tragic loss.
> Even now I am still in some doubt whether to send you only the passages I read, as you ask, or to add what I was intending to keep back to present on another occasion. A single composition is quite inadequate for my sentiments, if I am to do justice to the memory of one I loved and revered so much, and his fame will be more widespread if it is published abroad by degrees. But while debating whether to show you all I have written so far, or to withhold something until later, I have come to see that honesty and friendship alike constrain me to send everything; especially as you assure me that nothing shall leave your hands until I have made up my mind about publication.
> One thing remains: please be equally honest about telling me if you think there are any additions, alterations, or omissions to be made. It is difficult for you to concentrate on this at a time of sorrow, I know; but, nevertheless, if a sculptor or painter were working on a portrait of your son, you would indicate to him what features to bring out or correct; and so you must give me guidance and direction as I, too, am trying to create a likeness which shall not be short-lived and ephemeral, but one you think will last for ever. It is more likely to be long-lived the more I can attain to truth and beauty and accuracy in detail. (Pliny the Younger, *Ep.* 3.10 [Radice, LCL])

23. Cottius's name is not mentioned in this letter but is in *Ep.* 2.7. Pliny offers more information about Cottius's identity and his death in the latter.

Pliny recited only a portion of what he wrote. The multivolume panegyric was partially released, and only in recitation. Other written material did not reach the ears of Pliny's audience. This he "thought to reserve for another volume" (in aliud volumen cogito reservare).[24]

Spurinna and Cottia's grief compels Pliny to send the text that he planned for subsequent release. He is reluctant, but Spurinna's assurance that nothing will be leaked helps to assuage his conscience. Having sent the unpublished material, Pliny seizes this opportunity to request feedback on the discourse. He compares his textual tribute to two other physical commemorations: a sculpture and a painting.[25] Akin to physical representations in stone or image, a text is "not short lived and ephemeral" (non fragilem et caducam) (Pliny the Younger, *Ep.* 3.10 [Radice, LCL]). Its material existence affords it permanence. But a text's physical existence also opens it to various forms of misattribution. This is why Pliny labors over his decision to send Spurinna the unpublished and unrecited material. He does, assured that the text will be kept in confidence until he himself determines to make it public.

In this case, limited circulation is temporary, and the limit was removed. Limited circulation also came in another form. A text could be provided to select individuals with no intention to make it public. In these cases, it was not offered for comments and revisions but served a utilitarian or pedagogical purpose. Galen writes about this practice often: he gave texts to students or other individuals for private use.[26] On the one hand, limited circulation could be a holding period during which a text was revised for public release. To the frustration of interested readers, an author might interminably extend this period and never make a written discourse public. On the other hand, limited circulation could entail offering a text to an individual or a small network.

---

24. Text Radice, LCL; trans. my own.

25. The comparison to a sculpture is particularly apt since Pliny remarks on a public statue of Cottius in *Ep.* 2.7. There, he states that it is rare for an effigy of young man to be publicly on display, but that Cottius's virtue and Spurinna's grief occasioned the exception. Pliny wishes to "do justice to the memory of the one he loved and revered so much" with a physical text, just as a statue can "offer consultation in sorrow" and "recall men's fame and distinction as well as their forms and faces" with a physical likeness. Quotations from Pliny the Younger, *Ep.* 3.10.3 and 2.7.7 (Radice, LCL).

26. In *On My Own Books* 10K, Galen states that this was the origin of *Bones for Beginners*, *The Pulse for Beginners*, an untitled text on veins and arteries, another on nerves, and the *Outline of Empiricism*. All of these began as private discourses and were subsequently finished and circulated in authorized form.

226 • *Circulating*

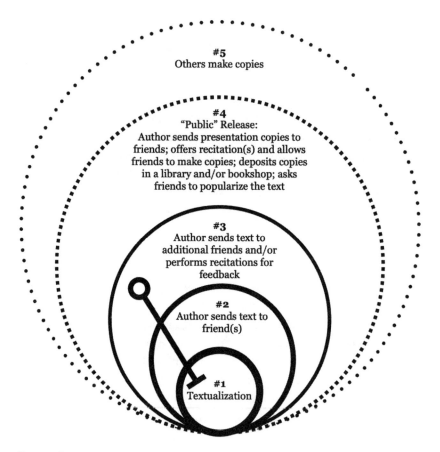

Figure 7. Suppression

As a holding period, limited circulation offered an author latitude to determine whether they would make their discourse public. If an author decided not to go public with a text after giving it to a limited number of confidants, they could suppress it. The fewer persons who had a physical version of the text and the more trusted they were, the easier this process was. After railing against dilettante poets, Horace writes that something written should enter the ears, not the eyes, of a select few and then the parchment hidden away in a closet. This is because "what you have not published you can destroy; the word once sent forth can never come back" (Horace, *Ars Poetica* 374–80 [Fairclough, LCL]).[27] If a text was suppressed, it was left to die with trusted confidants, represented by the open circle above.

27. I am dependent on Mitchell for this reference ("Exposing Textual Corruption," 7).

Pliny writes on both limited circulation and suppression in a letter to Pompeius Saturninus, who asked to review one of Pliny's latest works. Pliny obliges not by sending Saturninus something new, but a speech on which Saturninus had previously made some general comments. Pliny requests additional feedback on the work so that he can commit himself either "to publish or suppress it" (vel publicare vel continere) (Pliny the Younger, *Ep.* 1.8 [Radice, LCL]). His concern is that he might come off as self-aggrandizing by publishing the speech, since it was a private oration that he gave on the occasion of the opening of a library for which he was the benefactor. Floating the speech to Saturninus will help Pliny determine if he should move it beyond his innermost network. On this occasion Pliny is confident that the speech is still within his sphere of control. He does not express any concern about it leaking. Even if it did, Pliny would be cast in a positive light, given the events that occasioned the speech.

There were also failed attempts at suppressing speeches. This was the case with Cicero's slanderous text about Clodius. He attempted to suppress it but was unsuccessful and so determined to pass it off as a forgery. Similarly, Fronto informs Marcus Antoninus in a letter that he sent Verus three of his, Fronto's, published speeches. One of them contained a calumny against a friend of Verus, but Fronto learned only after circulating the speech that Verus did not think ill of this individual. When he learned as much, Fronto "did [his] best to have the speech suppressed. But it had already been circulated too widely to be called in" (Quod ubi primum comperi, curavi equidem abolere orationem. Sed iam pervaserat in manus plurium quam ut aboleri posset) (Fronto, *Ad Antoninum Imp.* 2.8 [Haines, LCL]).[28] Fronto wishes he could take back the text but that was impossible because it was in too many people's hands. He might have attempted to pass off the speech as a forgery, as Cicero did, but does not. Instead, Fronto takes the high road and proposes to make amends with the besmirched individual.

Following its limited circulation, an author may or may not successfully suppress a text. Likewise, they may or may not successfully revise a text that has been circulated, especially once it has been publicly released. Larsen cites two instances of "postpublication revision" from Cicero.[29] In one, Cicero instructs Atticus to replace "Eupolis" with "Aristophanes" for an attributed quotation in one of his speeches. The quotation comes from Aristophanes, though Cicero initially misattributed it to Eupolis. The error was stamped out, as all known

---

28. *Ad Antoninum Imp.* 2.8 reproduces a portion of the letter sent to Verus, which is extant as *Ad Verum Imp.* 2.9.

29. Larsen, *Gospels before the Book*, 50–51. These are Cicero, *Att.* 243 and 336.

manuscripts read "Aristophanes." In the other, Cicero requests that Atticus remove Lucius Corfidius as an individual who was directly addressed in the written version of the speech. It came to Cicero's attention that Corfidius could not have been addressed when the speech was delivered because he was not there. He was already dead. In this case, Cicero was not able to eradicate the error, as all known manuscripts mention Corfidius.

These are occasions of minor details being revised after a text has been publicly released. But revision could also be more thoroughgoing. For instance, Ovid writes that his *Amores* first existed as a five-volume work and was later pruned to three (Ovid, *Amores* 1.1).[30] Josephus continuously revised *Jewish Antiquities* and *Jewish War* after publication, and leaves open the possibility of updating *The Life*.[31] In these instances, revision was at the author's volition: they wished to update the authorized version of their already-published text. Alternatively, an author might revise and republish an unauthorized or leaked text.

"Not for Publication" and "For Publication"

The line between stages three and four in Starr's model represents the moment of "publication," or ἔκδοσις. Publication was the intentional act of making a discourse available to an audience that was both wide and not limited. As Sean Gurd puts it, "Ἔκδοσις in the ancient world meant nothing more than 'giving out' (ἐκδιδόναι) a text, usually to its dedicatee, on the understanding that it would be copied freely thereafter."[32] A text could be copied without the author's intention or knowledge. All the concentric circles are porous in Starr's model. Once a discourse is textualized, the possibility enters that the author might lose control of it.

Nonetheless, authors make a distinction between texts that are prepared for publication and those that are either not yet ready for publication or were not textualized for the purpose of publication. Some texts are created with no thought that they will be freely copied by whoever happens to want a copy. The author is not looking beyond stages one or two in the circulation model. Other texts are produced with uncertainty about their publication. Limited

---

30. I am dependent on Larsen ("Accidental Publication," 373) for this reference.
31. Larsen, "Accidental Publication," 374; see Josephus, *Ant.* 20.267; *Life* 363; 430.
32. Sean A. Gurd, "Galen on ἔκδοσις," in *Perceptions of the Second Sophistic and Its Times*, ed. Thomas Schmidt and Pascale Fleury (Toronto: University of Toronto Press, 2011), 170.

circulation helped an author determine whether they would publish the text or not. And still other texts are created from the outset with an eye to an open readership in the outer circles of the model. Preparing a text for publication involves imagining a wide readership with whom the author may not be familiar. To use Jan Assmann's language, authors imagine different "extended situations" for texts that are prepared for publication and those that are not, and they construct their discourses accordingly.[33]

The distinction between texts "for publication" and "not for publication" is acute in Galen's writings. His private texts that were first circulated in a limited manner to students and disreputably used by persons not named Galen were "not for publication" (οὐ πρὸς ἔκδοσιν). These were recovered, revised, and republished. The texts were plagiarized because they were a certain medium.[34] They were notes that were either taken down from an oral event or were dictated for students.

The Greek term that Galen uses for these notes is, in the plural, ὑπομνήματα (*hypomnēmata*) and in the singular ὑπόμνημα (*hypomnēma*). The word is translated several different ways. Reminders, memoirs, memoranda, records, drafts, texts, copies, and materials are all connotations of it.[35] The word is more categorical than it is descriptive. There were various kinds and forms of ὑπομνήματα. Commentaries, outlines, rough drafts, notes to self, or notes made by others could all be classified as ὑπομνήματα. I translate the term as "notes" for the plural and "set of notes" for the singular.[36] This is not because these are the most-accurate connotations of the term every time it is used, but because it well encapsulates its categorical function.

---

33. Jan Assmann, *Religion and Cultural Memory: Ten Studies*, trans. Rodney Livingstone (Stanford, CA: Stanford University Press, 2006), 103–8.

34. A modern comparandum is Nick Hornby and Ben Fold's 2010 song, "Levi Johnston's Blues" from the album *Lonely Avenue*. The song is written from the first-person perspective of Levi Johnston, who is the ex-fiancé of Bristol Palin, the daughter of 2008 vice-presidential candidate Sarah Palin. It chronicles his coming-of-age experience learning that his girlfriend is pregnant, and her mother has just been named the vice-presidential candidate of a major American political party. The chorus's lyrics were lifted and reused nearly verbatim from Johnston's Myspace page, a "not for publication" social media platform that once hosted personal webspace. The words existed in one medium before being transferred into another altogether by persons who did not write them, and are perduring.

35. LSJ, s.v. ὑπόμνημα.

36. The singular can refer to both a set of notes and a single note.

"Not for publication" was one of the essential characteristics of this category for Galen and for others. This kind of text was not produced with the intention that it would be made widely available, at least not initially. Notes are not publication media. "Compositions" (συγγράμματα) are publication media. Galen makes a distinction between notes and compositions, associating only the latter with publication. At the end of *The Art of Medicine*, Galen states his plan to write a bio-bibliography that will go over all of the "other compositions and notes" [ἄλλων συγγραμμάτων τε καὶ ὑπομνημάτων] that he has written in a one- or two-volume work tentatively titled "Galen, On My Own Compositions" (Γαληνοῦ περὶ τῶν ἰδίων συγγραμμάτων) (Galen, *Method of Medicine* 412K).[37] Galen delivered on this promise by writing *On My Own Books*.

It appears that Galen has mentally retained the division between "compositions" and "notes" in the writing of *On My Own Books*, but has flipped the order. The first half of the text, namely *On My Own Books* 1–23, addresses Galen's hypomnematic texts that were "given without inscription to friends or pupils, having been written with no thought for publication [οὐδὲ πρὸς ἔκδοσιν]."[38] These are all discourses that were leaked but made their way back to Galen for proper completion. They became "authorized" versions through this process, though premature circulation still impacted their final form. The second half of *On My Own Books* is mostly devoted to compositions.[39]

"Compositions" (συγγράμματα) were texts created for publication, while "notes" (ὑπομνήματα) were for private, limited use. Galen indicates this is the case for his own texts, as well as for Hippocrates's. On several occasions, the physician explains a feature from book 2 or 6 of Hippocrates's *Epidemics* based on their medium. Galen considered these two volumes to be private, hypomnematic texts that were not meant for publication, while books 1 and 3 were compositions created for publication.[40]

Commenting on a contextless saying from *Epidemics* 6.3.25, Galen writes, "It is no wonder that the support and even the whole account has been left out. For this document is not a composition created for publication [οὐ γὰρ

---

37. Text, Johnston, LCL; trans., my own. See also Kühn, *Claudii Galeni opera omnia*, vol. 1.
38. Trans. Singer, *Galen*, 3–4; Greek text, Kühn, *Claudii Galeni opera omnia*, 19:10–11.
39. It contains some compositions that began life as notes, and Galen makes sure to note as much when this is the case.
40. Kühn, *Claudii Galeni opera omnia* 17a:796; 18a:529–30; Gurd, "Galen on ἔκδοσις," 171; Tiziano Dorandi, "Ancient ἐκδόσεις: Further Lexical Observations on Some of Galen's Texts," *Lexicon Philosophicum: International Journal for the History of Ideas and Texts* 2 (2014): 4.

σύγγραμμά ἐστι τὸ βιβλίον τοῦτο πρὸς ἔκδοσιν γεγονὸς], but is more like drafts or outlines [παρασκευαί τινες ἢ ὑποτυπώσεις] which we would make for ourselves."[41] He offers the same rationale when commenting on the obscure line, "Watch for the sign of purification at the same time of the day."[42] Galen explains, "The text is unclear to us because, as I have already said several times, this book was not written for publication [οὐ πρὸς ἔκδοσιν] but as an outline sketch and draft [ὑποτύπωσίν τε καὶ παρασκευήν] for himself. If he were writing for publication [πρὸς ἔκδοσιν] he would have said everything he needed to say, specifically what time of day we should watch for the sign of the purification."[43] In these cases, Galen does not directly contrast the term "notes" with "composition." Rather, "drafts" (παρασκευαί) and "outlines" (ὑποτυπώσεις) constitute two sub-categories of "notes" (ὑπομνήματα).

Addressing the other volume of the *Epidemics* that was for Hippocrates's private use, namely book 2, Galen contrasts "notes" with "compositions" twice. The first time, he does so using two adverbs, declaring that book 2 was written "like notes, not like a composition" (ὑπομνηματικῶς, οὐ συγγραφικῶς).[44] The second time he uses noun forms: "We take the document to be certain notes for Hippocrates, not compositions" (τὸ βιβλίον ἐδείξαμεν ὑπομνήματά τινα τοῦ Ἱπποκράτους, οὐ συγγράμματα). Immediately following, Galen reminds the reader that only books 1 and 3 of the *Epidemics* were written for publication (ὡς πρὸς ἔκδοσιν πρὸς αὐτοῦ γέγραπται).

"Notes" are different kinds of texts than "compositions" and only one of the two categories is for public release.[45] This does not mean that Galen's notes were never meant to be seen or used by anyone else. Gurd writes, "Οὐ πρὸς ἔκδοσιν here *does* mean 'not for general release,' but it does *not* mean 'for the desk drawer' or 'never meant to see the light of day': at stake is the size and

---

41. Text Kühn, *Claudii Galeni opera omnia*, 17a:1001; trans., my own. I am dependent on Gurd for this reference ("Galen on ἔκδοσις," 172).

42. From Hippocrates, *Epidemics* 6.3.1.

43. Text, Kühn, *Claudii Galeni opera omnia* 17b:13; trans., Gurd, "Galen on ἔκδοσις," 172.

44. Text, Kühn, *Claudii Galeni opera omnia* 18a:529–30; trans my own. I am dependent on Dorandi for this reference ("Ancient ἐκδόσεις," 6).

45. Galen's comments on Hippocrates's texts, which were written some six centuries earlier, are probably not revelatory of publication and circulation patterns in Hippocrates's context, only Galen's. As modern scholars sometimes do for the first century, Galen is likely projecting his own experiences of distribution onto Hippocrates. Perhaps this is because Galen's Hippocratic commentaries began as notes (ὑπομνήματα) that he wrote for personal use (*On My Own Books* 35K).

nature of his intended readership, not its actual existence."[46] Hypomnematic texts were not usually created for a wide, public audience. They were created for a limited one; in some cases, the author alone.

Other Greco-Roman writers likewise contend that "notes" are not prepared for public consumption and they are reticent to use the noun "composition" (σύγγραμμα) and the verb "compose" (συγγράφω) with reference to them. Compositions, in contrast, are often directly associated with terms of publication or with a wide readership.[47]

Arrian, remarking on the composition and circulation of Epictetus's discourses, states that he did not "compose" (συγγράφω) them (Arrian, *Epict. diss.*, 1.pref.8–9 [Oldfather, LCL]). Four times in the preface he uses the verb to emphasize precisely what he did *not* do. Neither did he "publish" (ἐξήνεγκα) them. Instead, he wrote down Epictetus's words as notes (ὑπομνήματα) as he heard them so that he could personally use them.

Arrian makes this claim as a safeguard, lest someone like Lucian think him or Epictetus to be incapable of composing works. Lucian describes a "prosaic and ordinary" set of notes (ὑπόμνημα) compiled (συναγαγών), not composed, by an amateur Ionian historian in *How to Write History* 16 (Kilburn, LCL). They resembled what a soldier or craftsman might put together as a diary of the army's daily events. Among his critiques of this text is that it is largely written in "street-corner talk" (ἐκ τριόδου). This could be fixed by a later historian with greater literary skill.

Lucian outlines the process. The would-be historian should first collect the "facts" (πράγματα) into a set of notes (ὑπόμνημα) which are "as yet with no beauty or continuity" (ἀκαλλὲς ἔτι καὶ ἀδιάρθρωτον) (Lucian, *How to Write History* 48 [Kilburn, LCL]). These features are added later, when the notes are arranged in order (τὴν τάξιν). It is at this stage that the "history-composer" (τὸν ἱστορίαν συγγράφοντα) is less concerned with what to say and more concerned with how to say it. The task of the composer (τὸ τοῦ συγγραφέως ἔργον) is like that of a sculptor: they take raw material and beautify it (Lucian, *How to Write History* 51). Notes can become compositions through this beautification.

But not all writers have the skill or training to create such beautified documents. Philostratus claims that this was the case of Damis of Ninos, one of Apollonius of Tyana's companions. Damis's Greek was mediocre, and he lacked

---

46. Gurd, "Galen on ἔκδοσις," 174–75; italics in original.
47. Plutarch, *Cat. Min.*, 37.1–2 (777); Chariton, *Callirhoe*, 8.1.4; Strabo, *Geography* 1.22.

style on account of his schooling among the barbarians.⁴⁸ He could, however, "record a discourse and conversation" (διατριβὴν δὲ ἀναγράψαι καὶ συνουσίαν), as well as "draw up a set of notes" (ὑπόμνημα ... ξυνθεῖναι) of things that he heard and saw (Philostratus, *Vit. Apoll.* 1.19.2).⁴⁹ Such notes were the contents of Damis's *Scrap Book* (ἡ γοῦν δέλτος ἡ τῶν ἐκφατνισμάτων τοιοῦτον τῷ Δάμιδι).

According to Philostratus, the superiority of his own biography of Apollonius lies in the fact that he was able to acquire "the tablets of Damis's notes" (τῷ Δάμιδι τὰς δέλτους τῶν ὑπομνημάτων) and use them as the basis for his composition (Philostratus, *Vit. Apoll.* 1.3.1). These were never published and sat unknown until they were given to Apollonius to transcribe and "take care over their style, since the style of the man from Ninos was clear but rather unskillful." Gathering (ξυνήγαγον) these textual materials and others, Apollonius composed (ξυγγέγραπται) his own text on their basis.⁵⁰ Unpublished and unpolished notes written by one person could be transformed into a composition by another.

We learn much about the form and function of notes from Galen, Arrian, Lucian, and Philostratus. First, they came in multiple forms. Outlines, drafts, excerpts, and sketches all fit within this category. What unites them is their preliminary nature. Second, notes were contrasted with compositions, though they could become the latter. Notes were subliterary documents that might or might not be shaped into literature proper by their author or by someone else. Galen imputes moral impropriety to those who create compositions out of his notes, but Lucian and Philostratus do not appear to have the same qualms.⁵¹ Third, as preliminary and subliterary documents, notes were not publication media. They might be circulated prematurely, but they are not produced with a wide readership in mind. This could lead to a host of stylistic and content-related infelicities. The text might be unpolished, incomplete, relay events out of order, and contain obscure references. All these an author

---

48. Larsen cites Damis's notes as an example of unfinished "textual raw material" (*Gospels before the Book*, 34–36).

49. Text, Jones, LCL; trans. my own.

50. The whole account of Damis's tablets may in fact be fabricated by Apollonius. I tend to give authors the benefit of the doubt and trust that they are accurately relaying information unless there are compelling reasons to believe otherwise. Even if the account is a literary fiction, it is revelatory of Apollonius's imagination about writing, reuse, and circulation. As Larsen puts it, "Real or imagined, [Damis's tablets] reflect how some ancient readers understood *hypomnēmata* to function" (*Gospels before the Book*, 35).

51. Perhaps this is because their ideas were not the ones being reused.

might consider embarrassing in their published text. Fourth, notes were often a record of things that were said in a teaching context. This was the case for Galen's, Arrian's, and Damis's notes. The oral events could be textualized by the speakers themselves, but more usually this was done by a student. Fifth, and finally, the physical presentation and medium of notes differed from compositions. Damis's notes were written in tablets. At least some of Galen's notes were in codex form.[52] One important task in the process of turning notes into compositions was creating a clean, well-produced presentation copy.

Conclusion

While the practices addressed in this chapter might initially seem dissimilar to our modern notions and practices of circulating media, they are not. These are unfamiliar to publication practices for certain kinds of modern texts, namely printed books. For other media, these are acts and postures with which we are wholly familiar.

Just as an author in the first century might attempt to suppress a text, a modern "author" can de-publish or suppress a Tweet or other electronic post by deleting it. But this action does not guarantee its full de-publication, as others might have already screenshotted the discourse and made it available through channels the author has no control over. Similarly, an author can revise a blog post after publication. The digital medium facilitates revision, even after the discourse has been engaged by readers. Newspapers and magazines, in both physical and electronic versions, print retractions and corrections.

Galen begins *On My Own Books* with a dispute about whether or not a text titled "Galen the doctor" (Γαληνὸς ἰατρός) was written by him. A learned person looked at two lines and immediately recognized it as a farce.[53] The situation is not unlike recognizing a "mockbuster," a low-budget film that imitates one with high-production value. This is a simple task if one is familiar with the "authorized" material, but not if one is ignorant of it. In Galen's anecdote, it is the title that stirs suspicion about the text's authenticity. Likewise with mockbusters: the knockoff's title can be a dead giveaway. It usually resembles the real thing but is laughable if one is familiar with the official version: *Chop Kick Panda* to *Kung Fu Panda*; *Sunday School Musical* to *High School Musical*;

---

52. Clare K. Rothschild, "Galen's *De Indolentia* and the Early Christian Codex," *Early Christianity* 12 (2021): 28–39.

53. Text, Kühn, *Claudii Galeni opera omnia*, 19:8.

Snakes on a Train to *Snakes on a Plane*; and *Transmorphers* to *Transformers*. For Galen, a learned person who is familiar with Galen's work should be able to recognize what is authentic and what is not, and Galen writes *On My Own Books* to aid readers in that very task.

Like the literati of antiquity, academics will circulate pre-publication versions of orally delivered conference papers, articles, chapters, or even entire books to a limited audience. Many also make preliminary versions of their discourses available to their social networks on websites devoted to self-promotion and resource sharing. Oral academic events are often reduced to texts through live tweeters, frequently without speakers' explicit permission. All this is done not simply for the purpose of feedback, but also to establish and strengthen social ties.

Even with officious, printed publications, de-publication is possible, if rare. When it comes to light that an author has plagiarized major portions of a work, then a publisher might discontinue its distribution in electronic and print formats and even "destroy the remaining inventory" of that work.[54] Similarly, if a writer is known to have committed egregious immoral acts, they become a *persona non grata* in academic reading communities and their written works are not engaged or cited, even if they are never "officially" de-published.

Circulation and publication practices are multiple and complex in both ancient and modern contexts. They are, at their core, social acts realized in various ways for varying forms of media. This is no less true for the gospels. As different kinds of texts read and written in different kinds of ways, they will have also circulated in various ways and physical formats.

---

54. Destroying inventory was one of the actions Zondervan Academic took with respect to Peter T. O'Brien's commentaries, which were determined to contain plagiarized material (https://zondervanacademic.com/blog/statement-from-zondervan-academic). Eerdmans took similar actions regarding the same author's works (https://www.eerdmans.com/Pages/Item/59043/Commentary-Statement.aspx).

CHAPTER 8

Circulating the Gospels

Media Myth: The gospels were all circulated the same way and in the same physical format, whether it be a codex or roll.

Media Reality: The gospels, like other texts in their media context, were circulated textually in a variety of socially constructed ways and physical forms.

• • •

Addressing the publication of early Christian literature, Harry Y. Gamble emphasizes that it was circulated in ways similar to texts in the wider culture. "Christian writings were produced and disseminated in much the same way as other literature within the larger environment."[1] The publication and circulation of texts in Greco-Roman antiquity were complex and socially constructed. The circulation of early Christian gospels was likewise complex and socially constructed. The gospels do not fit into a single, idealized publication model.

The aim of the present chapter is to allow the complexity of ancient publication and circulation to inform the canonical gospels. Modulating Starr's model for the sociality inherent to circulating Greco-Roman texts fosters an appreciation for the diverse circumstances under which the gospels were distributed, as well as their relationships to one another. The gospels were not all released or circulated in identical ways. Nor were they distributed in the same physical medium. The gospels circulated in varying ways and physical forms. Mark was written as a set of notes that was initially offered for limited circulation and was "not for publication." Its native medium was the codex. Matthew, as a book composed for synagogue reading, modulated

---

1. Harry Y. Gamble, *Books and Readers in the Early Church: A History of Early Christian Texts* (New Haven: Yale University Press, 1995), 94. After surveying Greco-Roman and early Christian circulation mechanics, Timothy Mitchell similarly writes, "The methods employed by the Christians of the first and second centuries to distribute their literature were very similar to that found in Roman writers of the same era" ("Exposing Textual Corruption: Community as a Stabilizing Aspect in the Circulation of the New Testament Writings during the Greco-Roman Era," *JSNT* 43 [2020]: 16).

Mark's medium and created a new composition that circulated among early Christians. Luke likewise transformed the notes that Mark handed over into a composition. Writing for Theophilus, the author of Luke anticipated that the narrative would reach a wider audience. Creating texts "for publication" involved putting them into presentation form, which was a bookroll. The Johannine colophons indicate that the Fourth Gospel enters an environment in which the Synoptic Gospels are well known. John justifies its own existence alongside these texts by claiming that Jesus's deeds can never be exhausted in writing, whatever media they might come in.

I wish to state from the outset that the circulation of the gospels was textual. This is not to suggest that there were no communal readings or performances of gospel texts. There were. However, one cannot physically hold or distribute a performance or reading as one can a material text. Reading and performance are a mode of engaging a written text, not a manner of circulating it.

Circulating the Synoptics

Certain kinds of texts were written for publication. Notes were not. A variety of Greco-Roman authors contrast "compositions" with "notes" and consider only the former to be publication media. This does not mean that notes were not used by persons who did not write them. They were written for a limited audience and circulation, but they circulated nonetheless. The following characterize the form and function of notes, according to Galen, Arrian, Lucian, and Philostratus:

1. They came in multiple forms.
2. They were preliminary and subliterary.
3. They were often textualizations of oral teaching.
4. They could be shaped into literature proper by their author or another individual.
5. They were utilitarian and not produced for an anonymous readership.
6. Their physical form was not a presentation copy.

Several of these characteristics dovetail with arguments that have been made in this book about the Gospel of Mark and its reuse by Matthew and Luke. Mark's genesis was oral teaching events, and it was composed orally. Matthew's innovation was to present itself as a book. Luke likewise creates a new, more literary text using Mark, which is suggested by its preface. The Gospel of Mark, like other notes in its literary environment, was a subliterary textualization of oral teaching that was shaped into literature by other individuals.

Mark, as a set of notes, was utilitarian and not produced "for publication." Matthew and Luke were. Mark did not begin its circulation in presentation form. Matthew and Luke did. Not only is this the scenario that the early patristic writers present when they remark on the circulation of the gospels, but it is confirmed by internal evidence from Mark and the later Synoptics' redaction.

Here I wish to remind the reader that publication and circulation are not synonyms. When I write that Mark was not written for publication, I mean that the text was not prepared with a wide, anonymous readership in mind. When I write that the gospel was circulated, I mean that it was shared with individuals and communities. Mark did not march through the various stages of publication in the concentric circles model. Limited circulation, uncontrolled textualization, and accidental publication are all models that better illumine its distribution. When I write that Matthew and Luke were written for publication, I am importing intention into their act of composition. Both were writing for an extended readership.[2] Mark was composed as notes for limited circulation. Matthew and Luke wrote compositions for publication.

EXTERNAL EVIDENCE: EARLY ECCLESIASTICAL TESTIMONY

Early Christian remarks on Mark maintain that spoken teaching stands behind the gospel. The practice of making a set of notes from one or more oral events is its imagined composition scenario for these writers. In most instances of this testimony, Mark was not created for publication. It was a spoken discourse that was textualized and initially circulated to a limited group. While they differ on details about when, where, and why the text was written, these writers do not vary on who was involved in the process and how it happened: Mark wrote up Peter's oral teaching.

Papias, as reproduced in Eusebius's *Hist. eccl.* 3.39.15–16, is the first to claim that Mark is a textualization of Peter's oral discourses:

Μάρκος μὲν ἑρμηνευτὴς Πέτρου γενόμενος, ὅσα ἐμνημόνευσεν, ἀκριβῶς ἔγραψεν, οὐ μέντοι τάξει, τὰ ὑπὸ τοῦ κυρίου ἢ λεχθέντα ἢ πραχθέντα. οὔτε γὰρ ἤκουσεν τοῦ κυρίου οὔτε παρηκολούθησεν αὐτῷ, ὕστερον δέ, ὡς ἔφην, Πέτρῳ· ὃς πρὸς τὰς χρείας ἐποιεῖτο τὰς διδασκαλίας, ἀλλ᾽ οὐχ ὥσπερ σύνταξιν τῶν κυριακῶν ποιούμενος

---

2. This is not to imply that they were writing for a "general" public.

λογίων, ὥστε οὐδὲν ἥμαρτεν Μάρκος οὕτως ἔνια γράψας ὡς ἀπεμνημόνευσεν. ἑνὸς γὰρ ἐποιήσατο πρόνοιαν, τοῦ μηδὲν ὧν ἤκουσεν παραλιπεῖν ἢ ψεύσασθαί τι ἐν αὐτοῖς. (Eusebius, *Hist. eccl.* 3.39.15–16 [Lake, LCL])

Mark became Peter's interpreter and wrote accurately all that he remembered, not, indeed, in order, of the things said or done by the Lord. For he had not heard the Lord, nor had he followed him, but later on, as I said, followed Peter, who used to give teaching as necessity demanded but not making, as it were, an arrangement of the Lord's oracles, so that Mark did nothing wrong in thus writing down single points as he remembered them. For to one thing he gave attention, to leave out nothing of what he had heard and to make no false statements in them.

Papias does not detail several aspects of the composition scenario, such as when the text was written, whether Peter knew his teaching was textualized, if Mark attempted to represent Peter's words verbatim, and how thoroughly Mark edited what was written. Papias is clear that the textualization was not of one single event, though. Mark is created from a series of Peter's lectures (τὰς διδασκαλίας).

When insights from Josef Kürzinger about Papias's vocabulary in the passage are incorporated, it is apparent that Papias considers Mark to have created a set of notes of Peter's teaching.[3] When he states that Mark is Peter's "translator" (ἑρμηνευτής), he does not mean that Mark converts Peter's Aramaic into Greek. The term is a technical one referring to Mark's function as a literary middleman, transferring the oral teaching into the written modality.[4] When Papias claims that Mark did not write "in order" (τάξει), he does not have chronology in mind. The word refers to literary artistry. Using the same term, Lucian states that "order" is added to notes when the text is stylistically improved (Lucian, *How to Write History* 48). Mark wrote down what Peter taught without literary ambition, as is fitting a utilitarian text that is not meant for publication.

Candida Moss argues that Papias's presentation of Mark as Peter's "interpreter" would suggest to ancient readers that Mark is a servile worker.[5] This

---

3. Josef Kürzinger, "Das Papiaszeugnis und die Erstgestalt des Matthäusevangeliums," *BZ* 4 (1960): 19–38; Josef Kürzinger, "Die Aussage des Papias von Hierapolis zur literarischen Form des Markusevangeliums," *BZ* 21 (1977): 245–64.

4. Kürzinger, "Papiaszeugnis," 26.

5. Candida Moss, "Fashioning Mark: Early Christian Discussions about the Scribe and Status of the Second Gospel," *NTS* 67 (2021): 181–204.

allows Papias to connect the text to the apostolic memories of Peter and to justify the narrative's literary deficiencies.[6] Because servile workers do not emend the content dictated to them, Mark's inelegance "paradoxically serves as a guarantee of its accuracy."[7] In Moss's interpretation, Papias presents the gospel as an unpolished text that was dictated to a servile laborer.

Whether or not Papias presents Mark as enslaved or servile, the composition scenario resembles instances of oral events standing behind a written text. That Mark aimed "to leave out nothing of what he had heard" (τοῦ μηδὲν ὧν ἤκουσεν παραλιπεῖν) in his writing is similar to a claim that Philostratus makes of Damis's notes: that he included a surfeit of episodes "so as to leave nothing out" (ὑπὲρ τοῦ μὴ παραλελοιπέναι τι αὐτῶν) (Philostratus, *Vit. Apoll.* 7.28.1 [Jones, LCL]). According to Papias, the Gospel of Mark is textualized not to create something literary, but to capture the essence of Peter's teaching events.

Clement's account of Mark's composition, as presented in Eusebius's *Hist. eccl.* 2.15.1–2, resembles Papias's and may be derivative from it. It recalls the trope of a student textualizing a teacher's lecture for limited circulation and uses the term "notes" (ὑπόμνημα). According to Clement, a single event stands behind Mark's textualization of Peter's proclamation. The situation is that the teaching of Peter's rival, Simon, had taken root in Rome. The apostle arrives in the city, "preaching the proclamation of the Kingdom of Heaven" (τὸ κήρυγμα τῆς τῶν οὐρανῶν βασιλείας, εὐαγγελιζόμενος) and extinguishes Simon's influence. This gives rise to Mark's written gospel:

> τοσοῦτον δ' ἐπέλαμψεν ταῖς τῶν ἀκροατῶν τοῦ Πέτρου διανοίαις εὐσεβείας φέγγος, ὡς μὴ τῇ εἰς ἅπαξ ἱκανῶς ἔχειν ἀρκεῖσθαι ἀκοῇ μηδὲ τῇ ἀγράφῳ τοῦ θείου κηρύγματος διδασκαλίᾳ, παρακλήσεσιν δὲ παντοίαις Μάρκον, οὗ τὸ εὐαγγέλιον φέρεται, ἀκόλουθον ὄντα Πέτρου, λιπαρῆσαι ὡς ἂν καὶ διὰ γραφῆς ὑπόμνημα τῆς διὰ λόγου παραδοθείσης αὐτοῖς καταλείψοι διδασκαλίας, μὴ πρότερόν τε ἀνεῖναι ἢ κατεργάσασθαι τὸν ἄνδρα, καὶ ταύτῃ αἰτίους γενέσθαι τῆς τοῦ λεγομένου κατὰ Μάρκον εὐαγγελίου γραφῆς. γνόντα δὲ τὸ πραχθέν φασὶ τὸν ἀπόστολον ἀποκαλύψαντος αὐτῷ τοῦ πνεύματος, ἡσθῆναι τῇ τῶν ἀνδρῶν προθυμίᾳ κυρῶσαί τε τὴν γραφὴν εἰς ἔντευξιν ταῖς ἐκκλησίαις. (Clement *apud* Eusebius, *Hist. eccl.* 2.15.1–2 [Lake, LCL])

---

6. Moss, "Fashioning Mark," 186.
7. Moss, "Fashioning Mark," 198.

But a great light of religion shone on the minds of the hearers of Peter, so that they were not satisfied with a single hearing or with the unwritten teaching of the divine proclamation, but with every kind of exhortation besought Mark, whose Gospel is extant, seeing that he was Peter's follower, to leave them a set of notes of the teaching given them verbally, nor did they cease until they had persuaded him, and so became the cause of the Scripture called the Gospel according to Mark. And they say that the Apostle, knowing by the revelation of the spirit to him what had been done, was pleased at their zeal, and ratified the scripture for study in the churches.

According to Clement, Mark is a text written from an oral event without the speaker's knowledge, and it was handed over to a specific and limited audience. His comments cast Mark's Gospel within the trope of spoken teaching that became textualized by happenstance. Three aspects of Clement's account suggest as much. First, the document is the product of an agonistic context. Like other figures whose teaching was unintentionally textualized, Peter's lectures are in competition with Simon's, and his Roman hearers desire a textual monument of his didactic victory. Second, Peter's proclamation in the passage is referred to as "teaching" (διδασκαλία) in both its unwritten and its written forms. The unwritten teaching (τῇ ἀγράφῳ ... διδασκαλία) is the divine proclamation itself (τοῦ θείου κηρύγματος). The written version is explicitly labeled "*a set of notes* of the teaching" (ὑπόμνημα ... διδασκαλίας). Third, Clement emphasizes that Peter approved the text for study in the churches. Written versions of a lecture were textualized with and without a speaker's approval. A text could be re-employed in a variety of settings and in more or less reputable ways. By stating that Peter learned later that his proclamation had been textualized and that he approved of its reuse, Clement implies two things: (1) Peter did not revise the written text; (2) the written version of Peter's proclamation was not re-employed dubiously.

Later in the *Ecclesiastical History*, Eusebius embeds another account of Mark's origins from Clement's *Hypotyposes* that he, Clement, had received from the "primitive elders" (τῶν ἀνέκαθεν πρεσβυτέρων) (Eusebius, *Hist. eccl.* 6.14.5 [(modified) Lake, LCL]). Several details in this account differ from the other that Eusebius reproduces, but the core of the tradition remains the same:

τοῦ Πέτρου δημοσίᾳ ἐν Ῥώμῃ κηρύξαντος τὸν λόγον καὶ πνεύματι τὸ εὐαγγέλιον ἐξειπόντος, τοὺς παρόντας, πολλοὺς ὄντας, παρακαλέσαι τὸν Μάρκον, ὡς ἂν ἀκολουθήσαντα αὐτῷ πόρρωθεν καὶ μεμνημένον τῶν λεχθέντων, ἀναγράψαι τὰ εἰρημένα· ποιήσαντα δέ, τὸ εὐαγγέλιον μεταδοῦναι τοῖς δεομένοις αὐτοῦ· ὅπερ ἐπιγνόντα τὸν Πέτρον προτρεπτικῶς μήτε κωλῦσαι μήτε προτρέψασθαι. (Clement *apud* Eusebius, *Hist. eccl.* 6.14.6–7 [Lake, LCL])

When Peter had publicly preached the word at Rome, and by the Spirit had proclaimed the Gospel, that those present, who were many, exhorted Mark, as one who had followed him for a long time and remembered what had been spoken, to make a record of what was said; and that he did this, and distributed the Gospel among those that asked him. And that when the matter came to Peter's knowledge he neither strongly forbade it nor urged it forward.

Again Peter preaches the gospel in Rome, the hearers request a written version of the teaching, and the apostle only later learns that a text was left behind. The verbs "written up" (ἀναγράψαι) and "handed over" (μεταδοῦναι) are used rather than "composed" and "published."

The tradition is repeated a third and final time by Clement in his adumbrations on 1 Pet 5:12, extant only in Latin translation. Minor details of the tradition are flexible, but its core is fixed: "Mark, the follower of Peter, while Peter publicly preached the Gospel at Rome before some of Caesar's equites, and adduced many testimonies to Christ, in order that thereby they might be able to commit to memory what was spoken, of what was spoken by Peter, wrote entirely what was called the Gospel according to Mark."[8] Peter's audience has changed, as has the purpose for which his words are textualized, which in this instance is mnemonic. Nonetheless, the written version reproduces Peter's spoken words and is meant for a select and limited audience.

This is the distinctive feature of Mark in these witnesses: the gospel is the product of adapting oral discourses into a new, written modality that is shared with a limited group. In every instantiation of the tradition, two persons are involved in the composition process, one as a speaker and one as a writer, and the text is not prepared for publication. Mapping the patristic testimony about Mark's composition and circulation onto the publication models presented in the previous chapter thus looks like figure 1 below.

None of these writers indicate how Mark circulated beyond the select groups to whom the text was handed over. It is simply presumed that thereafter

---

8. William Wilson, "Clement of Alexandria," in *Ante-Nicene Fathers*, ed. Alexander Roberts, James Donaldson, and A. Cleveland Coxe, vol. 2 (Buffalo, NY: Christian Literature Publishing, 1885), 573.

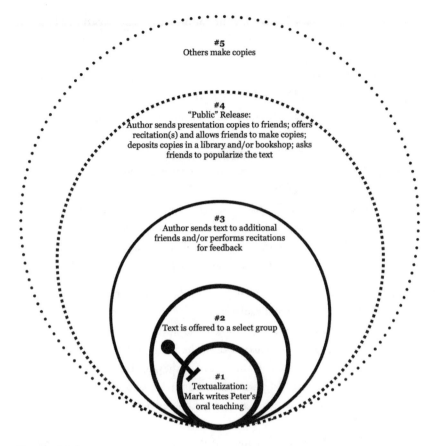

Figure 1. Mark

Mark was circulated more widely among the churches. The situation is different when the patristic writers remark on the other canonical gospels. Immediately following Papias's comments on Mark in *Hist. eccl.* 3.39.15, Eusebius embeds Papias's claims about Matthew's composition:

> Ματθαῖος μὲν οὖν Εβραΐδι διαλέκτῳ τὰ λόγια συνετάξατο, ἡρμήνευσεν δ' αὐτὰ ὡς ἦν δυνατὸς ἕκαστος. (Eusebius, *Hist. eccl.* 3.39.15 [(modified) Lake, LCL])
>
> Matthew composed the oracles in the Hebrew language, and each interpreted them as best they could.

Whereas Mark does not make "an arrangement of the Lord's oracles" (οὐχ ὥσπερ σύνταξιν τῶν κυριακῶν ποιούμενος λογίων), Matthew "composed" (συνετάξατο) his oracles. Papias does not apply a ταξ– root word to Mark but does to Matthew. That "each person" (ἕκαστος) interpreted Matthew as best they can, implies a readership that is not limited.

This is only a hint that Papias considers Matthew to be something more elegantly composed and "bookish" than Mark, but in Irenaeus's commentary on the composition of all four gospels, the claim is more explicit:

> ὁ μὲν δὴ Ματθαῖος ἐν τοῖς ἑβραίοις τῇ ἰδίᾳ διαλέκτῳ αὐτῶν, καὶ γραφὴν ἐξήνεγκεν εὐαγγελίου, τοῦ Πέτρου καὶ τοῦ Παύλου ἐν Ῥώμῃ εὐαγγελιζομένων, καὶ θεμελιούντων τὴν ἐκκλησίαν. μετὰ δὲ τὴν τούτων ἔξοδον, Μάρκος, ὁ μαθητὴς καὶ ἑρμηνευτὴς Πέτρου, καὶ αὐτὸς τὰ ὑπὸ Πέτρου κηρυσσόμενα ἐγγράφως ἡμῖν παραδέδωκε. καὶ Λουκᾶς δέ, ὁ ἀκόλουθος Παύλου, τὸ ὑπ᾽ ἐκείνου κηρυσσόμενον εὐαγγέλιον ἐν βίβλῳ κατέθετο. ἔπειτα Ἰωάννης, ὁ μαθητὴς τοῦ Κυρίου, ὁ καὶ ἐπὶ τὸ στῆθος αὐτοῦ ἀναπεσών, καὶ αὐτὸς ἐξέδωκε τὸ εὐαγγέλιον, ἐν Ἐφέσῳ τῆς Ἀσίας διατρίβων.[9]

> Matthew brought out a writing of the gospel among the Hebrews in their own dialect, while Peter and Paul were proclaiming the gospel in Rome and building the church. After their death, Mark, the disciple and interpreter of Peter, himself handed over to us in writing the things preached by Peter. And Luke, the follower of Paul, put down in a book the gospel proclaimed by him. Then John, the disciple of the Lord and the one who reclined on his chest, he also published his gospel, while staying in Ephesus of Asia.

Per Irenaeus, Matthew "brought out a writing of the gospel" (γραφὴν ἐξήνεγκεν εὐαγγελίου), and there is no suggestion that anything oral or note-like stands directly behind this composition. Mark, in contrast, hands over in writing the things that were preached by Peter. Paul's preached gospel stands behind Luke, and it was "put down in a book." Finally, John "published" (ἐξέδωκε) his gospel in Asia.

Of the four gospels, only Mark and Luke are based on antecedent, non-written material, according to Irenaeus. It might appear that Irenaeus presumes similar composition scenarios for the two. However, there are notable differences between what he writes about Mark and Luke. First, Mark is written

---

9. The most accessible Greek text of *Adv. Haer.* 3.1.1 is the one embedded in Eusebius's *Hist. eccl.* 5.8.1–4, which I use here from Lake LCL with my own translation. For a critical edition with the Greek and Latin text with French translation of book 3, see Adelin Rousseau and Louis Doutreleau, *Irénée de Lyon, Contre Les Hérésies. Livre III*, SC 211 (Paris: Les Éditions du Cref, 1974).

from "the things preached by Peter" (τὰ ὑπὸ Πέτρου κηρυσσόμενα) in the plural, whereas "the gospel preached by Paul" (τὸ ὑπ᾽ ἐκείνου κηρυσσόμενον εὐαγγέλιον), which is the basis for Luke, is in the singular. The former has a more diffuse, disconnected connotation than the latter. Second, and more significantly, Irenaeus uses different verbs to express what Mark and Luke do, respectively. Luke "puts down in a book" (ἐν βίβλῳ κατέθετο) Paul's gospel, whereas Mark "hands over" (παραδέδωκε) the written version of Peter's spoken discourses. The phrase that is applied to Luke has a more literary implication than the one used with respect to Mark. Demosthenes uses a nearly identical phrase (εἰς βιβλίον καταθεῖτο) to the one Irenaeus applies to Luke. He does so to characterize a discourse that is literature proper, which he directly contrasts to discourses that are composed for oral delivery (Demosthenes, *Eroticus* 2 [De Witt and De Witt, LCL]).[10]

The verb used with respect to Mark differs not only from what is applied to Luke, but also the other two canonical gospels. Irenaeus employs verbs of publication, ἐκφέρω ("brought out") and ἐκδίδωμι ("published"), for Matthew and John, respectively. Their proper preposition (ἐκ) connotes an outward release of written material. "Handed over" (παραδέδωκε) is lateral. The former verbs imply that the text is released beyond a limited audience.

Mark's gospel stands at the intersection between speech and writing in a way that its counterparts do not in early Christian testimony. It is produced from antecedent oral events and two people are involved in the textualization. There is not a hint in any of these writers' remarks on Mark that they consider it to have been prepared for publication. In most of the testimony, it is given to a limited audience as an afterthought. The later Synoptics and John are composed by individuals and published. They are premeditated.

I survey the patristic witness not to argue that it is accurate with respect to the details that it presents about the gospels' composition and circulation. Rather, it suggests that these authors, who wrote in a media context like the gospels', understood Mark to be the kind of document that was textualized from spoken events for limited circulation. They do not presume the same composition and circulation scenarios for the other gospels.

---

10. I am dependent on Matthew D. C. Larsen, *Gospels before the Book* (Oxford: Oxford University Press, 2018), 95, for the linguistic parallel between Irenaeus and Demosthenes.

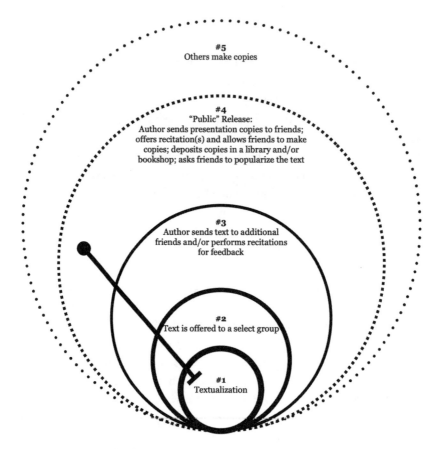

Figure 2. Matthew and Luke

INTERNAL EVIDENCE: MARK AND ITS REDACTION

There are several internal features of Mark that lend it to being understood as a set of notes textualized for limited circulation. Matthew and Luke alter each of these. While the early Christian writers do not mention these characteristics, they closely correspond to the comments made about notes by Galen, Arrian, Lucian, and Philostratus that were surveyed in the previous chapter. How Matthew and Luke revise and supplement their predecessor corresponds to what ancient authors claim about compositions that are prepared for publication in contrast to notes that are not. Early Christian writers were not reading the first three gospels synoptically, but they were able to recognize that Matthew and Luke are more polished, complete, and less obscure than Mark. I offer five reasons that suggest Mark was notes composed for limited circulation that were subsequently literaturized for publication by Matthew and Luke.

First, Mark's style is nonliterary, reflecting spoken norms. This is a result of its compositional mode. One can imagine Lucian describing Mark's style as "street-corner talk" (ἐκ τριόδου) or "as yet with beauty or continuity" (ἀκαλλὲς ἔτι καὶ ἀδιάρθρωτον), as he did other sets of notes (Lucian, *How to Write History* 16; 48 [Kilburn LCL]). One can similarly imagine Philostratus claiming that Mark's Greek was, like Damis's, "mediocre" (ξυμμέτρως) and "without style" (τὸ γὰρ λογοειδὲς οὐκ εἶχεν) on account of the author's education (Philostratus, *Vit. Apoll.* 1.19.2).[11] Both Damis and Mark could, however, draw up notes of what they heard and saw. Lack of literary polish is excusable for this kind of text.

Matthew and Luke systematically improve Mark's style. They change its paratactic structure and are more hypotactic. They also reduce the prominence of the historical present and the discourse marker "immediately" (εὐθύς) found in Mark. These oral stylistic features are considered objectionable in literary compositions. Lucian might consider Matthew and Luke to be future authors able to create a composition out of the "amateur's" (ὁ ἰδιώτης) prosaic and ordinary notes (Lucian, *How to Write History* 16). After "arranging the notes in order," they gave them beauty and enhanced them "with charms of expression, figure, and rhythm" (Lucian, *How to Write History* 48 [Kilburn, LCL]).

Second, Mark is bedeviled by a lack of precision and obscurity in several respects. Its evocations of Scripture are echoic. Rarely does the narrative quote the Septuagint verbatim and occasionally makes "mistakes" in how it is recalled.[12] Mark 1:2–3 ostensibly quotes "Isaiah the prophet," but proceeds to offer an amalgamation of Exodus, Malachi, and Isaiah. Matthew and Luke both correct this. In Mark 2, Jesus mistakenly states that David and his companions ate the bread of the presence when Abiathar was high priest. Ahimelech was high priest at the time. Matthew and Luke remove the reference to Abiathar. They also eliminate two seemingly contextless verses about the naked young man in Mark 14:51–52. Galen might have explained Mark's obscurity as he did Hippocrates's: "It is no wonder that the support and even the whole account has been left out. For this document is not a composition

---

11. Text, Jones LCL; trans. my own.

12. On Mark's "imprecise intertextuality" as a mark of its oral composition, see Nicholas A. Elder, *The Media Matrix of Early Jewish and Christian Narrative*, LNTS 612 (London: T&T Clark, 2019), 132.

created for publication."[13] Imprecision and obscurity are features of the text's limited circulation.

Third, in one instance Mark is not too obscure for Matthew and Luke, but too precise. Mark 15:21 identifies Simon from Cyrene as the "father of Alexander and Rufus." While Simon remains named in the later Synoptics, his sons are not.[14] Interpreters often understand the reference to Alexander and Rufus to result from the Markan audience's familiarity with them.[15] Joel Marcus proposes that they might have been members of the "Markan community."[16] The sons' omission by Matthew and Luke is then explained by their audience's unfamiliarity with these figures.[17] Simon and Rufus's presence or absence in each respective Synoptic is, in this line of thinking, dependent on the audience's acquaintance with them.

This logic presumes that the gospels were written with particular "communities" in mind, a premise that has been contested by Robyn Faith Walsh. She shows that the idea of such communities with authors as their figureheads is rooted more in our inherited methodologies than in ancient realities.[18] Even if one presumes that such communities did exist, it is difficult to explain Simon's perdurance in the later Synoptics. Were Matthew and Luke's communities familiar with Simon but not his sons?

Here the publication purview of the gospels is informative: extraneous and potentially obscure information is more appropriate in texts that are not meant for publication than those that are. One leaves extraneous information in a utilitarian text because that information may be useful at some later point. In streamlining a text for a wide readership, an author must decide whether or not such content is appropriate. In some instances, more information must

---

13. Text Kühn, *Claudii Galeni opera omnia*, 17a:1001; trans. my own.

14. Matt 27:32; Luke 23:26.

15. Gerd Theissen, *The Gospels in Context: Social and Political History in the Synoptic Tradition*, trans. Linda M. Maloney (Minneapolis: Fortress, 1991), 176–77; Adela Yarbro Collins, *Mark: A Commentary*, Hermeneia (Minneapolis: Fortress, 2007), 736; Joel Marcus, *Mark 1–8: A New Translation with Introduction and Commentary*, AB 27 (New York: Doubleday, 2008), 25; Richard Bauckham, *Jesus and the Eyewitnesses: The Gospels as Eyewitness Testimony* (Grand Rapids: Eerdmans, 2013), 51–52.

16. Marcus, *Mark 1–8*, 25.

17. Robert H. Stein, *Mark*, BECNT (Grand Rapids: Baker Academic, 2008), 709; Bauckham, *Jesus and the Eyewitnesses*, 52.

18. Robyn Faith Walsh, *The Origins of Early Christian Literature: Contextualizing the New Testament within Greco-Roman Literary Culture* (Cambridge: Cambridge University Press, 2021), 20–49.

be added to make the obscure clear. In other instances, it can be removed. Matthew and Luke do not follow Mark in mentioning Alexander and Rufus because they found the detail inappropriate for publication media.[19]

There are other extraneous Markan details that are removed or altered by Matthew and Luke and can be explained as inappropriate for publication media. The explanation about handwashing in Mark 7:3–4 is omitted in Matt 15:2 and Luke 11:38. Luke 5:27 does not name Alphaeus as Levi's father as Mark 2:14 does, and Matt 9:9 changes "Levi" to "Matthew," also with no mention of Alphaeus. Matthew and Luke omit both Jesus's Aramaic nickname for James and John and its translation from Mark 3:17. While Matthew and Luke both retain stories that resemble their predecessor's about blind Bartimaeus, only Mark provides his name.[20] While Matthew and Luke's alteration or omission of each of these might separately be explained in different ways, they all can be accounted for as extraneous details. Their redaction is akin to Philostratus omitting episodes that Damis had included "so as to leave nothing out" (ὑπὲρ τοῦ μὴ παραλελοιπέναι τι αὐτῶν) (Philostratus, *Vit. Apoll.* 7.28 [Jones, LCL]).[21]

Fourth, Mark begins and ends abruptly. After its prefatory material, the narrative commences *in medias res*, which is a common feature of oral narratives.[22] The original ending infamously concludes with the women at Jesus's tomb not saying anything to anyone because they were afraid. Mark 16:8 might be rhetorically effective, especially in oral recitation, but it was nonetheless found wanting by the authors of its multiple other endings. One can again imagine Galen claiming that Mark "would have said everything he needed to say" if the text was written for publication.

Matthew and Luke supplement the abrupt Markan beginning and ending. The genealogies and infancy narratives open their texts in a fulsome manner appropriate for publication media. The resurrection appearances, commissioning of the disciples, and the ascension all offer closure that is missing in Mark. What Sean Gurd writes about Galen's and Hippocrates's texts that are "for publication" (πρὸς ἔκδοσιν) in contrast to those that are not, makes excellent sense when applied to Matthew and Luke's completion of Mark: "A

---

19. Simon's name and act of carrying the cross, however, was a more stable memory that the later Synoptics did not wish to discard.
20. Mark 10:46 // Matt 9:27; 20:30; Luke 18:35.
21. See also Philostratus, *Vit. Apoll.* 1.3; 5.7; 5.26.
22. Walter J. Ong, "The Psychodynamics of Oral Memory and Narrative: Some Implications for Biblical Studies," in *The Pedagogy of God's Image: Essays on Symbol and the Religious Imagination*, ed. Robert Masson (Chico, CA: Scholars Press, 1982), 59.

text written πρὸς ἔκδοσιν ["for publication"] should attempt to provide an explanation useful to a 'normal,' that is, not expert but not ignorant, reader."[23] Unlike a set of notes, a text prepared for publication needs to provide enough information so as to be readily understood by someone with whom the author is not in immediate contact.

Fifth, and finally, that Mark is completed by at least two subsequent authors suggests that it was understood by them to be a medium appropriate for reuse. If one can imagine Lucian labeling Mark's style as completely prosaic and ordinary, one can likewise imagine him offering the caveat that Mark "was not so bad—it was quite obvious at the beginning what he was, and his work has cleared the ground for some future [evangelist] of taste and ability" (Lucian, *How to Write History* 16 [Kilburn, LCL]).[24] Galen is explicit that his hypomnematic texts were reused, reputably or disreputably, on account of their medium and composition scenario. While publication did not guarantee that a text would not be reused, it was a guard against it. We do not read of texts prepared for publication being reused nearly as often as we do notes that were not prepared for publication. That Matthew and Luke stylistically improve the first written gospel, remove or make precise its obscurities and extraneous information, and amend both its beginning and ending all suggest that they are creating compositions from a set of notes.

Circulation in Codex and Roll

Luke's dedication to Theophilus is another strong indication that it was written for publication and crosses the threshold between stages three and four in Starr's concentric circles model. Gurd writes, "Ἔκδοσις [publication] in the ancient world meant nothing more than 'giving out' (ἐκδιδόναι) a text, usually to its dedicatee, on the understanding that it would be copied freely

---

23. Sean A. Gurd, "Galen on ἔκδοσις," in *Perceptions of the Second Sophistic and Its Times*, ed. Thomas Schmidt and Pascale Fleury (Toronto: University of Toronto Press, 2011), 174.

24. This is not to disparage the Gospel of Mark. Different media are used for different purposes and ought to be judged in accordance with their specific form. The Gospel of Mark is masterful as a story, and particularly as a story retold in oral mode. The abiding success of texts such as *Mark as Story* and performances of the narrative are testaments to the former and latter, respectively (David Rhoads, Joanna Dewey, and Donald Michie, *Mark as Story: An Introduction to the Narrative of a Gospel*, 3rd ed. [Minneapolis: Fortress, 2012]).

thereafter."[25] A dedication marked the text as a complete composition ready for circulation to others.

The Third Gospel was written for an individual, and the dedication to this individual is also a signal that the text was complete and could be further distributed. The preface to Galen's *On Exercise with a Small Ball* exemplifies this circulation phenomenon well. The treatise is dedicated to Epigenes, who is its first reader. Second-person forms are used throughout the text. Galen is also clear about his expectations for a wider readership. He states his hope that the discourse will not only be useful to Epigenes, but will also be "employed by others to whom you [Epigenes] might transmit the work" (καὶ τοῖς ἄλλοις οἷς ἂν μεταδῷς τοῦ λόγου) (Galen, *Exercise with the Small Ball*, 1 [(modified) Johnston, LCL]).[26] The subjunctive verb μεταδῷς with the contingent particle ἄν indicates that the future readership of *On Exercise with a Small Ball* is both unknown and unlimited in Galen's mind. A discourse is composed and edited differently when it has a distant circulation horizon.

Offering a text to a dedicatee for further circulation involved more than simply releasing it. It also meant providing a presentation copy.[27] A version "for publication" was complete not only with respect to its content but also its form. It was characterized by "a more elegant style of handwriting, a more accurate arrangement of the columns, [and] some process of correction (διόρθωσις)."[28] This was a specialized task that, in most cases, was not performed by the author themself, but by a scribe or enslaved person trained to do so.[29]

Preparing a literary text for publication also meant putting it into the proper physical medium: a bookroll. If Matthew and Luke were creating compositions for publication, their presentation copies were in this form. The same is not true of Mark if it was a set of notes that was not prepared for publication.

It was not uncommon for utilitarian texts and rough drafts to be written in notebooks, otherwise known as "codices."[30] Quintilian recommended com-

---

25. Gurd, "Galen on ἔκδοσις," 170.
26. See also Kühn, *Claudii Galeni opera omnia*, 5:899.
27. Raymond J. Starr, "The Circulation of Literary Texts in the Roman World," *ClQ* 37 (1987): 215.
28. Tiziano Dorandi, "Ancient ἐκδόσεις: Further Lexical Observations on Some of Galen's Texts," *Lexicon Philosophicum: International Journal for the History of Ideas and Texts* 2 (2014): 8.
29. Starr, "Circulation," 214; William A. Johnson, "The Ancient Book," in *The Oxford Handbook of Papyrology*, ed. Roger S. Bagnall (Oxford: Oxford University Press, 2009), 261.
30. Loveday Alexander, "Ancient Book Production and the Circulation of the Gospels," in *The Gospels for All Christians: Rethinking the Gospel Audiences*, ed. Richard Bauckham (Grand Rapids: Eerdmans, 1998), 82–84.

posing initial drafts by hand on wax or parchment notebooks (Quintilian, *Inst.* 10.3.31). Damis's notes that served as the basis of Philostratus's biography of Apollonius were written in notebook form, as indicated by the title *Damis's Scrap Book* (ἡ γοῦν δέλτος ἡ τῶν ἐκφατνισμάτων τοιοῦτον τῷ Δάμιδι). The tablet notebook (ἡ δέλτος) was the proverbial medium for first drafts.[31] Since Damis's work was not written for publication, there was no reason for it to be put into presentation form. The codex had an "intersecting 'intermediate' status in terms of the practical processes of book production," and its contents could be transferred to rolls for publication.[32] But a literary text could also be in codex form when used personally. Surveying non-Christian manuscript evidence to codex texts in the second century, Larry Hurtado concludes that codices were most often used for "paraliterary texts" and "when codices were used for literary texts, it was often to provide workaday copies for annotation and handy aids such as excerpt collections."[33] The use of the text was related to its circulation medium. The codex was appropriate for limited, personal reading and paraliterary works.

If Mark first existed or circulated in codex form but the later Synoptics did not, then this has implications for book technology preferences in the first five centuries CE and the codex's eventual rise to prominence over the bookroll. In 1939, C. H. Roberts first associated Mark with the codex and then in 1954 argued that the gospel was the catalyst for the Christian preference for the codex. It was written as a parchment notebook in Rome that was taken to Alexandria, transferred into papyrus notebooks, and then exerted technological influence.[34] The argument was subsequently retracted in *The Birth of the Codex*, coauthored with T. C. Skeat, and has found little favor in recent scholarship.[35] However, Matthew D. C. Larsen and Mark Letteney have resurrected a form of Roberts's first argument, claiming that "he was not as far off track as later commentators have supposed."[36]

---

31. E. G. Turner, *Greek Papyri: An Introduction* (Oxford: Clarendon, 1968), 6–7.
32. Alexander, "Ancient Book Production," 83.
33. Larry W. Hurtado, *The Earliest Christian Artifacts: Manuscripts and Christian Origins* (Grand Rapids: Eerdmans, 2006), 51.
34. C. H. Roberts, "The Ancient Book and the Endings of St. Mark," *JTS* 40 (1939): 253–57; C. H. Roberts, "The Codex," *Proceedings of the British Academy* 40 (1954): 187–89.
35. C. H. Roberts and T. C. Skeat, *The Birth of the Codex* (London: Oxford University Press, 1983), 55–57.
36. Matthew D. C. Larsen and Mark Letteney, "Christians and the Codex: Generic Materiality and Early Gospel Traditions," *JECS* 27 (2019): 389.

Larsen and Letteney illuminate Christian media preferences with a concept they call "generic materiality," which connects a text's genre to its material form. They offer print newspapers as a modern analogue: "Just as a contemporary reader would be surprised to see her newspaper delivered either in looseleaf or in bound codex form rather than in the standard broadsheet or increasingly popular online format, the ancient Christian reader of 'gospel' would expect the text, based on its genre, to be transmitted as a codex, either in the older wooden or the increasingly popular papyrus format."[37] Larsen and Letteney understand Mark's genre to be notes, a contention with which I am in agreement.[38]

They then reject Harry Y. Gamble's influential argument that a Pauline letter collection was the initial impetus for the Christian preference for the codex. They do so citing the Acts of the Scillitan Martyrs, wherein Speratus carries "books and letters of Paul, a just man" in a *capsa*, which is a technology for holding rolls.[39] Per Larsen and Letteney, "The earliest unambiguous evidence actually depicts [the Pauline letters] circulating on rolls."[40]

But the same is true of the gospels. In the Acts of Peter, a late-second-century text, Peter comes upon a reading of "the gospel" (*euangelium*), which he "rolls up" (*inuolues eum*).[41] The gospel text is imagined to exist in roll form, just as the Pauline texts are in the Acts of the Scillitan Martyrs. In the passage from the Acts of the Scillitan Martyrs, there are two different kinds of textual objects in the *capsa:* books and letters of Paul (*libri et epistulae Pauli*). The phrase can be read either as "both books of Paul and also letters of Paul" or as "books and also letters of Paul." In the first, "Paul" (*Pauli*) modifies both textual objects; in the second, it modifies only "letters" (*epistulae*).

---

37. Larsen and Letteney, "Christians and the Codex," 386. A similar contention was made in 1941 by C. C. McCown who suggested that the parchment codex was "the proper medium in which to write *commentarii* and first drafts of works of all kinds" ("Codex and Roll in the New Testament," *HTR* 34 [1941]: 239). He claims it is "almost certain" that Mark was first written and circulated in a codex.

38. Larsen and Letteney, "Christians and the Codex," 399–404. I classify "notes" as Mark's media form, not its genre. Written artifacts from varying genres can exist in note form.

39. Larsen and Letteney, "Christians and the Codex," 412. Text, Antonius Adrianus Robertus Bastiaensen, ed., *Atti e passioni dei martiri* (Milan: Fondazione Lorenzo Valla, 1987), 102.

40. Larsen and Letteney, "Christians and the Codex," 412.

41. Text: R. A. Lipsius and M. Bonnet, eds., *Acta Apostolorum Apocrypha*, 2 vols. (Leipzig: H. Mendelssohn, 1891), 1:66–67.

It is possible that "books of Paul" refers either to canonical Acts or to the Acts of Paul. But it is more likely that the "books" is not modified by "Paul," and that the word refers to gospel materials, which also exist in roll form. Together, the Acts of Peter and the Acts of the Scillitan Martyrs imagine gospel and Pauline texts to exist in roll form in the second century. To this second-century evidence, Jan den Boeft and Jan Bremmer add that "codex" is missing from Tertullian's material vocabulary for Scriptural texts, but *volumen* is not.[42] The limited early literary evidence implies that New Testament texts of varying types existed as rolls.

This poses a problem for Gamble's Pauline letter collection theory, as well as Larsen and Letteney's Markan notes theory. Both presume, as Gamble puts it, "a precedent-setting development in the publication and circulation of early Christian literature that rapidly established the codex in Christian use."[43] According to Gamble, there is "substantial evidence" for dating the precedent-setting development of the Pauline letter collection to the early second century, but he tentatively pushes it back into the first.[44] Larsen and Letteney's big-bang moment is in the first century with the textualization of Mark.[45] Following Mark, subsequent gospel materials were produced in codices. They write, "It is all but certain that the earliest texts [of the gospels] circulated in codex form, and that later Christian communities continued the practice for all scriptural texts. On our theory the earliest textualized gospel material circulated on a codex in response to its genre, and the book form stuck, so to speak."[46]

Since all the literary evidence that alludes to the medium of New Testament texts in the second century imagines them to exist in roll form, claims that Christians were exclusively utilizing the codex in the first or second centuries should be tempered. The material evidence cannot confirm that Christians preferred the codex this early. The manuscript data from the period is limited and paleographically dated. Given the inexactitude of this method of dating,

---

42. Jan den Boeft and Jan N. Bremmer, "*Notiunculae Martyrologicae* IV," *VC* 45 (1991): 116–17.

43. Gamble, *Books and Readers*, 58.

44. Gamble, *Books and Readers*, 61. He also raises the possibility that Pauline letters were first written in small codices (*Books and Readers*, 64).

45. Graham Stanton labels these and others like it "big-bang" approaches to the Christian adoption of the codex (*Jesus and Gospel* [Cambridge: Cambridge University Press, 2004], 167–69). One major event, text, or collection instituted a sea change in practice.

46. Larsen and Letteney, "Christians and the Codex," 411.

both Eldon Jay Epp and Brent Nongbri caution against asserting that the Christian preference for the codex was established long before the rest of the Roman world.[47]

Even if early Christians did not invent the codex and its preference cannot be demonstrated in the second century, it is clear that, as Epp puts it, "early Christians picked up quickly on the use of the codex for their writings."[48] They were, in the terms of diffusion of innovations theory, "early adopters" of the technology.[49] According to diffusion of innovations theory, widespread adoption of new technologies happens on an S-shaped curve: initially few people or groups utilize a given technology, followed by a steep increase in its adoption, before it levels off at near-universal acceptance. According to Benjamin Harnett, the diffusion of the codex in the first five centuries CE maps onto this S-shaped curve.[50]

Early Christian manuscript data does not map onto the curve. The earliest manuscript evidence, which is in the form of codices, already shows widespread adoption. The data is already plotted at the top of the S curve. The issue is that there is limited early data to plot. It might be that the early Christian transition from rolls to codices, in practice, followed such a curve.[51] Alternatively, it might be that from the emergence of early Christianity, codices were in widespread use for Christian texts. The reality is likely in between these two options.

I submit that early Christian texts circulated in a variety of media, including codices and rolls. Certain texts, such as Matthew and Luke-Acts, were more likely to circulate as rolls because they were considered publication literature. Other texts, such as Mark, were more likely to circulate as codices because they were not considered publication literature. There was not a single text or set of texts that instituted a sea change in bibliographic practices among early

---

47. Eldon J. Epp, "The Codex and Literacy in Early Christianity and at Oxyrhynchus: Issues Raised by Harry Y. Gamble's Books and Readers in the Early Church," in *Perspectives on New Testament Textual Criticism: Collected Essays, 1962–2004*, ed. Eldon Jay Epp, NovTSup 116 (Leiden: Brill, 2005), 522–23; Brent Nongbri, *God's Library: The Archaeology of the Earliest Christian Manuscripts* (New Haven: Yale University Press, 2018), 23–24, 288nn5–6.

48. Epp, "Codex and Literacy," 523.

49. Benjamin Harnett uses diffusion of innovations theory to explain non-Christian adoption of the codex, and places Christians in just this category ("The Diffusion of the Codex," *ClAnt* 36 [2017]: 203–4). The standard work on diffusion of innovations theory is Everett M. Rogers, *Diffusions of Innovations*, 5th ed. (New York: Free Press, 2003).

50. Harnett, "Diffusion of the Codex," 192–99.

51. Harnett, "Diffusion of the Codex," 202.

Christians. Both a Pauline letter collection and the Gospel of Mark circulated in codex form. There is no reason we must choose between one or the other.[52]

This is even more likely if Pauline letters were not considered publication texts, which Gamble proposes. He writes, "It is misleading to suppose that the Christian step was to employ the codex for the transcription of literature. The Christians who made them and made use of them did not regard them as notebooks or as books of fine literature."[53] Under both Gamble's and Larsen and Letteney's theories, the texts that are circulated, whether they be Pauline letters or gospels, were not literature proper. The "generic materiality" of a Pauline letter collection was paraliterary.

If multiple Christian texts were known to exist and circulate in codex form, then this explains why Christians were early adopters of the technology.[54] It does not require that all New Testament texts were written in codices following a single originative event. There was a mixture of media use within early Christianity. In the terms of diffusion of innovations theory, early Christians were posed to be exposed to the technological innovation of the codex and later adopt it for other kinds of texts, including those that were "for publication."[55]

That New Testament texts existed in a variety of media, both codex and roll, was a claim made by C. C. McCown in 1941. His *Harvard Theological Review* article, "Codex and Roll in the New Testament," has been overshadowed by Roberts and Skeat's *The Birth of the Codex* and Gamble's *Books and Readers in the Early Church*.[56] But McCown makes several arguments that anticipate later propositions about the adoption of the codex. He suggests that Mark was first written and circulated in codices because the technology was well known in Rome "as a *memorialis libellus*, the proper medium in which to write *commentarii* and first drafts of works of all kinds."[57] McCown submits

---

52. Larsen and Letteney do just this, and so must contend that the "codex form of the gospel is likely primary, and that Pauline letter collections experienced a generic format attraction as the two corpora began to be transmitted together" ("Christians and the Codex," 412).

53. Gamble, *Books and Readers*, 66.

54. It also neither eliminates nor necessitates the proposition that the codex was adopted widely in the Roman world under later Christian influence.

55. Individuals and groups are more likely to adopt a technology early if others in their network have (Rogers, *Diffusion of Innovations*, 359).

56. McCown, "Codex and Roll," 219–49.

57. McCown, "Codex and Roll," 239.

that the codex was the most natural medium for a Pauline letter collection, which was also nonliterary.[58]

But this does not press him into claiming that all subsequent New Testament texts were circulated in codices. He draws the opposite conclusion with respect to Luke-Acts: it was written and circulated in rolls. The length of both narratives, the prefaces and dedications to Theophilus, and the style of both narratives all indicate as much.[59] When it comes to Matthew, McCown is not as confident, tentatively suggesting that a roll might have been preferred. Given Matthew's stylistic improvements upon Mark, that it labels itself a "book" (βίβλος), and was written as a composition, we can be confident that it was initially circulated in roll form. If it was not, this would be an innovation. Mark and Pauline letters were expected to circulate in codices on account of their "generic materiality." Matthew's and Luke's generic materiality implies their early existence as rolls. If Matthew followed Mark with respect to its medium, this would be the pioneering act that broke technological convention. It might have further influenced the early Christian preference for the codex.

The Synoptic Gospels circulated in a variety of physical forms. The codex was an appropriate technology for the Gospel of Mark, a hypomnematic text that was "not for publication." It would be unexceptional to find "orally proclaimed news" (εὐαγγέλιον) that had been textualized circulating in this medium. The roll was natural for the later Synoptics, which improve upon Mark stylistically and present themselves as literature "for publication." Both a "book" (βίβλος) and an "account" (διήγησις) with a literary preface would conventionally circulate in rolls.

Circulating John

John presents a crossroads with respect to the physical form of gospel texts. If John knew the Synoptic Gospels, which I shall argue below, and if the Synoptics circulated in varying book technologies, then the Fourth Gospel's physical form had the potential to impact that of gospel traditions moving forward. There are three options. First, John might have characteristically existed as a roll following the physical form of Matthew, Luke, and most literature in the first century. Second, John, if considered to be paraliterary, might have

---

58. McCown, "Codex and Roll," 243–49.
59. McCown, "Codex and Roll," 242.

followed Mark and characteristically existed as a codex. Third, John might have followed all three and circulated in both technologies simultaneously.

The third is most likely the case based on John's media self-designation and its relationship to the Synoptics. The Johannine colophons hint at the Synoptics' existence as mixed media. In chapter 3, I argued that the Fourth Gospel's self-designation as a "document" (βιβλίον) and the Johannine colophons' similarities to conventions in texts from Plutarch and Josephus indicate that the text presents itself as contributing to a wider tradition. There the question of John's relationship to the Synoptics was raised but left unanswered.

In this section, I argue that the Gospel of John is familiar with the Synoptics, but considers itself wholly distinct from them. This is not to suggest that John wishes to supplant other written Jesus traditions. The Fourth Gospel justifies its own existence in the colophons by claiming Jesus's signs and deeds can never be exhausted in writing.

The argument proceeds in four steps. First, I demonstrate that the Johannine colophons echo a repeated formula in 1–2 Kings. Second, I offer five arguments for John's knowledge not only of Mark but also of Matthew and Luke. I then explicate John's posture toward the Synoptics based on its media designation and the 1–2 Kings formula it echoes. Finally, I draw conclusions about John's physical medium and circulation in conjunction with the Synoptics'.

JOHN AND 1–2 KINGS

Thirty-three times 1–2 Kings refers to two different texts known only by their titles: "The Document of the Words of the Days of the Kings of Israel" and "The Document of the Words of the Days of the Kings of Judah."[60] These are literal translations of the Hebrew and Greek titles. What I have rendered "document" is the Hebrew term סֵפֶר. The Greek is βιβλίον, the same word with which the Fourth Gospel labels itself. What is often translated as "Annals" or "Chronicles" is properly the phrase "words of the days."[61]

Each time 1–2 Kings evokes these documents, it is at the end of a section in which a given king's deeds have been narrated and the reference occurs in a standardized, though flexible, formula. It first appears in 1 Kgs 14:29, which is representative of the basic arrangement:

---

60. 1 Kings 14:19, 29; 15:7, 23, 31; 16:5, 14, 20, 27; 22:39, 45; 2 Kings 1:18; 8:23; 10:34; 12:19; 13:8, 12; 14:15, 18, 28; 15:6, 11, 15, 21, 26, 31, 36; 16:19; 20:20; 21:17, 25; 23:28; 24:5.

61. This is דִּבְרֵי הַיָּמִים and λόγων τῶν ἡμερῶν in the MT and LXX, respectively.

וְיֶ֛תֶר דִּבְרֵ֥י רְחַבְעָ֖ם וְכָל־אֲשֶׁ֣ר עָשָׂ֑ה הֲלֹא־הֵ֣מָּה כְתוּבִ֗ים עַל־סֵ֛פֶר דִּבְרֵ֥י הַיָּמִ֖ים לְמַלְכֵ֥י יְהוּדָֽה

καὶ τὰ λοιπὰ τῶν λόγων Ροβοαμ καὶ πάντα, ἃ ἐποίησεν, οὐκ ἰδοὺ ταῦτα γεγραμμένα ἐν βιβλίῳ λόγων τῶν ἡμερῶν τοῖς βασιλεῦσιν Ιουδα;

And the rest of the acts of Rehoboam and all that he did, have these not been written in The Document of the Words of the Days of the Kings of Judah? (1 Kgs 14:29)

This oft-repeated expression indicates that additional words and deeds can be found about a given king in these titled works.[62] There are striking similarities between the formula, especially in its Septuagintal form, and the Johannine colophons. Based on these parallels, I suggest that the colophons intentionally echo 1–2 Kings.

Πολλὰ μὲν οὖν καὶ ἄλλα σημεῖα ἐποίησεν ὁ Ιησοῦς ἐνώπιον τῶν μαθητῶν αὐτοῦ, ἃ οὐκ ἔστιν γεγραμμένα ἐν τῷ βιβλίῳ τούτῳ· ταῦτα δὲ γέγραπται ἵνα πιστεύητε ὅτι Ιησοῦς ἐστιν ὁ χριστὸς ὁ υἱὸς τοῦ θεοῦ, καὶ ἵνα πιστεύοντες ζωὴν ἔχητε ἐν τῷ ὀνόματι αὐτοῦ.

Now Jesus did many other signs before his disciples, which have not been written in this document. But these things have been written that you might believe that Jesus is the Christ, the Son of God and that believing you might have life in his name. (John 20:30–31)

Ἔστιν δὲ καὶ ἄλλα πολλὰ ἃ ἐποίησεν ὁ Ιησοῦς, ἅτινα ἐὰν γράφηται καθ᾽ ἕν, οὐδ᾽ αὐτὸν οἶμαι τὸν κόσμον χωρῆσαι τὰ γραφόμενα βιβλία.

But there are many other things which Jesus did, and if each one were written I suppose the world itself would not be able to contain documents written. (John 21:25)

---

62. Whether or not these documents physically existed when 1–2 Kings was composed and what sorts of texts they were are interesting questions beyond the scope of this book. Menahem Haran makes a compelling case that the Deuteronomist's acquaintance with these texts is indirect and mediated ("The Books of the Chronicles 'of the Kings of Judah' and 'of the Kings of Israel': What Sort of Books Were They?" *VT* 49 [1999]: 160). He argues that the singular word סֵפֶר indicates that the document is available in only one copy, and it is highly unlikely that the Deuteronomist had access to it.

There are five persistent features of the formula in 1–2 Kings that overlap with one, the other, or both colophons in John. First, the perfect, passive participle "have been written" (γεγραμμένα) appears in all but two of the thirty-three occasions of the expression in 1–2 Kings. On those two occasions, the participle is replaced by the perfect, passive indicative form "were written" (γέγραπται).[63] John 20:30–31 contains both the passive participle and the passive indicative verb. This form of "have been written" (γεγραμμένα) is somewhat rare in the New Testament, appearing only six other times.[64] Notably, over half of the occasions of it in the LXX occur in this formula from 1–2 Kings.

Second, the neuter demonstrative "these things" (ταῦτα) is without exception the object of writing in the 1–2 Kings locution. It always directly precedes the verb. This is likewise the case in John 20:31, wherein the neuter demonstrative is the object of γέγραπται ("were written").

Third, and again without exception, the kind of text referenced in 1–2 Kings is a "document" (βιβλίον), a word that, among the gospels, is uniquely appended to John. The noun is used in both Johannine colophons. In John 20:30 it is applied to the Fourth Gospel, and in John 21:25 it refers to the hypothetical documents that the world could not hold if all of Jesus's deeds were textualized.

Fourth, on most occasions, the formula in 1–2 Kings includes either the relative phrase "that he did" (ἅ ἐποίησεν) or the correlative "as much as he did" (ὅσα ἐποίησεν). On these occasions, "the rest of the deeds" (τὰ λοιπὰ τῶν λόγων) and "all things" (πάντα) are the pronouns' antecedents. Both Johannine colophons contain the identical aorist form "he did" (ἐποίησεν) with a neuter plural object that precedes the relative ἅ or correlative ὅσα. In John 20:30, the object is "many other signs" (πολλὰ ... ἄλλα σημεῖα) and in John 21:25 it is simply "many other things" (ἄλλα πολλά).

In 1–2 Kings, the correlative pronoun ὅσα occurs twenty times in the formula and is thus more common than the relative ἅ, which is in the exemplar from 1 Kgs 14:29 reproduced above. The latter appears eight times in 1–2 Kings and once in each of the Johannine colophons.[65] Many important tex-

---

63. The indicative form occurs in 1 Kgs 22:46 and 2 Kgs 8:23.
64. Luke 18:31; 21:22; 24:44; John 12:16; Acts 13:29; Rev 1:3.
65. The correlative ὅσα ἐποίησεν ("as much as he did") appears in LXX 1 Kgs 22:46; 2 Kgs 1:18; 8:23; 10:34; 12:20; 13:8, 12; 14:15, 28; 15:6, 21, 26, 31, 36; 16:19; 20:20; 21:17; 21:25; 23:28; 24:5. The relative ἅ ἐποίησεν ("that he did") appears in LXX 1 Kgs 14:29; 15:7, 31; 16:5, 14, 27; 22:39; 2 Kgs 14:18.

tual witnesses to John 21:25 substitute the correlative ὅσα for the relative ἅ, perhaps to correspond with the pronoun that is more commonly found in the LXX formula.[66]

There is a striking constellation of participial forms of "write" (γράφω), the neuter demonstrative "these things" (ταῦτα), the term "document" (βιβλίον), and a relative or correlative phrase with the aorist verb "he did" (ἐποίησεν) in 1–2 Kings and the Johannine colophons. This unique combination signifies that the Fourth Gospel is echoing the formula. That John evokes the intertext near its end is also telling, since it always concludes a discrete literary unit in 1–2 Kings.

But there are also significant differences between the colophons and its forerunner. While both function as conclusions to a literary unit, the author of the Fourth Gospel does not continue to narrate the events of another individual's life, as 1–2 Kings does. In the latter, the expression concludes the account of a respective king, only to move to another. John, in contrast, is solely interested in the actions of Jesus.

Another difference is that in 1–2 Kings, the formula appears as a question on all but four occasions.[67] In Hebrew, the interrogative הֲ does not imply either a positive or negative answer, but the Septuagintal translation of it with οὐκ expects the former.[68] The implied answer is "Yes, these have been written in The Document of the Words of the Days of the Kings of Judah." 1–2 Kings names the text in which the other acts of a respective king might be found. The Fourth Gospel does not. Following the formula, both Johannine colophons refer to Jesus's other deeds. They do not, however, directly state that those have been textualized.

In 1–2 Kings, all the words and deeds of a particular king have been written down and exist in one of two physical documents: the one at hand or the one referenced. For the hyperbolizing author of the second Johannine colophon, all of Jesus's other deeds could not be contained in the world, much less a single document. Similarly, the author of the first colophon recognizes that Jesus

---

66. Per the NA28 apparatus, the correlative pronoun ὅσα appears in place of ἅ in A C³ D W Θ ƒ1.13 𝔐. The relative ἅ occurs in ℵ¹ B C* Ψ 33. ℓ 2211. However, on three other occasions one or more of these same witnesses replace ἅ with ὅσα: John 4:39; 11:46; 15:14.

67. 2 Kings 15:11, 15, 26, 31.

68. Though GKC §150e notes that the interrogative in 1 Kings is used for strong affirmation. "[I]t serves to express the conviction that the contents of the statement are well known to the hearer, and are unconditionally admitted by him."

performed many other signs that were not written in the Johannine text. In contrast to the texts that they echo, the Johannine colophons explicitly claim that Jesus's deeds cannot be exhausted in writing. By making this claim, the Fourth Gospel justifies its own existence. A new Jesus text can be produced because Jesus's deeds, per John 21:25, are an inexhaustible well.

JOHN'S KNOWLEDGE OF THE SYNOPTICS

But why might the Fourth Gospel be interested in justifying its own existence? Plutarch found it necessary to legitimate his Lives of Alexander and Caesar because these discourses contributed to extant traditions that transcended themselves. There were already collective memories and written texts about these two men's most famous deeds, and Plutarch aimed to supplement them with new foci. By writing "not Histories ... but Lives" (οὔτε γὰρ ἱστορίας γράφομεν, ἀλλὰ βίους) he textually contributed something new to the discourses about Alexander and Caesar (Plutarch, *Alex.* 1.1–3 [664–65]). He left it "to others" (ἑτέροις) to write about their great deeds and conquests. 1–2 Kings similarly presents its accounts as supplementing extant textual traditions. The author names these texts but does not directly engage with or reproduce them in their own writing.

The Fourth Gospel is similar. John knows written Jesus traditions in the form of the Synoptic Gospels and aims to supplement them by offering new material. Both colophons acknowledge that Jesus did (ἐποίησεν) many other things that were not written in the Johannine narrative. With a growing cadre of scholars, I reckon that John betrays knowledge of the Synoptics and engages them in the gospel.[69] The Synoptics are in the periphery when the colophons refer to Jesus's other actions and signs. Here I distill what I find to be the five most compelling reasons for John's knowledge of the Synoptics.

---

69. On John's knowledge, use, and transformation of Mark see the paradigm-shattering collection, Eve-Marie Becker, Helen K. Bond, and Catrin Williams, eds., *John's Transformation of Mark* (London: T&T Clark, 2021). It would be difficult to overstate just how significant and convincing the essays in this volume are with respect to John's relationship to Mark. Other significant texts taking the position that John knew one or more of the Synoptics include Thomas L. Brodie, *The Quest for the Origin of John's Gospel: A Source-Critical Approach* (New York: Oxford University Press, 1993); Richard Bauckham, "John for Readers of Mark," in *The Gospel for All Christians: Rethinking the Gospel Audiences* (Edinburgh: T&T Clark, 1998), 147–71; Udo Schnelle, *Das Evangelium nach Johannes*, 2nd ed., THKNT 4 (Leipzig: Evangelische Verlagsanstalt, 2000), 13–17; James Barker, *John's Use of Matthew* (Minneapolis: Fortress Press, 2015).

First, Mark had already been utilized by two other authors when the Gospel of John was composed. This reveals the profound influence of the first written gospel. Mark was well known by the time John was produced.[70] It also suggests that Mark was conducive for reuse and rewriting. A precedent had already been set for incorporating antecedent written Jesus traditions into new ones. As Catrin Williams shows, there is a "vast range of rewriting strategies" for Second Temple Jewish texts, and we should therefore not expect John's relationship to Mark to mirror Matthew's and Luke's.[71] This claim can be pressed a step further: if John knows Matthew or Luke's manner of Markan reuse, then they are even less likely to repeat it.

Second, the early Jesus movement was relatively small, well networked, and mobile. If Mark circulated widely and was a watershed for the transference of oral Jesus traditions into the written modality, then it is likely that the author of John would be aware of this development. News of Mark's written gospel is likely to have reached the author of John. Not only were travel routes well established in the first-century Roman world, but, per the New Testament texts themselves, leaders of the early Jesus movement were itinerant. They traversed the empire. As Michael B. Thompson concludes, "News and information could spread relatively quickly between the congregations in the great cities of the empire, and from there into the surrounding regions."[72] That Mark could have existed for several years or decades without John's knowledge of and access to it is unlikely.

Third, unlike the Synoptics, John does not indicate what kind of text it is at its beginning. If the Fourth Gospel was wholly unaware of the Synoptics and it independently textualized Jesus traditions, then the author would have considered their act innovative. In this situation, we would expect the author to give some indication about what kind of text they wrote. Instead, the Fourth

---

70. Bauckham argues similarly ("John for Readers of Mark," 148n2).

71. Catrin Williams, "John's 'Rewriting' of Mark: Some Insights from Ancient Jewish Analogues," in Becker, Bond, Williams, *John's Transformation of Mark*, 51–65, esp. 59–60. Jean Zumstein makes a similar case using intertextual theory from Gérard Genette, arguing that John is in a "hypertextual" relationship with Mark, which is the "hypotext" ("The Johannine 'Relecture' of Mark" in Becker, Bond, Williams, *John's Transformation of Mark*, 23–29). Unlike the Synoptics, "the relationship between John and Mark is one characterized by distance and freedom" (Zumstein, "Johannine 'Relecture,'" 23n5).

72. Michael B. Thompson, "The Holy Internet: Communication Between Churches in the First Christian Generation," in *The Gospels for All Christians: Rethinking the Gospel Audiences*, ed. Richard Bauckham (Grand Rapids: Eerdmans, 1998), 68.

Gospel presumes that its audience knows something about its content and genre.[73] The best explanation for such an assumption is that the author and audience have experience with comparable written Jesus traditions. John 1:1's "in the beginning" (ἐν ἀρχῇ) appears to be riffing on Mark 1:1's "the beginning of the gospel" (ἀρχὴ τοῦ εὐαγγελίου).[74]

Fourth, John follows the overarching structure of the Synoptics and shares important material in common with them.[75] In both John and the Synoptics, Jesus's ministry begins with the preaching of John the Baptist. In the middle of the narratives, Jesus performs miracles and teaches. Each gospel concludes with an extended passion narrative in which Jesus is crucified outside Jerusalem. This shared structure indicates an "essential continuity" between John and the Synoptics.[76] There were several other ways one could write Jesus traditions without following this structure, as other gospels, such as Thomas, demonstrate. Along with a shared general structure, John includes much parallel material from the Synoptics, even if it is stylistically and theologically transformed.[77] This is the case at the level of both episodes and words.[78]

---

73. Similarly, Chris Keith, riffing on Tom Thatcher's *Why John Wrote a Gospel: Jesus, Memory, History* (Louisville: Westminster John Knox, 2006), suggests that John chose the written medium because the author was aware that others had successfully harnessed the technology for their own Jesus narratives (*The Gospel as Manuscript: An Early History of the Jesus Tradition as Material Artifact* [Oxford: Oxford University Press, 2020], 147–48).

74. Christina Hoegen-Rohls, "The Beginnings of Mark and John: What Exactly Should Be Compared? Some Hermeneutical Questions and Observations," in Becker, Bond, Williams, *John's Transformation of Mark*, 102–5.

75. Similar arguments are made by Brodie, *Quest for the Origin*, 51; Bauckham, "John for Readers of Mark," 151; Andrew Lincoln, *The Gospel according to Saint John*, BNTC 4 (London: Continuum, 2005), 27; Williams, "John's 'Rewriting,'" 60; Mark Goodacre, "Parallel Tradition or Parallel Gospels?," in Becker, Bond, Williams, *John's Transformation of Mark*, 87.

76. Brodie, *Quest for the Origin*, 31.

77. Harold Attridge offers sixty instances of parallels between John and one or more of the Synoptics in a table divided into three sections: narrative parallels, sayings parallels, and miscellaneous parallels ("John and Mark in the History of Research," in Becker, Bond, Williams, *John's Transformation of Mark*, 10–12).

78. Raymond E. Brown documents the following shared material: the ministry of John the Baptist; Jesus gathering disciples; Jesus cleansing the Temple; Jesus's healing of the official's son; multiplication of loaves; Jesus walking on water; Peter's confession; debates with Jewish authorities; anointing of Jesus; entry into Jerusalem; the Last Supper; the passion, death, and resurrection of Jesus (*An Introduction to the Gospel of John*, ed. Francis J. Maloney, ABRL [New York: Doubleday, 2003], 94). At the level of individual words and phrases, Andrew T. Lincoln argues that in several places John is dependent on one or more of the Synoptics (*Gospel according*

Fifth, and finally, John makes several statements that make better sense in light of the Synoptics. This is the foundation upon which Richard Bauckham makes his argument in "John for Readers of Mark."[79] He cites four different "parenthetical explanations" for which knowledge of Mark is presumed but is not necessary for John's own narrative to make sense.[80] For those who have read Mark, these parenthetical statements in John supplement the antecedent text. As Chris Keith shows, Johannine material need not agree with the Synoptics to supplement it. Difference can indicate inheritance as much as similarity does.[81]

John knows the Synoptics, and particularly Mark, and references them in the composition of the Fourth Gospel. When the colophons allude to other hypothetical written Jesus traditions, the Synoptics cannot be far from view. But does this suggest that John presents itself as superior to its written predecessors?

The Johannine colophons do not claim superiority over antecedent written Jesus traditions.[82] The comparable text from Plutarch addressed in chapter 3 and the echo of the 1–2 Kings formula considered above suggest that John does not endeavor to supplant other Jesus traditions but to complement them. The author might hope that the Fourth Gospel is read more often and enjoys a reputation that is elevated over its predecessors. By merely writing a discourse about Jesus when others already exist, the Gospel of John enters a competitive textual environment. But it does not follow from this that the Fourth Gospel intends

---

to Saint John, 36), Chris Keith argues that John 12:27 takes a "posture of correction" toward Mark 14:34–36 (Keith, *Gospel as Manuscript*), James W. Barker argues for "John's literary dependence on Matthew" (*John's Use of Matthew*, 19), and Mark Goodacre calls attention to three minor verbal agreements between John and one or more of the Synoptics, an occasion where a Johannine passage functions as a fourth Synoptic ("Parallel Traditions or Parallel Gospels?" 79–84).

79. Bauckham, "John for Readers of Mark," 150–69.

80. Bauckham's four texts are John 1:32; 3:24; 6:67–71; 11:2 ("John for Readers of Mark," 150–69).

81. Chris Keith, "'If John Knew Mark': Critical Inheritance and Johannine Disagreements with Mark" in Becker, Bond, Williams, *John's Transformation of Mark*, 31–49.

82. Bauckham and Barker both conclude similarly (Bauckham, "John for Readers of Mark," 170; Barker, *John's Use of Matthew*, 16). That John presents itself as superior to the Synoptics in the colophons is the position of both Hans Windisch (*Johannes und die Synoptiker: Wollte der vierte Evangelist die älteren Evangelien ergänzen oder ersetzen?* UNT 12 [Leipzig: Hinrich, 1926], 121–24) and Keith (*Gospel as Manuscript*, 131–54). Windisch's argument is that John intended to displace the Synoptics. Keith's is that John understands itself as in competition with the Synoptics and that such a stance does not necessarily imply an effort on John's part to displace its predecessors.

to supplant these predecessors, only that it differs from them. By analogy, this book, *Gospel Media*, is "in competition" with other books written about the gospels and their ancient media environment. I hope its readers find that it contributes to an ongoing discourse, but I have no presumption that it will supplant other texts. It aims to accomplish something different than its predecessors do. As its author, I presume a reader has some familiarity with and access to those texts, even when I do not engage them directly.

The modern reading, writing, and publication culture in which *Gospel Media* participates differs from that of antiquity. The theory that John intends to displace the Synoptics nonetheless requires a romanticized view of ancient reading and writing, one that understands texts to be a limited good in short supply. In few other literate contexts does a newly written text attempt to replace its antecedents altogether.

In place of supplant theories for John's relationship to the Synoptics, James W. Barker offers a model he calls "gospel proliferation."[83] Barker begins with the overlooked fact that, with respect to their materiality, texts could last for 150 years or more.[84] An author therefore could not reasonably expect that rival texts would simply cease to exist in the author's own lifetime. Barker shows that works in antiquity that were similar to one another proliferated without intending to replace their predecessors.[85] This is also true of early Christian gospels, canonical and otherwise. What Barker writes of the infancy gospels equally applies to his assessment of the gospels generally: "[They] stand on their own, but they do not stand alone."[86] As early Christian gospels proliferated, they were meant to be read alongside one another and used in differing ways.

By opening a new avenue with written content that is not paralleled in the Synoptics, the Fourth Gospel is a decisive new step in gospel proliferation. If Mark's innovation was to textualize previously unwritten Jesus traditions and Matthew and Luke's was to make the tradition more bookish, then John's

---

83. James W. Barker, "Tatian's Diatessaron and the Proliferation of Gospels," in *The Gospel of Tatian: Exploring the Nature and Text of the Diatessaron*, ed. Matthew R. Crawford and Nicholas J. Zola, The Reception of Jesus in the First Three Centuries 3 (London: T&T Clark, 2019), 111–41.

84. Barker, "Tatian's Diatessaron," 114. Barker is himself dependent on George W. Houston, *Inside Roman Libraries: Book Collections and Their Management in Antiquity*, Studies in the History of Ancient Greece and Rome (Chapel Hill: The University of North Carolina Press, 2014), 74–75, 120–21.

85. Barker, "Tatian's Diatessaron," 111–21.

86. Barker, "Tatian's Diatessaron," 128; Barker, *John's Use of Matthew*, 32.

innovation was to charter new written territory. As a written Jesus narrative with content that differed from the Synoptics, the Fourth Gospel added new material to the archive.

Questions remain about how John circulated and in what physical form. The colophons, their echo of 1–2 Kings, and the Fourth Gospel's supplementation of the Synoptics do not answer these conclusively, but they do offer new data for rethinking the issue, as do expanded notions of publication and circulation practices in antiquity.

The strongest hints concerning the Fourth Gospel's circulation are found in its double colophons. Both bring narrative closure to the discourse. After the first ending at John 20:30–31, however, the narrative is resumed for another chapter. The closure is reopened. Questions about John 21's relationship to the preceding content are usually framed in terms of "originality." Was John 21 an "original" part of the gospel? Was it composed by the same "pen" or "hand" as John 1–20? "Originality" becomes a cipher for "authentic."[87]

This frame is anachronistic. It presumes that texts in antiquity have fixed boundaries and were the products of individual authors. Additions to a discourse become intrusions to the pure, authoritative original. But the production and circulation of texts is more complex than this.

John 21 betrays signs of being secondary to John 20. Raymond E. Brown's three reasons for considering the chapter an epilogue remain compelling.[88] First, John 20:31 is a fitting ending to the text. John 21 is an awkward and abrupt continuation. Second, John 20:29's blessing upon those who have not seen Jesus seems to preclude the narration of additional appearances. Third, the narrative logic of chapter 21 is disconnected from what precedes. The disciples have already seen Jesus risen in Jerusalem and have been commissioned. Their return to Galilee to resume their work as fishermen is peculiar. This all indicates that John 21, and the second colophon with it, was not likely composed when John 20 was.

Yet there is no material evidence or patristic testimony that John 1–20 ever circulated without John 21. This is the crux. In absence of material and testimonial evidence, interpreters conclude that John 21 must have been "original" to the Fourth Gospel.[89] But the complexity of ancient circulation permits

---

87. Keener, *The Gospel of John*, 2 vols. (Grand Rapids: Baker Academic, 2003), 2:1220.

88. Brown, *The Gospel according to John XIII–XXI*, AYBC (New Haven: Yale University Press, 1970), 1078.

89. Keith, *Gospel as Manuscript*, 132–33.

holding both of these data points together and complicating what is meant by "original." John 21 was likely added before the narrative began to circulate widely. Changes and additions to a textual tradition were made with varying levels of success. The more widely the text had been distributed, the more difficult it became to incorporate additions or emendations. John 21 is an instance in which an addition was made early in circulation, perhaps when it was still being used by a small network and perdured.[90]

The syntactical and stylistic similarities and differences between the final chapter of John and the rest of the gospel lead interpreters to two different conclusions about authorship: John 21 was written by the person who wrote John 1–20 or it was written by someone else.[91] The simple sentence structure reflects what is found in John 1–20, but several particularities of grammar and vocabulary are unique to John 21.[92] These particularities, as well as the third-person reference to "the one writing these things" and the "editorial we" (οἴδαμεν) in John 21:24, suggest that the author was at least one step removed from penning these words with their own hand. This does not mean, however, that the author was not involved in the creation of John 21, as one could compose by mouth in varying ways. The final chapter could have been composed by dictation or from an antecedent oral account. John 21 is secondary to the Fourth Gospel but still connected to the author of John 1–20.

This is not to claim that John 21 is inauthentic, unoriginal, non-authoritative, or some other such. The secondary epilogue is unremarkable with respect to ancient circulation practices. A secondary preface does, however, indicate something about the circulation of the Fourth Gospel, specifically that it happened in stages.

Finally, we return to the question regarding the medium of John's circulation, whether as a codex, roll, or both. Strong cases can be made for either John's circulation as a roll or as a codex. I will first present the points in favor of each, before suggesting that John most likely circulated in both media simultaneously.

---

90. Jennifer Knust and Tommy Wasserman argue similarly (*To Cast the First Stone: The Transmission of a Gospel Story* [Princeton: Princeton University Press, 2018], 71–72).

91. For an excellent summary of the various positions on the two colophons' author- or editorship, see Armin D. Baum, "The Original Epilogue (John 20:30–31), the Secondary Appendix (21:1–23), and the Editorial Epilogues (21:24–25) of John's Gospel," in *Earliest Christian History*, ed. Michael F. Bird and Jason Maston, WUNT 320 (Tübingen: Mohr Siebeck, 2012), 240–47.

92. Baum, "Original Epilogue," 243–47.

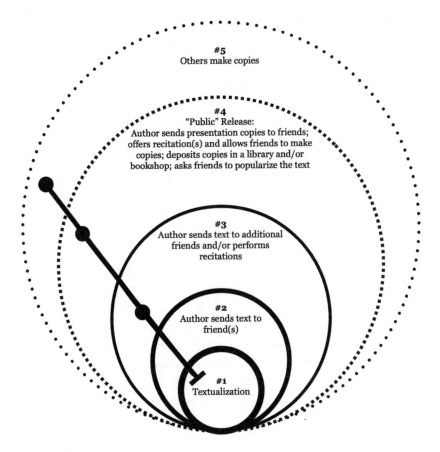

Figure 3. John

The strongest argument in favor of John's circulation as a roll is that in the first and second centuries CE this medium was the "standard vehicle for all literary texts."[93] If a text circulated in another physical form, it was usually because it was not "literary."[94] The roll was the natural medium for the Fourth Gospel if it was a literary text, which both the prologue and purpose statement in the epilogue suggest. If John was competing with other Jesus literature that

---

93. L. D. Reynolds and N. G. Wilson, *Scribes and Scholars: A Guide to the Transmission of Greek and Latin Literature*, 4th ed. (Oxford: Oxford University Press, 2014), 34.
94. Codices were anthological or utilitarian in nature, whereas rolls were suited for unified treatises (Clare K. Rothschild, "Galen's *De Indolentia* and the Early Christian Codex," *Early Christianity* 12 [2021]: 35–38).

existed as rolls, namely Matthew and Luke, then circulating as codex will have put it at a disadvantage in the competition. We ought to assume that John circulated as a roll unless there is compelling evidence otherwise.

Christian textual predecessors that circulated as codices might be compelling evidence. If Mark, a Pauline letter collection, Q, and other Christian texts characteristically existed as codices, then it might have been natural for John to follow suit. In this view, the early Christian addiction to the codex is quite early and it influenced the last written canonical gospel. This might be confirmed by manuscript evidence, namely P52, which, if one accepts an early date for the fragment, indicates the Fourth Gospel existed as a codex as early as the first half of the second century.[95] Finally, the Johannine aporias, or dislocations of literary material, as well as its supposed additions, specifically its prologue and epilogue, might be evidence of its materiality.[96] If John initially existed as a codex, a rearrangement of the leaves, whether intentional or unintentional, and an addition to them were easily facilitated.

The codex and roll are not mutually exclusive options, however. This is true of John, the Synoptic Gospels, other early Christian and Jewish literature, and Greco-Roman texts generally. Nothing precludes a written tradition from existing and circulating in multiple forms simultaneously. Because texts were reproduced and circulated in an ad hoc manner, their material form was flexible, though the cultural norm in the first two centuries CE was that literature existed in rolls. This being the case, the default assumption ought to be that John circulated as such.

Yet with the Synoptic Gospels and Pauline collections, there were different precedents for the materiality of Christian texts. When John was written and reproduced, both options were on the table. If early versions of John were utilized intramurally within a small network and were not yet considered "publication literature," then these might have been in the form of codices. The later stage of extended circulation that is reflected in the second colophon would more naturally have been in the form of a roll. The codex was a strong candidate for the materiality of the Fourth Gospel as it circulated in the inner

---

95. P52 is a papyrus fragment containing John 18:31–33 on one side and John 18:37–38 on the other. It is regarded by many to be the earliest extant New Testament text, though its early-to-mid-second-century date has been contested. See especially Brent Nongbri, "The Use and Abuse of P52: Papyrological Pitfalls in the Dating of the Fourth Gospel," *HTR* 98 (2005): 23–48; Brent Nongbri, "Palaeography, Precision and Publicity: Further Thoughts on P.Ryl. III.457 (P52)," *NTS* 66 (2020): 471–99.

96. McCown, "Codex and Roll," 241–42.

circles of the Johannine model presented above, and the roll was a strong candidate for its material form as it circulated more widely.

The Johannine colophons are nondescript when it comes to their label for the material form of both John and other hypothetical texts about Jesus that might exist. The term with which John labels itself, "document" (βιβλίον), does not connote one physical form or another. The term can mean a literary discourse that existed as a roll, it can indicate a codex text, and it can refer to a single page of papyrus. When the second colophon refers to hypothetical Jesus traditions that might be written, it does so with the same term, though in the plural: "documents" (βιβλία). If all of Jesus's deeds were textualized, the world could not contain the "written documents," no matter the book technology in which they circulated. This reflects the plurality of material forms of written Jesus traditions in the Fourth Gospel's media context.

Conclusion

Not only do different kinds of texts make for different kinds of reading events, but different kinds of texts are written and circulated in different kinds of ways. In no context is there only one mode of making written discourses public. Publication and circulation are complex and socially constructed phenomena. Their mechanics and materiality vary from culture to culture and intertwine in complicated ways.

In the gospels' media context, there were several ways and material forms in which texts were distributed. Some circulation practices were intentional, and others were not. Written discourses were more likely to circulate in incomplete and unauthorized forms if they were not prepared for publication. Publication was a guard, albeit an imperfect one, against dubious reuse of traditions. Certain book technologies were also more appropriate for certain kinds of texts than others. Texts created "for publication" characteristically circulated as rolls in their presentation versions. Texts that were for private use or were paraliterary in nature might also exist as rolls, but it was common for them to be found in codices as well.

The ways that the canonical gospels were read and composed dovetail with their circulation and materiality. Mark, as a text composed from antecedent oral events to be reactivated in subsequent events, was not a text composed "for publication." It was written for limited circulation. This impacted its style, which was oral, and its material form, which was the codex. The later Synoptics, in contrast, were created "for publication." This is indicated by the ways that they redact their predecessor, how they composed their own materials, and the media designations they append to themselves. Their style reflects written psychodynamics, and their native material form was the bookroll. The Fourth Gospel betrays knowledge of the Synoptics and their media diversity. It bears marks of being circulated in stages, first to a limited audience and then a wider one. It is the most likely of the four gospels to have circulated in multiple technologies, both codex and bookroll.

Conclusion

Ancient reading, writing, and circulation practices were diverse. There was not a single way to read, write, or circulate a text. Different kinds of media were produced, engaged, and reproduced in different kinds of ways. This was as true for the gospels as it was the culture in which their authors and readers participated. Romantic notions have obscured diverse and complex media realities. New Testament scholarship has exoticized the mechanics of ancient reading, writing, and circulation, perpetuating simplified myths about them. Rectifying these myths allows us to better understand the media culture in which the canonical gospels participate and the reading, writing, and circulation of the gospels themselves.

Literate cultures know a variety of reading modes. In antiquity, texts were not always read aloud. Both silent and vocalized reading were common, as were communal and private reading. Different kinds of texts made for different kinds of reading events. Texts were read in groups of varying sizes and in varying spaces, both public and private. But this was not to the exclusion of individuals reading by themselves, silently or aloud, also in a variety of settings and for myriad reasons.

Like reading practices, composition practices were multiple and diverse. Both handwriting and dictation played a role in the composition processes of different authors. Some writers preferred dictation to writing *sua manu*, and some preferred writing *sua manu* to dictation. Still others preferred to mix the two modes of composition in the various stages of writing literature. Authors varied their compositional mode based on the kind of text they were writing and to whom it was addressed. Social factors, writing technologies, and modes of composition all leave their marks on what is produced.

Whether created by hand or by mouth, writing transmits thought in an iterative medium. Once a discourse is reduced to a physical form, it can be reused across time and space. Persons who do not create a text can hold, see, read, and hear it. Texts make their way to other persons through a variety of channels. Authors have varying levels of control over these channels. Publication is a social mechanism by which an author brokers a text to a wide readership. But not all texts make their way to a wide readership through this mechanism, and not all texts that are published enjoy a wide readership. Texts are circulated in a variety of ways and physical forms. Publication endows texts with a medium and format that is socially conditioned. Published texts look and feel different from unpublished texts. The former is deemed officious and finalized; the latter is not.

The media complexity that characterizes Greco-Roman antiquity also characterizes the gospels. The gospels themselves indicate that they were different kinds of texts from one another. Mark declares itself "orally proclaimed news" in its opening sentence. It straddles the line between orality and textuality, reducing traditions to a written medium. But the text still betrays signs of spoken narrative. It is marked by an oral register on account of its composition by mouth. Two people were involved in the process, one as a speaker and one as a writer. It fits within the trope of a discourse that was textualized from oral teaching events and was reused for similar events. Being hypomnematic or note-like, it was not the kind of text composed for publication, but for utilitarian purposes. The codex was a fitting physical medium for its initial distribution.

The Gospel of Matthew rejects the label "gospel" and instead describes itself as a "book" in its opening sentence. Books were written, read, and circulated differently from notes. Matthew's innovation was to write the first gospel book. The author transformed the raw Markan material into a literary product. This involved a different method of composition. Matthew removes oral residues that are objectionable in literature. It is better written than Mark because it is a different kind of text. Matthew had high aspirations for itself as a book. Not only does the opening line indicate the discourse's medium, but it also places itself on the same level as Scriptural traditions. It was meant to be received in a manner similar to those traditions: in synagogue reading events. The physical form of the text mattered as it was put on public display in liturgical settings. Its native medium was a roll.

Luke follows neither Mark nor Matthew in its self-designation. It does not have a title, but a preface. The opening paratext addresses the Third Gospel to an individual. Theophilus is Luke's first reader. It was read privately and individually before it was read communally. That Luke was first written for an individual does not mean that it was a private text or was not meant for publication. Offering a text to an individual was one way to place it into the public domain, knowing that it could be copied by others thereafter. Addressed to an individual, the gospel was, like Matthew and unlike Mark, composed for publication. Luke went public with Theophilus's presentation copy, which was in roll form.

John betrays knowledge of the Synoptic Gospels and the variety of their media forms. The narrative is nondescript in its self-designation as a "document." The colophons that close the discourse nod to the existence of other gospel media while also justifying the Fourth Gospel's existence. John does not wish to supplant the Synoptics, but to supplement them. It is a literary and media metamorphosis of antecedent traditions. The double colophons and the narrative's statements about the Beloved Disciple's authorship indicate that it was used and circulated in multiple ways and stages. It was first read intramurally before it was circulated more widely.

Mark was a gospel, Matthew a book, Luke an account, and John a document. The canonical gospels were not all the same type of text. They were of various media forms. Different kinds of media are composed with different technologies and using different methods. They are engaged and made public in different ways.

The gospels were not all read, written, and circulated the same way.

Appendix: Papyri Letters

SB 14.11584:[1]

[. . . . . .Ἰσιδ]ώρωι τῶ ἀδελφῶι [χαίρει]ν.
[εὐθὺς ἐλθὼν εἰς] τὴν Ἀντίνου ἐκομι-
[σάμην σου] τὰ γράμματα δι' ὧν ἔδοξά
[σ]ε θεω[ρ]εῖν. διὸ παρακαλῶ τὸ αὐτὸ
ποιεῖν σ[υ]νεχῶς, οὕτως γὰρ αὐξηθή-
[σ]εται ἡμῶν ἡ φιλία. ὅταν δέ σοι βραδέως
[γ]ράφω, διὰ τὸ μὴ εὑρ[[υ]]ίσκειν μηδένα
πρὸς σὲ ἐρχόμενον ῥαδίως τοῦτο γίνε-
ται. περὶ οὗ σοι χρεία ἐστὶν ἐπίστελλέ μοι
[ε]ἰδὼς ὅτι ποιήσω ἀνυπερθέτως.
[εἰ] ἐπιστο[λὴν γ]ράφεις μοι, Ἑρμῆτι τῶι
φίλῳ παρὰ Ἀρτεμᾶν πέμπε ἵνα μοι
ἀναδῷ. [ἀ]σπάζεταί σε πολλὰ αὐτὸς Ἑρμῆ[ς]
καὶ Ταυσῖ[ρι]ς ἡ ἀδελφή.
ἔρρωσο.
v
(hand 2) [ἀπόδος τῷ] φίλῳ Χ Ἰσιδώρῳ ἐμ Φιλαδελφ(είᾳ) παρὰ

". . . to Isidoros, his brother, greetings.
As soon as I reached Antinoopolis, I
received your letter, through which I get the feeling of
seeing you. I therefore beseech you to do the same
constantly, for in this way our love will be increased.
Whenever I am slow to write to you, this happens easily because I find no one
going your way.
If you have need of anything, send me word since
you know that I will do it without delay.
If you write me a letter,

1. Text from Duke Databank of Documentary Papyri; https://papyri.info/ddbdp/sb;14;11584; translation slightly modified from APIS.

send it to my friend Hermes
at the house of Artemas so that he may deliver it to me.
Hermes himself
and his sister Tausiris greet you heartily.
Farewell.
(Verso in second hand): Deliver to my dear Isidoros in Philadelphia from ...

BGU 2.423:

Ἀπίων Ἐπιμάχῳ τῶι πατρὶ καὶ
κυρίῳ πλεῖστα χαίρειν. πρὸ μὲν πάντων εὔχομαί σε ὑγιαίνειν καὶ διὰ παντὸς
ἐρωμένον εὐτυχεῖν μετὰ τῆς ἀδελφῆς
μου καὶ τῆς θυγατρὸς αὐτῆς καὶ τοῦ ἀδελφοῦ
μου. εὐχαριστῶ τῷ κυρίῳ Σεράπιδι
ὅτι μου κινδυνεύσαντος εἰς θάλασσαν
ἔσωσε εὐθέως. ὅτε εἰσῆλθον εἰς Μη-
σήνους, ἔλαβα βιάτικον παρὰ Καίσαρος
χρυσοῦς τρεῖς καὶ καλῶς μοί ἐστιν.
ἐρωτῶ σε οὖν, κύριέ μου πάτηρ,
γράψον μοι ἐπιστόλιον πρῶτον
μὲν περὶ τῆς σωτηρίας σου, δεύ-
τερον περὶ τῆς τῶν ἀδελφῶν μου,
τρ[ί]τον, ἵνα σου προσκυνήσω τὴν
χεραν, ὅτι με ἐπαίδευσας καλῶς,
καὶ ἐκ τούτου ἐλπίζω ταχὺ προκό-
σαι τῶν θε[ῶ]ν θελόντων. ἄσπασαι
Καπίτων[α] πολλὰ καὶ τοὺς ἀδελφούς
[μ]ου καὶ Σε[ρηνί]λλαν καὶ το[ὺς] φίλους μο[υ].
ἔπεμψά σο[ι εἰ]κόνιν μ[ου] διὰ Εὐκτή-
μονος. ἐσ[τ]ι[ν] μου ὄνομα Ἀντῶνις Μάξιμος. ἐρρῶσθαί σε εὔχομαι.
κεντυρί(α) Ἀθηνονίκη.[2]

Apion to Epimachus his father and
Lord. Many greetings! Before all else
I pray that you are well and that you always
prosper in health with my sister

---

2. Reproduced from Hunt and Edgar, LCL, 304–6.

and her daughter and my brother.
I thank the Lord Serapis
that when I was in danger at sea
he immediately came to the rescue. When I came to
Misenum, I received from Caesar three gold pieces as traveling money
and it is well with me.
So I ask you, my lord and father,
write me a letter, first
about your health, second
about my siblings' health,
third so that I can adore your
handwriting, because you educated me well
and because of this I hope to quickly advance
should the gods will it. Greet
Kapiton very much, as well as my siblings
and Serenilla and my friends.
I am sending you a picture of me by way of
Euktemonos. My name is Antonius
Maximus. I pray that you are well.
Company Athenonike.[3]

BGU 2.632:[4]

Ἀν[τώνι]ος Μάξιμος Σαβίνῃ
τῇ ἀ[δ]ελφῇ πλεῖστα χαίρειν.
πρὸ μὲν πάντων εὔχομαί
σε ὑγιαίνειν, καἰγὼ γὰρ αὐτὸς
ὑγιαίν[ω]. μνίαν σου ποιούμενος παρὰ τοῖς [ἐν]θάδε θεοῖς
ἐκομισάμην [ἓ]ν ἐπι[σ]τόλιον
παρὰ Ἀντωνε[ί]νου τοῦ συν-
πολ[ε]ίτου ἡμῶν, καὶ ἐπιγνούς
σε ἐρρωμένην λίαν ἐχάρην··
καἰγὼ διὰ πᾶσαν ἀφορμὴν
ο[ὐ]χ ὀκνῶ σοι γράψαι περὶ

---

3. Trans. my own with reference to Hunt and Edgar, LCL, 304–6 and Klauck and Bailey, *Ancient Letters*, 10–11.

4. Text from Duke Databank of Documentary Papyri; https://papyri.info/ddbdp/bgu ;2;632; trans. my own.

τῆ[ς] σωτηρίας μου καὶ τῶν
ἐμῶν. ἄσπασαι Μάξιμον
πολλὰ καὶ Κοπρῆν τὸν κύριν
μ[ου. ἀ]σπάζεταί σε ἡ σύμβι-
ός [μου Ἀ]υφιδία καὶ [Μ]άξιμος
[ὁ υἱὸς μ]ου, [οὗ] ἐστι[ν] τὰ γενέ-
[σια Ἐ]πεὶπ τριακὰς καθ' Ἕλ-
[ληνα]ς, καὶ Ἐλπὶς καὶ Φορτου-
[νᾶτ]α. ἄσπ[α]σαι τὸν κύριον
[... several fragmentary lines ...]
[ἐρρῶσθαί σε εὔχο]μαι.

Antonius Maximus to Sabine
his sister. Many greetings! Before all else I pray that
you are well, and I myself am
well. Making mention of you
before the gods here,
I received a letter
from Antonius our fellow
citizen and learning
that you are in good health I rejoiced exceedingly.
And at every opportunity
I don't hesitate to write to you concerning
my health and that of my family.
Greet Maximus
very much and Kopres, my lord.
My wife Aufidia greets you
as does Maximus
my son, whose birthday
is the thirtieth of Epeiph according to
the Greek calendar, as well as Hope and Fortune.
Greet my Lord...
[... several fragmentary lines]
I pray that you are well.

P.Oxy. 1.119:[5]

Θέων Θέωνι τῷ πατρὶ χαίρειν.
καλῶς ἐποίησες οὐκ ἀπενηχες με μετε ἐ-
σοῦ εἰς πόλιν. ἠ οὐ θέλις ἀπενεκκεῖν <με> με-
τὲ σοῦ εἰς Ἀλεξάνδριαν οὐ μὴ γράψω σε ἐ-
πιστολὴν οὔτε λαλῶ σε οὔτε υἱγενω σε,
εἶτα ἂν δὲ ἔλθῃς εἰς Ἀλεξάνδριαν οὐ
μὴ λάβω χειραν παρὰ [σ]οῦ οὔτε πάλι χαίρω
σε λυπόν. ἂμ μὴ θέλῃς ἀπενέκαι μ[ε]
ταῦτα γε[ί]νετε. καὶ ἡ μήτηρ μου εἶπε Ἀρ-
χελάῳ ὅτι ἀναστατοῖ μὲ ἄρρον αὐτόν.
καλῶς δὲ ἐποίησες δῶρά μοι ἔπεμψε[ς]
μεγάλα ἀράκια πεπλάνηκαν ἡμως ἐκε[ῖ]
τῇ ἡμέρᾳ ιβ ὅτι ἔπλευσες. λυπόν πέμψον εἴ[ς]
με παρακαλῶ σε. ἂμ μὴ πέμψῃς οὐ μὴ φά-
γω, οὐ μὴ πείνω· ταῦτα.
ἐρῶσθέ σε εὔχ(ομαι).
Τῦβι ιη.

Verso: ἀπόδος Θέωνι [ἀ]πὸ Θεωνᾶτος υἱῶ

Theon to his father Theon, greetings!
It was a fine thing of you not to take me with
you to the city! If you don't want to take me
with you to Alexandria I won't write you
a letter or speak to you or wish you good health;
and if you go to Alexandria I won't
take your hand nor ever greet you again.
That's what will happen if you won't take me. My mother said to
Archelaus, "He's driving me crazy; take him!"
It was a fine present you sent me:
locust beans! They tricked us
on the 12th day, the day you sailed. Finally, send for
me, I implore you. If you don't,

---

5. Text: Duke Database of Documentary Papyri; http://papyri.info/ddbdp/p.oxy;1;119. Trans. my own on the basis of Grenfell and Hunt, *Oxyrhynchus Papyri* 1:186 and Klauck and Bailey, *Ancient Letters*, 26–27.

I won't eat, I won't drink; so there!
I bid you farewell.
The 18th of Tybi.

Verso: Deliver to Theon from Theon his son.

Appendix: Tables to Chapter 6

Conjunctions in the Synoptics and Other Texts

	καί alone	καί and δέ combined	δέ alone	δέ-καί ratio	Other conjunctions (not καί or δέ)
Mark	9.7% or 1 in 10.12 (1,078/11,138)	11.1% or 1 in 8.95 (1,244/11,138)	1.4% (157/11,138)	1:6.87	24.5% of Total Conjunctions (405/1,649)
Matthew	6.5% or 1 in 15.38 (1,194/18,363)	9.1% 1 in 10.89 (1,688/18,363)	2.7% (494/18,363)	1:2.42	26.4% of Total Conjunctions (607/2,295)
Luke	7.6% or 1 in 13.14 (1,483/19,495)	10.4% 1 in 9.63 (2,025/19,495)	2.8% (542/19,495)	1:2.74	21.3% of Total Conjunctions (547/2,572)
John	5.5% or 1 in 18.05 (868/15,671)	6.9% or 1 in 14.50 (1,081/15,671)	1.4% (213/15,671)	1:4.08	47.3% of Total Conjunctions (973/2,054)
Mark Paralleled in Matthew	9.7% or 1 in 10.34 (1,033/10,679)	11.1% or 1 in 8.99 (1,188/10,679)	1.5% (155/10,679)	1:6.66	24.6% of Total Conjunctions (388/1,576)
Matthew Paralleled in Mark	6.9% or 1 in 14.47 (841/12,173)	9.5% or 1 in 10.51 (1,158/12,173)	2.6% (317/12,173)	1:2.65	24.2% of Total Conjunctions (370/1,528)
Mark Paralleled in Luke	9.7% or 1 in 10.32 (985/10,170)	11.1% or 1 in 8.93 (1,133/10,170)	1.4% (144/10,170)	1:6.84	24.6% of Total Conjunctions (370/1,503)
Luke Paralleled in Mark	7.5% or 1 in 13.31 (794/10,569)	10.7% or 1 in 9.37 (1128/10,569)	3.2% (334/10,569)	1:2.38	20.5% of Total Conjunctions (291/1,419)
Matthew Paralleled in Luke	5.5% or 1 in 18.32 (208/3,811)	8.2% or 1 in 12.13 (314/3,811)	2.9% (106/3,811)	1:1.96	33.3% of Total Conjunctions (157/471)

Conjunctions in the Synoptics and Other Texts, continued.

	καί alone	καί and δέ combined	δέ alone	δέ-καί ratio	Other conjunctions (not καί or δέ)
Luke Paralleled in Matthew	7.1% or 1 in 14.04 (273/3,834)	8.9% or 1 in 11.1 (343/3,834)	1.8% (70/3,834)	1:3.9	27% of Total Conjunctions (127/470)
Unique Matthew	5.4% or 1 in 18.63 (135/2,515)	9.4% or 1 in 10.61 (237/2,515) Excluding Matt. 1:1–17: 194/2,248 (8.6% or 1 in 11.59)	4.0% (102/2,515) Excluding Matt. 1:1–17: 64/2,248 (2.8%)	1:1.32 (Excluding genealogy: 1:2.10)	24.7% of Total Conjunctions (78/315) Excluding Matt. 1:1–17: 74/271 (27.3%)
Unique Luke	8.0% or 1 in 12.56 (420/5,275)	10.4% or 1 in 9.59 (550/5,275)	2.5% (130/5,275)	1:3.23	19.2% of Total Conjunctions (131/681)
P.Oxy. 56.3860	10.8% or 1 in 9.26 (41/380)	11.1% or 1 in 9.05 (42/380)	0.2% (1/380)	1:41	28.8 % (17/59)
P.Oxy 903	9.1% or 1 in 10.97 (36/395)	10.6% or 1 in 9.40 (42/395)	1.5% (6/395)	1:6	32.3% (20/62)
Philo, On the Life of Moses	6.1% or 1 in 16.4 (1916/31,452)	8.7% or 1 in 11.38 (2,765/31,452)	2.7% (849/31,452)	1:2.25	35.3% (1,511/4276)
Philo, On the Life of Joseph	6.3% or 1 in 15.8 (813/12,846)	8.8% or 1 in 11.37 (1,130/12, 846)	2.5% (317/12,846)	1:2.56	36.7% 655/1785
Philo, Against Flaccus	6.1% or 1 in 15.8 (546/8,931)	8.4% or 1 in 11.91 (750/8,931)	2.2% (204/8,931)	1:2.67	34.4% (394/1,144)

Conjunctions in the Synoptics and Other Texts, continued.

	καί alone	καί and δέ combined	δέ alone	δέ-καί ratio	Other conjunctions (not καί or δέ)
Aristeas	5.9% or 1 in 17.07 (758/12,943)	9.5% or 1 in 10.51 (1,231/12,943)	3.7% (473/12,943)	1:1.6	32.4% (590/1821)
3 Macc	5.5% or 1 in 18.07 (281/5080)	8.1% or 1 in 12.33 (412/5,080)	2.6% (131/5,080)	1:2.14	17.6% (88/500)
Josephus, *The Life*	4.4% or 1 in 22.9 (689/15,836)	7.8% or 1 in 12.81 (1,236/15,836)	3.5% (547/15,836)	1:1.25	33.2% (615/1851)
Josephus, *Jewish War*	5.2% or 1 in 22.06 (6,593/125,595)	9.1% or 1 in 11.04 (11,381/125,595)	3.8% (4,788/125,595)	1:1.38	31.9% (5,334/16,715)

Parataxis in Mark

	καί alone	καί and δέ combined	δέ alone	δέ-καί ratio	Other conjunctions (not καί or δέ)
Mark	9.7% or 1 in 10.12 (1,078/11,138)	11.1% or 1 in 8.95 (1,244/11,138)	1.4% (157/11,138)	1:6.87	24.5% of Total Conjunctions (405/1,649)
P.Oxy. 56.3860	10.8% or 1 in 9.26 (41/380)	11.1% or 1 in 9.05 (42/380)	0.2% (1/380)	1:41	28.8% (17/59)
P.Oxy 903	9.1% or 1 in 10.97 (36/395)	10.6% or 1 in 9.40 (42/395)	1.5% (6/395)	1:6	32.3% (20/62)

Parataxis in Matthew and Luke

	καί alone	καί and δέ combined	δέ alone	δέ-καί ratio	Other conjunctions (not καί or δέ)
Mark	9.7% or 1 in 10.12 (1,078/11,138)	11.1% or 1 in 8.95 (1,244/11,138)	1.4% (157/11,138)	1:6.87	24.5% of Total Conjunctions (405/1,649)
Matthew	6.5% or 1 in 15.38 (1,194/18,363)	9.1% 1 in 10.89 (1,688/18,363)	2.7% (494/18,363)	1:2.42	26.4% of Total Conjunctions (607/2,295)
Luke	7.6% or 1 in 13.14 (1,483/19,495)	10.4% 1 in 9.63 (2,025/19,495)	2.8% (542/19,495)	1:2.74	21.3% of Total Conjunctions (547/2,572)
Mark Paralleled in Matthew	9.7% or 1 in 10.34 (1,033/10,679)	11.1% or 1 in 8.99 (1,188/10,679)	1.5% (155/10,679)	1:6.66	24.6% of Total Conjunctions (388/1,576)
Matthew Paralleled in Mark	6.9% or 1 in 14.47 (841/12,173)	9.5% or 1 in 10.51 (1,158/12,173)	2.6% (317/12,173)	1:2.65	24.2% of Total Conjunctions (370/1,528)
Mark Paralleled in Luke	9.7% or 1 in 10.32 (985/10,170)	11.1% or 1 in 8.98 (1,133/10,170)	1.4% (144/10,170)	1:6.84	24.6% of Total Conjunctions (370/1,503)
Luke Paralleled in Mark	7.5% or 1 in 13.31 (794/10,569)	10.7% or 1 in 9.37 (1128/10,569)	3.2% (334/10,569)	1:2.38	20.5% of Total Conjunctions (291/1,419)
Matthew Paralleled in Luke	5.5% or 1 in 18.32 (208/3,811)	8.2% or 1 in 12.13 (314/3,811)	2.9% (106/3,811)	1:1.96	33.3% of Total Conjunctions (157/471)
Luke Paralleled in Matthew	7.1% or 1 in 14.04 (273/3,834)	8.9% or 1 in 11.1 (343/3,834)	1.8% (70/3,834)	1:3.9	27% of Total Conjunctions (127/470)

Parataxis in Matthew and Luke, continued.

	καί alone	καί and δέ combined	δέ alone	δέ-καί ratio	Other conjunctions (not καί or δέ)
Unique Matthew	5.4% or 1 in 18.63 (135/2,515)	9.4% or 1 in 10.61 (237/2,515) Excluding Matt. 1:1–17: 194/2,248 (8.6% or 1 in 11.59)	4.0% (102/2,515) Excluding Matt. 1:1–17: 64/2,248 (2.8%)	1:1.32 (Excluding genealogy: 1:2.10)	24.7% of Total Conjunctions (78/315) Excluding Matt. 1:1–17: 74/271 (27.3%)
Unique Luke	8.0% or 1 in 12.56 (420/5,275)	10.4% or 1 in 9.59 (550/5,275)	2.5% (130/5,275)	1:3.23	19.2% of Total Conjunctions (131/681)

Use of εὐθύς and Historical Present in Matthew and Luke

	Historical Present to Total Indicative Verbs	Historical Present to Total Indicative Verbs in Non-Speech Margins	Historical Present to Total Indicative Verbs in Speech Margins	Historical Present to Non-speech Margins to Historical Present Speech Margins	Use of εὐθύς
Mark	150/1,520 (9.9%)	77/808 (9.5%)	73/1,712 (10.6%)	1.05:1	41
Matthew	94/2,245 (4.2%)	28/1,215 (2.3%)	66/1,030 (6.4%)	1:2.35	5
Luke	11/2,445 (0.4%)	3/1,257 (0.2%)	8/1,188 (0.6%)	1:2.7	1

Glossary of Terms

These terms appear frequently in this book. Many of these are closely related but are not synonyms.

Circulation sharing a written discourse. Circulation involves a written text being passed around to different individuals and groups. Like distribution, circulation can happen under authorial control or not.

Communal reading a reading event with two or more people present. Communal reading can be either public or private. In most communal reading events, the text is read aloud.

Composition a translation of the Greek word σύγγραμμα (*syngramma*) in the singular and συγγράμματα (*syngrammata*) in the plural. In most cases, compositions were created with the intention that they would be published.

Dictation the intentional act of composing by mouth. When dictating, the speaker knows that a written text is being created and may or may not alter how they speak accordingly.

Discourse a message experienced at discrete points in time. A discourse can exist in multiple forms and be activated at different times by various means. A discourse is a message that can be contained in a variety of media.

Distribution making a written discourse accessible to people who did not author it. Distribution can happen intentionally or unintentionally. It is an umbrella term that connotes the text "getting out" to other persons.

Media/medium a conduit for experiencing a discourse, such as a speech, a note, a book, a codex, or a roll. No medium is neutral. Marshall McLuhan famously quipped, "The medium is the message."[1] A discourse is affected by its medium and cannot be cleanly extracted from it. A given discourse can exist and be experienced in several

---

1. Marshall McLuhan, *Understanding Media: The Extensions of Man* (Cambridge: MIT Press, 1994).

different media. One can hear a story or a speech in an oral event and, if that story or speech also exists in manuscript form, read it. The versions will differ on the basis of their medium.

Notes a catchall translation of the Greek word ὑπόμνημα (*hypomnēma*) in the singular and ὑπομνήματα (*hypomnēmata*) in the plural. This category of text had several different connotations in antiquity, including reminders, memoranda, records, rough drafts, texts, and copies. In most cases, notes were not created with the intention that they would be published.

Oral event a discourse that is vocalized. The discourse may or may not also be textualized. "Oral event" is an umbrella term that can refer to both the reading of a text or the vocalizing of a discourse with no text present. Oral events typically happen communally but can also be solitary. For example, an individual can read aloud or perform a speech with no one else present.

Performance event a discourse that is vocalized with no text present and with audience engagement. The absence of a text is what characterizes a performance event, but a text may have been used in preparation for the performance event. Performance events also pay heed to the "social biosphere" of the performer and the audience. Performance events are rightly or wrongly stereotyped as livelier than reading events. This is because the former is often more attuned to matters such as prosody, gesturing, movement, and audience engagement.

Private reading a reading event in which a text is read, either silently or aloud, in a space that is not easily accessible to anyone, such as a private residence.

Publication making a text available to a wide, anonymous readership. Publication is narrower than distribution and circulation. It involves intention on the author's or distributor's part.

Public reading a reading event in which a text is read, usually aloud, in a space where persons can be present without much difficulty.

Reading the social act of engaging a text. Reading comes in a variety of forms and events. It can be solitary and vocalized, solitary and non-vocalized, or communal and vocalized. Individuals and communities read different kinds of texts in different kinds of ways for a variety of purposes. When I use the term "reading," I imply that a text is present at the reading event. A text can be read performatively, but if no text is present at the event, then the social act is not reading but rather a performance or oral event.

Reading event a specific instance of reading in time and space. While reading is a generalized social construct, reading events are specific instantiations of this construct. As with reading, reading events can be solitary or communal, vocalized or non-vocalized.

Silent reading reading a text without vocalizing its words. Silent reading can be done in public or private spaces and with other persons present or not.

Solitary reading one person reading to themself. Solitary reading can be public or private, silent or vocalized.

Text a written form of a discourse. I avoid using the word "text" for nonwritten discourses. There is potential for confusion here as others use the term "text" to refer to a discourse, irrespective of its written-ness. Sometimes the seemingly oxymoronic phrase "oral text" is found in New Testament scholarship. I avoid this designation.

Tradition a constellation of similar or identical discourses. Traditions are both stable and flexible. There are certain recognizable features that constrain a tradition to being singular rather than multiple, but these features are malleable and can be removed or supplemented with other components.

Vocalized reading reading a text aloud. Vocalized reading can be done in public or private spaces and with other persons present or not.

Writing by hand a compositional mode in which the author personally inscribes the text, whether in part or in whole.

Writing by mouth a compositional mode in which the author does not personally inscribe the text. Writing by mouth can be intentional, as in the case of dictation, or unintentional, as in the case of an oral event being textualized by another individual without the speaker's knowledge.

Bibliography

Achilles Tatius. *Leucippe and Clitophon*. Translated by S. Gaselee. LCL. Cambridge: Harvard University Press, 1969.

Achtemeier, Paul J. "*Omne Verbum Sonat*: The New Testament and the Oral Environment of Late Western Antiquity." *JBL* 109 (1990): 3–27.

Aland, Kurt. *Synopsis Quattuor Evangeliorum*. 13th ed. Stuttgart: Deutsche Bibelgesellschaft, 1985.

Alexander, Loveday. "Ancient Book Production and the Circulation of the Gospels." Pages 71–111 in *The Gospels for All Christians: Rethinking the Gospel Audiences*. Edited by Richard Bauckham. Grand Rapids: Eerdmans, 1998.

———. "Luke's Preface in the Context of Greek Preface-Writing." *NovT* 28 (1986): 48–74.

———. *The Preface to Luke's Gospel: Literary Convention and Social Context in Luke 1.1–4 and Acts 1.1*. SNTSMS 78. Cambridge: Cambridge University Press, 1993.

Allen, Willoughby C. *A Critical and Exegetical Commentary on the Gospel according to Saint Matthew*. 3rd ed. ICC 26. Edinburgh: T&T Clark, 1912.

Aristophanes. *Acharnians; Knights*. Translated by Jeffrey Henderson. LCL. Cambridge: Harvard University Press, 2000.

Aristotle. *Problems*. Translated by Robert Mayhew. 2 vols. LCL. Cambridge: Harvard University Press, 2011.

Assmann, Jan. *Religion and Cultural Memory: Ten Studies*. Translated by Rodney Livingstone. Stanford, CA: Stanford University Press, 2006.

Athenaeus. *The Learned Banqueters*. Translated by S. Douglas Olson. 8 vols. LCL. Cambridge: Harvard University Press, 2007.

Attridge, Harold W. "John and Mark in the History of Research." Pages 9–22 in *John's Transformation of Mark*. Edited by Eve-Marie Becker, Helen K. Bond, and Catrin Williams. London: T&T Clark, 2021.

Augustine. *Confessions*. Translated by Carolyn J. B. Hammond. 2 vols. LCL 26–27. Cambridge: Harvard University Press, 2014.

Aune, David E. "Genre Theory and the Genre-Function of Mark and Matthew." Pages 145–75 in *Mark and Matthew I*. Edited by Eve-Marie Becker and Anders Runesson. WUNT 271. Tübingen: Mohr Siebeck, 2011.

———. *Greco-Roman Literature and the New Testament: Selected Forms and Genres*. SBLSBS 21. Atlanta: Scholars Press, 1988.

———. *The New Testament in Its Literary Environment*. LEC 8. Philadelphia: Westminster, 1987.

Bagnall, Roger S., and Raffaella Cribiore. *Women's Letters from Ancient Egypt, 300 BC–AD 800*. Ann Arbor: University of Michigan Press, 2009.

Bakker, Egbert J. "How Oral Is Oral Composition?" Pages 29–47 in *Signs of Orality: The Oral Tradition and Its Influence in the Greek and Roman World*. Edited by Anne E. Mackay. Leiden: Brill, 1999.

Balogh, Josef. "*Voces Paginarum*: Beiträge zur Geschichte des lauten Lesens und Schreibens." *Philologus* 82 (1927): 84–109, 202–40.

Barker, James W. *John's Use of Matthew*. Minneapolis: Fortress Press, 2015.

———. "Tatian's Diatessaron and the Proliferation of Gospels." Pages 111–41 in *The Gospel of Tatian: Exploring the Nature and Text of the Diatessaron*. Edited by Matthew R. Crawford and Nicholas J. Zola. The Reception of Jesus in the First Three Centuries 3. London: T&T Clark, 2019.

Barnard, L. W. "The Heresy of Tatian—Once Again." *JEH* 19 (1968): 1–10.

Bastiaensen, Antonius Adrianus Robertus, ed. *Atti e passioni dei martiri*. Milan: Fondazione Lorenzo Valla, 1987.

Bauckham, Richard, ed. *The Gospels for All Christians: Rethinking the Gospel Audiences*. Grand Rapids: Eerdmans, 1998.

———. *Jesus and the Eyewitnesses: The Gospels as Eyewitness Testimony*. Grand Rapids: Eerdmans, 2013.

———. "John for Readers of Mark." Pages 147–71 in *The Gospels for All Christians: Rethinking the Gospel Audiences*. Edited by Richard Bauckham. Edinburgh: T&T Clark, 1998.

Baum, Armin D. "Mark's Paratactic καί as a Secondary Syntactic Semitism." *NovT* 58 (2016): 1–26.

———. "The Original Epilogue (John 20:30–31), the Secondary Appendix (21:1–23), and the Editorial Epilogues (21:24–25) of John's Gospel." Pages 227–70 in *Earliest Christian History*. Edited by Michael F. Bird and Jason Maston. WUNT 320. Tübingen: Mohr Siebeck, 2012.

Beaman, Karen. "Coordination and Subordination Revisited: Syntactic Complexity in Spoken and Written Narrative." Pages 45–80 in *Coherence in Spoken and Written Discourse*. Edited by Deborah Tannen. Advances in Discourse Processes 12. Norwood, NJ: Ablex, 1984.

Beavis, Mary Ann. *Mark*. Paideia. Grand Rapids: Baker Academic, 2011.

Becker, Eve-Marie, Helen K. Bond, and Catrin Williams, eds. *John's Transformation of Mark*. London: T&T Clark, 2021.

Berg, Deena. "The Mystery Gourmet of Horace's 'Satires 2.'" *CJ* 91 (1995): 141–51.

Best, Ernest. "Mark's Narrative Technique." *JSNT* 37 (1989): 43–58.

Bird, Michael F. *The Gospel of the Lord: How the Early Church Wrote the Story of Jesus*. Grand Rapids: Eerdmans, 2014.

Black, C. Clifton. *Mark: Images of an Apostolic Interpreter*. Studies on Personalities of the New Testament. Columbia: University of South Carolina Press, 1994.

Black, Matthew, and Albert Marie Denis, eds. *Apocalypsis Henochi Graece*. PVTG 3. Leiden: Brill, 1970.

Bock, Darrell L. *Acts*. BECNT. Grand Rapids: Baker Academic, 2007.

———. *Luke 1:1–9:50*. BECNT. Grand Rapids: Baker Academic, 1994.

den Boeft, Jan, and Jan N. Bremmer. "*Notiunculae Martyrologicae IV*." *VC* 45 (1991): 105–22.

Bond, Helen K. *The First Biography of Jesus: Genre and Meaning in Mark's Gospel*. Grand Rapids: Eerdmans, 2020.

Boring, M. Eugene. *Mark: A Commentary*. NTL. Louisville: Westminster John Knox, 2006.

———. "Mark 1:1–15 and the Beginning of the Gospel." *Semeia* 52 (1990): 43–81.

Botha, Pieter J. J. "'I Am Writing This with My Own Hand . . .': Writing in New Testament Times." *Verbum et Ecclesia* 30 (2009): 115–25.

Boudon-Millot, Véronique. "Un traité perdu de Galien miraculeusement retrouvé, Le *Sur l'inutilité de se chagriner*: texte grec et traduction française." Pages 72–123 in *La science médicale antique: Nouveaux regards. Études réunités en l'honneur de Jacques Jouanna*. By Véronique Boudon-Millot, Alessia Guardasole, and Caroline Magdelaine. Paris: Beauchesne, 2007.

Boudon-Millot, Véronique, Jacques Jouanna, and Antoine Pietrobelli. *Galien, Œuvres, Tome IV: Ne pas se Chagriner*. Paris: Les Belles Lettres, 2010.

Bovon, François. *Luke 1: A Commentary on the Gospel of Luke 1:1–9:50*. Translated by Christine M. Thomas. Hermeneia. Minneapolis: Fortress, 2002.

Bradshaw, Paul F., Maxwell E. Johnson, and L. Edward Phillips. *Apostolic Tradition*. Hermeneia. Minneapolis: Fortress, 2002.

Bremmer, Jan N. "Aspects of the Acts of Peter: Women, Magic, Place and Date." Pages 1–20 in *Apocryphal Acts of Peter: Magic, Miracles and Gnosticism*. Edited by Jan N. Bremmer. Leuven: Peeters, 1998.

Brent, Allen. *Hippolytus and the Roman Church in the Third Century: Communities in Tension before the Emergence of a Monarch-Bishop*. VCSup 31. Leiden: Brill, 1995.

Brinton, Laurel J. *Pragmatic Markers in English: Grammaticalization and Discourse Functions*. Topics in English Linguistics 19. Berlin: de Gruyter, 1996.

Brodie, Thomas L. *The Quest for the Origin of John's Gospel: A Source-Critical Approach*. New York: Oxford University Press, 1993.

Brown, Raymond E. *An Introduction to the Gospel of John*. Edited by Francis J. Maloney. ABRL. New York: Doubleday, 2003.

———. *The Gospel according to John, XIII–XXI*. AYBC. New Haven: Yale University Press, 1970.

Bruce, F. F. *The Book of Acts*. NICNT. Grand Rapids: Eerdmans, 1988.

Bryan, Christopher. *A Preface to Mark: Notes on the Gospel in Its Literary and Cultural Settings*. New York: Oxford University Press, 1993.

Buck, P. Lorraine. "Justin Martyr's Apologies: Their Number, Destination, and Form." *JTS* 54 (2003): 45–59.

Burfeind, Carsten. "Wen hörte Philippus? Leises Lesen und lautes Vorlesen in der Antike." *ZNW* 93 (2002): 138–45.

Burnyeat, M. F. "Postscript on Silent Reading." *ClQ* 47 (1997): 74–76.

Busch, Stephan. "Lautes und Leises Lesen in der Antike." *Rheinisches Museum für Philologie* 145 (2002): 1–45.

Cadbury, Henry J. "Commentary on the Preface of Luke." Pages 489–510 in *The Beginnings of Christianity: Part I, The Acts of the Apostles*. Edited by F. J. Foakes-Jackson and Kirsopp Lake. New York: Macmillan, 1922.

Cameron, Averil. *Christianity and the Rhetoric of Empire: The Development of Christian Discourse*. Berkeley: University of California Press, 1994.

Celsus. *On Medicine*. Translated by W. G. Spencer. 3 vols. LCL. Cambridge: Harvard University Press, 1935.

Chafe, Wallace L. *Discourse, Consciousness, and Time: The Flow and Displacement of Conscious Experience in Speaking and Writing*. Chicago: University of Chicago Press, 1994.

———. "Integration and Involvement in Speaking, Writing, and Oral Literature." Pages 35–53 in *Spoken and Written Language: Exploring Orality and Literacy*. Edited by Deborah Tannen. Advances in Discourse Processes 9. Norwood, NJ: Ablex, 1982.

---. "Linguistic Differences Produced by Differences between Speaking and Writing." Pages 105–23 in *Literacy, Language, and Learning: The Nature and Consequences of Reading and Writing*. Edited by David R. Olson, Nancy Torrance, and Angela Hildyard. Cambridge: Cambridge University Press, 1985.

---. "Linking Intonation Units in Spoken English." Pages 1–27 in *Clause Combining in Grammar and Discourse*. Edited by Sandra Thompson and John Haiman. Typological Studies in Language 18. Philadelphia: John Benjamins, 1988.

---, ed. *The Pear Stories: Cognitive, Cultural, and Linguistic Aspects of Narrative Production*. Norwood, NJ: Ablex, 1980.

Chafe, Wallace, and Deborah Tannen. "The Relation Between Written and Spoken Language." *Annual Review of Anthropology* 16 (1987): 383–407.

Chafe, Wallace, and Jane Danielwicz. "Properties of Spoken and Written Language." Pages 83–113 in *Comprehending Oral and Written Language*. Edited by Rosalind Horowitz and S. Jay Samuels. San Diego: Academic Press, 1987.

Champlin, Edward. *Fronto and Antonine Rome*. Cambridge: Harvard University Press, 1980.

Chang, Anne-Marie, Daniel Aeschbach, Jeanne F. Duffy, and Charles A. Czeisler. "Evening Use of Light-Emitting EReaders Negatively Affects Sleep, Circadian Timing, and Next-Morning Alertness." *Proceedings of the National Academy of Sciences of the United States of America* 112 (2015): 1232–37.

Chariton. *Callirhoe*. Translated by G. P. Goold. LCL. Cambridge: Harvard University Press, 1995.

Cicero. *In Catilinam 1–4; Pro Murena; Pro Sulla; Pro Flacco*. Translated by C. Macdonald. LCL. Cambridge: Harvard University Press, 1976.

---. *Letters to Atticus*. Translated by D. R. Shackleton Bailey. 4 vols. LCL. Cambridge: Harvard University Press, 1999.

---. *Letters to Friends*. Translated by D. R. Shackleton Bailey. 3 vols. LCL. Cambridge: Harvard University Press, 2001.

---. *Letters to Quintus and Brutus; Letter Fragments; Letter to Octavian; Invectives; Handbook of Electioneering*. Translated by D. R. Shackleton Bailey. LCL. Cambridge: Harvard University Press, 2002.

---. *Tusculan Disputations*. Translated by John Edwards King. LCL. Cambridge: Harvard University Press, 1927.

Clark, W. P. "Ancient Reading." *CJ* 26 (1931): 698–700.

Collins, Adela Yarbro. *Mark: A Commentary*. Hermeneia. Minneapolis: Fortress, 2007.

Cribiore, Raffaella. *Gymnastics of the Mind: Greek Education in Hellenistic and Roman Egypt*. Princeton: Princeton University Press, 2001.

---. *Writing, Teachers, and Students in Graeco-Roman Egypt*. American Studies in Papyrology 36. Atlanta: Scholars Press, 1996.

Davenport, Caillan, and Jennifer Manley, eds. *Fronto: Selected Letters*. Classical Studies Series. New York: Bloomsbury, 2014.

Davies, W. D., and Dale C. Allison. *Matthew 1–7*. ICC. London: T&T Clark, 2004.

Decker, Rodney J. "Markan Idiolect in the Study of the Greek of the New Testament." Pages 43–66 in *The Language of the New Testament: Context, History, and Development*. Edited by Andrew W. Pitts and Stanley E. Porter. Linguistic Biblical Studies 6. Leiden: Brill, 2013.

———. "The Use of Εὐθύς ('immediately') in Mark." *Journal of Ministry and Theology* 1 (1997): 90–120.

Deissmann, Adolf. *Light from the Ancient East: The New Testament Illustrated by Recently Discovered Texts of the Graeco-Roman World*. Translated by Lionel Richard Mortimer Strachan. London: Hodder & Stoughton, 1910.

Demosthenes. *Orations*. Translated by J. H. Vince et al. 7 vols. LCL. Cambridge: Harvard University Press, 1926.

Dewey, Joanna. "From Storytelling to Written Text: The Loss of Early Christian Women's Voices." *BTB* 26 (1996): 71–78.

———. "The Gospel of Mark as Oral Hermeneutic." Pages 71–87 in *Jesus, the Voice, and the Text: Beyond "The Oral and the Written Gospel."* Edited by Tom Thatcher. Waco, TX: Baylor University Press, 2008.

———. "Mark as Interwoven Tapestry: Forecasts and Echoes for a Listening Audience." *CBQ* 53 (1991): 221–36.

———. *The Oral Ethos of the Early Church: Speaking, Writing, and the Gospel of Mark*. Biblical Performance Criticism Series 8. Eugene, OR: Cascade Books, 2013.

———. "Oral Methods of Structuring Narrative in Mark." *Int* 43 (1989): 32–44.

Dickson, John P. "Gospel as News: Εὐαγγελ- from Aristophanes to the Apostle Paul." *NTS* 51 (2005): 212–30.

Dio Cassius. *Roman History*. Translated by Earnest Cary. 8 vols. LCL. Cambridge: Harvard University Press, 1914.

Dio Chrysostom. *Discourses*. Translated by J. W. Cohoon and H. Crosby Lamar. 5 vols. LCL. Cambridge: Harvard University Press, 1932.

Diodorus Siculus. *Library of History*. Translated by C. H. Oldfather et al. 12 vols. LCL. Cambridge: Harvard University Press, 1933.

Donahue, John R., and Daniel J. Harrington. *The Gospel of Mark*. SP 2. Collegeville, MN: Liturgical Press, 2002.

Doole, J. Andrew. *What Was Mark for Matthew? An Examination of Matthew's Relationship and Attitude to His Primary Source*. WUNT 2 344. Tübingen: Mohr Siebeck, 2013.

Dorandi, Tiziano. "Ancient ἐκδόσεις: Further Lexical Observations on Some of Galen's Texts." *Lexicon Philosophicum: International Journal for the History of Ideas and Texts* 2 (2014): 1–23.

Downing, F. Gerald. "Theophilus's First Reading of Luke–Acts." Pages 91–109 in *Luke's Literary Achievement: Collected Essays*. Edited by C. M. Tuckett. JSNTSup 116. Sheffield: Sheffield Academic, 1995.

Dronsch, Kristina. "Transmissions from Scripturality to Orality: Hearing the Voice of Jesus in Mark 4:1–34." Pages 119–29 in *The Interface of Orality and Writing: Speaking, Seeing, Writing in the Shaping of New Genres*. Edited by Annette Weissenrieder and Robert B. Coote. WUNT 260. Tübingen: Mohr Siebeck, 2010.

Duke Databank of Documentary Papyri. https://papyri.info/docs/ddbdp.

Dunn, James D. G. "Altering the Default Setting: Re-Envisaging the Early Transmission of the Jesus Tradition." Pages 41–79 in *The Oral Gospel Tradition*. Edited by James D. G. Dunn. Grand Rapids: Eerdmans, 2013.

Dupont, Florence. "*Recitatio* and the Reorganization of the Space of Public Discourse." Pages 44–59 in *The Roman Cultural Revolution*. Edited by Thomas Habinek and Alessandro Schiesaro. Cambridge: Cambridge University Press, 1997.

Dus, Jan A. "Papers or Principles? Ignatius of Antioch on the Authority of the Old Testament." Pages 151–63 in *The Process of Authority: The Dynamics in Transmission and Reception of Canonical Texts*. Edited by Jan Dušek and Jan Roskovec. DCLS 27. Berlin: de Gruyter, 2016.

Elder, Nicholas A. *The Media Matrix of Early Jewish and Christian Narrative*. LNTS 612. London: T&T Clark, 2019.

———. "The Synoptic Gospels as Mixed Media." *Biblical Research* 64 (2019): 42–66.

Ellingworth, Paul. "The Dog in the Night: A Note on Mark's Non-Use of KAI." *BT* 46 (1995): 125–28.

Elliott, J. K., ed. *The Apocryphal New Testament: A Collection of Apocryphal Christian Literature in an English Translation*. Oxford: Oxford University Press, 1993.

Engelbrecht, J. "The Language of the Gospel of Matthew." *Neot* 24 (1990): 199–213.

Epictetus. *Discourses*. Translated by W. A. Oldfather. 2 vols. LCL. Cambridge: Harvard University Press, 1925.

Epp, Eldon Jay. "The Codex and Literacy in Early Christianity and at Oxyrhynchus: Issues Raised by Harry Y. Gamble's Books and Readers in the Early Church." Pages 521–50 in *Perspectives on New Testament Textual Criticism: Collected Essays, 1962–2004*. Edited by Eldon Jay Epp. NovTSup 116. Leiden: Brill, 2005.

Euripides. *Children of Heracles; Hippolytus; Andromache; Hecuba*. Translated by David Kovacs. LCL. Cambridge: Harvard University Press, 1995.

Eusebius. *Ecclesiastical History*. Translated by Kirsopp Lake. 2 vols. LCL. Cambridge: Harvard University Press, 1926.

Evans, Craig A. "'The Book of the Genesis of Jesus Christ': The Purpose of Matthew in Light of the Incipit." Pages 61–72 in *Biblical Interpretation in Early Christian Gospels. Vol. 2: The Gospel of Matthew*. Edited by Thomas R. Hatina. LNTS 310. New York: T&T Clark, 2008.

———. *To See and Not Perceive: Isaiah 6.9–10 in Early Jewish and Christian Interpretation*. JSOTSup 64. Sheffield: Sheffield Academic, 1989.

Eve, Eric. *Writing the Gospels: Composition and Memory*. London: SPCK, 2016.

Faivre, Alexandre. "La documentation canonico–liturgique de l'Eglise ancienne." *RevScRel* 54 (1980): 273–97.

Fitzmyer, Joseph A. *The Acts of the Apostles: A New Commentary and Translation*. AB 31. New York: Doubleday, 1998.

———. *The Gospel according to Luke I–IX*. AB 28. New York: Doubleday, 1981.

———. *The Gospel according to Luke X–XXIV*. AB 28A. New York: Doubleday, 1981.

Fleischman, Suzanne. *Tense and Narrativity: From Medieval Performance to Modern Fiction*. Austin: University of Texas Press, 1990.

Fludernik, Monika. "The Historical Present Tense in English Literature: An Oral Pattern and Its Literary Adaptation." *Language and Literature* 17 (1992): 77–107.

———. "The Historical Present Tense Yet Again: Tense Switching and Narrative Dynamics in Oral and Quasi-Oral Storytelling." *Text: An Interdisciplinary Journal for the Study of Discourse* 11 (1991): 365–97.

France, R.T. *The Gospel of Mark*. NIGTC. Grand Rapids: Eerdmans, 2002.

Freisenbruch, Annelise. "Back to Fronto: Doctor and Patient in His Correspondence with an Emperor." Pages 235–55 in *Ancient Letters: Classical and Late Antique Epistolography*. Edited by Ruth Morello and A. D. Morrison. Oxford: Oxford University Press, 2007.

Fronto. *Correspondence*. Translated by C. R. Haines. 2 vols. LCL. Cambridge: Harvard University Press, 1919.

Galen. *Hygiene; Thrasybulus; On Exercise with a Small Ball*. Translated by Ian Johnston. LCL. Cambridge: Harvard University Press, 2018.

———. *Method of Medicine*. Translated by Ian Johnston and G. H. R. Horsley. 3 vols. LCL. Cambridge: Harvard University Press, 2011.

———. *Oeuvres complètes: Tome IV, Ne pas se chagriner*. Translated by Véronique Boudon-Millot and Jacques Jouanna. Paris: Les Belles Lettres, 2010.

Gamble, Harry Y. *Books and Readers in the Early Church: A History of Early Christian Texts*. New Haven: Yale University Press, 1995.

———. "Literacy, Liturgy and the Shaping of the New Testament Canon," Pages 27–39 in *The Earliest Gospels: The Origins and Transmission of the Earliest Christian Gospels—The Contribution of the Chester Beatty Gospel Codex P45*. Edited by Charles Horton. JSNTSup 258. New York: T&T Clark, 2004.

García Martínez, Florentino, and Eibert J. C. Tigchelaar, trans. *The Dead Sea Scrolls: Study Edition*. 2 vols. Grand Rapids: Eerdmans, 1998.

Gavrilov, A. K. "Techniques of Reading in Classical Antiquity." *ClQ* 47 (1997): 56–73.

Genette, Gérard. *Paratexts: Thresholds of Interpretation*. Translated by J. E. Lewin. Lecture, Culture, Theory 20. Cambridge: Cambridge University Press, 1997.

Gibson, Eleanor J., and Harry Levin. *The Psychology of Reading*. Cambridge: MIT Press, 1975.

Gibson, Roy K., and Ruth Morello. *Reading the Letters of Pliny the Younger: An Introduction*. Cambridge: Cambridge University Press, 2012.

Gilliard, Frank D. "More Silent Reading in Antiquity: *Non Omne Verbum Sonabat*." *JBL* 112 (1993): 689–96.

Goodacre, Mark. "Parallel Tradition or Parallel Gospels?" Pages 77–89 in *John's Transformation of Mark*. Edited by Eve-Marie Becker, Helen K. Bond, and Catrin Williams. London: T&T Clark, 2021.

———. *Thomas and the Gospels: The Case for Thomas's Familiarity with the Synoptics*. Grand Rapids: Eerdmans, 2012.

Gray, W. S. *The Teaching of Reading: An International View*. Cambridge: Harvard University Press, 1957.

Green, Joel B. *The Gospel of Luke*. NICNT. Grand Rapids: Eerdmans, 1997.

Grenfell, Bernard P., and Arthur S. Hunt. *Oxyrhynchus Papyri*. London: Egypt Exploration Society, 1898.

Grønli, Janne, Ida Kristiansen Byrkjedal, Bjørn Bjorvatn, Øystein Nødtvedt, Børge Hamre, and Ståle Pallesen. "Reading from an IPad or from a Book in Bed: The Impact on Human Sleep. A Randomized Controlled Crossover Trial." *Sleep Medicine* 21 (2016): 86–92.

Gundry, Robert H. *Mark: A Commentary on His Apology for the Cross*. Grand Rapids: Eerdmans, 1993.

Gurd, Sean A. "Galen on ἔκδοσις." Pages 169–84 in *Perceptions of the Second Sophistic and Its Times*. Edited by Thomas Schmidt and Pascale Fleury. Toronto: University of Toronto Press, 2011.

Hägg, Tomas. *The Novel in Antiquity*. Berkeley: University of California Press, 1983.

Hagner, Donald A. *Matthew 14–28*. WBC 33B. Dallas: Thomas Nelson, 1995.

Haran, Menahem. "The Books of the Chronicles 'of the Kings of Judah' and 'of the Kings of Israel': What Sort of Books Were They?" *VT* 49 (1999): 156–64.

Harnack, Adolf von. *Bible Reading in the Early Church*. Translated by J. R. Wilkinson. Crown Theological Library 36. London: Williams and Norgate, 1912.

Harnett, Benjamin. "The Diffusion of the Codex." *ClAnt* 36 (2017): 183–235.

Hawkins, John C. *Horae Synopticae: Contributions to the Study of the Synoptic Problem*. Oxford: Clarendon, 1909.

Hays, Richard B. *Echoes of Scripture in the Gospels*. Waco, TX: Baylor University Press, 2016.

Heilmann, Jan. "Reading Early New Testament Manuscripts: *Scriptio Continua*, 'Reading Aids,' and Other Characteristic Features." Pages 177–96 in *Material Aspects of Reading in Ancient and Medieval Cultures: Materiality, Presence and Performance*. Edited by Anna Krauß, Jonas Leipziger, and Friederike Schücking-Jungblut. Berlin: de Gruyter, 2020.

Heine, Bernd. "On Discourse Markers: Grammaticalization, Pragmaticalization, or Something Else?" *Linguistics* 51 (2013): 1205–47.

Heinric, Carol, and Eduard Lommatzsch, eds. *Origenis opera omnia*. Vol. 8. Berlin: Sumtibus Haude et Spener, 1838.

Held, Heinz Joachim. "Matthew as Interpreter of the Miracle Stories." Pages 165–299 in *Tradition and Interpretation in Matthew*. Edited by Günther Bornkamm, Gerhard Barth, and Heinz Joachim Held. London: SCM, 1963.

Helmreich, Georg, Johannes Marquardt, and Iwani Müller. *Claudii Galeni pergameni scripta minora*. Vol. 3. Leipzig: Teubner, 1891.

Henderson, John. *Pliny's Statue: The Letters, Self-Portraiture and Classical Art*. Exeter: Liverpool University Press, 2002.

Hendrickson, G. L. "Ancient Reading." *CJ* 25 (1929): 182–96.

Hengel, Martin. *The Johannine Question*. London: SCM, 1989.

Hercher, Rudolf, and Jean François Boissonade, eds. *Epistolographi Graeci*. Paris: Didot, 1873.

Hicks-Keeton, Jill. *Arguing with Aseneth: Gentile Access to Israel's "Living God" in Jewish Antiquity*. Oxford: Oxford University Press, 2018.

Hock, Ronald F. "The Greek Novel." Pages 127–46 in *Greco-Roman Literature and the New Testament*. Edited by David E. Aune. Atlanta: Scholars Press, 1988.

Hoegen-Rohls, Christina. "The Beginnings of Mark and John: What Exactly Should Be Compared? Some Hermeneutical Questions and Observations." Pages 101–19 in *John's Transformation of Mark*. Edited by Eve-Marie Becker, Helen K. Bond, and Catrin Williams. London: T&T Clark, 2021.

Holmes, Michael W., ed. *The Apostolic Fathers: Greek Texts and English Translations*. 3rd ed. Grand Rapids: Baker Academic, 2007.

Horace. *Satires*; *Epistles*; *The Art of Poetry*. Translated by H. Rushton Fairclough. LCL. Cambridge: Harvard University Press, 1926.

Horner, Timothy J. "*Listening to Trypho*": *Justin Martyr's Dialogue Revisited*. CBET 28. Leuven: Peeters, 2001.

Horsfall, Nicholas. "Rome without Spectacles." *Greece & Rome* 42 (1995): 49–56.

Horsley, Richard A. "Oral and Written Aspects of the Emergence of the Gospel of Mark as Scripture." *Oral Tradition* 25 (2010): 93–114.

Houston, George W. *Inside Roman Libraries: Book Collections and Their Management in Antiquity*. Studies in the History of Greece and Rome. Chapel Hill: The University of North Carolina Press, 2014.

Hurtado, Larry W. "Oral Fixation and New Testament Studies? 'Orality,' 'Performance' and Reading Texts in Early Christianity." *NTS* 60 (2014): 321–40.

———. *The Earliest Christian Artifacts: Manuscripts and Christian Origins*. Grand Rapids: Eerdmans, 2006.

Iverson, Kelly R. "Oral Fixation or Oral Corrective? A Response to Larry Hurtado." *NTS* 62 (2016): 183–200.

Jerome. *Select Letters*. Translated by F. A. Wright. LCL. Cambridge: Harvard University Press, 1933.

Johnson, Luke Timothy. *The Acts of the Apostles*. SP. Collegeville, MN: Liturgical Press, 1992.

———. *The Gospel of Luke*. SP. Collegeville, MN: Liturgical Press, 1991.

Johnson, William A. "The Ancient Book." Pages 256–81 in *The Oxford Handbook of Papyrology*. Edited by Roger S. Bagnall. Oxford: Oxford University Press, 2009.

———. *Readers and Reading Culture in the High Roman Empire: A Study of Elite Communities*. Oxford: Oxford University Press, 2010.

———. "Toward a Sociology of Reading in Classical Antiquity." *AJP* 121 (2000): 593–627.

Johnson, William A., and Holt N. Parker. *Ancient Literacies: The Culture of Reading in Greece and Rome*. Oxford: Oxford University Press, 2009.

Josephus. *Jewish Antiquities*. Translated by H. St. J. Thackeray et al. 8 vols. LCL. Cambridge: Harvard University Press, 1930.

———. *The Jewish War*. Translated by H. St. J. Thackeray. 3 vols. LCL. Cambridge: Harvard University Press, 1927.

———. *The Life*; *Against Apion*. Translated by H. St. J. Thackeray. LCL. Cambridge: Harvard University Press, 1995.

Jouanna, Jacques. "Galen's Reading of the Hippocratic Treatise *The Nature of Man*: The Foundations of Hippocratism in Galen." Pages 313–34 in *Greek Medicine from Hippocrates to Galen: Selected Papers*. Edited by Philip van der Eijk, Translated by Neil Allies. Leiden: Brill, 2012.

Kautzsch, Emil, ed. *Gesenius' Hebrew Grammar*. Translated by Arther E. Cowley. 2nd ed. Oxford: Clarendon, 1910.

Keener, Craig S. *Acts: An Exegetical Commentary 3:1–14:28*. Grand Rapids: Baker Academic, 2013.

———. *The Gospel of John*. 2 vols. Grand Rapids: Baker Academic, 2003.

Keith, Chris. *The Gospel as Manuscript: An Early History of the Jesus Tradition as Material Artifact*. Oxford: Oxford University Press, 2020.

———. "'If John Knew Mark': Critical Inheritance and Johannine Disagreements with Mark." Pages 31–49 in *John's Transformation of Mark*. Edited by Eve-Marie Becker, Helen K. Bond, and Catrin Williams. London: T&T Clark, 2021.

———. *Jesus against the Scribal Elite: The Origins of the Conflict*. Grand Rapids: Baker Academic, 2014.

———. *Jesus' Literacy: Scribal Culture and the Teacher from Galilee*. LNTS 413. New York: T&T Clark, 2011.

Kelber, Werner H. *The Oral and the Written Gospel: The Hermeneutics of Speaking and Writing in the Synoptic Tradition, Mark, Paul, and Q*. Bloomington: Indiana University Press, 1983.

Kelly, Benjamin. *Petitions, Litigation, and Social Control in Roman Egypt*. Oxford: Oxford University Press, 2011.

Kilpatrick, George D. "Some Notes on Markan Usage." Pages 159–74 in *The Language and Style of the Gospel of Mark: An Edition of C. H. Turner's "Notes on Marcan Usage" Together with Other Comparable Studies*. Edited by J. K. Elliott. NovTSup 71. Leiden: Brill, 1993.

Klauck, Hans-Josef. *The Apocryphal Acts of the Apostles: An Introduction*. Translated by Brian McNeil. Waco, TX: Baylor University Press, 2008.

Klauck, Hans-Josef, and Daniel P. Bailey. *Ancient Letters and the New Testament: A Guide to Context and Exegesis*. Waco, TX: Baylor University Press, 2006.

Kleist, James A. *The Gospel of Saint Mark Presented in Greek Thought-Units and Sense-Lines with a Commentary*. New York: Bruce Publishing Company, 1936.

Knox, Bernard M. W. "Silent Reading in Antiquity." *GRBS* 9 (1968): 421–35.

Knust, Jennifer, and Tommy Wasserman. *To Cast the First Stone: The Transmission of a Gospel Story*. Princeton: Princeton University Press, 2018.

Köstenberger, Andreas J. *John*. BECNT. Grand Rapids: Baker Academic, 2004.

Kühn, Karl Gottlob, ed. *Claudii Galeni opera omnia*. 22 vols. Leipzig: Car. Cnoblochii, 1821–1833.

Kürzinger, Josef. "Das Papiaszeugnis und die Erstgestalt des Matthäusevangeliums." *BZ* 4 (1960): 19–38.

———. "Die Aussage des Papias von Hierapolis zur literarischen Form des Markusevangeliums." *BZ* 21 (1977): 245–64.

Larsen, Matthew D. C. "Accidental Publication, Unfinished Texts and the Traditional Goals of New Testament Textual Criticism." *JSNT* 39 (2017): 362–87.

———. *Gospels before the Book*. Oxford: Oxford University Press, 2018.

Larsen, Matthew D. C., and Mark Letteney. "Christians and the Codex: Generic Materiality and Early Gospel Traditions." *JECS* 27 (2019): 383–415.

Leung, Mavis. "The Narrative Function and Verbal Aspect of the Historical Present in the Fourth Gospel." *JETS* 51 (2008): 703–20.

Levin, Harry, and Ann Buckler-Addis. *The Eye-Voice Span*. Cambridge: MIT Press, 1979.

Levine, Lee I. *The Ancient Synagogue: The First Thousand Years*. 2nd ed. New Haven: Yale University Press, 2005.

Lewis, R. G., trans. *Asconsius: Commentaries on Speeches of Cicero*. Oxford: Oxford University Press, 2006.

Libanius. *Selected Orations*. Translated by A. F. Norman. 2 vols. LCL. Cambridge: Harvard University Press, 1969.

Lincoln, Andrew. *The Gospel according to Saint John*. BNTC 4. London: Continuum, 2005.

Lipsius, R. A., and M. Bonnet, eds. *Acta Apostolorum Apocrypha*. 2 vols. Leipzig: H. Mendelssohn, 1891.

Llewelyn, Stephen R. *A Review of the Greek Inscriptions and Papyri Published in 1982–83*. New Documents Illustrating Early Christianity 7. Sydney: The Ancient History Documentary Research Centre, Macquarie University, 1994.

Lucian. *The Dead Come to Life or The Fisherman; The Double Indictment or Trials by Jury; On Sacrifices; The Ignorant Book Collector; The Dream or Lucian's Career; The Parasite; The Lover of Lies; The Judgement of the Goddesses; On Salaried Posts in Great Houses*. Translated by A. M. Harmon. LCL. Cambridge: Harvard University Press, 1921.

———. *How to Write History; The Dipsads; Saturnalia; Herodotus or Aetion; Zeuxis or Antiochus; A Slip of the Tongue in Greeting; Apology for the "Salaried Posts in Great Houses"; Harmonides; A Conversation with Hesiod; The Scythian or The Consul; Hermotimus or Concerning the Sects; To One Who Said "You're a Prometheus in Words"; The Ship or The Wishes*. Translated by K. Kilburn. LCL. Cambridge: Harvard University Press, 1959.

———. *Lucians von Samosata Sämtliche Werke*. Translated by Christoph Martin Wieland. 6 vols. Leipzig: Im Verlag der Weidmannischen Buchhandlung, 1788.

Luijendijk, Anne-Marie. "Sacred Scriptures as Trash: Biblical Papyri from Oxyrhynchus." *VC* 64 (2010): 217–54.

Luz, Ulrich. *Matthew 1–7*. Translated by James E. Crouch. Hermeneia. Minneapolis: Fortress, 2007.

———. *Matthew 21–28*. Translated by James E. Crouch. Minneapolis: Fortress, 2005.

Magne, Jean. *Tradition apostolique sur les charismes et Diataxeis des saints Apôtres*. Origines chrétiennes 1. Paris: Magne, 1975.

Maloney, Elliott C. *Semitic Interference in Marcan Syntax*. SBLDS 51. Chico, CA: Scholars Press, 1980.

Manson, T. W. *The Teaching of Jesus: Studies of the Form and Content*. Cambridge: Cambridge University Press, 1943.

Marcus Aurelius. *Marcus Aurelius*. Translated by C. R. Haines. LCL. Cambridge: Harvard University Press, 1916.

Marcus, Joel. *Mark 1–8: A New Translation with Introduction and Commentary*. AB 27. New York: Doubleday, 2008.

———. *The Way of the Lord: Christological Exegesis of the Old Testament in the Gospel of Mark*. Louisville: Westminster John Knox, 1992.

Marshall, I. Howard. *The Acts of the Apostles: An Introduction and Commentary*. Tyndale Commentary. Grand Rapids: Eerdmans, 1980.

Martial. *Epigrams*. Translated by D. R. Shackleton Bailey. 3 vols. LCL. Cambridge: Harvard University Press, 1993.

McCown, C. C. "Codex and Roll in the New Testament." *HTR* 34 (1941): 219–49.

McCutcheon, R. W. "Silent Reading in Antiquity and the Future History of the Book." *Book History* 18 (2015): 1–32.

McDonnell, Myles. "Writing, Copying, and Autograph Manuscripts in Ancient Rome." *ClQ* 46 (1996): 469–91.

McLuhan, Marshall. *Understanding Media: The Extensions of Man*. Cambridge: MIT Press, 1994.

Metso, Sarianna. "Whom Does the Term Yahad Identify?" Pages 63–84 in *Defining Identities: We, You, and the Other in the Dead Sea Scrolls*. STDJ 70. Leiden: Brill, 2008.

Miller, Shem. *Dead Sea Media: Orality, Textuality, and Memory in the Scrolls from the Judean Desert.* Leiden: Brill, 2019.

Mills, Ian N. "Pagan Readers of Christian Scripture: The Role of Books in Early Autobiographical Conversion Narratives." *VC* 73 (2019): 481–506.

Mitchell, Timothy. "Exposing Textual Corruption: Community as a Stabilizing Aspect in the Circulation of the New Testament Writings during the Greco-Roman Era." *JSNT* 43 (2020): 1–33.

Montessori, Maria. *Dr. Montessori's Own Handbook: A Short Guide to Her Ideas and Materials.* Cambridge, MA: Robert Bentley, 1964.

Moss, Candida. "Fashioning Mark: Early Christian Discussions about the Scribe and Status of the Second Gospel." *NTS* 67 (2021): 181–204.

Mount, Christopher N. *Pauline Christianity: Luke-Acts and the Legacy of Paul.* Leiden: Brill, 2002.

Munier, Charles. "A Propos des Apologies de Justin." *RevScRel* 61 (1987): 177–86.

Nachtergaele, Delphine. "Variation in Private Letters: The Papyri of the Apollonios *Strategos* Archive." *GRBS* 56 (2016): 140–63.

Nässelqvist, Dan. *Public Reading in Early Christianity: Lectors, Manuscripts, and Sound in the Oral Delivery of John 1–4.* NovTSup 163. Leiden: Brill, 2016.

Neirynck, Frans, Theo Hansen, and Frans van Segbroeck, eds. *The Minor Agreements of Matthew and Luke against Mark: With a Cumulative List.* BETL 37. Leuven: University Press, 1974.

Neville, David. *Mark's Gospel—Prior or Posterior? A Reappraisal of the Phenomenon of Order.* LNTS 222. New York: T&T Clark, 2002.

Nickelsburg, George W. E. *1 Enoch.* Hermeneia. Minneapolis: Fortress, 2001.

Nickelsburg, George W. E., and James C. VanderKam. *1 Enoch: The Hermeneia Translation.* Minneapolis: Fortress, 2012.

Nolland, John. *Luke 1:1–9:20.* WBC 35A. Dallas: Word Books, 1989.

Nongbri, Brent. *God's Library: The Archaeology of the Earliest Christian Manuscripts.* New Haven: Yale University Press, 2018.

———. "Palaeography, Precision and Publicity: Further Thoughts on P.Ryl. III.457 (P52)." *NTS* 66 (2020): 471–99.

———. "The Use and Abuse of P52: Papyrological Pitfalls in the Dating of the Fourth Gospel." *HTR* 98 (2005): 23–48.

Norden, Eduard. *Die Antike Kunstprosa.* Leipzig: Teubner, 1898.

Nutton, Vivian. "Avoiding Distress." Pages 43–106 in *Galen: Psychological Writings.* Edited by P. N. Singer, Daniel Davies, and Vivian Nutton. Cambridge: Cambridge University Press, 2014.

———. Introduction to "Avoiding Distress." Pages 45–76 in *Galen: Psychological Writings.* Edited by P. N. Singer, Daniel Davies, and Vivian Nutton. Cambridge: Cambridge University Press, 2014.

Ong, Walter J. "The Psychodynamics of Oral Memory and Narrative: Some Implications for Biblical Studies." Pages 55–73 in *The Pedagogy of God's Image: Essays on Symbol and the Religious Imagination.* Edited by Robert Masson. Chico, CA: Scholars Press, 1982.

O'Rourke, John J. "The Historic Present in the Gospel of John." *JBL* 93 (1974): 585–90.

Osiek, Carolyn. *Shepherd of Hermas: A Commentary.* Hermeneia. Minneapolis: Fortress, 1999.

Östman, Jan-Ola. "The Symbiotic Relationship Between Pragmatic Particles and Impromptu Speech." Pages 147–77 in *Impromptu Speech: A Symposium; Papers of a Symposium Held in Åbo, Nov. 20–22, 1981.* Edited by Nils Erik Enkvist. Åbo: Åbo Akademi, 1982.

Overman, J. Andrew. *Matthew's Gospel and Formative Judaism: The Social World of the Matthean Community.* Minneapolis: Fortress, 1990.

Ovid. *Heroides; Amores.* Translated by Grant Showerman. LCL. Cambridge: Harvard University Press, 1914.

Park, Yoon-Man. *Mark's Memory Resources and the Controversy Stories (Mark 2:1–3:6): An Application of the Frame Theory of Cognitive Science to the Markan Oral-Aural Narrative.* Leiden: Brill, 2010.

Parker, Holt N. "Books and Reading Latin Poetry." Pages 186–229 in *Ancient Literacies: The Culture of Reading in Greece and Rome.* Edited by William A. Johnson and Holt N. Parker. Oxford: Oxford University Press, 2009.

Paton, W. R., trans. *Greek Anthology.* 5 vols. LCL. Cambridge: Harvard University Press, 1917.

Perrot, Charles. "The Reading of the Bible in the Ancient Synagogue." Pages 137–59 in *The Literature of the Jewish People in the Period of the Second Temple and the Talmud*, Volume 1 *Mikra.* Leiden: Brill, 1988.

Pesch, Rudolf. *Das Markusevangelium: Einleitung und Kommentar zu Kap. 1,1–8,26.* 4th ed. 2 vols. HThKNT. Freiburg: Herder, 1984.

Philo. *Every Good Man Is Free; On the Contemplative Life; On the Eternity of the World; Against Flaccus; Apology for the Jews; On Providence.* Translated by F. H. Colson. LCL. Cambridge: Harvard University Press, 1941.

———. *On Flight and Finding; On the Change of Names; On Dreams.* Translated by F. H. Colson and G. H. Whitaker. LCL. Cambridge: Harvard University Press, 1934.

———. *On the Special Laws; On the Virtues; On Rewards and Punishments.* Translated by F. H. Colson. LCL. Cambridge: Harvard University Press, 1939.

Philostratus. *Apollonius of Tyana.* Translated by Christopher P. Jones. 3 vols. LCL. Cambridge: Harvard University Press, 2005.

Plautus. *Amphityron; The Comedy of Asses; The Pot of Gold; The Two Bacchides; The Captives.* Translated by Wolfgang de Melo. LCL. Cambridge: Harvard University Press, 2011.

Pliny the Younger. *Letters.* Translated by Betty Radice. 2 vols. LCL. Cambridge: Harvard University Press, 1969.

Plotinus. *Ennead, Volume I: Porphyry On the Life of Plotinus.* Translated by A. H. Armstrong. LCL. Cambridge: Harvard University Press, 1969.

Plutarch. *Lives.* Translated by Bernadotte Perrin. 11 vols. LCL. Cambridge: Harvard University Press, 1914.

———. *Moralia, Volume IV: Roman Questions; Greek Questions; Greek and Roman Parallel Stories; On the Fortune of the Romans; On the Fortune or the Virtue of Alexander; Were the Athenians More Famous in War or in Wisdom?* Translated by Frank Cole Babbitt. LCL. Cambridge: Harvard University Press, 1936.

Poirier, John C. "The Roll, the Codex, the Wax Tablet and the Synoptic Problem." *JSNT* 35 (2012): 3–30.

Quintilian. *The Orator's Education.* Translated by H. E. Butler. 5 vols. LCL. Cambridge: Harvard University Press, 1920.

———. *The Orator's Education*. Translated by Donald Russell. 5 vols. LCL. Cambridge: Harvard University Press, 2002.

Reardon, B. P., ed. *Collected Ancient Greek Novels*. Berkeley: University of California Press, 1989.

Reece, Steve. *Paul's Large Letters: Paul's Autographic Subscription in the Light of Ancient Epistolary Conventions*. LNTS 561. New York: Bloomsbury, 2016.

Reed, Stephen. "Physical Features of Excerpted Torah Texts." Pages 82–104 in *Jewish and Christian Scripture as Artifact and Canon*. Edited by Craig A. Evans and H. Daniel Zacharias. Library of Second Temple Studies 70. London: T&T Clark, 2011.

Reynolds, L. D., and N. G. Wilson. *Scribes and Scholars: A Guide to the Transmission of Greek and Latin Literature*. 4th ed. Oxford: Oxford University Press, 2014.

Rhoads, David. "Performance Events in Early Christianity: New Testament Writings in an Oral Context." Pages 166–93 in *The Interface of Orality and Writing: Speaking, Seeing, Writing in the Shaping of New Genres*. Edited by Annette Weissenrieder and Robert B. Coote. WUNT 260. Tübingen: Mohr Siebeck, 2010.

Rhoads, David, Joanna Dewey, and Donald Michie. *Mark as Story: An Introduction to the Narrative of a Gospel*. 3rd ed. Minneapolis: Fortress, 2012.

Roberts, C. H. "The Ancient Book and the Endings of St. Mark." *JTS* 40 (1939): 253–57.

———. "The Codex." *Proceedings of the British Academy* 40 (1954): 169–204.

Roberts, C. H., and T. C. Skeat. *The Birth of the Codex*. London: Oxford University Press, 1983.

Rodríguez, Rafael. *Oral Tradition and the New Testament: A Guide for the Perplexed*. London: Bloomsbury, 2014.

Rogers, Everett M. *Diffusions of Innovations*. 5th ed. New York: Free Press, 2003.

Rothschild, Clare K. "Galen's *De Indolentia* and the Early Christian Codex." *Early Christianity* 12 (2021): 28–39.

Rothschild, Clare K., and Trevor W. Thompson, eds. *Galen's De Indolentia: Essays on a Newly Discovered Letter*. Studien und Texte zu Antike und Christentum 88. Tübingen: Mohr Siebeck, 2014.

Rousseau, Adelin, and Louis Doutreleau, eds. *Irénée de Lyon, Contre Les Hérésies. Livre III*. SC 211. Paris: Les Éditions du Cref, 1974.

Runesson, Anders. *The Origins of the Synagogue: A Socio-Historical Study*. ConBNT 37. Stockholm: Almqvist & Wiksell, 2001.

Scheck, Thomas P., trans. *Apology for Origen: With On the Falsification of the Books of Origen by Rufinus*. Washington, DC: The Catholic University of America Press, 2010.

Schiffrin, Deborah. *Discourse Markers*. Studies in Interactional Sociolinguistics 5. Cambridge: Cambridge University Press, 1987.

———. "Tense Variation in Narrative." *Language* 57 (1981): 45–62.

Schmidt, Carl. "Zur Datierung der alten Petrusakten." *ZNW* 29 (1930): 150–55.

Schnelle, Udo. *Das Evangelium nach Johannes*. 2nd ed. THKNT 4. Leipzig: Evangelische Verlagsanstalt, 2000.

Seneca. *Epistles*. Translated by Richard M. Gummere and H. Crosby Lamar. 3 vols. LCL. Cambridge: Harvard University Press, 1917.

Seneca the Elder. *Declamations*. Translated by Michael Winterbottom. 2 vols. LCL. Cambridge: Harvard University Press, 1974.

Shin, Hyeon Woo. "The Historic Present as a Discourse Marker and Textual Criticism in Mark." *BT* 63 (2012): 39–51.
Shiner, Whitney Taylor. *Proclaiming the Gospel: First-Century Performance of Mark*. Harrisburg, PA: Trinity Press International, 2003.
Singer, P. N. "The Diagnosis and Treatment of the Affections and Errors Peculiar to Each Person's Soul." Pages 203–332 in *Galen: Psychological Writings*. Edited by P. N. Singer, Daniel Davies, and Vivian Nutton. Cambridge: Cambridge University Press, 2014.
———, trans. *Galen: Selected Works*. The World's Classics. Oxford: Oxford University Press, 1997.
———. General introduction to *Galen: Psychological Writings*. Edited by P. N. Singer, Daniel Davies, and Vivian Nutton. Cambridge: Cambridge University Press. 2014.
———. "New Light and Old Texts: Galen on His Own Books." Pages 91–131 in *Galen's Treatise Περὶ Ἀλυπίας ("De Indolentia") in Context*. Edited by Caroline Petit. Leiden: Brill, 2019.
Singer, P. N., Daniel Davies, and Vivian Nutton, eds. *Galen: Psychological Writings*. Cambridge: Cambridge University Press, 2014.
Smith, D. Moody. *John among the Gospels*. 2nd ed. Columbia, SC: University of South Carolina Press, 2001.
Soyars, Jonathan E. *The Shepherd of Hermas and the Pauline Legacy*. NovTSup 176. Leiden: Brill, 2019.
Stanton, Graham M. *Jesus and Gospel*. Cambridge: Cambridge University Press, 2004.
Starr, Raymond J. "Reading Aloud: Lectores and Roman Reading." *CJ* 86 (1991): 337–43.
———. "The Circulation of Literary Texts in the Roman World." *ClQ* 37 (1987): 213–23.
Stein, Robert H. *Mark*. BECNT. Grand Rapids: Baker Academic, 2008.
Stephens, Susan A., and John J. Winkler, eds. *Ancient Greek Novels: The Fragments: Introduction, Text, Translation, and Commentary*. Princeton: Princeton University Press, 1995.
Stewart-Sykes, Alistair. *Hippolytus: On the Apostolic Tradition: An English Version with Introduction and Commentary*. Crestwood, NY: St Vladimir's Seminary, 2001.
Suetonius. *Lives of the Caesars*. Translated by J. C. Rolfe. 2 vols. LCL. Cambridge: Harvard University Press, 1914.
Tannen, Deborah, ed. *Analyzing Discourse: Text and Talk*. Washington, DC: Georgetown University Press, 1982.
———. "Oral and Literate Strategies in Spoken and Written Narratives." *Language* 58 (1982): 1–21.
———, ed. *Spoken and Written Language: Exploring Orality and Literacy*. Advances in Discourse Processes 9. Norwood, NJ: Ablex, 1982.
Thatcher, Tom. *Why John Wrote a Gospel: Jesus, Memory, History*. Louisville: Westminster John Knox, 2006.
Theissen, Gerd. *The Gospels in Context: Social and Political History in the Synoptic Tradition*. Translated by Linda M. Maloney. Minneapolis: Fortress, 1991.
Thompson, Michael B. "The Holy Internet: Communication Between Churches in the First Christian Generation." Pages 49–70 in *The Gospels for All Christians: Rethinking the Gospel Audiences*. Edited by Richard Bauckham. Grand Rapids: Eerdmans, 1998.
Thyen, Hartwig. *Das Johannesevangelium*. HNT 6. Tübingen: Mohr Siebeck, 2005.

Trelenberg, Jörg. *Tatianos, Oratio Ad Graecos Rede an Die Griechen*. BHT 165. Tübingen: Mohr Siebeck, 2012.
Turner, E. G. *Athenian Books in the Fifth and Fourth Centuries BC*. London: H. K. Lewis & Co., 1952.
———. *Greek Papyri: An Introduction*. Oxford: Clarendon, 1968.
Vatri, Alessandro. "The Physiology of Ancient Greek Reading." *ClQ* 62 (2012): 633–47.
Venema, G. J. *Reading Scripture in the Old Testament: Deuteronomy 9–10, 31, 2 Kings 22–23, Jeremiah 36, Nehemiah 8*. OtSt 48. Leiden: Brill, 2004.
Walsh, P. G., trans. *Pliny the Younger, Complete Letters*. Oxford World's Classics. Oxford: Oxford University Press, 2009.
Walsh, Robyn Faith. *The Origins of Early Christian Literature: Contextualizing the New Testament within Greco-Roman Literary Culture*. Cambridge: Cambridge University Press, 2021.
Watson, Francis. *Gospel Writing: A Canonical Perspective*. Grand Rapids: Eerdmans, 2013.
Watts, Richard J. "Taking the Pitcher to the 'Well': Native Speakers' Perception of Their Use of Discourse Markers in Conversation." *Journal of Pragmatics: An Interdisciplinary Monthly of Language Studies* 13 (1989): 203–37.
Weissenrieder, Annette, and Robert B. Coote, eds. *The Interface of Orality and Writing: Speaking, Seeing, Writing in the Shaping of New Genres*. WUNT 260. Tübingen: Mohr Siebeck, 2010.
White, L. Michael, and G. Anthony Keddie, eds. *Jewish Fictional Letters from Hellenistic Egypt: The Epistle of Aristeas and Related Literature*. Atlanta: SBL Press, 2018.
White, Peter. *Promised Verse: Poets in the Society of Augustan Rome*. Cambridge: Harvard University Press, 1993.
Wikgren, Allen. "ΑΡΧΗ ΤΟΥ ΕΥΑΓΓΕΛΙΟΥ." *JBL* 61 (1942): 11–20.
Williams, Catrin. "John's 'Rewriting' of Mark: Some Insights from Ancient Jewish Analogues." Pages 51–65 in *John's Transformation of Mark*. Edited by Eve-Marie Becker, Helen K. Bond, and Catrin Williams. London: T&T Clark, 2021.
Wilson, William. "Clement of Alexandria." *Ante-Nicene Fathers*. Edited by Alexander Roberts, James Donaldson, and A. Cleveland Coxe. Vol. 2. Buffalo, NY: Christian Literature Publishing, 1885.
Windisch, Hans. *Johannes und die Synoptiker: Wollte der vierte Evangelist die älteren Evangelien ergänzen oder ersetzen?* UNT 12. Leipzig: Hinrich, 1926.
Winkler, John J. Introduction to Leucippe and Clitophon. Pages 170–284 in *Collected Ancient Greek Novels*. Edited by B. P. Reardon. Berkeley: University of California Press, 1989.
Winsbury, Rex. *Pliny the Younger: A Life in Roman Letters*. London: T&T Clark, 2014.
———. *The Roman Book: Books, Publishing and Performance in Classical Rome*. Classical Literature and Society. London: Duckworth, 2009.
Winter, J. G. "In the Service of Rome: Letters from the Michigan Collection of Papyri." *CP* 22 (1927): 237–56.
Wire, Antoinette Clark. *The Case for Mark Composed in Performance*. Biblical Performance Criticism Series 3. Eugene, OR: Cascade, 2011.
Witherington, Ben, III. *Jesus the Sage: The Pilgrimage of Wisdom*. Minneapolis: Fortress, 2000.
Wolfson, Nessa. "A Feature of Performed Narrative: The Conversational Historical Present." *Language in Society* 7 (1978): 215–37.

———. *CHP: The Conversational Historical Present in American English Narrative.* Topics in Sociolinguistics. Dordrecht: Foris, 1982.

Wright, Brian J. *Communal Reading in the Time of Jesus: A Window into Early Christian Reading Practices.* Minneapolis: Fortress, 2017.

Yonge, C. D., trans. *The Works of Philo.* Peabody, MA: Hendrickson, 1993.

Zumstein, Jean. "The Johannine 'Relecture' of Mark." Pages 23–29 in *John's Transformation of Mark.* Edited by Eve-Marie Becker, Helen K. Bond, and Catrin Williams. London: T&T Clark, 2021.

Zumthor, Paul. *Oral Poetry: An Introduction.* Translated by Kathy Murphy-Judy. Theory and History of Literature 70. Minneapolis: University of Minnesota Press, 1990.

Index of Authors

Achtemeier, Paul J., 8–9, 38–39, 123n2, 140
Alexander, Loveday, 93, 103–5
Allison, Dale C., 84n24, 95n56, 95n57
Assmann, Jan, 56n52, 85, 229
Attridge, Harold W., 264n77
Aune, David E., 82n14, 93n54

Bagnall, Roger S., 158
Bailey, Daniel P., 133n14
Balogh, Josef, 8n3, 10–11, 15, 29n74
Barker, James W., 202, 265n78, 265n82, 266
Bauckham, Richard, 111n118, 265
Baum, Armin D., 114n128
Berg, Deena, 170n57
Bock, Darrell L., 34n86
Boeft, Jan den, 254
Botha, Pieter J. J., 99n74
Boudon-Millot, Véronique, 108n109
Bovon, François, 22, 187
Bremmer, Jan N., 75n113, 254
Brodie, Thomas L., 264n75
Brown, Raymond E., 114n128, 264n78, 267
Bruce, F. F., 35n90
Bryan, Christopher, 196
Burfeind, Carsten, 7n1, 23n53, 35n88
Burnyeat, M. F., 9n7
Busch, Stephan, 9n8, 28n72

Cadbury, Henry J., 103n89
Cameron, Averil, 73n108
Chafe, Wallace, 177n10, 180
Clark, W. P., 23n54
Cribiore, Raffaella, 133n13, 158

Davies, W. D., 84n24, 95n56, 95n57
Decker, Rodney J., 182n30
Deissmann, Adolf, 132n10, 134n15

Dewey, Joanna, 99, 175n6, 250n24
Dickson, John P., 84n26
Doole, J. Andrew, 95n57
Dorandi, Tiziano, 231n44, 251
Downing, F. Gerald, 104n99, 105
Dronsch, Kristina, 11n12
Dus, Jan A., 52n45

Elder, Nicholas A., 84n24, 167n52, 178n11, 180n18, 181n21, 182n27, 187n50, 191n60, 200n97
Ellingworth, Paul, 179n16
Engelbrecht, Johan, 184n40
Epp, Eldon Jay, 255
Eve, Eric, 194, 200

Fitzmyer, Joseph A., 22–23, 103n89
Fleischman, Suzanne, 183n33
Fludernik, Monika, 184n37, 205
Forshey, Susan, 134n21

Gamble, Harry Y., 8n5, 10–11, 47n23, 47n26, 48, 123, 236, 253, 254, 256
Gavrilov, A. K., 7n1, 15n31, 17n37, 18n39, 23
Genette, Gérard, 82, 263n71
Gibson, Roy K., 27
Gilliard, Frank D., 9n9, 16n32, 81n8
Goodacre, Mark, 173n3, 265n78
Grenfell, Bernard P., 135
Gurd, Sean A., 228, 231–32, 249–50, 250–51

Hägg, Tomas, 19n42
Haran, Menahem, 259n62
Harnack, Adolf von, 49n34
Harnett, Benjamin, 255
Hays, Richard B., 196n81, 201–2, 202–3
Heilmann, Jan, 12n15
Held, Heinz Joachim, 100

Hendrickson, G. L., 29n74
Hicks-Keeton, Jill, 97n64
Hoegen-Rohls, Christina, 114n126
Horner, Timothy J., 51n43
Horsfall, Nicholas, 57n55, 148n5
Houston, George W., 266n84
Hunt, Arthur S., 135
Hurtado, Larry W., 9n9, 39n3, 46n21, 102, 252

Iverson, Kelly R., 39n3

Johnson, Luke Timothy, 103n89
Johnson, Maxwell E., 48n32
Johnson, William A., 1n1, 4n2, 5, 8n3, 14, 15n30, 15n31, 21n46, 23n52, 36n9, 56n49, 81–82
Jouanna, Jacques, 108n109

Keener, Craig S., 10n10, 35
Keith, Chris, 21, 23, 56n52, 80–81, 82n19, 85, 92n47, 98n66, 101, 176n6, 264n73, 265
Kelber, Werner H., 173n4
Kelly, Benjamin, 159
Kilpatrick, George D., 182n24
Klauck, Hans-Josef, 133n14
Kleist, James A., 180n21
Knox, Bernard M. W., 8n3, 16n34, 17n37, 18, 23n54, 29n74
Kürzinger, Josef, 239

Larsen, Matthew D. C., 75n116, 88n36, 139, 165n44, 169, 214–15, 216n9, 227, 228n30, 233n48, 233n50, 245n10, 252–54, 256
Letteney, Mark, 252–54, 256
Leung, Mavis, 204
Luijendijk, Anne-Marie, 5n2
Luz, Ulrich, 93n50, 99

Manson, T. W., 198n92
Marcus, Joel, 94n55, 248
Marshall, I. Howard, 103n89
McCown, C. C., 253n37, 256–57

McCutcheon, R. W., 9, 10n10, 12n14, 24n56, 25n57, 25n60, 28n72
McDonnell, Myles, 136–38
McLuhan, Marshall, 84–85, 289–90
Michie, Donald, 250n24
Miller, Shem, 71n101
Mills, Ian N., 49n37, 50n38
Mitchell, Timothy, 134n21, 220n14, 221n17, 226n27, 236n1
Montessori, Maria, 142n39
Morello, Ruth, 27
Moss, Candida, 239–40
Mount, Christopher N., 112n121

Nachtergaele, Delphine, 135n23
Nässelqvist, Dan, 40n6, 54n47, 74n112
Nolland, John, 104n97, 198n90
Nongbri, Brent, 82, 255, 270n95
Norden, Eduard, 8n3, 16n33

Osiek, Carolyn, 32n82
Overman, J. Andrew, 100–101

Parker, Holt N., 24n54, 41, 42, 59n64, 61n72
Pietrobelli, Antoine, 108n109
Poirier, John C., 193

Reece, Steve, 139n32
Rhoads, David, 38–39, 250n24
Roberts, C. H., 193, 252, 256
Rodríguez, Rafael, 9n9
Rogers, Everett M., 255n49, 256n55
Rothschild, Clare K., 110
Runesson, Anders, 71

Schiffrin, Deborah, 182n26, 184n37, 205
Shin, Hyeon Woo, 183n36
Shiner, Whitney Taylor, 11n12, 39n4
Singer, P. N., 4n2, 87–88, 89n40, 90, 108n106, 108n108, 110n117, 167
Skeat, T. C., 193, 252, 256
Smith, D. Moody, 101n85
Soyars, Jonathan E., 31n79
Stanton, Graham M., 73n106, 254n45
Starr, Raymond J., 57n55, 111n120, 211–15

Thompson, Michael B., 263
Turner, E. G., 16n34

Vatri, Alessandro, 12n15
Venema, G. J., 63n78, 63n79, 65

Walsh, Robyn Faith, 248
Watson, Francis, 172–73
Wheatley, Paul, 134n21
White, Peter, 59n62, 59n63

Williams, Catrin, 262n69, 263
Windisch, Hans, 114n127, 265n82
Winkler, John J., 18n40
Winsbury, Rex, 26n61, 26n63
Winter, J. G., 133n12
Wire, Antoinette Clark, 179n16
Wright, Brian J., 38, 40n6, 40n7, 61n71

Zumstein, Jean, 263n71

Index of Subjects

accidental publication, 88n36, 165, 214–17, 238

book (βίβλος), 91–93, 95–96, 115, 120, 172, 186, 236–37, 257, 274

bookroll, 21, 74–75, 237, 250–57, 268–71, 274

circulation: aims of, 211–13; concentric circles model of, 2; defined, 209; diversity of, 214; limited, 225–27, 238, 240, 245; multiplicity, 220; public, 56; revision and feedback, 211–12; social networks, 211–13

codex, 234, 250–57, 268–71, 274

competitive textualization, 92, 98, 101, 265–67, 269–70

compositions (συγγράμματα), 230–34, 237, 243–44, 246–50

copying texts, 33, 137–39, 150, 213

correcting texts, 166, 172

dictation, 145, 268; excuses for, 126, 127, 147; letters, 147–60; literary compositions, 160–65; style and, 176

diffusion of innovations theory, 255–56

direct discourse, 159, 176

discourse markers, 182

document (βιβλίον), 31, 81n10, 114–20, 172, 258, 275

extended situation (*zerdehnte Situation*), 56n52, 85, 89, 229

for publication (πρὸς ἔκδοσιν), 217, 228–34, 237–38, 245–50, 256–57, 274

generic materiality, 253

gospel (εὐαγγέλιον), 84–85, 89–90, 120, 172, 257

handwriting, 44, 125–43, 172, 268; sentimentalized, 127, 129, 131–32, 133, 147; shift into or out of one's own hand, 126, 149, 151

historical present, 183–84, 191, 204–6, 247

imagined reading, writing, and circulation practices, 3, 129, 146, 169–70, 238

immediately (εὐθύς), 181–82, 191–92, 247

intertextuality, 164, 194–203, 247, 258–62

John's knowledge of the Synoptics, 119, 262–68

letters, 125, 147–60, 221

literary posturing, 28, 108

literary routines, 26–29, 57, 140, 163

materiality, 46, 82, 222, 225, 266, 270

media myths: ancient practices compared to modern, 22n48; circulation, 211, 236; communal reading, 8, 38, 105; defined, 1; dictation, 124, 125; handwriting, 125; scanning texts, 22n48; vocalized reading, 7–10, 33, 105, 123; writing, 123, 172

modern media, 60, 82, 124, 229n34, 234–35, 266

navigating a text, 21–22, 35, 45

nonreading uses of texts, 5, 22, 78

notes (ὑπόμνημα, ὑπομνήματα), 67–68, 90–91, 167–68, 217, 229–34, 236–37, 240–41, 246–50, 274

not for publication (οὐ πρὸς ἔκδοσιν), 217, 228–34, 274

novels, 18–20, 129–32

orality, 87–90, 120, 159, 165–70, 172–85, 219, 237–38, 274

parataxis, 159, 176, 178–81, 187–90, 203, 247
paratexts, 82–83, 113–14
performance criticism, 38–39, 99
personal possession of texts, 34, 35n87, 44–47
plagiarism, 88n36, 130, 216, 227
Pliny the Younger, 3, 26–27
prefaces, 102–4, 112, 186, 274
presentation copies of texts, 213, 234, 237, 251, 275
private texts, 195, 216, 225, 274
publication, 26n64, 58, 59, 166, 209, 213, 222, 228–34, 244–45, 270, 273

reading: communal, 38–40, 54–76, 273; diversity of, 5–6, 10, 36, 38–39, 54, 68, 70, 76; eye-voice span and, 13; familial, 69–70; health and, 33–34, 57; large-group, 54–57, 63–67; liturgical, 80, 99–101, 274; meals and, 48, 74; moderately sized group, 67–76; normalcy of, 42; one's own writing, 58, 60; private or personal, 40–41, 68, 273; public, 40–41, 80; serially, 45; silent, 7–25, 273; sleep and, 42–44, 68; small-group, 29, 40, 57–63, 68; solitary, 27–28, 34, 39, 41–54; synagogue, 71, 97–101, 274; travel and, 34, 58; vocalized, 25–36, 38, 80, 273; well or poorly, 34, 55, 56n50, 60
recitations, 213, 222, 225
residual orality, 172
revising, 58–59, 170, 184, 201, 212, 221, 233

scribal literacy, 23, 31n79
scriptio continua, 9, 10–13, 14, 35n90
slavery, 29, 58, 137, 144, 168, 192, 222, 239–40, 251
sociality of media, 1, 5, 36–37, 41, 76, 123, 128, 139, 145, 153, 158, 167, 209, 236, 271
sociolinguistics, 177–92
speeches, 85–87
suppression or de-publication, 215–16, 226–28

textual self-consciousness, 80–83, 114
Theophilus, 111–13, 274
titles, 83, 92–93, 166, 217, 274

vernacular Greek, 179, 232, 247, 274

wax tablets, 141, 144, 194–95
writing: by mouth, 165–70, 268; characteristics of, 172, 272; diversity of practice, 2, 136, 206; solitary, 142; travel and, 126, 139, 148, 163; well or poorly, 133, 135, 141, 153, 154n18, 158, 160–61, 164, 166, 169, 174, 185, 186n43, 192, 216, 232–33, 246–50

Index of Scripture

OLD TESTAMENT

Genesis
2:4	93–94
5:1	93n50, 94

Exodus
3:20	196

Leviticus
22:27	69

Deuteronomy
6:4–5	196n81
17:18	43
24:1–3	93n50
30:10	116n132
31:10–13	64–65

2 Samuel
11:14–15	93n50

1 Kings
14:19	258n60
14:29	258–59, 260n65
15:7	258n60, 260n65
15:23	258n60
15:31	258n60, 260n65
16:5	258n60, 260n65
16:14	258n60, 260n65
16:20	258n60
16:27	258n60, 260n65
20:8–9	93n50
22:39	258n60, 260n65
22:45–46	258n60, 260n63, 260n65

2 Kings
1:18	258n60, 260n65
5:5–7	93n50
8:23	258n60, 260n63, 260n65
10:34	258n60, 260n65
12:19–20	258n60, 260n65
13:8	258n60, 260n65
13:12	258n60, 260n65
14:15	258n60, 260n65
14:18	258n60, 260n65
14:28	258n60, 260n65
15:6	258n60, 260n65
15:11	258n60
15:15	258n60
15:21	258n60, 260n65
15:26	258n60, 260n65
15:31	258n60, 260n65
15:36	258n60, 260n65
16:19	258n60, 260n65
20:20	258n60, 260n65
21:17	258n60, 260n65
21:25	258n60, 260n65
22	64–65
22:8	64
23:2	64
23:28	258n60, 260n65
24:5	258n60, 260n65

2 Chronicles
34:14	64
34:30	64

Nehemiah
8:1–3	63–64

Psalms
69:12	164n42
78:2	200
104:29	164n43
164:4	164n43

Proverbs
10:9	164n42

Isaiah
6:9–10	198–99, 199n96, 202
40:3	196
40:4–5	197–98, 200
42:1–4	199n95

Jeremiah
2:22	164n42
3:3	164n42
39:10–16	93n50
39:44	93n50

Nahum
1:1	93n52

Zechariah
9:9	202

Malachi
3:1	196

Index of Scripture

Apocryphal / Deuterocanonical Books

Tobit
1:1   93n52

Baruch
1:1   93n52

2 Maccabees
8:23   68n94

1 Esdras
8:1–3   63n79

New Testament

Matthew
1:1	81n10, 83, 92–93, 96
1:2–17	92
3:3	197–98
3:16	192n66
4:23	71n102, 100n78
8:28–34	100n76
9:1–8	100n76
9:9	249
9:35	71n102, 100n78
10:17	100, 100n78
11:10	197n87
12:3	45n17
12:5	45n17
12:9	100, 100n78
12:18–21	199n95
12:25–37	100n77
13:13–15	199–200
13:15	199n96
13:20–21	192n66
13:35	200
13:54	71n102, 100n78
14:3–12	100n76
14:13–21	100n76
14:27	192n66
15:2	249
17:14–21	100n76
19:1–12	100n77
19:4	45n17
19:7	115n130
20:25–28	100n77
21:3	192n66
21:16	45n17
21:33–46	100n77
21:42	45n17
22:31	45n17
23:1–36	100n77
23:34	100
24:9–14	100n77
24:15	80, 81n10, 113
26:17–19	100n76
27:9–10	200
27:32	248n14
27:37	77

Mark
1:1	83–85, 93, 173, 264
1:2–3	196–98, 200, 247
1:10	182n25
1:12	182n25
1:18	181n23
1:20	182n25
1:21	71n102, 181, 182n25, 183n36
1:21–28	181n21
1:23	181, 182n25
1:28	182n25
1:30	182n25
1:39	71n102
1:42	181n23
1:43	182n25
2:1–12	100n76
2:8	182n25
2:12	182n25
2:14	249
2:23–28	247
2:25	45n17
2:26	200n97
3:6	182n25
3:13	183n36
3:17	249
3:20	183n36
3:23–30	100n77
4:5	181n23
4:10–11	100n77
4:12	198–200
4:15–17	181n23
5:1–20	100n76
5:2	182n25
5:21–43	100n76
5:25–29	181n21, 181n23
5:30	182n25
5:42	181n23
6:2	71n102
6:17–29	100n76
6:25	181n23
6:27	182n25
6:30	183n36
6:30–44	100n76
6:45	182n25
6:50	182n25
6:54	181n23
7:1	183n36
7:3–4	249
7:25	182n25
8:10	182n25
8:22	183n36
9:2	183n36
9:14–29	100n76
9:15	182n25
9:20	181n23, 182n25
10:1	183n36
10:1–12	100n77
10:4	115n130
10:35	183n36
10:42–45	100n77
10:46	183n36
10:52	182n25
11:1	183n36
11:2–3	182n25

318 • Index of Scripture

11:15	183n36	6:3	45n17	10:34	201n100, 202n105
11:27	183n36	6:6	71n102	11:2	265n80
12:1–12	100n77	7:27	197n87	11:38	204n116
12:10	45n17	8:10	199	11:46	261n66
12:13	183n36	10:26	45n17	12:13–15	201n100, 202, 202n104
12:18	183n36	10:27	197n88		
12:29–30	196n81	11:38	249	12:22	204n113
12:39–40	100n77	12:26	95	12:38–40	201n100, 202, 202n104
13:9–13	100n77	13:10	71n102		
13:14	80, 81n10, 113	18:31	260n64	13:4	204n116
14:12–16	100n76	18:35	249n20	13:6	204n113
14:17	183n36	20:42	96	13:18	201n100, 202n104
14:21	200n97	21:20	113	13:24	204n113
14:27	200n97	21:22	260n64	13:26	204n113
14:29	200n97	23:26	248n14	13:38	205n118
14:32–33	183n36	23:28	77	15:14	261n66
14:43	182n25	24:44	260n64	15:25	201n100, 202n105
14:45	182n25			17:12	201n100, 202n106
14:51–52	247	**John**		18:3	204n113, 204n116
14:66	183n36	1:1	114n126, 264	18:20	71n102
14:72	182n25	1:1–18	114	18:28	204n116
15:1	182n25	1:23	201n100, 202n104	18:38	204n116
15:20	183n36	1:29	204n113	19:19–20	77
15:21	248	1:32	265n80	19:24	201n100, 202n104
16:2	183n36	1:41	204n113	19:28	201n100, 202n106
16:8	249	1:43	204n113, 204n116	19:36	201n100, 202n105
		1:45	204n113	19:37	201n100, 202n105
Luke		2:9	204n113	20:1	204n116
1:1	186	2:17	201n100, 202n105	20:2	204n113, 204n116
1:1–4	81n10, 102–13	3:24	265n80	20:18	204n116
1:3	103	4:5	204n116	20:29	267
1:63	40n6	4:7	204n113	20:30–31	81n10, 83, 103, 114, 115n130, 117, 258–62, 267
3:4	95	4:39	261n66		
3:4–6	100	5:2	204n116		
4:4–6	197–98	5:14	204n116	21	267–68
4:15	71n102	6:19	204n113	21:13	205n118
4:16–20	21–23	6:31	201n100, 202n105	21:20	204n113
4:16–30	71n102, 72, 98	6:45	201n100, 202n105	21:24–25	83, 114
4:17	115n129, 115n130	6:59	71n102	21:25	115n130, 258–62
4:18–19	197n88	6:67–71	265n80		
4:20	115n129	7:37	201n100	**Acts**	
4:31–33	71n102	7:38	202n105, 202n106	1:1	102n88, 103n89
4:44	71n102	8:17	201n100, 202n105	1:2	103n89
5:27	24	9:13	204n113, 204n116	1:15	103n89

Index of Scripture

1:20	96	28:26–27	199n96	10:7	115n130
7:42	96				
8:26–40	10n10, 34–35, 41	**Romans**		**Revelation**	
9:20	71n102	12:17	164n42	1:3	260n64
13:5	71n102			1:11	115n130
13:14–16	71n102	**Galatians**		3:5	96n58
13:14–41	72, 98	3:10	115n129, 115n130	5:1–9	115n130
13:29	260n64			6:14	115n130
14:1	71n102	**Philippians**		10:8	115n130
15:21	71n102, 72	4:3	96n58	12:9	51n41
17:2–3	71n102			13:8	115n130
17:10–11	71n102	**2 Timothy**		17:8	115n130
17:17	71n102	4:13	115n130	20:12	115n130
18:4–6	71n102			20:15	96n58
18:26	71n102	**Hebrews**		21:27	115n130
19:8	71n102	9:19	115n130	22:18–19	115n130
19:19	96				

Index of Other Ancient Sources

Greco-Roman Writings

Achilles Tatius

The Adventures of Leucippe and Cleitophon
1.6	18–19
5.18–20	131–32

Apollonius of Tyana

Testimonia
258	116n135

Appian

Civil Wars
2.98–99	42
2.116	116n135

Apuleius

Apologia
87.2	130n7

Metamorphoses
5.22	19n41

Aristophanes

Equites
115–28	15n31
115–50	17–18

Aristotle

Problems
1.18.1	43

Athenaeus

Deipnosophistae
10.450–51	16–17

Asconsius

Commentary on Pro Milone
42C	220–21

Aulus Gellius

Attic Nights
18.5	55

Celsus

De Medicina
1.8	33–34

Chariton

Chaereas and Callirhoe
1.1.5–10	19n41
4.4.5–10	3, 19–20, 129
4.5	129
5.1.1	102n88
8.4.6	130

Cicero

De amicitia
3	150
93.3	150
193	28
401	149n8
402	149n8

De finibus
3.7–10	42

De Naturo Deorum
3.30.74	130n7

Epistulae ad Atticum
40	126n12, 149
43	126, 147, 148
57	214–16
60	214n7
89	126n12, 148
107	126n12, 148n3
110	126n12, 148n4
123	149n6
125	148
137	126n12
151	151
162	126n12
163	148n5
199	126
206	148n5
212	126n12, 149
234	149, 151
243	227
271	126
299	151
336	227
426	148n2

Epistulae ad Quintum fratrem
21	151
23	148n4

In Catilinam
3.12.10–11	130n7
4	149n7

Index of Other Ancient Sources • 321

4.3	130n7	**Epictetus**		39	109n112
10–11	149n7	*Discourses*		51	109n112
12	149n7	1.pref.8–9	216, 232	54–55	109n112
Phillipicae		1.4	116n135	79	109
2.4.7–9	130n7			*Differences of Pulses*	
2.7.16–17	130n7	**Euripides**		591–92K	21–22
		Hippolytus		*Method of Medicine*	
Pro Milone	220	856–75	17	1K	106–8
Tusculanae disputationes		874–75	15n31	412K	230
5.40	23			456K	107–8
5.116	15n31	**Fronto**		*My Own Doctrines*	
		De Bello Parthico		14	110n117
Claudius Ptolemy		10	128, 147	*On Exercise*	
Judiciaris		*De feriis alsiensibus*		*with a Small Ball*	
5.2	15n31	3	29, 126	1	105–6, 251
		Epistolarum ad Antoni-		2	110n117
Cornelius Nepos		*num Imperatorem*		*On My Own Books*	
Cato	3.3	1.2	128, 147	10K	88n37, 166, 185,
		Epistolarum ad Marcum			225n26
Demosthenes		*Caesarem*		11K	166
Eroticus		3.3	127	11–13K	216n10
2	245	4.9	127, 147	12K	217–18
		Epistolarum ad Verum		13K	167
Dio Cassius		*Imperatorem*		14–15K	89, 166
Orations		2.1	87	17K	88, 89, 216n10,
18	61	2.8	227		216n11
		2.9	227	21–22K	88
Roman History				34K	194–95
42.11.2–5	42	**Galen**		34–37K	216n10
62.29.1	55	*The Affections and Errors*		42K	216n10
		of the Soul		43K	216n10
Dio Chrysostom		1K	87, 167	*Thrasybulus*	
Discourses		*Avoiding Distress (De*		1	3, 87, 168
18.19–20	162, 176	*Indolentia)*		**Horace**	
		2	109	*Epistles*	
Diodorus Siculus		8–9	111n119	2.1.108–17	140, 163n41
Library of History		11	109n112	*Satires*	
40.8	215–16	12	109n112	1.4.9–13	141, 161, 176
		16	109n112	1.6.122–23	42

322 • Index of Other Ancient Sources

1.10.72	140–41, 193	2.10	137	56.3860	158–59, 179, 180n20
2.4	169, 170n57	4.2	128		
		4.6	14	67.4633	5n2
Juvenal		4.8	128, 150n9	903	158–59, 179
Satires		5.41	137	*SB*	
1.12	59n63	5.47	128, 148	14.11584	132, 277–78
4.70	59n63	**Martial**		**Philostratus**	
13	130n7, 149n7	*Epigrams*		*Vita Apollonii*	
Libanius		2.6	42	1.3.1	233, 249n21
Orations		3.68.11–12	42	1.19.2	247
18.175	34	3.86.1–2	42	5.7	249n21
		4.6.4–5	59n63	5.26	249n21
Lucian		11.16.9–10	42	7.28.1	240, 249
Herodotus		**Ovid**		**Plautus**	
1–8	54–55	*Amores*		*Bacchides*	
How to Write History		1.1	228	724–55	144–45
16	232, 247, 250	*Heroides*		**Pliny the Elder**	
48	239, 247	2.1.1–2	25		
51	232			*Natural History*	
The Ignorant Book-Collector		**Papyri**		13.83	136
2	12–13, 29–30	*BGU*		**Pliny the Younger**	
		2.423	132–35, 153n16, 278–79	*Epistles*	
Marcus Aurelius		2.632	132–36, 153n16, 279–80	1.1	27
Ad Amicos				1.2	60n66, 211–12
2.3	137	4.1204	154–56	1.6	140
De feriis alsiensibus		4.1205	154–56	1.7	222n21
4	128n6, 151–52	4.1206	154–56	1.8	227
De Nepote Amisso		4.1207	154–56	1.20	85, 87
1.2	128, 147	*P.Brem.*		2.3	61n73
Epistles		61	152–53	2.7	225n25
9.36	3	*P.Mich.*		2.10	222
		8.482	158n30	2.19	59n63, 86
Epistolarum ad Marcum Caesarem		8.490	156–57	3.1	58
1.6	62, 87, 137	8.491	156–57	3.5	57, 139
1.7	62n77, 137	*P.Oxy.*		3.10	224–25
2.4	137	1.119	135–36, 281–82	3.15	61, 222n22
				4.7	56, 60n70
				4.14	162–63, 176

Index of Other Ancient Sources • 323

4.16	15n31, 24	*De Alexandri magni fortuna aut virtute*		10.3.19	146
4.19	59n63, 85			10.3.19–27	142, 160, 176
4.23	27–28	7 [340A]	24	10.3.31–32	193, 252
5.3	59n63	*De capienda ex inimicis utilitate*		10.4.1	193
5.10	223			11.3.2–4	15n31
5.12	58, 59n63, 60n66	1 (86c)	116n133		
6.6	59n63			**Seneca the Elder**	
6.15	59	*Demetrius*		*Controversiae*	
6.16	42	1.7 (889)	116n133, 116n134	10.pref.8	15n31
6.17	59	*Lucullus*			
6.20	42	42.4 (519)	116n133	**Seneca the Younger**	
7.4	85, 176	*Lysander*		*Epistles*	
7.17	58–59, 213	19.6–7 [444]	116	1.46.3	62n74
7.20	60n66, 212–13	*Non posse suaviter vivi secundum Epicurum*		65.1	42
8.7	213				
8.9	148n3	1 (1086c)	116n132	**Strabo**	
8.12	59n63			*Geography*	
8.21	59n63	*Pericles*		17.5 (C790)	116n136
9.34	59n63, 60	2.4	116n133		
9.36	33–34, 57, 163, 176	*Polybius*		**Suetonius**	
9.40	163, 176	*Histories*		*Augustus*	
		30.8.4	130n7	80.3	136
Plotinus				81	130n7
Ennead		**Porphyry**		87.1	136
1.4.10	42	*Vita Plotini*		88	136
Plutarch		8.1–13	141, 160n39	*Caesar*	
				17	130n7
Adversus Colotem		**Quintilian**		*Domitian*	
1 (1107d)	116n133	*Institutio Oratoria (The Orator's Education)*		12	130n7
30 (1124e)	116n133			*Gaius Caligula*	
Alexander		1.pref.3	185	24	130n7
1.1–3	117–19, 262	1.pref.7–8	168–69, 185, 219	*Nero*	
		1.1.27–29	141–42, 160	10.2	55
Brutus		1.1.35	13	15.1	24
5.2–3 [986]	24	1.7.20–22	136	52	141
		7.2.24	218–19	52.3	136
Cato the Younger		10.1.8	25		
20.4–5	137	10.1.8–10	15n31	*Suasoriae*	
28.1	116	10.3.1–18	142	6.27	59n63
68–70	42	10.3.17	141n38		

Index of Other Ancient Sources

Titus
3   130n7

Tacitus

Annals
3.49.1   59n63
30   130n7

Dialogus de oratoribus
9.3   59n63

Xenophon of Athens

Anabasis
2.1   102n88
3.1   102n88
4.1   102n88
5.1   102n88
7.1   102n88

Xenophon of Ephesus

Anthia and Habrocomes
1.1.35   13
1.3.1   19n41

JEWISH WRITINGS

Dead Sea Scrolls
1QIsa^a   22–23

1QS
6:1–8   70–71, 97n65, 98

1QSa
1:4–5   66

1 Enoch
13:7–10   43, 67–68

Josephus

Against Apion
Pref.   112–13
1.1   96n62
1.1–18   104n92
1.40   115n129
1.101   116n131
1.164   116n131
1.176   116n131
1.182   116n131
1.320   116n131
2.1   116n131
2.173–75   97n65, 98
2.175   71n102
2.183   116n131
2.296   116n131, 117

Antiquities
1.5   112
1.8–9   112n124
1.15   116n131
1.26   96
1.82   96n62
1.139   96n62
1.159   116n131
2.347   96n62
3.81   96n62
3.105   96n62
4.304   115n129
4.326   96n62
8.44   115n129
8.159   115n129
9.28   96n62
9.46   96n62
10.58   96n62
10.63   96n62
10.94   115n129
10.210   115n129
10.218   115n129
10.267   115n129
11.15   115n129
11.99   116n131
12.110   68n95
14.4   130n7
16.4   130n7
16.43–45   71n102
16.146   71n102
16.164   96n62
16.256   116n131
20.17–53   44
20.44   35n87
20.261   96n62
20.267   116n131, 228

Jewish War
1.1   112, 130n7
1.17   104n92
1.30   112, 116n131
2.289–92   71n102
3.352   96n62

The Life
216–17   20
218   115n129
222–24   41
236–61   66–67
361   116n131
363   228
430   228

Letter of Aristeas
310–11   65–66

3 Maccabees
1:13   68n94

4 Maccabees
18:10–18   35n87, 70

Philo

Embassy to Gaius
1.19   116n132
1.83   43, 69n99
156–57   71n102, 72
311–13   71n102

Flaccus
100   68n94

Heir
258   96n59

Hypothetica
7.11–13   71n102, 72, 98

Legum allegoriae
1.83   24

Index of Other Ancient Sources • 325

On the Cherubim	
124	96
On the Contemplative Life	
30–31	71n102, 72
On the Creation of the World	
128	71n102, 72
On the Decalogue	
1	96n59
154	96n59
On Dreams	
2.127	71–72, 96n59, 97n65, 98
2.175	116n132
On Drunkenness	
208	96n59
On the Eternity of the World	
19	95, 96n59
On the Life of Abraham	
1	95
156	96n59
177	96n59
258	96n59
On the Life of Moses	
2.11	96n59
2.36	96n59
2.45	96
2.95	96n59
2.215–16	71n102, 72
On the Migration of Abraham	
14	96n59
On Planting	
1	116n132
On the Posterity of Cain	
127	95

On the Preliminary Studies	
20	69n99
On the Sacrifices of Cain and Abel	
1	116n132
On Sobriety	
17	96n60
On the Special Laws	
1.214	24, 44, 69n99
2.60–62	71n102, 72
2.150	96n59
3.110–14	69n96
4.160–67	43, 44, 116n132
4.175	96n59
On the Virtues	
34	96n59
95	96n60
131–33	69
That Every Good Person Is Free	
80–83	71, 97n65, 98
That the Worse Attacks the Better	
161	96n59

Testament of Job

1:1	93n52

EARLY CHRISTIAN WRITINGS

Acts of Peter

19–21	73–76, 80, 97n65

Augustine

Confessions

6.3.3	7–10
8.12.29	7–8

The Trinity

11.8.15	42

Clement of Alexandria

Miscellanies

7.7	48

Cyril

Catechetical Lectures

4.36	44

Epistle of Barnabas

12	116n135

Eusebius

Ecclesiastical History

2.14.6–2.15.2	90n43
2.15.1–2	75n115, 91n45, 240–41
2.16	75n115
2.16.1	91
3.4.6	91n45
3.24.5	91n45
3.24.6	91n45
3.24.7	91n45
3.24.15	91n45
3.39.14–16	75n115, 91n45, 238–40, 243–44
4.26.13–14	53
5.8.2	91n45
5.8.3	91n45
5.8.4	91n45
6.12.1–4	80
6.14.5	241
6.14.6–7	75n115, 91n45, 241–42
6.25.3	91n45
6.25.9	91n45

Hippolytus

The Apostolic Tradition

41	48

Ignatius

To the Ephesians
5:3   53n45

To the Magnesians
12:1   53n45

To the Philadelphians
8:2   50

Irenaeus

Against Heresies
2.27.1   80
3.1.1   75n115, 244n9

Jerome

De Viris Illustribus
8   75n115

Epistles
117.12   164, 176, 194
127.14   164, 176, 194

John Chrysostom

Homiliae in Joannem
11.1   47

Justin Martyr

1 Apology
28   50
67   73, 76, 80, 97n65, 101

2 Apology
3   50

Dialogue with Trypho
10   50
18   50

Origen

Homily in Exodus
12.2   48n29
12.27   28n29

Homily in Genesis
10.1   48n29
11.3   47–48
12.5   48n29

Homily in Leviticus
11.7   48n29

Homily in Numbers
2.1   48n29

Shepherd of Hermas

1.2.2 [2.2]   30
1.3.3–4 [3.3–4]   30
1.4.3 [4.3]   32
2.1.3–4 [5.3–4]   31, 31n79, 32–33
2.2.1 [6.1]   32
2.4.3 [8.3]   31n79
2.4.5 [8.3]   31n79
5.1.5–7 [25.5–7]   31n79

Tatian

Oratio ad Graecos
29   49
31   49

Tertullian

Against Marcion
2.1–2   75n115
3.4   75n115
4.1   75n115
5.3–4   75n115

Apology
31   50